The STICKNEY

She eases my disappointment and frustration when things don't go right, and shares in the joy when everything comes together.

The research for Benjamin Franklin Stickney's biography has taken the better part of 20 years and strained the friendship of many of the librarians that I have come to respect. Appreciation for the hours of research that they have provided go to librarians Mike Lora, Donna, Greg, Laura, Irene, Ann, and retired Jim Marshall at the Toledo Lucas County Public Library. Thanks to Ken Levin, Fred Folger, Randy Buchman, Larry Nelson, Larry Michaels, the Schroeders and Judy Justus for having the skill and talent to tell a good story. Special thanks to Renee Bachmann, Bob & Ann Foeller, Steve Crouse, and Jim Johnson for providing all the last minute assistance. Last but not least, thanks to good friend Gerald C. Hill for providing the best artwork that we have had the good fortune to enjoy.

A very special appreciation and recognition is extended to John Robinson Block and the Block Family, for THE BLADE's tireless quest of Toledo's future potential by providing a truthful journal of Toledo's past.

It has been almost a year since the final draft of Stickney's biography was completed. Since that time, many of our good friends have read the manuscript and offered numerous suggestions, but Bonnie my best friend and lover for over 40 years, would always ask if I was satisfied with the finished effort. Since the final draft has been completed, *Stickney's* biography has been rewritten 12 times, culminating with Dave Murray's penciled editorial suggestions and comments. Sometimes critical, but always supportive, Dave strived to make a good story better.

I'll end with the comments by Judith Justus, President, Perrysburg Historical Society about *STICKNEY and the maumee valley.*

"This is an outstanding compendium of the early history of the Maumee Valley drawn from various published and first hand sources. Its environs and inhabitants interact to produce a complete picture of its formation. Woven throughout the narrative is the little known story of a man who was pivotal in calming the volatile relationship between the settlers and the Native Americans – Benjamin Franklin Stickney."

contents
Benjamin Franklin Stickney

	contents		i
	preface	Dr. Larry Nelson	ii
	introduction		iv

those that came before...

1	earthworks, the maumee valley, & the french	1
2	the first son of the maumee valley	15
3	rebellion & pontiac's days on the maumee	29
4	conflict on the maumee & another son is born	45
5	blue jacket, little turtle & the capitol	59

eighty miles north of the boundary of the white population

6	new hampshire, canada, & fort wayne	67
7	fort wayne, war, & whistler's grandfather	85
8	upper sandusky, whiskey, & doubt	107
9	whistler, richardville, & politics	119
10	letters from home	139
11	a disputed territory, redemption, & expedition	161
12	the boundary, settlers, & a task unfinished	175
13	tradition, canals, & manhattan	193
14	boundaries, canal talk, & development	213
15	vistula, boundaries, & preparations	233
16	war fever, robins, & prison	257
17	a wedding, the stabbing, & a dead horse	287
18	harve, manhattan, & lectures	317
19	epilog ....bush street	351
20	index	361

1st Printing October 2009, ZKDATT Publishing
Point Place, Ohio. Copyright 2009

All photographs and other visual images are from various collections as noted, and remain the property of their respective owners and or holders. No part of this work may be copied in any form, unless the work is to be quoted in a review or other fair usage that complies with the current copyright laws. Mistakes have a way of avoiding detection in a work like this. Please forgive any errors that you may find, they are totally without malice, and please inform the author that they be corrected, Thank You.

The cover illustrating *Fort Industry 1803* is by renowned watercolor artist Gerald C. Hill, and is available in a limited edition print. Please contact your favorite gallery for availability.

Benjamin Franklin Stickney

preface
Dr. Larry Nelson

Benjamin Franklin Stickney was an exceptional man. He lived during a remarkable era and his life reveals an extraordinary story about Toledo and northwest Ohio. Stickney came to the Maumee Valley as an Indian agent in 1811, a time when European settlement had barely penetrated the region and much of the area remained a sparsely inhabited and untamed wilderness. At his death in 1852, roads, canals, and railroads laced the region in a sophisticated and interconnected transportation network that had brought people, material, jobs, and wealth to those living in northwest Ohio. Toledo was a large, vibrant, and expanding city. Ships from its port linked the town to destinations across the Great Lakes, along the eastern seacoast, and throughout the globe. And its boosters predicted that it would only be a brief time before Toledo took its rightful place as one of the nation's grand commercial emporiums.

Benjamin Franklin Stickney took part in, or, in many cases, actually planned and directed the events that had led directly to this astonishing transformation. A politician and judge by profession, Stickney was one of the region's earliest champions for a canal system that would link the region economically to the rest of the state. Further, he actively participated in the events that both brought about and then resolved the infamous "Michigan War," the 1835 quarrel between Ohio and its northern neighbor over a disputed boundary separating the two states. Ohio's modern boundary, established in 1836, and the subsequent develop of the Miami and Ohio and the Wabash and Erie canal systems, both of which terminated in Toledo, were essential both to Toledo and the lower-Maumee Valley's subsequent economic development. Moreover, it was Stickney who first proposed that, in return for ceding the disputed territory to Ohio, Michigan should receive its present-day Upper-Peninsula. Stickney's foresight and vision, shrewd judgment, and political acumen contributed positively to the development of not only Ohio, but also Michigan and the entire Old Northwest. Further, these events continue to reverberate. Toledo's and northwest Ohio's present-day economic vitality is, in large measure, the result of actions first proposed and then undertaken by Stickney.

Stickney was more than an activist. He retained a penetrating interest in the region's Native peoples throughout his entire life. He interviewed Indians living along the Maumee Valley until their removal from Ohio and recorded his conversations and observations in a series of documents that contain traditions and customs of the Wyandot and Ottawa Nations found in no other sources.

Moreover, Stickney embodied the unbridled optimism and intensely individualistic character that defined *ante-bellum* America. He named his sons One and Two and his daughter Indiana.

In *STICKNEY and the Maumee valley,* local historian and well-known author Ken Dickson has created an outstanding study of one of Toledo's most significant, flamboyant, and idiosyncratic founders. His biography is grounded in writings from the period that, in many cases, are published here for the first time. Readers will be delighted with this well-crafted, insightful biography that provides a unique, revealing, and always entertaining glimpse into Toledo's beginnings and earliest history.

Dr. Larry L. Nelson

Benjamin Franklin Stickney

introduction
Benjamin Franklin Stickney

Benjamin Franklin Stickney, defender of Fort Wayne during the War of 1812, renowned Indian Agent, architect of the Ohio Michigan Boundary dispute, and direct descendant of Benjamin Franklin is rapidly leaving the historical consciousness of the famed gateway to the west, the Maumee River Valley.

As each succeeding generation gathers familiar landmarks to celebrate their own passing, the footprints of the original inhabitants and pioneers are rapidly disappearing as the waves of time and historians continually reinvent the past to fit the demands of the present.

Benjamin Franklin Stickney is not the only player on the historical stage of the Maumee Valley that has become a dying ember in a long discarded campfire. Pontiac and Tecumseh, sons of the Maumee Valley barely fifty years apart, provided the will and leadership to thwart the immigrant's migration through their ancestral way of life. The thunder and lightning that once followed Pontiac and Tecumseh as they tried to rekindle the dignity inherent in the Indian way of life have been reduced to mere shadows that faintly flicker through the streams of historical perception.

An unintended consequence of their failure to ultimately stem the westward migration resulted in the historical fragments of the first inhabitants of Northwest Ohio having been relegated to the archives as ancient memories and lines of antiquated text.

The biography of Benjamin Franklin Stickney is the story of the historical giants that walked through the towering forests and paddled over the Maumee Valley's broad highways before Stickney appeared *…80 miles north of the boundary of white population…*. Stickney's biography is the story of those that shaped the land and those that created the dilemmas that faced the immigrants that used the Maumee Valley as the Gateway to the West. And lastly Stickney's biography is the story of the land speculators who used greed, whisky, and bigotry to remove the Indians from their ancestral homes.

If Benjamin Franklin Stickney is mentioned or remembered at all it is because of the whimsical way in which he named his five children. His sons were named One and Two, and his daughters were Mary after his wife, Louisa who died in childhood, and Indiana. Only his last child was named after a State.

Stickney Hall, one of Toledo's celebrated landmarks of the mid 1880's is gone and barely remembered, if at all. Stickney's brick home at Bush and Summit Streets on the banks of his beloved Maumee River was demolished to make way for Toledo's Women and Children's Hospital, and his vineyards which were prominently featured in the Toledo War have long since become a pockmarked asphalt parking lot for the closed Riverside Hospital. A beautiful silver tankard which at one time was prominently displayed by the Toledo Museum of Art as a legacy from Benjamin Franklin to his namesake has been relegated to a non-descript shelf in a forgotten storage area. Stickney Elementary School which proudly bore his name has been closed for years and awaits the wrecker's ball. Stickney Avenue, which was once the major pathway between Detroit and Maumee, slowly awaits a name change in honor of the Jeep Chrysler Plant that has been constructed along its broad shoulders.

Before the sands of time completely eliminate Benjamin Franklin Stickney's footprints from the Maumee Valley, the historical foundation that Stickney constructed and future generations built on needs to be permanently carved in the historical consciousness of the Maumee Valley.

Benjamin Franklin Stickney was born into privilege on April 1st 1773, and while his New Hampshire parents were relatively poor they were prosperous with well placed relatives in the forthcoming American government.[1] With the name and countenance of what passed for royalty in the fledgling United States, it would be almost forty years before Dr. Benjamin Franklin's namesake would begin his westward trek from New Hampshire to write his name across the gateway to New Orleans …. the Maumee Valley.

For perhaps a thousand years before Stickney's birth, the land surrounding the Great Lakes was cut by numerous rivers and streams, interspersed with vast forests and immense prairies teeming with game. The French *coureurs de bois* made their way through the forests and mountains using the natural highways to Lake Huron and Superior in search of the pelts.

The western end of Lake Erie isolated by a vast swamp to the south and east made it one of the last areas to be revealed. Virtually inaccessible except to the Indian tribes that called the Maumee Valley their home, the opening of travel on Lake Erie from the east brought Benjamin Franklin Stickney and thousands of white settlers eager for cheap land and the promise of a new life to the entrance to the gateway to the west.

They found the Maumee Valley filled with promise, but they also found layers of Indian cultures long vanished, coupled with Indian tribal identities that would be eventually crushed under the waves of white migration. This was the *old northwest territory.*

…those that came before…

Elias Fassett, Toledo pioneer and Benjamin Franklin Stickney's Vistula paperboy, often recalled the autumn's pallet of brilliant red hues intermixed with the shades of yellow from the two hundred mature sugar maple trees that were scattered throughout the three acres that comprised the earthen mound enclosure on Charles Crane's East Toledo farm. Fassett's farm

Benjamin Franklin Stickney

house was the next house south of the Cranes, and for as long as Elias could remember the earthen mounds had always been on the high bluffs of the Maumee River with Crescent Street on the south, centered around Fort Street[2].

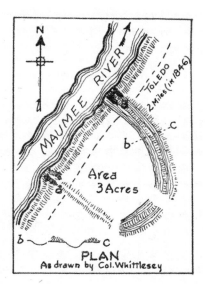

The Mound at Miami and Fassett Streets as drawn by Col. Whittlesey. Courtesy of *The History of the Maumee River Basin*, C. E. Slocum

Captain William Nason, early Toledo fireman from Toledo's Number 10's engine house, remembers as a young lad playing in the remains of semicircular mounds that made up the walls of the fort on the Maumee's high bluffs. *"... Standing on the very edge of the dirt mound you could see up and down the Maumee for miles.... They destroyed our fort when they cut Miami Street through from the city to Rossford."*[3]

Charles Whittlesey[4] of Cleveland said in 1848 that there were a string of such forts commencing at Conneaut, Ohio, and ending at Charles Crane's farm.[5] After years of farming, erosion, and benign neglect the only thing left of the mounds is a bronze plaque mounted on a huge boulder in front of the grain elevators at Miami and Fassett Streets, and sometimes the plaque was stolen for scrap value.

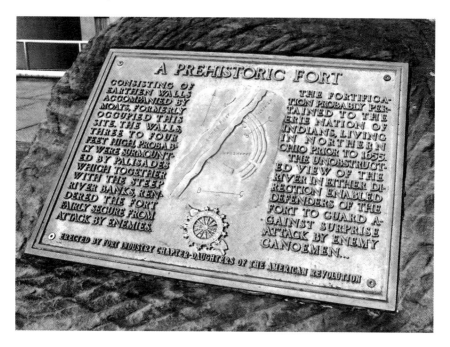

Historical plaque at Miami and Fassett Streets. Plaque placed by the Fort Industry Chapter of the Daughters of the American Revolution. Courtesy of the author.

Another of the earth mounds dating from about the early seventeenth century was located close to the Summit Street entrance to the Anthony Wayne or High Level Bridge. The mound extended from approximately Clayton and Oliver Streets to the high banks of Swan Creek. According to Dr. Slocum the established earthen works were almost eradicated by 1871 from present memory by the grading and usage of the streets.

Benjamin Franklin Stickney

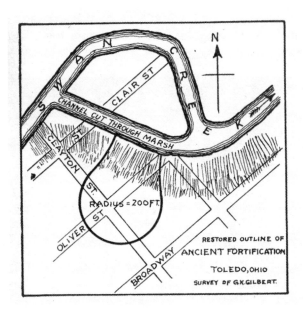

The Mound at Oliver and Clayton Streets at the Broadway entrance to Toledo's High Level Bridge, as drawn by G. K. Gilbert. Courtesy of *The History of the Maumee River Basin*, C. E. Slocum

Dresden Howard, who came into the Maumee Valley as a six year old youngster in 1821, befriended many of the Indians and learned their languages and customs. Dresden would later recall, as he gazed northward from his home on the knoll just above the *Council Oak,* that in those corn and bean fields there were twelve mounds that had been leveled by the plow.

Earthen works from two to three feet in height and thirty to thirty-five feet in diameter were mentioned in *The Mounds at Winameg* an article that Dresden Howard wrote in 1892.

".... In the late twenties my occupation as a fur trader and Indian interpreter led me over the trail from the banks of the Maumee to the Pottawatomie village ruled over by the grey

Benjamin Franklin Stickney

haired old chief, Winameg. The village was situated along the banks of Keg Creek, now called Bad Creek, and the site of our humble home. .... My curiosity was directed to several circular knolls or mounds nearly in the center of one of the villages, upon some of these mounds large oaks were growing at the time of my earlier visits. ..... I made inquiry of the old chief, whose head was white with the snows of a hundred winters, as to who made them..... His answer was "that no one was old enough to remember who made them." The trees growing on them were three times older than Winameg."

Map of the French American Empire from the book *The Conquest* by Dr. Randolph Downes, Vol. One of the Lucas County Historical Series, published by the Historical Society of Northwestern Ohio, 1948.

Benjamin Franklin Stickney

Archaeologists prefer to hedge their conclusions by saying *"... the cultural material of these ramparts we believe pertains to the Eries .... However, we prefer to call these Indians "the Whittlesey Indians."* Their name derives from the same Charles Whittlesey who wrote about the earthen works on Miami Street in 1848, and who was hesitant to label the Indians of the mounds as the ancestors of the Erie Indians.

Historian Randolph Downes said that if the *Whittlesey Focus People* and the Eries were one and the same or descendants this would place the Maumee Valley on *the stage of history.*[6] Recognizing the travel routes of the early French *coureurs de Bois*[7] it is easy to observe that of the five Great Lakes, Lake Erie or the Lake of the Cat, as it was known, was the last one to be discovered. The French explorers that encountered the *Nation of Bobcats or Cat Indians* named the lake after the Indians that lived along its southern shores.

Present historical research places the Five Nations of the Iroquois and the Indians of Lake Erie at odds with each other. The animosity arose because the Erie Indians of the *Lake of the Cat* would not pay the required tribute to the Iroquois in the number of beaver pelts and deer hides that the established trade with Dutch and English of the Mohawk Valley required. The *Erie* people preferred to ignore the demands of the Iroquois and trade directly with the French. The direct trade with the French gave them better prices for their pelts and improved prices for the trade goods. Allied with the Huron, and other Algonquin tribes the Eries knew they were taking a risk in going against the Iroquois. Finally the refusals by the Erie Indians, coupled with the Iroquois's internal conflict with the Huron people[8] in 1644, made war inevitable.[9]

Facing a forest with peltry of their own almost depleted and a significant loss of income as middlemen in the business venture, the Five Nations decided to follow their historical preferences of the past and eliminate the competition.[10] Traveling through the shores and back country of Lake Erie they killed every one of

Benjamin Franklin Stickney

the Erie or Cat Indians that they could find. As their warriors trekked westward along Lake Erie's shores they completely exterminated everyone they encountered. What Erie Indians survived were either forced into slavery or assimilated into other tribes, never again to gather as a cultural entity. The Iroquois had created "... a solitude, and called it peace. ..."[11]

For the next fifty years the Five Nations of the Iroquois carried war to all the tribal entities in the Great Lakes/ St. Lawrence River region, and all of them avoided the southern shores of Lake Erie.

The Maumee Valley was dormant till the Miami Indians cautiously reentered their ancestral homes on the Wabash River. The Miami had fled the Wabash region during the Iroquois wars to Iowa and then to the Fox River section of Wisconsin. Finding that they weren't welcome by the Fox Indians, the Miami once again moved to the St. Joseph River in southern Michigan. By 1701 the French and the Iroquois, weary of war, arranged a peace through the efforts of the French Governor, Count de Callieres. This peace enabled Antoine de la Mothe Sieur de Cadillac to build a fort at *de Troit* between Lakes Erie and Huron. The peace, Fort Detroit, and tribal confederacies enabled the French to begin trading for furs and pelts. With the French seemingly in control of the Great Lakes region the Miamis began to migrate into the Maumee Valley.

Led by Pierre le Moyne Sieur D'Iberville, the French traders established themselves on the lower Mississippi River. This created the final link in a trade route that coupled the Maumee/Wabash corridor with the Gulf of Mexico and the Great Lakes. With this link in place the sophisticated thinking of Antoine LaSalle and his trading routes began to flourish and prosper.

The Fox Indians[12] of Wisconsin under the leadership of Kiala resented the French and their trading policies. Much like Neolin, Pontiac, and Tecumseh, the Fox in an early attempt to preserve the Indian way of life laid waste to the Wisconsin and Fox Rivers fur trade in 1714. The trade routes which connected Green Bay to the Mississippi River and to Fort Michilimackinac were bankrupt. For over twenty years the Fox and their allies to the south kept the Wisconsin and Illinois countryside in confusion and chaos. This turmoil almost ruined the upper western fur trade to Fort Mackinac.

This disruption in the Wisconsin/Illinois fur trade only strengthened the Wabash/Maumee corridor. Within a couple of years after the Fox uprising, the French had set up a trading outpost at present day Fort Wayne, Indiana called Fort Miami[s]. What was good for the Wabash/ Maumee corridor was not necessarily good for the French. The comparative positions of the British and French, relative to the Maumee Valley, would later provide the fuse that would ignite the British and the French conflict in North America, with the Indians caught in the middle.

During the last year of King George's War of 1748, Chief Orontony or Nichols[13] , as he was sometimes called, found out that the British paid more for the pelts than the French. Incensed at their duplicity, The Wyandot under Orontony began to organize an Indian confederacy based in Sandusky that would remove the French from the Maumee Valley. Even with great cunning on the part of their leadership, the Wyandot stratagem was discovered before it could be implemented. With King George's War ending, the advantage that had brought Orontony to the forefront in trade relations had disappeared. Within the year the Wyandot leader traveled to Detroit to ask the French for clemency. One of the outcomes dictated by the French commanding officer was the creation of a French fortification on the north side of the Sandusky Bay. The military at Fort Sandouski were like the cork in the bottle that prevented further access to the Ohio country through the lakes and rivers of northern Ohio. The second part of Orontony's escape from death at the hands of the French was the burning of his village in April of 1748 as 119 families left for White River, in the Indiana territory.

Benjamin Franklin Stickney

In an effort to solidify French control over the Ohio Country Pierre Joseph Sieur de Celoron[14], in a *shock and awe* campaign, left Montreal with 20 French regulars, 200 Canadian Militia, and a few domesticated Indians for the Ohio Country. Celoron's orders were to visit all the Indian towns south and west of Lake Erie, and at the head and mouth of all the major rivers erect posts with leaden plates bearing the arms of France. The plates also asserted France's authority and power over the area, but instead of posting the proclamations Celoron buried them. With all the pageantry associated the typical *savoir faire* of the French, Celoron and his military force accompanied by vibrantly hued flags and banners held aloft left Montreal.

Everywhere Celoron traveled he received enthusiastic welcomes and promises of ever lasting friendship to France. When Celoron's expedition reached Pickawillany, near present day Piqua, Ohio, the Miami leader La Demoiselle or old Britain[15] as he later would be called, professed friendship. An old chief of the Miamis would later confide to Celoron *"I hope I'm mistaken, but I'm sufficiently attached to the interests of the French to say that La Demoiselle[16] lies."*[17] As Celoron descended the Maumee River he wrote in his Journal *"... The Indians in council made a conciliatory reply, with which the Governor of New France would be satisfied if one could believe in their sincerity; but it is to their interest to trade with the English, whose goods are so much cheaper than those of the French."* [18]

During the 1740's the tremendous advance in the British fur trade in western Pennsylvania was made possible by King George's War. The French were so short of trade goods during the war with England that they were unable to pay the Indians for their furs.[19] George Croghan was the first of the British traders to take full advantage of the past French failures in the region. By 1750 Croghan and the British had complete control of the Miami River, the Scioto River, the Cuyahoga River, and finally the Sandusky River. In effect the British controlled the eastern access to the Ohio country.

Benjamin Franklin Stickney

Traders from Pennsylvania and Virginia were crowding into the eastern Ohio country.[20] The Miami Indians at Pickawillany did not return to the Maumee to hunt and fish in as promised. Instead La Demoiselle was flying the British Union Jack when traders from Pennsylvania and Virginia were welcomed into his village on Loramie Creek. In a deliberate effort to keep the French in Detroit, George Croghan at the behest of Pennsylvania arrived to seal an alliance with the Miami's at Old Britain's Pickawillany. Fortified with a stockade, Pickawillany[21] became the center of British influence and trading for the Ohio country by 1750. In a demonstration of his loyalty to the English, Old Britain humiliated four Ottawa Indians when they arrived at Pickawillany with banners touting the French colors.

With the illusion of French influence over the Indians of the Ohio Country in jeopardy, Montreal sent Bellestre to destroy Pickawillany. By the time he reached the Maumee River his large band of Indians was reduced to 17 through the influence of the Ottawas that he encountered along the way.

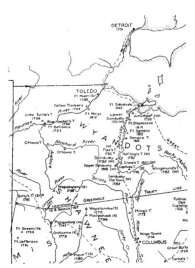

The Ohio Country of the Historic Indian Period
Compiled by H. C. Shetrone, Drawn by R. B. Sherman.
From Ohio Archaeological & Historical Quarterly, July 1918.

Benjamin Franklin Stickney

With the Bellestre expedition a failure, Montreal sent Charles Langlade[22] against Pickawillany in 1751. Previously Langlade as a young cadet in the French militia had gone to Pickawillany with three others with French banners flying to trade[23] when Old Britain had disgraced and brutally beaten them before the entire village. On his return Langlade told his friend Pontiac about his treatment and they both vowed revenge against Old Britain or LaDemoiselle.[24]

When Langlade accompanied by his long time friend Pontiac[25] and 240 Indians and militia on their way to Pickawillany entered the territory of the Ottawas, Langlade let Pontiac confer with the Ottawa Indians. Intimidated by Pontiac's mounting reputation as a warrior, the Ottawas debated the merits of Langlade's mission. Awed by Pontiac's oration skills, the Ottawas gave their permission.

An ink sketch of a warrior that would have followed Pontiac.
Shetrone, The Indian in Ohio, OAHQ, July 1918.

Benjamin Franklin Stickney

With most of the village's warriors hunting, the attack on Pickawillany was a complete surprise. The women were still working in the lush cornfields when the British traders were taken captive after only a few shots fired. Their trade goods worth over 3,000 pounds were seized, and fourteen Miamis were killed. During the celebration that followed Langlade's crushing success, one of the wounded English traders and Old Britain were burned and eaten. With their village and the English trader's stockade reduced to ashes, the Miamis returned to the Maumee River region.

On the 21st of June 1752, with Langlade and Pontiac projecting their vision of the future, the first of many conflicts for control over the lucrative fur trade of America had begun on the banks of the Miami River.[26] Coupled with the defeat of the Miami's Old Britain and his British support, the Ottawa warrior known as Pontiac grew in stature among his own.

The French attack on Pickawillany shifted the quiet war of *skirmish and reprisal* that was bubbling just beneath the surface to undeclared hostilities. The quarrel was altered from a British superiority in trade goods to French military control of the region. The Indians carefully watched the British response to the French military incursion, and they soon realized that the British would not always defend its allies. General Braddock emphasized that point when he said: *"... no Savage should inherit the land."* Braddock soon learned from the Delaware at Fort Duquesne the meaning of Shinga's reply: *"... if they could not live on the land, they would not fight for it."*

Many of the tribes from the major Indian groups that inhabited the Ohio Country[27] moved freely through the region. In any war party there were always several tribal affiliations, a climate that promoted loyalty to the individual not a cultural faction. What the Indians really shared was a lifestyle that was becoming increasingly dependent on trade with either England or France. One fine edge of the sword that the Indians encountered was the accommodation as to which of the European Nations would let them keep mastery over their ancestral land. The other edge of the sword was the dependence on the trade goods which were slowly destroying their way of life. They soon learned that without losing a single skirmish or battle, they would lose everything.

Endnotes from Chapter One
earthworks, the maumee valley, & the french

[1] Anthony and Dorcas [Davenport] Stickney had a son which they named Anthony Somerby Stickney, and on March 6th of 1770 he married Ruth [Brown Coffin]. Dr. Benjamin Franklin was Dorcas Stickney's favorite uncle, and as a result Dr. Benjamin Franklin offered the newly weds a bequest of sixty Spanish silver dollars if they would name their first born male child Benjamin Franklin Stickney.

[2] Fort Street was renamed Hathaway Street in honor of Dr. Harrison Hathaway of 1233 Miami Street.

[3] The Toledo BLADE, May 2, 1945.

[4] Squire and Davis, authors of the book *Ancient Monuments of the Mississippi Valley* published in 1848, contained a section by Whittlesey called *Ancient Forts of Northern Ohio*.

[5] Whittlesey went on to say that the forts as he called them all were constructed on principal rivers three to five miles from the lake.

[6] The Conquest, Randolph Downes, Lucas County Historical Series, p 13.

[7] The French in order to avoid the Iroquois turned inland and used the Ottawa River in Canada to reach the Great Lakes Country. This is why Lake Erie was the last to be discovered.

[8] Allies of the French.

[9] The date of 1644 is an educated guess on the part of the author.

[10] In 1609, French explorer Samuel de Champlain using fire arms in the Battle of Lake Champlain gains the lasting hostility of the devastated Iroquois.

[11] The Conquest, Randolph Downes, Lucas County Historical Series, p 14.

[12] The Fox Indians were called *Reynards* by the French.

[13] Orontony or Nichols of the Wyandot negotiated peace with the French on extremely favorable terms, and promised to keep the peace in the future. The Wyandot could trade with the British if they wished; however the French did not think that Orontony would. Finding the his band of the Wyandot deserted by their allies, Orontony made plans to leave the Ohio country. In April of 1748 Orontony destroyed his village and 119 warriors and their families left for the White River in the Indiana Territory. Soon after arriving Orontony died.

[14] Former French commander of Detroit and Mackinac.

[15] The Wyandot knew him as Pianguisha, the French as La Demoiselle, and the British as Old Britain.
[16] La Demoiselle translated means the lady.
[17] The Conquest, Randolph Downes, Lucas County Historical Series, p 21.
[18] The Conquest, Randolph Downes, Lucas County Historical Series, p 21.
[19] The reality of the situation was that the British with their command of the oceans captured the French ships bringing the trade goods to America. Also the French ships returning with the furs were captured and sunk.
[20] In 1748, Pennsylvania sent George Croghan with gifts for the *Twightees* [Miami] and the Miamis sent their delegates to Lancaster. The outcome of this understanding was that the Miamis at Pickawillany were to serve their trade relations with the French.
[21] Pickawillany is correct using Slocum, however Dr. R. Downes used Pickawillani. Since I am from northwest Ohio, I will use the "Y."
[22] Charles Langlade was a mixed blood from Michilimackinac with an Indian wife. Catholic, he was the maternal nephew of Ottawa Leader Lafourche. During Pontiac's uprising he remained neutral and rescued many of the English that were taken prisoner.
[23] An important series of councils between Gist and the Miamis had just concluded when *"... four Ottawas with a French flag, a gift of brandy and tobacco, and an invitation to the Indians to visit Detroit...."* The American Colonies in the 18th Century, Herbert Osgood, Columbia University Press, 1924, pages 288-9.
[24] The American Colonies in the 18th Century, Herbert Osgood, Columbia University Press, 1924, pages 288-9. Along with Sieur Charles Michel de Langlade, Lost Cause, Lost Culture, by Sandra J. Zipperer, appeared in the Voyageur, Historical Review of Brown County and Northwest Wisconsin, Winter/Spring 1999. Zipperer sights in a footnote *The Wisconsin Creoles*, by Russ Rentmeester, published 1987, pgs 33-39.
[25] New research places Pontiac along with Langlade in their raid on Pickawillany. Ohio Archaeology Blog, Bill Pickard, Ohio Historical Society, July 17, 2008. Also Sieur Charles Michel de Langlade, Lost Cause, Lost Culture, by Sandra J. Zipperer, appeared in the Voyageur, Historical Review of Brown County and Northwest Wisconsin, Winter/Spring 1999. Zipperer sights in a footnote *The Wisconsin Creoles*, by Russ Rentmeester, published 1987, pgs 33-39.
[26] Many historians believe that this marks the real start of the French and Indian War, 1754-1763.
[27] Ottawa, Delaware, Wyandot, Shawnee, Miami, and Mingo had intermingled so much that is was difficult to not find a village that did not have Iroquois long houses and Algonquin wigwams.

the first son of the Maumee Valley
chapter two

The southwesterly winds of spring, confused with the changing of the seasons, changed their direction to the northeast and began to sweep the waters of Lake Erie from the Falls of Niagara, down the entire length of the Cat [1]. Angered by the change of seasons, the *Cat* would halt the flow of the Maumee River and would raise the water in the *old Miami of the Lake* [2] as far west as the rock bar [3] some fourteen miles inland. The willow lined sand ridges of the Mud Creek estuary [4] familiar with the repeated onslaught of the wind driven waves, would easily have given way to the raging nor'easters. While many of the storms destroyed the early settler's dwellings and crops, the aftermath was a bonanza for those that knew where to look for evidence of the Ottawa Indians.

"… In 1853 a family by the name of Applegate lived for some years on what is now known as the Yeslin Farm at the mouth of the Mud Creek, below the Casino. After a severe wind on Lake Erie, which made a heavy sea that washed the bank away in front of the farm, the two Applegate boys would pick up Indian relics and trinkets on the beach from the Indian graves. Mr. Roselie Cowdrey, of this city, and myself, saw one of their collections that was sold to Joseph Canneff [5], then a jeweler in Toledo. … In this collection were massive silver earrings, bracelets and necklaces. …" [6]

Noted Historian Lyman Draper[7] using the recollections and memories of the Maumee Valley pioneers, chronicled a glimpse into the Ottawa Indians and Pontiac from the echoes of their lives along high banks of the Maumee River. The recovered relics and memories of the Maumee Valley's first inhabitants provided the threads from which Draper wove the historical cloth that changed the memories into the Maumee's recorded history.

"… Thursday, Oct. 4th, 1866, spent the evening on invitation, with Henry Hall [8]*, Esq. Merchant, Toledo. … Mr. Hall also showed me a somewhat smaller British Silver Medal which once belonged to Pontiac - struck in the reign of George III- with his images - with a legend on the reverse side*

Benjamin Franklin Stickney

representing a church and steeple and the insignia of Christianity and civilization guarded by a lion - and at the back a gaunt Indian cur evidently feebly attempting to protect the Indian wilderness in his rear from the advance of civilization. This medal was worn by Pontiac's widow, and by his son Otussa, in whose grave it was buried, and from which obtained by some of the old French settlers long since the Ottawa migrated to the west.

At Presque Isle, on the southern bank of the Maumee, a little below Toledo [for distance see Vol. 1 -- trip 1863] where the Ottawas formerly lived -- and, I doubt not, Pontiac -- the bank of the river keeps caving in, thus has exposed many relics -- one a large silver crucifix some nine or ten inches long with the initials J.M. yet dimly seen engraved thereon. Mr. Hall supposes it may have been James Marquette -- perhaps possessed by his old companion Joliet, a Jesuit -- whose final fate is involved in doubt and mystery after returning with Marquette and losing the latter's journals, etc. in the St. Lawrence -- and who perhaps may have retired, lived and died among the Ottawas, and buried on the bank of the Maumee at Presque Isle. Mr. Peter Navarre informed Mr. Hall, that the ancient Ottawas spoke of a black gown a priest, who lived and died among them, whose name is not now known. This crucifix undoubtedly belonged to that priest, whoever he was. If he was Joliet, then this crucifix may have been given him by that noted explorer, Marquette, whose initials it bears, at their final parting, as a friendly keepsake."

Conversely, almost fifty years before Stickney's birth, the Maumee Valley had already found its way into the rapidly growing historical consciousness of the country through the efforts of an Ottawa who had aligned himself and the future of his Algonquian *Outaoues* with the French. The son of an Ottawa father and a Chippewa mother raised in the great Ottawa village a little north of present day Detroit on the Canadian side of the Detroit River, Pontiac would forever leave his mark on the Maumee Valley. Known as *Obwondiyag*, *Pontiague*, or *Pondiac* his birth was generally conceded to have occurred between

1718 and 1725. [9] Pontiac's formative years absorbed the best traditions of his Ottawa and Chippewa heritage filtered through the customs of the French trappers and traders.

Intermarriage between the various tribal identities that surrounded the *throat or De'troit* was fairly common in the early 1700s', and by 1718 the Ottawa village that raised Pontiac was described in an early recorded memoir.

"... the village of the Outaoues was described as having a number of cabins constructed entirely of bark, very strong and solid, and very long with arched like arbors and an interior portioned into [family] *sleeping areas. In all, the village was completely enclosed within a palisade and contained approximately one hundred men and a number of women...."*[10]

By 1720 an agreement had been reached between the Wyandot, Chippewa, Pottawatomie, and Ottawa which provided the Ottawas with winter hunting grounds along the Maumee River. [11] Chief Quinousaki [Canoe-es-kee] reported that by 1748 the Wyandot and Ottawa were leaving their summer villages at Detroit, and traveling along the northern shores of Erie from the Sandusky Bay westward to the St. Josephs' River in Indiana. The Miami Nation reported to the French that the Ottawas were planning on establishing a permanent village at Roche de Bout in order to be closer to the English who were promising to give them better trade terms. [12]

One of first recorded instances of Pontiac's leadership abilities began with opposition to General Braddock's punitive military excursion into the Ohio County to drive the French out of Fort Duquesne [13] in 1755. For the estimated 60,000 French farmers and fur trappers in Canada and the Upper Great Lakes in 1750 to defend or hold the territory that France claimed was impractical considering the million plus population of the British Colonies in North America.

In 1754, Governor Duquesne asked the sometime trapper and militia cadet Charles Langlade to ask the Ottawas at Detroit to assist the French command at Fort Duquesne. The western Pennsylvania Iroquois, Delaware, Shawnee, and Huron were under the influence of the New York Iroquois who had decided that the Indians always suffered when they took part in the *"the White-Man's war."* Initially refused, Langlade turned to his friend from the Pickawillany skirmish, Pontiac, and together they gathered 637 Ottawas to their cause.

A personalized ink drawing that was sketched into a copy of the book *Ohio Indian Trails* by Frank Wilcox on September 30, 1963. From the author's collection.

General Edward Braddock assisted by Lt. Col. George Washington and 2,500 men arrived at the Monongahela River on July 9, 1755. Believing the intelligence from the Iroquois that had filtered through the woods "... *that the British were far superior to the French and would win without their help,*" Braddock continued to experience confidence. Even after narrowly escaping two ambush attempts, Braddock felt secure with the British *file and fife* march. Patiently waiting in their well camouflaged noose were 72 French regulars, 146 Canadian militia, and 637 Indians. The Ottawa contingent was led by Langlade and Pontiac. As Braddock reportedly ate lunch, Lt. Gage crossed the Monongahela and found his troops in a lightly wooded ravine flanked with steep prominent sides. Hidden by the hillside's undergrowth were the deadly muskets of the French and Indian militia. At the agreed upon signal the murderous fire reigned down on the unprotected British. Holding their ranks without an adversary in sight, the carnage was inescapable.

As the smoke of the battle's confusion settled over the Monongahela ravine and surrounding countryside, those men that were not killed in the initial volleys were still holding their ranks. With no order to fire against an invisible force that offered no target, the next cascade of shots started a rolling retreat among those that were left standing. The panic gained momentum as the volleys intensified, cutting down what was left of the advance column as they ran past Braddock's main force. Without waiting for orders as the carnage reigned around them, Braddock's central force, wheeled, and rushed for the safety of the teamster's wagons. Dropping their weapons and supplies as they ran to the rear, delivered added seconds of safety in their flight. After firing their muskets into the thinning throng, the Indians stopped to pick up the discards before reloading. The route to the safety of the rear became a headlong race for their lives as officers, soldiers, teamsters, and others added to the force that was racing towards possible survival.

All the stores of food, cannon, powder, balls, muskets, ammunition, horses, cattle, clothing, liquor and other items considered baggage, were captured as the Indians and militia plundered the retreating column of men. Almost 2,000 officers and men of the punitive expedition were either killed or wounded

Benjamin Franklin Stickney

along with General Braddock. Braddock was defeated by a force of 72 French, 146 Canadians, and 637 Indians coupled with his manifest arrogance. And of those 637 Indians Pontiac stood out as the leader of the Ottawas. The losses suffered by the French forces amounted to only 30. And most of the Indians that were killed, resulted from falling tree branches that were cut off by stray British cannon balls. [14]

Located among the papers of Sir William Johnson, the British Superintendent of Northern Indians was a speech dictated in 1757 and written in French by *Pontiague, Ottawa Chief, at Fort Duquesne*. The contents inferred that George Croghan had tried to lure the western tribes away from the French by a false story that Quebec had fallen to the British. Pontiac, fluent in French and English, would later keep two secretaries to handle his correspondence. One of his secretaries wrote all of Pontiac's dictated messages, while the other would read the letters that he received.

Most of the Indians throughout the *old northwest* believed that the French military would prevail over the British forces. As the years and eastern conflicts developed, battles in places like Pittsburgh, Niagara, and Quebec turned to the British forces. When the governor of French Canada surrendered to Lord Jeffery Amherst, the British commander in America, on September 8, 1760 a tenuous calm spread across what was to become the Northwest Territories and Pennsylvania. Confirmed by the Treaty of Paris in 1763, Canada and the Maumee Valley had become British and the Indians, who never lost a battle, had become British subjects.

The majority of the Indians that sided with the French viewed the British as their enemy, and even the Indians that aided the British felt used, abused, and unfairly treated. Regardless of the French and British outcome, the Indian elders from both sides predicted a renewed westward migration of white settlers on their fore-fathers lands. Predicted by the Northern Iroquois at the start of the French and Indian War, the tribal land holders would suffer as a result of the white-man's war.

Benjamin Franklin Stickney

One of Amherst's first official duties was to order Robert Rogers into the western territories to meet with the conquered Indians and take possession of the French forts at Detroit and Michilimackinac. The forts existed because the Indians allowed the French and now the British to use a little waste ground for construction of their dwellings. As a consequence, the forts were considered by the Indians as a convenient place to trade furs for the European goods that the Indians now considered essential in their day to day existence. The land still belonged to the respective tribes; after all they had never been conquered by the British, let alone the French. The Indians of the old northwest did not consider themselves subjugated by any European Nation, and as for the French and British they largely ignored the Indians and dealt with each other. When the Ottawas finally met with Rogers, the Indians were not supplicants seeking relief from their conquerors, but dealt with Rogers from a position of strength and dignity.

George Croghan Journal of 1760 November 23:
"... we embarked and sailed about three leagues and half to Ceedar Point where is a large Bay, here was a large encampment of Indians Wayondotts and Ottawas. ..." Croghan would later indicate that this leader was indeed Pontiac.

From Robert Rogers' Journal 1760 November 23:
"We rowed ten miles the next day on a course N:W& by W: to Point Cedar, & then formed a camp. Here we met some of the Indian messengers to whom we had spoken two days before ... A Sachem [Chief] of the Outawawa's was amongst them. ..."

Five years later when Robert Rogers rewrote his 1760 Journal titled *Concise Account of North America, Philadelphia, 1765* his notes had been changed or clarified to read:
"... I was met in my way by an embassy from him, of some of his warriors, and some chiefs of the tribes that are under him; the purport of which was to let me know that Ponteack was at a small distance, coming peaceably, and that he desired me to halt my detachment till such time as he could see me with his

Benjamin Franklin Stickney

own eyes. His ambassadors had also orders to inform me that he was Ponteack, the King and Lord of the country I was in."

When Robert Rogers arrived at the mouth of the Detroit River near *Brownstown* on November 27th he was met by a delegation of Indian leaders. Deferred to by the other Indian leaders present, Pontiac *"... demanded my business into his country, and how it happened that I dared enter it without his leave. ..."* Rogers replied that his mission was to remove the French from the area and had no designs against the Indians.

Though the Indian leaders did not see themselves as the conquered allies of the French, they realized that some accommodation had to be reached with the British. Robert Rogers reported that Pontiac indicated his willingness to *"Reign in his country in subordination to the King of Great Britain, and was willing to pay him such annual acknowledgement as he was able in furs, and to call him uncle.* On the other hand, Rogers said that Pontiac warned him that if the English neglected him he would shut off their route to the interior. Rogers would later write that Pontiac's demeanor indicated that *"... he was far from considering himself as a conquered Prince, and that he expected to be treated with the respect and honor due to a King or Emperor, by all who came into his country, or treated with him."*

At first, the shift from French to British rule did not change life at Detroit. The French continued to gather at Detroit to trade and exchange news. The Indians continued to trade with the French traders for blankets, kettles, knives, and guns. Even Captain Campbell, the British commander, hosted parties with dancing and card playing that lasted well into Sunday morning. However, there was one significant difference between the French and British rule. In the past the French secured the loyalty of their Indian allies, by among other things, giving them ammunition and other provisions. With the change in authority Campbell was under strict orders to change the status quo. Amherst had directed Campbell to withhold all such gifts. Nothing was to be given away, everything was to be bartered and paid for.

Benjamin Franklin Stickney

In Campbell's defense the decision was not his to make. Even Sir William Johnson wrote Amherst *"..It is very necessary and will always be expected by the Indians, that the commanding officer of every post have it in his power to supply them in case of necessity with a little clothing, some arms and ammunition to hunt with; also some provisions on their journey homewards, as well as a smith to repair their arms and working utensils."* On the other side, Amherst was determined to stop the practice of supplying the Indians free of charge. *"...I do not see why the Crown should be put to that expense. Services must be rewarded; it has ever been a maxim with me. But as to purchasing the good behavior either of Indians or others, that is what I do not understand. When men of whatsoever race behave ill, they must be punished but not bribed."*

The economic chaos caused by the British military's economy was also felt among the more western tribes, where Pontiac's influence was strong. The tribes centering around Detroit, the St. Joseph River, the Sandusky, the Wabash, and Maumee rivers were so numerous and so remote from the sources of British trading supplies, that it would have required a far greater expenditure than England was capable of making to satisfy even the nearer tribes. It was among these tribes that the French had recruited most of their Indian warriors during the French and Indian War. And it was a confederation of these tribes that was to provide the backbone of the forces that took part in Pontiac's war.

The Indians might have accepted the British policy with regards to powder and supplies if it would not have been for the English policy of rewarding officers with grants of land. The French had told them long ago that the British regarded the conquered Indians and their land as Crown property. And to confirm that policy, Amherst gave some grants of Seneca land near the Niagara Falls to some of his officers as a reward for services rendered. Amherst's action and that of the British land policy violated a treaty between the Six Nations and the colony of New York. Although the land grants were later invalidated in the

London courts, the damage was clear evidence of the Indians uncertain future in their own country. There were other subtle injustices that the Indians felt. The Indians were no longer welcome in the forts, and interracial mingling, especially marriage, was discouraged. In short, unlike the French, the British acted as if they had no obligation towards what they considered as conquered Indians.

The attitude of the Indians of the *old Northwest* was captured by Minavavana a Chippewa leader.[15]

"Englishman, although you have conquered the French, you have not conquered us! We are not your slaves! These lakes, these woods, and mountains were left to us by our ancestors. These are our inheritance. We will give them to no one ..."[16]

Agents and traders who knew the Indians best began to hear rumors of plots against the British. In western Pennsylvania, Neolin[17] a Delaware prophet was urging the Indians to return to the old ways and throw off the trappings of the white man. Along with the crop failure of 1762 came famine, and when the smallpox swept through the Ohio River Valley, inflicting misery on the Native Americans, more and more credence was given throughout the Indian territories to Neolin's teachings. When the Ohio Indians sought supplies and aid from the British, they were met with rejection. The Mingo complained that in times of crisis, fathers eagerly helped their children, brothers aided brothers, and that the unwillingness of the British to help them in time of dire need clearly indicated that they had *"bad designs"* against them. The current British actions proved that they were neither fathers nor brothers, but rather an evil people who wished only ill on the Indians in the Ohio country. In 1763, Newcomer, chief of the Turtle Clan of the Delaware, reflected the general sense of betrayal when he proclaimed that the British had *"grown too powerful & seemed as if they would be too strong for God himself."*

Neolin's mixture of Christianity and native religion, with references to visions, heaven, hell, sin, and God, while urging a return to a lifestyle that existed prior to contact with European civilization, appealed to the Shawnee and Delaware. But Neolin's message affected the British even more. The British recognized this new religion as a threat to the deerskin and fur trade which they had become accustomed to, and their inability to continue the missionary work among the Ohio Indians.

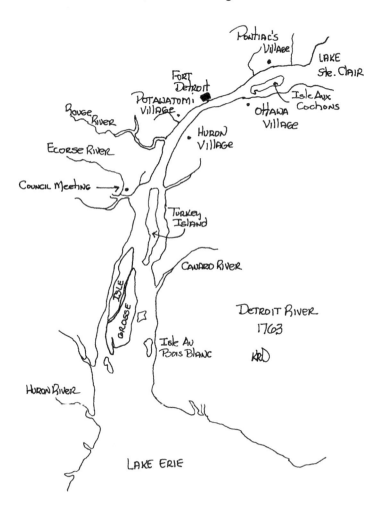

Map of the Detroit River circa 1760 from Lake Erie to Lake Ste. Clair. From the author's collection.

At the Indian Council on the banks of the Ecorse River near Detroit on April 27, 1763, Pontiac mixed and used parts of Neolin's revelations which aided his own ambitions and views of the western future. What follows is a part of Pontiac's address.

I am the Maker of Mankind, and because I love you, you must do my will. The land on which you live I have made for you, and not for others. Why do you suffer the white men to dwell among you? My Children, you have forgotten the customs and traditions of your forbearers. Why do you not clothe yourselves in skins, as they did, and use the bows and arrows, and the stone pointed lances, which they used? You have bought guns, knives, kettles, and blankets, from the white men, until you can no longer do without them; and, what is worse, you have drunk the poison fire water, which turns you into fools. Fling all these things away; live as your wise forbearers lived before you. And as for these English, -- these dogs dressed in red, who have come to rob you of your hunting grounds, and drive away the game, --- you must lift the hatchet against them. Wipe them from the face of the earth, and then you will win my favor back again, and once more be happy and prosperous.[18]

Pontiac, an Ottawa war chief, whom a French contemporary called *"... A proud, vindictive, war-like, and easily offended man ...,"* chose to combine Neolin's call for spiritual purification through prayer, and a return to the old ways of living with military power that would enable the western Indians not only to reject European culture, but also to drive the whites from their lands and keep them away forever. ....." Croghan wrote to William Johnson, who directed British Indian Policy in the colonies, that *"..Pontiac is a shrewd sensible Indian of few words, & commands more respect amongst those Nations, than any Indian I ever saw could do amongst his own tribe."* Pontiac was quite clear. He said the *"the Master of life put Arms in our hands,"* a variation on the Christian concept that God helps those who help themselves. Pontiac also told his followers, *".... It is important for us, my brothers, that we exterminate from our lands this nation which seeks only to destroy us."*

Benjamin Franklin Stickney

chapter two

Pontiac's Rebellion was just minutes away from sweeping through the Northwest Territories and the Maumee Valley.

Endnotes from Chapter Two
the first son of the Maumee Valley

---

[1] Early maps referred to Lake Erie as Lake of the Cat.
[2] Maumee River was referred to on old maps as *Miami of the Lake*.
[3] The location of the future towns of Perrysburg and Maumee on the Maumee River.
[4] The estuary of Mud Creek is widely recognized as Detwiler Marsh or the land reserved to Wasaonoquette. The area makes up the northern mouth of the Maumee River. *Birds of Lucas County, Louis W. Campbell, Toledo Zoological Society, October 1940, pages 8-9.*
[5] Canneff Jewelers, 240 Elm Street, Toledo. Jewelry, Watches, & Musical Instruments.
[6] From an article: *INDIANS OF THE MAUMEE VALLEY*, George A. Chase, Toledo BLADE, June 5, 1908.
[7] BIOGRAPHICAL FIELD NOTES of Dr. Lyman C. Draper, Toledo & Vicinity 1863-1866. Historical Society of Northwestern Ohio, Vol 5 No.4, October 1933.
[8] Henry Hall esq. October 4, 1866, In the 1872 City of Toledo Directory: Henry M. Hall, residence 328 Huron St. Mrs. Henry M. Hall, home east corner Madison & 13 Hall & Kellogg House, Sign and Ornamental Painters.
[9] With apologies to the 1949 Encyclopedia AMERICANA, Professor Emeritus Randall Buchman of Defiance College and my mentor sides with the current historical research that indicates Pontiac was born and raised on the Canadian side of the Detroit River in the shadow of the French fort, not at the confluence of the Auglaize and Maumee Rivers.
[10] Michigan Pioneer and Historical Collection, Volume 33, pages 679-680.
[11] Tanner, 1974, 12.
[12] Tanner, 1974, 22.
[13] Fort Duquesne located at the confluence of the Allegheny and Monongahela Rivers at the foot of the Ohio River. [Pittsburgh, Pennsylvania] The French seizing the location for a fort, constructed Fort

Benjamin Franklin Stickney

Duquesne. Fort Duquesne was an assertion of the French to claim ownership over land already stolen from the Indians by the British, and claimed by Pennsylvania and Virginia. Most Historians claim that this seizure and creation of Fort Duquesne and Washington's activities a year earlier was the start of the French and Indian War.

[14] The survivors of General Braddock's defeat on the Monongahela on July 9, 1755, south of Fort Duquesne of Fort Pitt, read like a who's who of the American Revolution. *Col. George Washington, Daniel Boone, Horatio Gates, Thomas Gage, Lt. Henry Gladwin, Christopher Gist, Dr. James Craik, Daniel Morgan, Captain Roger Morris, George Croghan, Ralph Burton, William Crawford, Dr. Thomas Walker.* For further information please read: BRADDOCK'S ALUMNI, Robert C. Alberts, American Heritage, February 1961, page 40.

[15] The following was given by Minavavana, a Chippewa leader, when Alexander Henry an Englishman was discovered impersonating a French trader at Mackinac in 1761.

[16] W.H.C.[State Historical Society of Wisconsin] 7, 155; William Joseph Seno, ed. Up Country. Voices from the Great Lakes Wilderness. Minocqua: Heartland, 1989, 165.

[17] Noted as the *Delaware Prophet*, Neolin related to all Indians that they must return to the ways of their ancestors and urged the Indians to reject the French, English, and all white men and their trade goods. If the Indians followed his teachings the animals would return to the forests and they would have dominion over their land once again.

[18] Francis Parkman, Conspiracy of Pontiac, Vol.1, page 206.

With an end to the overt hostilities of the French and Indian War, which was really between the British and the French, the Treaty of Paris in 1763 had effectively transferred all of the French land claims in the *Northwest Territories* to England. Without losing a single battle the Indians that had aligned themselves with the French had lost all of their tribal land claims. Like the cold winds that swept in from the north with winter's arrival, the Treaty brought the realization that the Indians had no influence in the disposition of their ancestral land. According to witnesses, Newcomer, the leader of the Delaware, was *"struck dumb for a considerable time"* when he learned of the Treaty of Paris. Along with the English proprietors came the rumors of secret deals that swirled across the meadows and through the forests before they vanished, leaving the Indians alone and huddled around a deteriorating campfire.[1]

British trader George Croghan in an attempt to deflect the anger that was building amongst the Indians against the English insisted: *"… that the French had no right to give away their [the Indians] country; as, they say, they were never conquered by any nation."*

Almost overnight the British charged higher prices for the inferior trade goods that replaced the French items, and the powder and lead used for hunting was no longer free. The Indian's dependence on the European trade goods, coupled with the vanishing beaver pelts and deer hides, was a downward spiral that was rapidly leading to the destruction of the Indian's way of life in the northwest. These changes that the Indians faced at the hands of the haughty British brought credibility to Pontiac and the teachings of Neolin. Along with the authority came the inevitable acceptance of Pontiac's call for warrior purification.

The men who really knew the Indians, the agents and trappers, saw first hand the devastation of the crop failures of 1762 and the death and destruction that accompanied the smallpox epidemics that had swept through the Ohio River Valley. The response to the tribal cries for help was met with indifference by the British. In September of 1762 Thomas Hutchins visited the

Shawnee and reported *"... People sick and dying everyday."* The Mingo complained about the British and their lack of assistance in a time of need. The tribal confederations indicated that the British were an evil people, and that in times of difficulty fathers eagerly came to the aid of their children, and brothers helped brothers.

> This paper was handed to me with other papers which belonged to Major B. F. Stickney of late of Toledo. Major S. was appointed Indian Agent by President Madison in 1812, and from that time to the time of his death in 1851, was much among the Ottawas, Pottawatamies, the tribes composing his agency, Miamis and Wyandots. He was an Enthusiastic searcher after Indian antiquities, and spent several years in the compilation of an Indian Dictionary that was never published. The history of Pontiac, as herein narrated, I have no doubt was collected from the Ottawa Indians by Major S. in compliance with a request made of him by Gen. Cass many years ago. This Valley (the Maumee) was the home of the Ottawas until 1839. Otusso one of the Chiefs of that tribe, who died in 1830 claimed to be a regular descendant of Pontiac. He was a man of fine talents, and great pride of character. Atoka or Ottokee, the last Chief in this Valley was also a descendant of Pontiac, but a miserable specimen of the indian. He died soon after the removal of the tribe west of the Mississippi.
>
> H. L. Hosmer.
>
> I send the original Manuscript, not having time to copy.

Cover letter by H.L.Hosmer, early editor of the BLADE, to Francis Parkman concerning the *Tradition of the Ottaway Indians.* Courtesy of the Massachusetts Historical Society.

Benjamin Franklin Stickney

chapter three

The tribes that gathered around the French trading posts were the same Indians that desperately needed the trade goods that England's military command refused to supply. These were the same Indians that the French had supplied and then recruited as warriors for the French and Indian War. The rise in the price of trade goods coupled with the demands for more and more land, was a deadly blend. Once again brought together by necessity, this was the same confederation of tribes that would provide the warriors for Pontiac's Rebellion.

Pontiac's Rebellion has been viewed from scarce glimpses and accounts that were written from British military records, several first hand accounts from the survivors of the siege of Fort Detroit, and conjecture from the historians that gathered the material together. Even the description of Pontiac comes from noted historian Howard Peckham. [2]

Fort Detroit circa 1705. Excerpted from Charles Richard Tutle's History of Michigan, Tyler & Co., 1873

Benjamin Franklin Stickney

Another son of the Maumee Valley who would write about the Ottawas and Pontiac was Benjamin Franklin Stickney. Raised in New Hampshire, Stickney would find himself calling the Maumee Valley his home. Employed as agent to the Ottawa Indians at Presque Isle, Stickney was ordered by Lewis Cass to write a history of the Ottawa Nation and Pontiac. [3]

The Ottawas in 1825 resided near Little Cedar Point where Rogers and Croghan would first make contact with Pontiac. Conversant in the Ottawa language Stickney met with Pontiac's widow Ken-tuck-ee-gun [4] and her son by Pontiac, Otusa [5]. Together, mother and son orally recalled the Ottawa Traditions as Stickney wrote them on paper. Filed away from the historical mainstream, the *Oral Tradition of the Ottawas* added new insights into Pontiac's Rebellion from the Ottawa's point of view. What follows is a portion of the Ottawa history transcribed by Stickney that pertained to the French & Indian War, and the events leading to Pontiac's Rebellion.

"... In about this stage in the order of events, the collaborator Pontiack appears acting as sole Shing[6] over the Chippewas, Ottawas, and Potawatomies who was an Ottawa by birth. The line of the other Shing M-cut-ta-mauke had disappeared. Pontiac was probably born about the time the French came to Detroit, or not long afterward. The first concessions out of Pontiack, that the Ottaways appear originated with us, when the French were preparing a force to meet the English at Fort Niagara. The Indians were called together, and requested to take a part with them against the English. Pontiack answered, this is a quarrel between you and people with skins of the same color as your own - we know nothing of the cause or merits of your contest. Why should we expose ourselves in a case of this kind? Why should I place my warriors in a situation to be covered with blood, that you may not be able to wash off? No one has done me injury: I have no cause to seek revenge.

The invitation by the french to join in the war, had been in the usual indian mode, by, presenting a belt of wampum made red by vermillion. When the french commanding officer understood that Pontiack declined receiving the belt; the officer

Benjamin Franklin Stickney

urged it upon him in the strongest terms. If you are covered with blood, or have the best quantity fall upon you, I am able to wash it off. Or if thorns should be put in your path, or any kind of brush: I will clear it out of your way. And then laid the belt across the lap of Pontiack as he was sitting. It was still refused: and again urged with additional promises. But an unequivocal refusal. However, after the close of the council Pontiack called a general meeting in council of all the old men and warriors, to make himself originated with their feelings upon the subject. They were not united in opinion. But, a leaning was discovered toward yielding to the wishes of the french. Again the french and Indians met in council: and again the Indians refused the tomahawk (as the belt of wampum is called). At length invited the french to meet in council - They met. Pontiack continued his speech by reciting all the great promises the French had made. And called upon them in an impartial manner to remember them. Which the French promised. Now said Pontiack, I will take hold of your tomahawk, since you push me so hard. You will not let me have any peace otherwise.

The Indians joined the French and marched to near Fort Niagara. When they arrived in the neighborhood of the British force: they found the six nations had joined the British. The Indians of the two confederacies had a secret interview. And it was agreed, that they should not charge their pieces with anything but powder in firing upon each other, when they should be brought into action. But, that they might charge with ball respectively in their aim upon the English or French. When this understanding was brought to practical test the six nations were found to charge with lead. It does not appear that the whites on either side became acquainted with the agreement; or the want of good faith on the front of the six nations. For all it appears that hostilities took place in consequence of the Indians.

After the return of the French and Indians to Detroit, and the orders for the surrender of the military post to the English, and the Indians informed of the change to take place; Pontiack complained to the French of the non-fulfillment of their engagement to wipe away the stains of blood received in the late expedition, and to protect and take care of them as children. He was told that the English were under obligation to do to, and for them, all such things as they the French were bound to do. Although not satisfied, he found further complaint useless. After the change of fathers took place, Pontiack went to visit his new father the British commanding officer at Fort Detroit. Upon entering the quarters of the officer, he saw the chief of the six nations, who presented his hand to him, to shake hands. Instead of receiving it, he took him by the back of the neck, and thrust him out of the room without speaking a word. The Seneca chief understood the matter, without making inquiry. He recollected the charging with ball, instead of powder alone.

Origin, progress, and termination of the war of Pontiack. A brother of Pontiack died. And Pontiack visited the commanding officer of Fort Detroit (Col. Campbell) to ask for assistance to clothe his brother, and other wise to perform such ceremonies as he should think proper for the internment of the important individual deceased. Upon asking for aid, the english officer asked him lightly why he did not call upon his french father? The feelings of Pontiack were wounded. He answered, yes, he could, the wound inflicted was perceived. The english father said he was only in jest. Pontiack could not submit to jesting on such an occasion. He left the room, and fort immediately without compromise. After the performance of the ceremonies of internment of his brother: Pontiack called a secret council of all the chiefs of the four nations, who were near. And in laying before them the business of the council, said, I am now about to speak to you of a very important matter - I wish no one of you to speak otherwise than as I speak. This new father has treated me as a very little child he has told me to go to my french father. That I will do. I will not ask him again for anything. He thinks me very small, and very weak. He shall know that is not true. He shall have enough of the trial of my strength to know what it is. When he had finished speaking, other chiefs spoke. The general sentiment expressed, was, in the indian mode. "You have spoken and you shall not lie." Pontiack again said. A speech must be prepared, and sent to all the other indians with whom I am connected. It must pass under ground, in the manner of the ground mole. I will tell them what is to be done. After some time, an other council was assembled. It met at the common council house. But, they were removed into a valley, a small distance from the left bank of the Detroit River, opposite hog island [7]. To avoid observation. There the plan of attack of the British Forts was settled. Great care was taken to prevent the disclosure of the secret proceedings. But, a women approached unperceived, so near them as to hear what passed. This women went to the commanding officer at Detroit and communicated what she had heard. She being a worthless straggler among the private soldiers, the officer paid no attention to what she said. Just before the time fixed for the execution of the design an Indian chief came to Col. Campbell and informed him of all the particulars.[8] And he set about making preparations to render abortive the plans of Pontiack.

The scheme of Pontiack was to have a simultaneous attack made at Detroit, Michillimackinac, and Lower Sandusky. "

The tribal elders, counseled by Pontiac, had come to the conclusion that war with the British was the only way to preserve the Indian way of life. And on May 7th, 1763 the followers of Pontiac from the various tribes and confederations of the old northwest arose as one and attempted to drive the British from the Northwest Territories. By the end of June, all of the British outposts throughout the Great Lakes and the greater northwest, with the exception of Fort Detroit and Fort Pitt, had fallen to the tribal confederation led by Pontiac.

Fort Detroit was able to hold out against Pontiac because of the advance warning given to Major Gladwin, and Fort Pitt was able to resist because smallpox was introduced among the Indians. [9]

The British considered this outbreak of war in the northwest so serious that the region beyond the Appalachian Mountains was closed to settlement and trade by Royal Edict. Migration and trade resumed in October of 1763 when Pontiac failed in his attempt to destroy Fort Detroit.

After failing in their plan of deception to gain entry to Fort Detroit using a popular Indian game, some of Pontiac's warriors had gone directly to the Isle au Cochon[10] and took their revenge on retired Sergeant James Fisher and his family. This early incident

Benjamin Franklin Stickney

in the siege of Fort Detroit would have ramifications that would ripple through the courts and would form the basis for Indian tribal relations to this day.

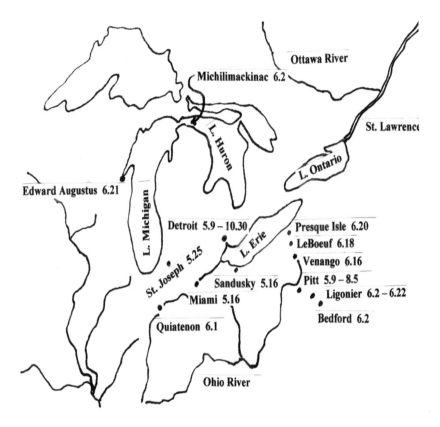

British forts that fell to Pontiac in May & June 1763. Courtesy of the Author's Collection.

Intending to butcher the cattle which grazed on Hog Island the warriors brought their canoes to rest on an outcropping of sand that had formed at Fisher's landing. On the island at the time and unaware of what had transpired at Fort Detroit were three soldiers, two of whom were on leave acting as herdsmen and a third, Francois Goslin, who was squaring some building timbers.

Retired James Fisher, his wife and four children, and their maid called the island their home. [11] Within minutes the Ottawas had killed and scalped Fisher along with two of the soldiers His wife was hanged with a raw-hide thong, and one of the Fisher children was brained. The maid who was Goslin's wife and the three remaining children of the Fisher Family were taken prisoners. The maid, not believing the Indians, attempted to escape and was killed on the spot.

Of the remaining three Fisher children; Millie who was one at the time, was taken to the Saginaw Bay and adopted by the Chippewa. Marie, 15 months, was returned to Fort Detroit after the siege failed and died of smallpox in October. Only six year old Betty Fisher remained with her Ottawa captors. [12]

One of the last to be killed on Hog Island was Francois Goslin who was dragged from his hiding place and killed. The next day two Canadians crossed over to the island to bury the early victims of Pontiac's Rebellion. They returned several days later and found Francois Goslin's hands thrust above the ground entreating God's mercy. Once again they covered Goslin's remains and not believing what they had previously witnessed they returned again and found Goslin's hands above the ground seeking God's mercy. This time they told a priest who hastened to the grave, sprinkled Goslin with holy water, and performed the overlooked rites of burial. [13]

By the Fall of 1763, Pontiac came to the realization that if France's promise of aid did not arrive as promised, the various tribes that supported the confederacy would disband and prepare for the coming winter. At the end of October a messenger arrived from Mons. Neyon, Commander of Fort Chatres on the Mississippi River, and informed Pontiac that the promised help from France would not arrive. France was at peace with the English. [14]

Benjamin Franklin Stickney

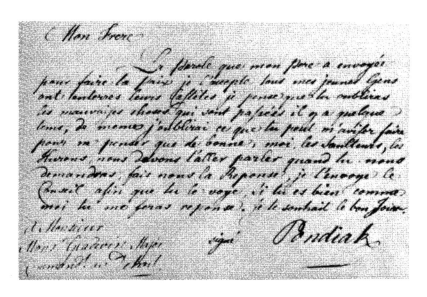

Pontiac's note of surrender in French October 31, 1763.. From Howard Peckham's *Pontiac and the Indian Uprising.* The English translation follows:

My Brother
The word which my father has sent me to make peace I have accepted; all my young men have buried their hatchets. I think you will forget the bad things which have taken place for some time past. Likewise I shall forget what you may have done to me, in order to think of nothing but good. I, the Chippewas, the Hurons, we are ready to go speak with you when youask us. Give us an answer. I am sending this resolution to you in order that you may see it. If you are as kind as I, you will make me a reply. I wish you a good day. "Pontiac" Signed with his symbol. [Amherst Papers, vol. 7, Clements Library.]

As the significance of the message rippled through the tribes, Pontiac's siege of Fort Detroit drifted into the darkness of the coming night. Pontiac along his most trusted followers and seven year old captive Betty Fisher moved their camp from Detroit to the islands of the Maumee River. According to Peckham, the Ottawas had made two winter villages on the Maumee. On the north bank opposite Roche de Bout Island, stood the village of pro-English Atawang. Pontiac's village was

further up the Maumee on an island which is now divided in two.
[15] [16]

As winter settled in the Maumee River valley, Pontiac and his followers found the Maumee River partially frozen on the 17th of November 1763 as they arrived on the island[17]. Betty Fisher with only rags for clothing and a blanket for warmth, tried to gather closer to the campfire. Frequently soiled with her constant diarrhea, Betty had tried to wash the feces from her meager clothing. As her clothing dried the smell of excrement permeated the crowded lodge adding to Pontiac's already foul mood.

In an obvious rage over the repugnant odor from Betty's soiled clothing, Pontiac focused his pent up anger as he roughly picked her up in an effort to throw her into the coldness of the night. As Pontiac's hands tightened around the object of his scorn, Betty's bowels weakened by dysentery and fear, sprayed feces everywhere.

Still holding her away from his body, Pontiac walked out of the lodge to the river's edge, and threw Betty into the ice-encrusted Maumee River. Pontiac called to Mushett Cuerie [18] to go and drown the struggling child. *"… You bragged of your courage. Show me now if you are a man or not! …"* Cuiellierie took no notice till Pontiac in a menacing voice spoke a second time. Mushett waded into the cold water and held Betty under the dark waters of the Maumee till she stopped moving. [19]

According to later testimony Alexis Cuiellierie then picked up the child from the water and carried her past Pontiac in the woods behind the lodge where he was joined by his friend Jean Maiet. [20] Using their tomahawks and knifes they tore at the frozen earth till a suitable grave had been fashioned. As they laid Betty in her grave her legs began to shake, and Maiet took this as a rebuke from God for what they had done. [21]

In the Spring of 1765 Jean Maiet left Pontiac's village on the Maumee and traveled to Detroit were he told the story of Betty Fisher's death to Lt. George McDougall and two prominent

Frenchmen traders who resided with the British. The British were able to realize that the death of Betty Fisher at the hands of Alexis Cuiellierie was an opportunity to assert the rule of the Crown over Detroit's ethnic French. Especially against those who had aided Pontiac. They also thought that this investigation would provide an opportunity to make a legal distinction between the French and Euro-American inhabitants and the Indians

Alexis Cuiellierie was the son of Antoine Cuiellierie a prominent leader of Detroit's French community and friend of Pontiac. Alexis had aided the enemies of the Crown and fought against the English, so it was no surprise that when Alexis risked a summer visit to Detroit in 1767, he was arrested and thrown in jail.

Informed that he was being charged with the murder of British subject Betty Fisher some four years earlier, Alexis's family began to plan his defense. Denied bail by the court, Alexis's jailers weighed the importance of the British Fisher family against the expanding business interests of the French Cuiellierie family and promptly released Alexis. Pontiac, ordered to Detroit by the British arrived on August 29th, said that he would neither confirm nor deny who had drowned Betty Fisher. Furthermore, Pontiac asked the British to drop the charges against Alexis.

After days of testimony from Alexis Cuiellierie and Jean Maiet and others present during Betty Fisher's murder, the British declined to show any interest in prosecuting Pontiac. "*The fact was that Pontiac, though he lived within the Ling's claimed realm and under the Crown's claimed sovereignty and protection, was not in anyone's view a Crown subject. ... He [Pontiac] was instead the leading member of a separate nation, a nation that, however subordinate, had just made peace with Great Britain, a peace that obliterated the acts of war.*"[22]

The Belt of Friendship that Pontiac carried formalized the relationship between tribes and the Crown and that the peace that had been negotiated had buried all "*...that had happened* *during the war. ...*" If Pontiac's Rebellion had been a revolt, Pontiac and others would have died at the end of a hangman's noose. Instead no Great Lakes or other Indian of the Northwest was ever brought to trial for rising against Great Britain.

Within four years after the siege of Detroit Pontiac had gone from a respected enemy of the Crown to an influential leader among the Indian tribes of the northwest. Pontiac became a man to be courted and respected by the Crown, a man to be brought into their realm of interest. Or, perhaps *"knocked in the head."* [23]

Endnotes from Chapter Three
rebellion and pontiac's days on the Maumee

---

[1] In November of 1762 a secret provision in the Treaty of Fontainebleau between France and Spain, gave Spain the Louisiana Territory.

[2] *Description of Pontiac: "At maturity Pontiac was not attractive in appearance by the beauty standards of the white race. A fairly reliable source testified that he was a tall man and not handsome yet another reporter calls him a remarkably well-looking man: nice in his person, and full of taste in his dress, and in the arrangement of his exterior ornaments. He was physically strong, as would be expected of a good warrior, and his frame was solidly filled out. Of course, his hair was black and straight, and his face was free of beard. His skin was said to be lighter than average and probably was shiny from frequent oiling with bear fat. His body must have been considerably tattooed in conformity with custom. On ceremonial occasions he also painted his face according to his own design. His hair was worn in a narrow short pompadour, diminishing from front to back. The Ottawas told Cadillac it gave his enemies less to take hold of. Besides the beads in the ears, the stone in his nose and silver bracelets on his arms, Pontiac may have worn a collar of white plumes or beads around his neck and a few feathers tied in his short hair."* Howard H. Peckham, *Pontiac and the Indian Uprisings*, 1947, p28.

[3] According to Willard Carl Klunder in his book [*Lewis Cass and the Politics of Moderation, Kent State University Press, 1966, page ix, 52]* Secretary of War, Lewis Cass, planned to write a biography of Pontiac

but did not proceed beyond the status of gathering material. Cass at the urgings of Henry Whiting and Henry R. Schoolcraft in the early 1820s' realized that within another generation or less the Indian way of life was coming to an end. In an attempt to gather information on the tribes under their control, each Indian agent was sent a circular letter of over sixty pages detailing the questions that were to be answered and retained. For some unknown reason Benjamin Franklin Stickney complied with the request but never sent the completed content to Lewis Cass.

[4] With Pontiac's first wife he had a daughter that was named Meck-ke-sic-ko-qua. After his first wife died Pontiac married another women who died childless. His second wife before she died made him [Pontiac] promise to marry her 12 year old sister Ken-tuck-ee-gun. Ken-tuck-ee-gun was the third wife of Pontiac, and their son was named O-tusa, the youngest of Pontiacs three known sons. Ken-tuck-ee-gun lived into her advanced years and was a renowned elder often sought for advice.

[5] According to noted historian Lyman Draper Otussa, Pontiac's son died at Toledo's Presque Isle around 1828 as a result of being poisoned by Oquanoxa, an Ottawa village chief on the Auglaize River near present day Defiance, in revenge for having been removed as council chief. Otussa is reputed to have said *"I know the man who has poisoned me."* Draper goes on to say that Otussa was buried on the east bank of the Maumee River near the town of Manhattan.

[6] It appears that the term *Shing* is a prefix meaning leader or chief in the Ottawa language.

[7] Hog Island or Belle Island, as it is presently known, is located at the northern end of the Detroit River, opposite Sandwich, Ontario and about two miles north of Detroit.

[8] The story of the lone Indian girl betraying the planned onslaught of Fort Detroit has been the crux of Francis Parkman's work *The Conspiracy of Pontiac*. However the French Priest's *"Pontiac Manuscrpt"* attributes Major Gladwin's warning to *"... the plot was disclosed to Gladwin by a man of the Ottawa Tribe..."* Continuing he states that the next day Pontiac sent several of his warriors to the Pottawatomie camp at Springwells to seize an Ojibwa girl who was questioned, and later severely beaten, before being allowed to return to her camp. In a brief letter to General Amherst, Major Gladwin states *"... on the 7th he [Pontiac] came, but I was luckily informed the night before he was coming to surprise us."*

The truth of the warning account in Indian agent Stickney's narrative probably lies with William Tucker. Tucker, a white settler, was captured by a Pottawatomie raiding party and adopted into the tribe. Learning of Pontiacs intentions from his adopted sister, Tucker passed the information to Major Gladwin, and his adopted sister was in all probability the women that Pontiac had beaten senseless. For further clarity please read: *The Gladwin and Pontiac Fable*, by Henry A. Ford, Michigan Pioneer Collection, Vol. 10, page 104-6.

[9] Captain Ecuyer, a Swiss soldier of Fortune, aiding the British in the defense of Fort Pitt [Fort Duquesne] suggested that the Indians be allowed into the fort to talk about terms of surrender. The British gave blankets and other cloth items infected with smallpox to the Indians as evidence of their sincerity, and within a short period of time a smallpox epidemic spread through the Indian population surrounding Fort Pitt.

[10] Isle au Cochon or Hog Island was located in the Detroit River, and is known today as Belle Isle.

[11] Howard Peckham, *Pontiac and the Indian Uprising*, page 135.

[12] Howard Peckham, *Pontiac and the Indian Uprising*, page 135. Also St. Aubin's account in Michigan Pioneer & Historical Collection, Vol 8, page 352.

[13] St. Aubin's Account, Michigan Pioneer & Historical Collection.

[14] LaJeunesse, 1960, Vol LXXIX.

[15] From Captain Thomas Morris' Journal dated August 1764 *"... on leaving this village and going upstream, Morris passed that same day an island on which Pontiac's village was located. The Maumee River widens just above Roche de Bout and is divided by two large islands. ..."* Most likely present day Indianola Island.

[16] As noted earlier Ken-tuk-ee-gun, Pontiac's third wife's village was at Presque Isle the site of Toledo's CSX coal loading facility. In an article from the Toledo City Directory 1858-9 said: *"Chief Pontiac lived at Presque Isle [which is now the Toledo Port Authority]. Before 1769 the Pontiac encampment was on Front Street between the Norfolk and Western Rail Road Bridge and Millard Avenue."* Another article in the Toledo BLADE by S. S. Knabenshue, dated December 12, 1903 said *"An Ottawa village occupied a location on the East Side, below Ironville, probably near the northern corporation line. It was on the site of Pontiac's encampment after he left Detroit in 1764. Peter Navarre described it as consisting of about sixty whitewashed log cabins, arranged in two rows, occupying a grassy ploy of ground opposite Manhattan"*

[17] Indianola Island was also known as Missionary Island and consisted of 315 acres. Off of its south end and separated by an extremely narrow creek is Grave Island. The two largest islands were at one time joined and together they made Pontiac's Village. Fred Vollmar, the man who developed Vollmar's Amusement Park, found arrowheads, stone pipes, silver broaches, skinning stones, and other relics of village life.

[18] Mushett Cuerie was the name that Pontiac had given Alexis Cuiellierie.

Benjamin Franklin Stickney

[19] Jean [John] Maiet's Accusation, August 4, 1767. Received by General Gage by way of Trumbull April 25, 1768. Gage Papers.
[20] Howard Peckham calls him Maiet; Richard White calls him Maret, but Gregory Evans Dowd in his book, *War under Heaven*, suggests that it may have been Jean Morad who was reported to have wintered [1767-1768] with the St. Joseph Pottawatomi.
[21] Gregory Evans Dowd, *War under Heaven*, John Hopkins University, 2002.
[22] Gregory Evans Dowd, *War under Heaven*, John Hopkins University, 2002, page 345, note 19.
[23] General Thomas Gage, North American Indians, Thomas Hoxie, Houghton Mifflin, 1996, page 496.

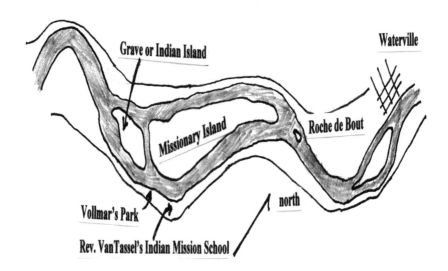

Pontiac's village below Waterville on Missionary or Indianola Island. Courtesy of the author.

Benjamin Franklin Stickney

conflict on the maumee
chapter four

A respected Indian elder, revered within his own tribe and throughout the northwest, reflected on the European intrusion into his way of life. *"The British and the French were the scissors and we were the cloth. Each cut reduced what had been given to our ancestors by the Great Spirit. Our world was coming to and end and we didn't even realize it."* [1]

The great Indian Confederacies of the Iroquois and the Algonquin should have realized that when Louis XIV, a king from across the great salt sea, gave Cadillac a grant of fifteen acres on the *"the throat"* [2] for a fort to house the French soldiers, that this was Indian land that he was giving away. Not only was there an assault on the land, but with the explorers came the *Black Robes* and the outright rejection of the Indians belief system.

The inherent wars between the matrilineal Iroquois and patrilineal Algonquin confederacies had almost come to an end by the 1700's and the Algonquin aligned Indians over a period of several generations began to use the Ohio region without great fear of Iroquois reprisal. The Ottawa, Delaware, Wyandot, Shawnee, Miami, and the Mingo were beginning to see the possibilities of the Ohio land and its mild climate, and began to establish enduring villages and tribal territories.

Frequent contact with the *whites* provided an increased dependence on the iron pots, needles, knives, and other trade goods which over time became the necessities of everyday Indian life. The Indians used the British and French to gain an advantage over ancient enemies and tribal loyalties, and as a result these loyalties were exploited by the Europeans. Each side used the Indians to their advantage, and every time the Indians tried to reach an accommodation with the Europeans a larger part of their lifestyle and lands was devoured.

After each conflict between the British and French in North America, regardless of the nation that they fought for, the Indians would lose their traditional land along with their ancestral graves to the advancing plow and axe. Within a decade of Pontiac's Rebellion, the American Revolution of 1776 would

Benjamin Franklin Stickney

remove the British land claims and further the *thirteen fire's*[3] incursion into the Indian lands of the northwest.

After each war, the Indians were faced with a new and more powerful adversary, and their recent antagonists were now their allies. Each conflict that the Indians faced, whether it was European or American in nature, resulted in a reduction in their numbers and territory. The tribal elders began to realize that each conflict against the Americans resulted in less European support, and that the Americans *were more numerous than the leaves of the forest*. The Indians were on their own …. they were now fighting for their very survival.

About a mile from Marietta on the Ohio River, twelve settlers were by American standards of warfare brutally murdered[4] by the Indians. However, the reality of the situation was that the Indians and settlers had learned how to kill from each other. The resulting publicity of the massacre resulting from the Indian depredations in the Eastern press caused the flow of settlers and land sales for the Ohio Company to trickle to a stop. Previously the lookouts at Fort Harmar[5] on the Ohio River reported that they had counted eight or nine hundred flatboats carrying twenty-thousand settlers, horses, cows, and other livestock bound for Kentucky. They also estimated that there were more than 4,000 settlers located in the area northwest of the Ohio River and north to the Wabash River. To continue the flow of settlers and land sales to the speculators, the sun had risen on what was to be the final incursion against the Indians. The drive against the Indians originated at the Ohio Company's [6] settlement at the confluence of the Muskingum and Ohio Rivers at Marietta.[7]

General Josiah Harmar, fresh from his success in routing a band of Cherokees who were plundering flatboats on the Ohio River in April, left Fort Washington[8] with a battalion of regulars, and twelve hundred Kentucky and Pennsylvania volunteers to punish the Indians. Leading the advance guard[9], Colonel John Hardin marched north on September 26th and by the 15th of October, 1790, Hardin, without firing a shot, was camped in the Indian village of Kekionga[10] at the head of the Maumee River. Three hundred houses and numerous storehouses of the Miami Indian village were deserted, but the advance force kept complaining that their horses were wandering off.[11] When Harmar's expedition left Kekionga they burned over 20,000 bushels of corn.

General Harmar. Courtesy of the Ohio Archaeological and Historical Publications, Vol 21, 1912.

The British system of intelligence, aware that an American force was coming into the Maumee Valley, forwarded the information to Alexander McKee,[12] who then informed Little Turtle of the Miami Confederation.[13] The exaggerated reports of Harmar's Expedition had been tested and when Colonel Hardin returned from destroying two Delaware towns up the St. Joseph River, Little Turtle and his Miami tribal confederation were waiting. Little Turtle completely surprised Colonel Hardin before chasing the punitive expedition southward from the Maumee Valley, leaving twenty-four dead. When General Harmar and Colonel Hardin rejoined each other about a day's march from the burned Indian village of Kekionga, Hardin demanded a chance to return and teach Little Turtle a lesson. Aware that the soldiers were returning, Little Turtle again routed the Americans. This time General Harmar left Kekionga with 183 killed, 31 wounded and his army in a head long retreat to Cincinnati's Fort Washington. Harassed all the way south, the expeditionary force was in complete disarray and bedraggled when they arrived at Fort Washington. [14]

Friday, November 4th, 1791
A little over a year later, General Arthur St. Clair, Governor of the Northwest Territories, was under extreme pressure to punish the Miami Indians under Little Turtle for General Harmar's defeat. Another more important reason was to make the territory once again safe for settlement and increased land sales.

After visiting with President Washington for counsel, and pleased with his appointment to Major General, Arthur St. Clair was conferring with his officers to rid the land from the Ohio River to the Wabash of Indians. At the same time that St. Clair was in Washington, Cornplanter,[15] a Seneca Indian leader, and British Colonel Henry Proctor were in Detroit trying to arrange for peace.

After waiting what they thought was a sufficient amount of time for results from the peace initiative, General Charles Scott with Colonel James Wilkinson set out to rid the Wabash River region of any Indians they found. The resulting hostilities convinced the Indians that once again any talk of peace was a ruse to take more land. St. Clair ordered Wilkinson to cut a swath of destruction throughout northern Indiana from Kankakee to the Little River.

Benjamin Franklin Stickney

conflict on the maumee
chapter four

General Arthur St. Clair. Excerpted from *Howe's Historical Collections*, Howe, 1896

With orders from President Washington to advance on Fort Wayne from Fort Washington, General St. Clair left Cincinnati in the middle of September with 2,300 men. After building Fort Hamilton[16] and with the militia already deserting, St. Clair sent the main force north with General Butler. Armed with diluted powder that would not carry bullets the length of the musket, axes made out of soft metal, clothing that disintegrated when washed, and wine that was of a terrible quality General St. Clair ordered his men to advance. He would follow with proper supplies. Two weeks later, on the 13th of October St. Clair's troops were on half rations of flour when they began building Fort Jefferson six miles south of Greenville.

Like General Harmar, General St. Clair's horses were disappearing at an alarming rate, but Indians were not noticed till the 28th when the expedition was in the swampy headwaters of the Wabash River.[17] At night the sentries fired so many volleys at an unseen enemy that the officers thought the main battle was imminent. It was not till the morning of November 4th, 1791 just before sunrise that Little Turtle and his confederation of

Indians fell upon 1,400 of St. Clair's forces. Of the 1,400 men on the field St. Clair lost 890 killed or wounded. Once again Little Turtle demonstrated his prowess against the Americans. [18] It was said that some of the survivors did not stop running till they reached Cincinnati, and when the burial detail returned they found many of the 600 dead staked to the ground and others with their mouths filled with dirt. [19] This act was viewed by the Indians as a macabre way to give the soldiers the land they so desired.

Within weeks after St. Clair's defeat the aligned tribes [20] met on the banks of the Ottawa River [and Miami of the Lake or Maumee River]. According to the written record two respected leaders with opposing viewpoints were chosen to debate the path that future relations with the settlement and trade *thirteen fires* should take.

"... *fome of their wife and moft experienced chiefs, as is their cuftom on like occafions, were appointed to repeat to the council, the reafons which ought to operate, on the minds of nations, for and against the meafure propofed. Two fpeakers were named on each fide, and thefe were directed not to confult their refentments on one hand, nor their doubts on the other; but be guided folely by the interfetf, honour, and glory, of the nations; ...*" [replace the "f" with "s", ie: "*some, most, etc.*"]

After listening to the history of the present conflict and the reasons for war it was decided to try once more to reach an accommodation with the United States.

"... *Now let us listen to that ancient wife peace chief; Ab, beth, din, Wyrofh, Tefhivo, my cousin, whom you have appointed to fpeak in favor of you fending to your elder brethren, of the United States, to tell them you are ready to liften to peace....*"

In the ensuing three years between St. Clair's Defeat and Wayne's Expedition, settlement of the Northwest Territory had continued almost unabated and as a result unprincipled traders and Indian leaders brought whisky along with their trade goods

Benjamin Franklin Stickney

into the region. The resulting profits were too high to stop the flow of whisky that cascaded across the region.

Despite the efforts of Simcoe [21], British Governor of Canada, to disrupt and eventually stop the flow of spirits into the Indian villages of the Maumee, the trader's profits were too high to stop the whiskey sales. Miami Indian leader Little Turtle and probably Shawnee leader Blue Jacket disrupted the whisky trade only at instances that suited them, and profited from whisky as the opportunities surfaced. This lack of moral conviction frustrated Alexander McKee, the British agent at the rapids of the Maumee.

A letter from Alexander McKee to Colonel England[22] on Tuesday, July 22nd and the 25th of 1794 confirms the flow of liquor.
"... notwithstanding the respectability of his appearance, (he Little Turtle) is as great a trader in rum as any amongst them, and he[Little Turtle] actually brought a considerable quantity from Detroit with him, with which he has made great numbers drunk and stripped them of their clothing for payment. ..."

Another letter from Colonel England on July 9th of 1794 to Governor Simcoe contained the following warning: *"... and the intelligence of Colonel McKee received of a large reinforcement having crossed the Ohio, for General Wayne's Army. ... The prisoners all agree that General Wayne intended moving forward for this Post [23] at the full of the present moon; say that he has received considerable reinforcements and that his Army is in great spirits. ... The Fort at the Miamis[24] is not yet in a situation to make a defense. ..."* In another letter from R. G. England dated July 22nd contained in the archives of Governor Simcoe was the following: *"Little Turtle, A Miamis Chief, paid me a visit, ... the object of his visit was clearly to discern what assistance he and the other Indians were to expect from us, ... if not assisted by the British they would be obliged to desist in their plan of attempting to stop the progress of the American Army. ..."*

Benjamin Franklin Stickney

After training his men rigorously for almost three years after St. Clair's Defeat, General "Mad Anthony" Wayne's army is finally on the move against the Indians and British in the Ohio region.

General "Mad" Anthony Wayne. Excerpted from Howe's *Historical Collections of Ohio,* Vol. 1, 1896.

Thus, when Wayne's Army left Greenville and reached the confluence of the Auglaize and the Maumee Rivers on August 8th, the Shawnee, Miami and other Indian villages were found deserted. From the journal of volunteer George Will: *"... We have marched four or five miles in cornfields down the Auglaize and there is not less than a thousand acres of corn around the town."* General Wayne would later write: *The margins of these beautiful rivers, the Miamis of the Lake and the Auglaize, appear like one continuous village for a number of miles above and below this place, and I have never seen such immense fields of corn in any part of America from Canada to Florida."* [25].

From present day Defiance, Ohio General Wayne sent runners to Little Turtle with one last offer of peace: ... *the arm of the*

United States is strong and powerful, but they love mercy and kindness more than war and desolation." While General Wayne waited for an answer his troops built Fort Defiance.

As Wayne's Army moved toward the mouth of the Maumee, the Indian runner with Little Turtle's answer arrived. Requesting a delay of ten days for their answer, Wayne pushed ahead forty-one miles and built Fort Deposit. Their advance was past numerous deserted villages till resistance was finally met. The killing ground of fallen timber that was scattered in every direction by a tornado was well chosen by Little Turtle. Knowing that cavalry were ineffective in the heavy downed timber and brush, the thirteen hundred Indians led by Little Turtle and his Miamis, Tecumseh and Black Wolf with the Shawnees, the *three fires* of the Ottawa, Chippewa, and Potawatomi under Blue Jacket, Sauk and Fox from Lake Superior, a few Iroquois, seventy white Canadian Rangers, and a few British waited for the approaching Army of General Wayne.

Wednesday, August 20th, 1794 [26]
In the resulting Battle of Presque Isle [27] or Fallen Timbers [28] as it was later called, General Wayne's Army took perhaps 25 to 30 minutes to set the Indians to flight. The well trained volunteers of Wayne's Army destroyed those Indians that remained in its path. The Indians left the battlefield in droves and headed for the safety and protection of Fort Miamis. Less than a ten minute run from the battlefield, the fort closed its gates and refused admittance to those that sought shelter. General Wayne proved to the Indians that the British would not come to their aid as General Wayne taunted the British from outside the fort's closed gates.

Historians have long debated the number of men lost at the Battle of Fallen Timbers and have concluded that General Wayne's losses were 38 killed and about 100 wounded, and about the same for the Indians.

For the Indian Confederacy it was not the number of losses, but the way in which General Wayne crushed their warrior spirit, and the humiliating way the British allies refused to come to their aid.

Benjamin Franklin Stickney

Without the British, the Indians were defeated, and it would be almost twenty years before any effective resistance could be mounted. Blue Jacket almost thirteen years later remembered *"They have often promised to help us, and at last, when we could not withstand the army that came against us, and went to the English fort for refuge, the English told us, "I cannot let you in, you are painted too much, my children."*[29]

Adding to the defeat, and ensuring that the Indians would come to Fort Greenville[30] and ask for peace, General Wayne ordered that the luxurious fields of corn, orchards, and villages that his Army had traveled through along the Maumee River were to be burned and utterly destroyed. Recognizing that Wayne waged war not only on the Indian warriors, but on their families only a very few Indian leaders acknowledged privately that their way of life had ended. Starvation had come to the once plentiful Maumee Valley.

Howard Chandler's *Treaty of Greenville*. Courtesy of the Ohio Historical Society.

Benjamin Franklin Stickney

At the treaty conference on August 3rd, 1795 which would be called the Treaty of Greenville, the whisky flowed and the food was plentiful as over 5,000 Indians gathered to decide their future. What they did not realize was that their future had already been decided. In early 1795 Jay's Treaty[31] effectively transferred all British military posts on American Territory to the United States. Joseph Brant leader of the Iroquois Confederacy was quoted as saying *"This is the second time the poor Indians have been left in the lurch."*[32]

During the ensuing discussions, Little Turtle powerfully fortified the Indian's right to the Northwest Territories. Little Turtle took great pains to define the extensive Miami land holdings that encompassed all of Indiana, western Ohio, and parts of southern Michigan and eastern Illinois. Wayne and the other Indian leaders knew this description to be false because the Miamis' had shared this land with the other Indian tribes. The leaders also knew that Winimac and Topinbee, two pro-American Potawatomi leaders had already negotiated Miami land. With white enclaves carved out in twelve mile squares and settlement allowed south of the Greenville line, the Treaty of Greenville opened the floodgates to the northwest.

With the Treaty of Greenville in place the flood of western migration turned into a torrent.

Benjamin Franklin Stickney

Battle of Fallen Timbers Monument. The battle took place about 1000 yards behind the monument. Courtesy of the author.

Benjamin Franklin Stickney

Endnotes from Chapter Four
conflict on the maumee

[1] SCOOUWA, James Smith's Indian Captivity Narrative, Ohio Historical Society, 1978.
[2] The Detroit River.
3. The thirteen fires refers to the United States original thirteen colonies.
[4] . The mutilation of the bodies during warfare was intended by the Indians to strike fear into the very being of their enemy, and the Indians considered the flood of white settlers into their home lands as an act of war.
[5] Located at the confluence of the Muskingum and Ohio Rivers.
[6] The Ohio Company of Associates was led by Revolutionary War veteran Rufus Putnam of Massachusetts.
[7] First named Adelphia, which translates to brotherhood, was soon changed to Marietta in honor of France's Queen Marie Antoinette. The Revolutionary War soldiers were honoring the French participation in America's Revolutionary War against Britain.
[8] Cincinnati, Ohio.
[9] The militia was badly armed and equipped. *The Conquest of Ohio,* History of Ohio, Rowland H. Rerick, 1905.
[10] Fort Wayne, at the headwaters of the Maumee and Wabash Rivers.
[11] The narrative of one of the volunteer's claimed that an Indian was killed and decapitated as he attempted to steal a staked out horse. The head was then placed on a pole near General Harmar's tent to remind him that he had promised a dozen bottles of wine for the first Indian head brought in. *The Conquest of Ohio,* History of Ohio, Rowland H. Rerick, 1905.
[12] For further information on British Agent Alexander McKee, try *A Man of Distinction Among Them,* Larry Nelson, Kent State University, 1999.
[13] The Confederation consisted mainly of the Miamis and Shawnees and Indians from other tribal affiliations that continued a border war aided by the British against the United States.
[14] With their horses either killed of stolen by the Indians, the soldiers had been forced to carry all of their luggage.
[15] In 1790 Cornplanter and several other Seneca leaders met with President George Washington to urge the President to adopt treaty making as the method of dealing with the Indians. After St. Clair's defeat Cornplanter led a delegation of the Six Nations at the AuGlaize to act as peace makers between the United States and the Miamis and Shawnees. The other leaders from the opposing side treated Cornplanter and the Six Nations with contempt.

[16] Located at the joining of the Great Miami River and the Four Mile River at present day Hamilton, Ohio.
[17] Fort Recovery, Ohio
[18] William Henry Harrison, 18 years old in 1791, was the son of Benjamin Harrison.
[19] Little Turtle, Calvin M. Young, a Unigraphic Reproduction, 1917, p62.
[20] Various historians have placed those Indians that attended as high as 8,000 and as low as 200. The leaders that were there included Little Turtle and others that were responsible for St. Clair's defeat.
[21] John Graves Simcoe was the first Governor of Upper Canada [Ontario] and throughout America's War of Independence he remained on the British side. Simcoe encouraged British Loyalists to settle in Canada.
[22] Commander of the British at Fort Detroit.
[23] British Fort Detroit.
[24] British Fort Miami is located in Maumee, Ohio on the Maumee River.
[25] *The Conquest of Ohio,* History of Ohio, Rowland H. Rerick, 1905, p132.
[26] General Wayne knew their method of fighting, and from the scouting reports and previous experience that the Indians were lying in wait. Wayne decided to wait several days till the Indians food and water supplies were exhausted before attacking.
[27] Extensive research by Dr. G. Michael Pratt of Heidelberg University has revealed that the high ground north and west of the intersection of US 23 and US 24 was the battle site. For a long time the battlefield was thought to be the flood plain below US 24 and the Maumee River.
[28] It should be noted that early accounts always referred to the Battle of Presque Isle not Fallen Timbers. It has been surmised that the name, Fallen Timbers, was not applied till much later perhaps as a result of Andrew Coffinberry's book "The FOREST RANGERS, 1842. It has been described as *"This is an original contribution in poor verse to the history of Wayne's Campaign in Northwestern Ohio and Indiana in 1794."*

[29] Blue Jacket, John Sugden, University of Nebraska, 2000, page 179.
[30] . Built as base camp for Wayne's Army it is located at present day Greenville, Ohio.
[31] Signed in London on November 1794 and published in Philadelphia in 1795, the treaty resolved many of the outstanding U.S.-British issues, especially the British forts in the northwest.
[32] . The Conquest, Lucas County Historical Series, Randolph Downes, MVHS, 1948, pg 64. Those Indian tribes that had sided with the French had lost their lands and now those Indians that had sided with the British had lost to the United States, thus losing twice.

blue jacket, little turtle, & the capitol
chapter five

The future direction of the Maumee Valley region in 1795 rested with the tribal confederations of the Miami and Shawnee. More specifically, the Maumee Valley depended on the actions and concerns of Little Turtle of the Miami Nation and Blue Jacket of the Shawnee Nation. They were both proven war leaders who had planned and executed the destruction of Generals Harmar and St. Clair. With the third expedition against them in as many years, Little Turtle advocated peace with General Wayne, while Blue Jacket did not; they both fought the common enemy ... the United States.

Defeat at the hands of General Anthony Wayne at the Battle of Fallen Timbers had brought them to the Treaty of Greenville. With almost a year of thoughtful insight since their defeat at Fallen Timbers, Blue Jacket and Little Turtle still differed on their vision of the Indian's future. Both of the men envisioned positions of power and personal wealth, but they differed greatly as to how their brothers and sisters meshed with the migration of white settlers.

Witnessed by 143 Shawnees, 91 Ottawas and Ojibwas, 180 Wyandot and Iroquois, 381 Delaware, 240 Potawatomi, 85 Miami, Eel Rivers, Wea, and Piankeshaw, and 10 Kickapoo and Kaskaskia the Treaty of Greenville was like the wind that constantly blew across the grasslands. ... a lot of noise without much sustenance... the terms had already been decided. When the Shawnee reached Fort Defiance, the once proud warriors separated from their civil chief Red Pole[1] and quickly bartered their goods for whisky from the corrupt traders. The gift of the Shawnee land from their hereditary spirit, Waashaa Monetoo would have been traded for a mere twenty horse loads of treaty goods, if it wouldn't have been for the commander of Fort Defiance, Major Hunt interceding with a trader named Felix. The Shawnee Nation would have left with nothing but the United States' promise of future annuities.[2] A day after the Shawnee had their goods returned, Mr. Abbott from Fort Wayne arrived with a newspaper containing the terms of Jay's Treaty which was designed to smooth relations with the British.[3]

Benjamin Franklin Stickney

Blue Jacket had been promised a share of the presents, a house, and a visit with the President of the United States. With the overt and covert deals made with the United States, Blue Jacket had lost a majority of the Shawnee and gained as much support among the political leadership of the United States. Blue Jacket's last words as war chief of the Shawnee as he surrendered his power to the civilian leadership left many to speculate about his probable responsibility to the Shawnee. "... Remember Brothers, you have buried your war hatchets. Your Brothers the Shawanese now do the same good act. We must think of war no more." [4]

The reality was that Blue Jacket from his American built cabin in Fort Wayne, would continue to manage the Shawnees by acting as a negotiator over the distribution of the Shawnee annuities. Even the pro-British faction led by Captain Johnny which settled at Swan Creek and had access to the fertile grounds of the Maumee River for crops, needed Blue Jacket's assistance the first year. In an effort to reduce British influence among the dissidents, General Wilkinson citing the wisdom of Blue Jacket, ordered that the Shawnee be allowed to draw on the food supplies at Fort Greenville until the harvests were in place.

Stressing that only the Shawnee that offered their loyalty to the Americans would be able to collect their share of the Greenville Treaty's annuities, Blue Jacket and Red Pole traveled to Fort Miamis on July 11th to witness the British in their scarlet tunics abandon the American soil. [5] War chief Blue Jacket and civil chief Red Pole wanted the assembled Shawnee to recall the humiliation when the British wouldn't aid or give sanctuary to the Indians after the Battle of Fallen Timbers.

Recognizing the importance of meeting with the President of the United States, Blue Jacket and Red Pole of the Shawnee, Little Turtle of the Miamis, and an Eel River leader named Soldier in October of 1796 assembled in Detroit for their trip to Philadelphia. As they prepared to board the vessel SWAN[6] for Presque Isle and then by land to Pittsburgh and Philadelphia, Little Turtle confused and troubled by the escaping clouds of

Benjamin Franklin Stickney

steam refused to board, and made the entire journey by horse. This seemingly innocent last minute change in travel caused Little Turtle to arrive in early December; weeks after the discussions had begun.

Blue Jacket and Little Turtle's disillusionment with travel plans had little to do with escaping clouds of steam, but probably centered on Little Turtle's plan to gradually reduce the Miami land holdings. The reduction in acreage would completely finance the Miami tribal change from a hunter/gatherer society to an agricultural community. General Anthony Wayne had always speculated that Little Turtle understood the value of the Miami's land holdings and the concept of land ownership through William Wells, [7] adopted son of Kaweahatta of the Eel River Miami.

Captain William Wells. Excerpted from Calvin Young's Little Turtle, 1917.

Benjamin Franklin Stickney

The conferences that started around November 28th, 1796 with President Washington did not change the terms of the Greenville Treaty. Red Pole, hoping to change the Treaty, said that the line was too far west and should have followed the Great Miami to the Ohio River. President Washington maintained that the Treaty could not be changed, because the presents that had been promised were ready to be delivered.

As to when Little Turtle and Wells arrived in Philadelphia is open to speculation, but they were housed on Market Street with the government paying for their stay[8]. In all probability they were given a separate audience with President Washington. An indication of this meeting was the ceremonial sword presented to Little Turtle by President Washington.

Returning home without the desired changes in the treaty was one thing, but the death of Red Pole from an illness that baffled the doctors of Pittsburgh was another matter. Blue Jacket was politically astute to know that it was through Red Pole that he was able to maintain his relationship with Little Turtle and sustain his power among the Shawnees.

With his return to the Ohio country in 1797, Blue Jacket inherited a dismal harvest and a dreadful winter of meager hunting. Blue Jacket also learned that his friend Anthony Wayne had died, but the assembled Shawnee were eager to hear the results of their trip to Philadelphia and perhaps more importantly the death of Red Pole. Once again Blue Jacket had to turn to General James Wilkinson to issue provisions to sustain the Shawnee till the fall harvest.

Retiring from the political turmoil, Blue Jacket abandoned his Fort Wayne home and moved to the new home of the American Shawnee, Wapakoneta. Blue Jacket supplemented his farming and hunting by trading heavily in whiskey brought from Cincinnati to such an extent that he was asked to leave. Blue Jacket moved within the year to the area around Brownstown where he started again renewing his acquaintances with the British agents who were his friends from his youth. [9] Before the

Benjamin Franklin Stickney

end of 1797 the Indians of the *old northwest* were looking to Little Turtle, the Miami, for leadership and guidance.

The political leadership of the United States was so impressed with Little Turtle that General Wilkinson suggested to his brother-in-law Owen Biddle on December 24th, 1797 that Little Turtle be introduced to the American Philosophical Society.

"The bearer of this letter, the Miamis Chief, the Little Turtle, who is at once the most distinguished warrior, the ablest Counselor among the Indian nations, is forcibly impressed by these truths, and is anxious to cooperate in a fair experiment at a reform of his tribe; it is with this view, particularly, that I introduce him to you, In the hope that you may think proper to recommend him to the patronage of the Benevolent Society[10] of which you are a member."

It was also during this visit that Vice-President Thomas Jefferson suggested that Dr. Benjamin Rush vaccinate Little Turtle and Wells against smallpox that would periodically sweep through the Indian and settlers of the *old northwest territories.*

During their second stay in Philadelphia President Adams in a letter dated February 4th, 1798 wrote *"... I have received the Miami Chief, the Little Turtle ... He is certainly a remarkable man. ..."* According to author Calvin Young, Little Turtle during this meeting with President Adams pleaded for protection against the whisky traffic that was flooding into the Indian villages. *"We had better be at war with the white people, for this liquor that they introduce into our country is more to be feared than the gun and tomahawk. ... More of us have died since the Treaty of Greenville, than we lost by the years of war before, and it is all owing to the introduction of this liquor among us."*[11]

Two little known events occurred in Philadelphia during the first three months of 1798 pertaining to Little Turtle's visit. The first is that William Wells arranged for renowned artist Gilbert Stuart to paint a portrait of Little Turtle. The painting hung for several years in the Secretary of War's office and was destroyed when

Benjamin Franklin Stickney

the British burned Washington on August 24th, 1814. The other aside occurred when Thaddeus Kosciosko [12] presented Little Turtle with a matched brace of pistols with this caution: "*... use them against the first man who ever comes to subjugate you. ...*" [13]

Little Turtle. This steel engraving by Hopkins is similar to the painting by Gilbert Stuart. Courtesy of Knapp's *History of the Maumee Valley 1872.*.

General Wilkinson in his letter of December 24th, 1797 to his brother-in-law Owen Biddle made his views quite clear on future of the Indian race.

"*My late intercourse with various tribes & nations from their neighborhood to Lake Superior, convince me that the*

Benjamin Franklin Stickney

corruptions of the Savages, are derived from those who stile themselves Christians - because, the further they are advanced from communication with white people the more honest, temperate, and industrious I have found them. When we contemplate the fortune of the Aborigines of this, our Country, the Bosom of philanthropy must heave with Sorrow, and our sympathy be strongly excited. What would not that man, of community, merit, who reclaims the untutored Indian, opens his mind to sources of happiness unknown, and makes him useful to Society? Since it would be in effect, to save a whole race from extinction; for surely, if this people are not brought to depend for subsistence on their fields, instead of their forests, and to realize ideas of distinct property, it will be found impossible to correct their present habits, and the needs of their extinction already sown, must be matured."

With the assurance of the President of the United States Little Turtle, William Wells, and the entire Miami delegation left Philadelphia with the belief that they had reached an agreement. The Miami tribal confederation would convert from a hunter/gather culture to an agricultural society.

Endnotes from Chapter Five
blue jacket, little turtle, & the capitol

[1] Red Pole and Blue Jacket had the same Shawnee mother. Red Pole was the Shawnee civil chief.
[2] *The Journal of Joseph Gardner Andres*, Surgeon's Mate at Fort Defiance, edited by Richard Knopf, O.H.S., 1957, pages 55-6
[3] Jay's Treaty eased tensions between Great Britain and the United States. For our purposes the treaty removed the British and their posts from United States soil. Popular thinking at the time considered the treaty humiliating to the United States.
[4] Minutes of the Treaty of Greenville.
[5] President Washington's Secretary of War, James McHenry wrote to Anthony Wayne on July 16, 1796 just five days after the British left Fort Miamis. "... *it has been stated to me that Fort Miamis has proved fatal to a*

Benjamin Franklin Stickney

majority of the British troops stationed there, ... if Fort Miamis is not absolutely essential as a place of depot .... It should be left ungarrisoned." Anthony Wayne Papers, Vol. XLV, p499-500.

[6] Commanded by Captain John Heth.

[7] *The Life and Times of Little Turtle,* Harvey Lewis Carter, University of Illinois, pages 157-8.
Chief Little Turtle in one of his Kentucky raids captured a boy about eleven years of age, William Wells, from the family of Nathaniel Pope. As the boy grew he earned the affection of Little Turtle and was adopted into his family. William later married Little Turtle's daughter, Waumaughapith or Sweet Breeze. William was a prominent factor in the defeat of General Harmar and St. Clair along with Little Turtle.
Realizing that the whites would eventually win, Wells changed sides and worked as a scout for General Wayne. Later became rejoined with Little Turtle, and was slain near Chicago's Fort Dearborn in August of 1812.
Descendants of William Wells and Sweet Breeze can be traced to the Wolcott family in Maumee, Ohio.

[8] For one four week period coming home Little Turtle, Wells, and three Indian companions had a tavern keeper bill of $80.00 for lodgings and a liquor bill of $86.62 ½ . Their daily consumption was one quart of wine, one pint of brandy, one half gill of gin, and a pint of bounce. While they implored abstinence their consumption was no more than most of the military officers at that time. *The Life and Times of Little Turtle,* Harvey Lewis Carter, University of Illinois, page 7.

[9] Exerted from *Blue Jacket,* John Sugden, University of Nebraska, page 305. [John Johnston to Lyman C. Draper, July 10, 1848 Tecumseh Papers, IIYY33; also *Notes on the early Settlement of the North-Western Territory,* Burnet, pages 68-71.]

[10] Wilkinson is referring to the American Philosophical Society. Dr. Benjamin Rush and Thomas Jefferson were members, and Wilkinson was elected to membership January 18, 1798.

[11] *Little Turtle The Great Chief of the Miami Indian Nation,* Calvin Young, 1917, page 149.

[12] A Polish patriot who volunteered his services during the American Revolution .

[13] *The Life and Times of Little Turtle,* Harvey Lewis Carter, University of Illinois, page 5.

Benjamin Franklin Stickney

chapter six

eighty miles north of the boundary of white population

While Benjamin Franklin Stickney was born into privilege on April fool's day of 1773, his New Hampshire parents were relatively poor. They were prosperous with well placed relatives and friends in the growing American legislative bureaucracy, and Washington City was the place to be recognized in society. With recognition came governmental patronage in the political system and employment. A government position rather than a trade apprenticeship suited Stickney and his ambition.

During Benjamin Franklin Stickney 27th year, Samuel Blodget[1] a friend of the Stickney Family introduced their son to the society of politicians and families that provided Washington City's culture. Benjamin must have made quite an impression on Mrs. Anna Marie [Brodeau] [2] Thornton [3], because he was mentioned in the newspapers as well as her personal journal throughout the months of October, November, and December of 1800.

With the needed social and political connections firmly in hand, Benjamin Franklin Stickney returned to Pembroke, New Hampshire and courted Mary, the daughter of Revolutionary War hero, General John Stark[4]. They were both 27 when they invited the entire countryside to celebrate their wedding and subsequent reception. General Stark considered his daughter late in life for marriage, but finally gave in to Stickney's persistence.

Stickney initially tried to make his fortune the old fashioned way through marriage, but his father-in-law General John Stark had other plans for his son-in-law. After almost a year of diligence and hard work on General Stark's farm, the Stickney's were blessed with a child. One[5] Stickney was born on August 20th, 1803, followed by a daughter, Louisa, in 1805 who died just three years later. To augment their meager income and provide for his growing family, Stickney became the postmaster and Justice of the Peace for Pembroke.

Benjamin Franklin Stickney

new hampshire, canada, & fort wayne
chapter six

With a widening circle of social acquaintances, one of Stickney's earliest known letters from Pembroke was written to Revolutionary War author Thomas Paine [6]. Notably older than Stickney, and known for his 1776 *Common Sense* writings, Stickney wanted to know if the rumors of Paine becoming a Christian were true. Thomas Paine's reply to Stickney was printed in the regional newspapers. *"... to check Federal Rumors..."* and Paine denied all such accusations.

The Stickney's moved across the Merrimack River to Bow, New Hampshire where their third child, Mary, was born on May 23rd, 1808. Their fourth child, Two, was also born in Bow on April 16th, 1810 a month before Stickney's biography [7] of General John Stark was published in the *NEW ENGLAND PATRIOT* and the *NEW HAMPSHIRE REGISTER*.

Either in consideration for his brilliant work on his biography or to secure Benjamin Franklin Stickney a position that would support the growing Stickney family, General Stark wrote to either President James Madison or Secretary of State James Monroe and requested that his son-in-law be appointed an Indian Agent.

The position of Indian Agent was put on hold as the entire country began to read of General William Henry Harrison's exploits on the Tippecanoe River at Prophetstown. Tecumseh had been traveling throughout the *old northwest* trying to arrange a confederacy of Indians similar to Pontiac that would rid the country of the whites. Tecumseh's main concern was for the well-being of the tribes that were slowly being squeezed out of existence.

As Tecumseh spoke of the Greenville Treaty and its aftermath, more and more of the land in Indiana was jointly assembled by additional treaties at the hands of General Harrison and lost to the tribes. Tecumseh's message as he traveled from village to village remained the same – the whites must be stopped.

Tecumseh arrived in Vincennes on the Wabash River in August of 1810 with four hundred warriors instead of the invited thirty for another round of scheduled talks. Angered by the attempt at intimidation, General Harrison and Tecumseh both knew that the discussions were aimed at the Indians relinquishing more land, and Tecumseh absolutely refused any future territory considerations.

Benson J. Lossing's portrait of Tecumseh which was published in 1869 was based on a sketch by Pierre Le Dru.

As an eager lieutenant in General Anthony Wayne's 1794 expedition, General Harrison remembered Wayne's tactics of intimidation. A year later in 1811 when Harrison and Tecumseh met in a grove of mature walnut trees at Grouseland[8], Indiana Territory's government center at Vincennes. Tecumseh's three hundred warriors were intermingled with six hundred of Harrison's well trained militia. Seated outside under the traditional sun shade of woven grape vines, Tecumseh talked of the future and boasted about his plans for a Grand Confederation of Indians, and then Tecumseh asked Harrison to delay any surveys or further settlements in the disputed territory until the spring. In granting the delay, Harrison realized that all of Tecumseh's plans for an Indian Confederacy were completed.

Benjamin Franklin Stickney

new hampshire, canada, & fort wayne
chapter six

The Greenville Treaty. Knabenshue, *Indian Land Cessions in Ohio,* O.A.H.S. VolXI, 1903.

The delay was the last indication that Harrison needed to assume that Tecumseh's revolt would occur in the Spring, and for that very reason Harrison was determined to establish a military presence in Tecumseh's backyard. Harrison's army took fourteen days to travel the sixty-five miles along the Wabash River to the high ground that Harrison's engineers had selected for Fort Harrison[9]. In the territory ahead of Harrison's advancing army was the confluence of the Wabash and Tippecanoe Rivers known as Prophetstown[10].

At some point Governor Harrison had made the decision to destroy Prophetstown, and with it Tecumseh's plans for an

Indian confederacy. Severely challenged by Harrison, Tenskwautawa[11], Tecumseh's brother also known as the Prophet, sent a delegation of Indians on the 5th of November and invited Harrison and his army to camp near Prophetstown so that talks could begin. Accepting the invitation Harrison's men slept that night with their muskets loaded and bayonets fixed.

Shabonee[12], a Potawatomi leader, would later testify that two British men in officers' red urged the assembled Indians to fight. With Tenskwautawa's [13] assurance that the American's gun powder would turn to sand and their bullets into mud, the assembled Indians attacked General Harrison's army in the early hours of the morning.

As the dawn's red sun revealed the horrors of the hand to hand struggle, the Prophet's influence dissolved like the wisps of fog that still hung over the bloodied ground. Harrison would be declared the victor because he had repulsed the Indians and held his ground. However, as Prophetstown burned to the ground, Harrison's critics were wondering how Harrison's Army with almost two hundred casualties remained the victor against an enemy with only 38 fatalities. On the other hand, Harrison's presidential supporters were already shouting *Tippecanoe and Tyler too*.

A little more than a month later on December 11th, 1811 President James Madison's Secretary of War, William Eustis[14], remembering General Stark's plea for a job for his son-in-law, summoned Stickney to Washington. Believing that war with England was close at hand, Eustis sent Stickney on a secret mission to Canada. His orders were to make a comprehensive report on the Canadian defenses against a possible invasion by the United States, and to determine which side the Canadians would assist.

Reporting back on Monday, February 3rd, 1812 Benjamin Franklin Stickney's comprehensive thirteen page report entitled *On, Canada, 1812* was given to William Eustis.

Benjamin Franklin Stickney

The critical problem, though, was the ability of the British to reinforce weaker areas from Quebec, and, on the size of the garrison there, the administration's informants had no reliable knowledge. …. Concentrated on Montreal and Quebec, assessing the British garrison at the later place to be no more than 4,000 men; and that force, he claimed, was "more nominal than real." With few exceptions, the King's Guard being the most notable, Stickney regarded the British regulars as being of little consequence, dismissing them as "much debilitated by intemperance" through long years of garrison duty. The troops drawn from the local population he found little better; "the Canadians," he wrote, "appear to be the meanest among the refuse of men." Stickney reckoned the militia of Lower Canada to be 50,000 strong, but, not being armed, they were totally ineffective and were trained only "in drunken frolics on common week days." On the basis of this unflattering opinion, Stickney argued that "it would not be difficult for brave men to penetrate" to Quebec, while the legendary fortifications of the city, he felt, though formidable in parts, were overrated in strength and had been neglected in recent years.[15] In the area between Montreal and Kingston, however, a very different situation existed. Montreal itself had no fortifications, the British having destroyed them after 1760, but the regular troops defending it were in Stickney's words, "pretty good men," while the Scottish forces guarding the approach through the Trois Rivieres region merited a similar description. Moreover, the militia forces were more formidable than their lower Canadian counterparts consisting mainly of Scottish settlers "possessed of some information, habituated to personal exposure and abstemious living." Finally, there, were a large number of Americans settled in the areas west of Kingston, many of whom were descended from Loyalists, and they would be, Stickney concluded, "very dangerous enemies."[16]

Stickney's last statement was in direct contradiction to Governor Daniel Thomkins of New York who earlier in 1811 confidently asserted that "… one-half of the Militia of both provinces [of Canada] would join our standard [cause]. …"[17]

Benjamin Franklin Stickney

Yet for all its wealth of information, it seems unlikely that Stickney's report had any great impact on President James Madison's administration thinking about how to conquer Canada, except possibly to confirm President Madison's preference for concentrating American forces on Montreal. Montreal still offered the easiest access to an invading army, it controlled the region of Canada that had recently become of great economic value to Great Britain, and Americans had actually occupied the city at the outset of the Revolutionary War in 1775.[18]

After returning from Canada, Secretary of War Eustis appointed Stickney to the post of Indian Agent at Fort Wayne thus fulfilling Stark's request of a year ago. On Saturday, March 7th, 1812, Stickney was given his commission as Indian Agent at the Fort Wayne, Indiana reservation. Indian Agents represented the United States government in all disputes between the Indian Nations that surrounded the government's reservations as granted by the treaties and the government. They were also responsible for the distribution of government annuities or monies to the Indians. In reality the army commands that were quartered in the reservations considered the Indian Agents as a necessary evil in dealings with the Indians.

It is interesting to note that both Stickney and Indian Agent John Johnston were in Washington at the same time, and that Johnston received his promotion to Piqua, Ohio as Indian Agent. Whether they met or not is a matter of conjecture. Later in a letter to Eustis, Johnston related that he had given Stickney all the necessary information about the machinery of the Fort Wayne Indian Agency, and the current political structure of the Indian leaders of the Maumee and Wabash Valleys.

The Indian Agencies, or Factories as they were sometimes called, were mostly built or located next to the existing military posts on the frontier. Other governmental agencies were located in the Reservations set aside in the Indian Lands for the incoming settlement. The Indian Agents were largely political appointments that used the attending military to symbolize the

Benjamin Franklin Stickney

power of the United States to strengthen their position in dealing with the Indians. The activities of the Agent were many, and unfortunately the Agents were expected to operate in their day to day relations with the Indians on a moral basis as no printed regulations existed with regards to legal and fiscal responsibility. Agents and subagents performed the same duties, but at greatly reduced wages. Agents received $1200 to $1800 a year, while subagents received only $500, along with housing and food rations.

There were three areas in which civilian and military authority clashed. The first was the construction of Agency buildings by the military, the second concerned jurisdiction over the lands reserved to the United States by treaty, and third was the problem of private land claims and just plain squatters in the government reserves or Indian lands. Because of the seemingly overlapping or ill defined regions of responsibility and authority, the military commanders and Indian agents instead of working together for the common good, often clashed over what they considered their fields of authority. The impending conflict between Fort Wayne's Commander Major John Whistler and Stickney was not unique to their strong personalities. Indian Agent Henry Schoolcraft had the same difficulties with Colonel Brady, and later with Lt. William Lawrence, at the Sault.

On Sunday, March 8th, 1812 with his family safely under the protection and guidance of General John Stark, Benjamin Franklin Stickney left Washington City for Pittsburgh.

Later Stickney would write: *"... At Pittsburgh I took a detachment of troops for the relief of Fort Wayne. We descended the river to Cincinnati in arks, arrived there 1st of April; found it a tolerable sized village. ... it was 120 miles to Fort Wayne, which was, of course, marched by land, passing the places where are now the large towns of Dayton, Troy, and Piqua – a few white inhabitants at each. At Dayton they had a tavern kept in a log cabin. At this time the line dividing the State of Ohio and the Territory had not been run, and Fort Wayne was supposed to be in Ohio, and*

Ohio did not extend north of the Black Swamp. Very little was known of the topography of the country. ..."[19]

Stickney arrived at Fort Wayne on Saturday, April 11th and was greeted by Captain James Rhea, Fort Wayne's commander. Stickney would later describe his first impressions of Fort Wayne as *"... eighty miles north of the boundary of white population ..."* [20]

A great amount of correspondence exists detailing Stickney's tenure as Fort Wayne's Indian Agent. At times Stickney would write four or more letters a day to Sec. of War Eustis, other government officials, other intellectuals that he corresponded with. Many of the letters described in great detail life at Fort Wayne, while others described the botanical and rock formations found nearby. Some letters were quite detailed, while others described the progress or lack of that he was making with the Indians. An example of the progress was contained in the following excerpt:

"…. The Little Turtle has sent his son to Wells and Wells has wrote a note to me. ..." Tuesday, April 21st, 1812 B. F. Stickney to William Eustis.

With war with the British and their Indian allies looming over the frontier, Stickney became conversant with the day to day activities of the Fort. Throughout April and May Stickney was aware of an Indian trying to settle in with the rhythm of the fort that gave his name as Isadore Chaine. With no help from Little Turtle, Stickney had correctly assumed that Chaine was in reality the Wyandot leader, Shetoon. The influential Wyandot was sent by British agent Matthew Elliot [21] to observe the workings of Fort Wayne, but more importantly to try and convince Little Turtle to return to the British.

With the daily letters to William Eustis, Stickney also managed to write letters to his family. On May 2nd, 1812 Stickney wrote to his brother-in-law, Caleb Stark[22] and John McKinstry [23] Stark's business partner, detailing the possibilities of the Miami River [Maumee] being navigable throughout the year from Fort Wayne to Lake Erie. Continuing, he informed them that during times of high water canoes laden with cargo had been able to pass from the Maumee River to the Wabash River without the 8 mile portage. Stickney confirmed the stories of the early French trappers that a water route from Lake Erie to New Orleans existed. Stark and McKinstry were thrilled with this latest bit of intelligence from the western frontier.

A Grand Council of the twelve tribes on the Wabash River was held in May of 1812 and Stickney's warnings about Isadore Chaine [Shetoon] were confirmed in a letter to Governor William Hull [24] of the Michigan Territory.

"The time appears to have arrived when it is necessary, if possible, to cut off all communication between the Indians within the Territory of the United States, and Canada. ..... It has for some time been well understood, that the British Government has agents among the Indians within the United States; but it has been almost impossible to distinguish them. .... There is a man here now, who is called Shetoon, [Esidore Chaine] who represents himself to be a Wyandot Chief from Brownstown. .... But it appears from the collected mass of circumstances, that he has been sent by his nation to preach peace to the rest, and that he has been employed by Elliot to preach peace in general, and tell the real views of the British Government to a few. He carries many speeches of war, as well as peace. .... He told to one Indian, where he thought he was safe, that he was employed by the British Indian agent to go and advise all the Indians of this western country to be at peace with the United states; and to form a system, by which they all may be united as one nation. .... P.S. I shall keep Shetoon amused here as long as I can, hoping to obtain more from him."

The 12 Indian Tribes on the Wabash also wanted the flow of liquor into their country stopped, and on Monday, May 25th, 1812 Stickney wrote to Eustis:

Benjamin Franklin Stickney

"…. This grand council came to an agreement in their meeting on the Wabash, and have made a formal request to me, to have some measures taken more effectively to suppress the sale of spirituous liquors to Indians in the State of Ohio, Indiana Territory, and other places inhabited by white men. The chiefs complain, that the white men come out and put their foot to the Indian boundary line, and hold out the kegs of whiskey in their hands, and young men are so foolish as to go and suck, till they become drunk, and while they are drunk, they kill the white people, and that in this way a great part of the mischief has been done. I am satisfied that large quantities of whiskey are sold by the licensed Indian Traders, and cannot be proven but by Indian testimony. ……"

While Stickney was using his time posting handbills throughout Fort Wayne and its reservation area: "… forbidding all persons from selling, or causing to be sold, or given as a present or under any other pretext aiding or assisting any Indian or Indians in obtaining any spirituous liquor: even in the smallest quantity." Tecumseh was summoned by Sir George Provost, the British Governor General of Canada, to Fort Malden [Amherstburg, Ontario Canada] and told that war with the United States was imminent.

A little more than a week after leaving Fort Malden in June of 1812, and two days before President James Madison declared war on Great Britain[25], Tecumseh traveled to Fort Wayne and conferred with Stickney.[26] When questioned, Tecumseh stated that he was going to Malden for powder and lead, and emphatically denied that he was going there to plan for war with Matthew Elliot.[27] Stickney correctly deduced the true reason for the visit was to try and persuade the Miami Indians under Little Turtle to join with Tecumseh. Also, Stickney understood that Tecumseh and his followers were surveying Fort Wayne's defenses. Several times in the coming days Stickney considered the idea of placing Tecumseh under arrest until the hostilities ceased, and decided that he does not have the men or authority.

Benjamin Franklin Stickney

According to E. O. Randall in his writings, *Tecumseh, the Shawnee Chief,* Tecumseh while in Fort Wayne was invited to dinner by Mr. Stephen Johnston, a government clerk and brother to Piqua's Indian Agent John Johnston. Tecumseh is reputed to have said: *"I am the enemy of the white man -- I will not eat with you."* John Sugden in his book *Tecumseh* adds that Tecumseh refused all food except for potatoes at the dinner. Tecumseh considered the potato an Indian food and therefore acceptable to the Great Spirit. Sugden also asserted that the dinner was hosted by Captain James Rhea, Fort Wayne's commander. Ann Forsyth, who had been raised by Indians, attended the dinner. She recalled that Tecumseh was quite charming, and spent the greater part of the evening trying to deduce the tribe of her intended husband.

Stickney communicated with Governor Hull on the 20th with all the information that Stickney could gather together concerning the plans of the Indians should war commence with England. The next day Tecumseh regaled Fort Wayne's populace with a three hour speech which detailed the grievances the Indians have suffered at the hands of the United States since the Treaty of Greenville. Tecumseh, leaving one his followers behind for medical treatment, left Fort Wayne without notifying Rhea or Stickney. This affront to frontier hospitality left the same warning to everyone … that the coming war was about to plunge the western border into chaos.

"Your Blood is white. You have taken my talk, and the sticks, and the wampum, and the hatchet, but you do not mean to fight. I know the reason. You do not believe the Great Spirit has sent me. You shall know. I leave Tuckhabatchee [Tecumseh's birth village was a Creek Indian town on the Tallapoosa River in present day Georgia.] *directly, and shall go straight to Detroit. When I arrive there, I will stamp on the ground with my foot and shake down every house in Tuckhabatchee."* [28]

Any doubt that remained that the Indian tribes had aligned themselves with the British was removed with the burning of the daily or thirtieth red stick since the comet or *panther crossed the sky*. Tecumseh, when he addressed the Creek Indians, predicted what has since been called the New Madrid earthquake in December of 1811. Measuring an 8.0 on the Richter scale the quake's effects were felt over an area of two million square miles. After the earth shook and the Mississippi River ran backwards would there be any doubt about Tecumseh and war with the whites.

As they made their way to Fort Malden, Tecumseh and his followers learned that war had been declared between the United States and Great Britain. Invited to attend a last minute conference of influential settlers, traders, and Indians at Brownstown at the mouth of the Detroit River in an effort to find a way out of this mess, Tecumseh refused and said *" No I have taken sides with the King, my father, and I will suffer my bones to bleach upon this shore before I will cross that stream to join any council of neutrality with the Americans."*

With less than 100 days at Fort Wayne, Stickney had come to believe that Little Turtle's agricultural concept for the future of the Indians was correct and they became very good friends. When Little Turtle died in July of 1812, perhaps of complications from gout, Stickney arranged for his friend to have a military funeral. Little Turtle was brought from his Eel River village to William Well's home[29] in the Spy Run section and buried[30]. Captain Rhea and the officers of Fort Wayne's garrison were present.

The death of Little Turtle could not have come at a more unfortunate time. Like Tecumseh, Little Turtle was against any further land acquisitions by the Americans; however they differed in everyday implementation. Tecumseh advocated a return to the old ways of living, while Little Turtle was pressing for the Miamis to learn the ways of agriculture and live side by side with the white migration.

Since the Treaty of Greenville in 1795, Little Turtle had counseled continuously against war, and advocated peace with the Americans. After his death, Little Turtle's restraining

Benjamin Franklin Stickney

influence on the Miamis began to wither, and the Miamis were beginning to become responsive to the British and their allies. William Henry Harrison reflecting on the above mentioned differences said: *"It was the rock upon which the popularity of Tecumseh was founded, and that upon which the influence of Little Turtle was wrecked."*

End notes from Chapter Six
new hampshire, canada, & fort wayne

---

[1] Born in Goffstown, New Hampshire, the son of Samuel Blodget and Hannah White. Became a partner in the mercantile trade in Exeter, New Hampshire and Boston with Daniel Gilman. Daniel Gilman is the youngest son of an Exeter family prominent in New Hampshire politics. Blodget was an early advocate for the District of Columbia, both financially and architecturally. In spite of President Washington's reservations, Blodget was appointed Superintendent of Buildings.

[2] Daughter of Ann Brodeau of Philadelphia. She married William Thornton in 1790.

[3] William Thornton, born in the Virgin Islands and a graduate of the University of Edinburgh, practiced medicine, and designed the Capitol at Washington City. He was interested in the early attempts to harness steam power for navigation. Dr. Thornton was employed as Commissioner and his agency drew nearly all the leading men who where visitors to the seat of Government.

[4] Revolutionary soldier of Scottish parents, John Stark was well suited to the rigors of frontier, or Indian, style fighting. During the French and Indian Wars he saw extensive service with Roger's Rangers and was promoted to Captain. When the news of Lexington and Concord hit he mounted his horse and set out for Cambridge. He participated in the Battle of Bunker Hill, Trenton, and Princeton. Stark later resigned his commission because Congress had promoted junior officers past him. John believed that ability should determine promotions. During the rest of the Revolutionary War, especially when he attacked Baum with his New Hampshire volunteers, he is said to have exclaimed. *"There, my boys*

are your enemies, the red coats and tories, you must beat them or my wife sleeps a widow tonight." Stark is later censured for disregarding orders for a different movement of his men, later receives the thanks of Congress. Stark was promoted to the rank of Brigadier General in the Continental Army in 1777 and a Major General in 1783.

[5] Benjamin Franklin Stickney did not believe that he knew the children well enough to give them a proper Christian name. He was reputed to have said they the boys can choose their own names when they see fit. However, Benjamin's wife Mary always chose the names for her daughters.

[6] Revolutionary political author and agitator, wrote *The Age of Reason*, most known for his 47 page booklet *Common Sense* (January 9, 1776). Raised a Quaker, he soon became an atheist. The first copy of *Rights of Man*, published in France, to arrive in America was lent by its recipient J. Beckley, to Thomas Jefferson with the request that he pass it on to the publisher as soon as possible. Earlier on Wednesday, August 1, 1775, Thomas Paine advocated women's rights in an article appearing in the *Pennsylvania Gazette*. It probably did not hurt that he was the paper's editor.

[7] Considered by scholars to be the definitive biography of General Stark. Stickney's work is used as a primary source for information on General Stark.

[8]. Built in 1803 on a hill above the Wabash River in Vincennes by Indiana's Territorial Governor Harrison, it was considered the White House of the western frontier.

[9] Location of present day Terre Haute, Indiana.

[10] Located about 5 miles northeast of West Lafayette, Indiana.

[11] The Prophet and Tecumseh's brother.

[12] Shabonee, *built like a bear*, was a Potawatomi chief and the grand nephew of Pontiac, became one of Tecumseh's leaders and was with Tecumseh at the Battle of Thames. Incensed at the treatment of the Indians by the British he transferred his allegiance to the Americans.

[13] Tecumsch's brother was originally known as Lalawethika before changing his name to Tenskwatawa after he predicted an eclipse of the sun. While conferring with Crane at Upper Sandusky Rev. Badger wrote on the 16th of June 1806: *Sun eclipsed, total darkness for eight minutes, this was a matter of great surprise to the Indians.* But it was the Indian belief that the Prophet had caused the eclipse that added to his power among the Indians. The prophet also taught that the Americans were children of the devil, and advised all Shawnees to abolish all contact with the white. After the debacle at Prophetstown he was literally abandoned.

Benjamin Franklin Stickney

[14] William Eustis studied medicine, helped to care for the wounded at Bunker Hill, and then performed as a surgeon for the Revolutionary Army. Eustis served two terms in Congress beating John Quincy Adams for one of the terms. In 1807 President Jefferson named Secretary of War to succeed Henry Dearborn. Eustis continued in the same position in President Madison's cabinet. Eustis was in charge of the U.S. military during the critical period leading up to the War of 1812. The War Department was poorly equipped for the task, and after the Declaration of War was passed everybody joined in the denunciation of Eustis. When asked to resign on December 3, 1812, the War Department was taken over by James Monroe who was also serving as Secretary of State.

[15] This assessment of the British position at Quebec agrees closely with that made at about the same time by the governor of Lower Canada, Lieutenant General Sir George Provost.

[16] This is based on a letter from Benjamin Franklin Stickney to Eustis, February 3, 1812. This letter is in fact a thirteen page memorandum bearing the title *"On Canada, 1812."* Stickney was the son in law of President Madison's friend John Stark of New Hampshire, who had been asking the President to give him an appointment of some sort for over a year. After Stickney's return from Canada, William Eustis, President Madison's Secretary of War, appointed him Indian Agent at Fort Wayne, Indiana Territory.

[17] *1812,* Walter R. Borneman, Harper Collins, page 57.

[18] These points were emphasized in the *National Intelligencer* editorial on December 3, 1811.

[19] Benjamin Franklin Stickney, Historical Sketches, Toledo BLADE, August 20, 1850.

[20] Benjamin Franklin Stickney, Historical Sketches, Toledo BLADE, August 20, 1850.

[21] Matthew Elliot was born in Ireland, and raised in eastern Pennsylvania. At the close of the French and Indian War Elliot became a trader at Fort Pitt. Lord Dunmore's War found him with the Shawnees on the Scioto, and was one of the messengers for the Indians to the Virginia forces. On behalf of Cornstalks forces he asked for the terms of peace. After the war returned to Pittsburgh and traded with the Indians on the Muskingum.

Elliot was taken prisoner by a band of Wyandot, and escaped to Detroit where Governor Hamilton sent him as a prisoner to Quebec. This whole episode was believed to be a ruse on behalf of the British to infiltrate

Benjamin Franklin Stickney

Elliot as a spy. In reality Elliot had a Captains commission when he returned to Pittsburg in 1778.
Continues in this capacity in Malden where he openly pursues the British cause.

[22] Caleb Stark was the brother of Mary, Stickney's wife.

[23] John McKinstry was the brother of General Stark's wife. Stark & McKinstry were business partners in Boston.

[24] William Hull displayed bravery in the Revolutionary War and was commended by Washington and was advanced to rank of lieutenant colonel. Afterwards he practiced law in Newton, Mass. On March 22, 1805 he was appointed governor of the newly created Michigan Territory. Hull's land cessions from the Indians formed the basis of their discontent. In the spring of 1812 he was persuaded to accept a commission as brigadier general in the army designed to defend the Michigan Territory and attack Upper Canada. Instead Hull surrendered to General Proctor at Detroit. Severely censured for his activities in Detroit Hull was tried for treason and sentenced to be shot. President Madison approved the sentence but remanded his sentence at the last moment because of his service in the Revolution.

[25] Stickney will not be aware of war with Great Britain being declared until July 19th, 1812.

[26] . Alan Eckert in his book, *A Sorrow In The Heart*, described the meeting as lasting four days.

[27] It was later learned that after his meeting at Fort Malden Tecumseh received twelve horse loads of ammunition for his followers.

[28] Excerpted from James Mooney's book "Ghost Dance Religion."

[29] According to Charles Poinsatte in his book *OUTPOST IN THE WILDERNESS: FORT WAYNE 1706-1828*, the grave of Little Turtle was believed to have been discovered in 1912 at the home of Dr. George Gillie in the Spy Run section of Fort Wayne.

[30] It has been recorded that Stickney paid $2 to Cunningham & Howell for the coffin and $1 to Burney & Milligan for digging the grave.

Benjamin Franklin Stickney

Little Turtle, General Wayne, and settler. Courtesy of the author.

The sweltering days of August brought grim news from the frontier. Just two days before the soldiers of Fort Wayne knew that a state of war existed between the United States and Great Britain, Michilimackinac had been surrendered to the British on the 17th of July. The early August mornings conveyed a thin fog that permeated Fort Wayne, and as the miasma traveled through the fort it struck Stickney with malaria or ague as it was then called, rendering him bed-ridden till mid-month,

Fearing British General Brock's 2,000 man Canadian Army and his Indian supporters, General Hull withdrew his entire 2,200 man army from a siege on Canada's British Fort Malden and retreated across the Detroit River. Within days Fort Dearborn [Chicago] capitulated, and its inhabitants with a promise of safe passage ... were massacred. Notified of the fall of Michilimackinac and the failure of two supply detachments from the Maumee to meet an advance military escort, General Hull[1] surrendered his entire force to General Brock without a shot being fired. [2] The British in the first stages of the war defeated General Hull and seized control of the Lake Erie - Lake Michigan supply routes.

With the constant turmoil affecting the routine of Fort Wayne, Indian Agent Stickney believed that his orders should come from William Eustis, Secretary of War, not William Henry Harrison, Territorial Governor of Indiana. Eustis in a letter to Harrison on the 18th said that: *"... the Error into which Mr. Stickney appears to have fallen will be corrected."* [3] With the knowledge of the massacre of Fort Dearborn and the death of his mentor William Wells, Stickney either instigates or agrees with the orders of Captain Rhea[4], and sent the women and children under the protection of Captain John Logan, a Shawnee, to the safety of Agent John Johnston at Piqua.

Summoned and still weak from his bout with ague, Stickney made his way in the midnight darkness to the home of his friend Antoine Bondie just outside the fort's stockade. Waiting for him in the feeble light of a single candle was Meta, a Potawatomi leader, who was seated at the rough hewn table. The French

Benjamin Franklin Stickney

trader and trapper Bondie and his Miami wife had disregarded Meta's offer of safety, and sought the advice of Stickney. Stickney immediately outlined Meta's warning to Captain Rhea.

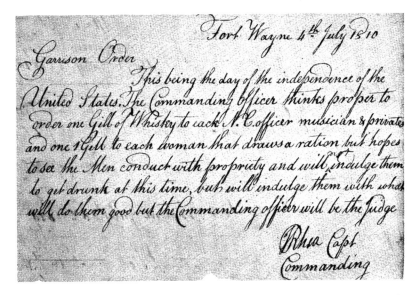

General order for Fort Wayne from Captain Rhea for July 4th. Courtesy of *Fort Wayne: Gateway of the West*, Bert Griswold, Indiana Historical Society, 1927.

Talking into the small hours of the morning with Captain Rhea and Captain Zachary Taylor[5], Antoine Bondie and Stickney both failed in their combined attempt to convince the military command that an attack on the fort was imminent. When Stickney added that French trader Charles Peltier had quietly informed him of the 500 Potawatomi that had been quietly gathering in the woods surrounding Fort Wayne, Captain Rhea refused the warning and discredited both Bondie and Peltier.

The last communications that were sent from Fort Wayne by both Stickney and Rhea to General Worthington and Governor Meigs of Ohio asked for immediate help from the impending attack.[6]

Benjamin Franklin Stickney

fort wayne, war & whistler's grandfather
chapter seven

Two days before the attack on Fort Wayne was to begin; Steve Johnston, Pete Oliver, and a recently discharged soldier used the early morning darkness to head for safety at Piqua. As the men approached the Hana homestead a short distance from the fort, a series of shots rang from the darkness at the edge of the heavy woods. The musket shots found their mark disabling Johnston and gave added fleetness to Oliver and the soldier as they gained the darkness of the impenetrable woods. Once the Indians reached Johnston they tomahawked and scalped him despite his pleas. Awakened to Johnston's murderous screams, White Raccoon accepted Bondie's offer of twenty dollars to retrieve Johnston's mutilated body.

After White Raccoon dumped Johnston's bloody body at the gates of the fort, the Potawatomi that had been quietly hiding in the woods attacked Fort Wayne with reckless fury. The bravado was met with well aimed musket balls from within the fort. Both sides had quietly prayed for a delay – the Americans for the arrival of General Harrison and the Indians for the arrival of the British with their cannon, but when the Indians saw Johnston's disfigured body discarded in the dirt the Indian's bravado crackled like lightning. Wave after wave of musket balls from the Fort created the expected deadly results as the unprotected Indians sprinted across the fort's killing ground. The heavy gray smoke from the gunpowder quickly covered the lines of fire which allowed the Indians to retreat to the cover of the dense forest and the opportunity to formulate another plan of attack.

Sunday morning brought a halt to the sniping gunfire that had originated from the limbs of the high trees that circled the fort. The lull in the fighting brought a delegation of Indians that cautiously approached the fort's gates. When they got within speaking distance, the Indians told the soldiers that they wanted to be admitted to the fort to talk with their good friend Stickney. Instead of falling for their deception, Stickney offered them a white flag of truce to be used when their intentions were honest. An unnatural silence had descended over the area as the Indians slowly returned to the safety of the forest. As the last of

Benjamin Franklin Stickney

the delegation melted into the woods, the silence was shattered as the sporadic sniping returned.

Early Wednesday morning after several days of continued gunfire, Stickney sent a message to the Indians demanding the return of his white flag. *"... they had soiled his flag, and he could not suffer them to have it any more."*

Less than an hour later the whole body of Indians moved to the Fort under Stickney's white flag of truce. Stickney, still weak from the ague slowly walked to the gates, and carefully designated the Indian leaders to be admitted inside the Fort. As the thirteen chosen Indians passed through the gate they were carefully examined for weapons. Under Stickney's order, Captain Rhea, kept the soldiers parading in front of the headquarters with weapons and fixed bayonets.

Lt. Curtis[7], Captain Rhea's second in command, would later write: *"We poor soldiers, either from cowardice or some other agency in our Captain, were not suffered to fire a gun but obliged their repeated insults to pass with impunity.."*

With the gates firmly closed behind them, the thirteen leaders were led under heavy guard formation to the Officer's Mess. The usual offering of tobacco was offered and as the smoke drifted towards the ceiling, Stickney asked the Great Spirit to guide the meeting to peace. Winamac[8] rose and gazed slowly at each officer in the room. When his eyes locked on Stickney he said that the Potawatomi did not kill Stickney's clerk Johnston[9], but the young Indians could not be controlled. *"But,"* as his voice rose to almost a shout, *"If my Father wishes war, I am a man."* With this, Winamac pulled out a knife concealed under his blanket. Stickney, who at this time did not understand the language, knew from the tension in the room and the barred knife that something was not right. Antoine Bondie who understood the Potawatomi language, had accompanied them into the crowded Officer's mess, immediately sprang to his feet, pulling out his own knife, shouting *"I am a man also."*

Benjamin Franklin Stickney

Surprised at Bondie's reaction, Winamac looked at An-ouk-sa for direction, and received a pre-arranged sign aborting their vicious intentions. Bondie would later tell Stickney that he was to have been assassinated by Winamac, while the other twelve leaders were to kill the other military officers in the room. Once the leaders were assassinated the fort's gates were to be opened, and the Indians would rush in and massacre those that remained.

Once their planned deception was uncovered, the Indians expected instant death from their captors. Confused, the Indians were relieved when Stickney, looking only at Winamac, ordered that Winamac and his band of murderers were to be allowed to leave the Fort. Using the same white flag of truce that they entered by, Winamac and his followers were startled by four riders that swiftly approached the fort from the banks of the St. Mary's River. Troubled, Winamac believed that the riders were the advance party of a large relief force coming to the aid of Fort Wayne. Winamac was truly confused when William Oliver dismounted, greeted him warmly, and shook hands with him. Completely bewildered with the turn of events, Winamac fled to the safety of the forest with his twelve supporters.

William Oliver[10], and three Shawnee -- Captain John Logan, Captain Johnny and Brighthorn, arrived at the fort with news that General Harrison [11] was on his way with the expected relief force.

On Thursday, September 3rd with the fort still under siege, Captain Rhea's final garrison order was posted. *"It is earnestly hoped by the Commanding Officer that for this night every man will be at his post, -- relief is at hand but means may be taken to cut us off from that relief. Should any man be found inattentive to his duty, punishment ensues; For on this night, our fame, our honor and everything that is near & dear depends. Be therefore Cautious and brave."* This was the last entry in Fort Wayne's *Orderly Book* for the next 27 days.

Benjamin Franklin Stickney

On the 4th Winamac again approached the fort under a flag of truce, and informed Stickney and Rhea: *"You know that Mackinaw is taken, Detroit is in the hands of the British, and Chicago has fallen; and you must expect to fall next, and that in a short time! Immediately!"* Completely disheartened, Captain Rhea with a sense of impending doom invited Winamac to his headquarters. According to Lt. Curtis, after three glasses of wine, the following words were uttered to Winamac by Captain Rhea. *"My Good Friend. I love You. I will fight for you. I will die by your side. You must save me."* Captain Rhea then gave Winamac a half dollar in an effort to seal the friendship.

The entire force of Indians that surrounded Fort Wayne attacked in concert on the 6th. The Indians attempted to scale the walls of the Fort but were repulsed. Further attempts to scale the palisades proved futile, so once again the Indians reverted to subterfuge. Forming two logs into the shape of a cannon, they placed the *guns* in battery formation before the gates of the fort. Approaching under a white flag, the Indians informed Captain Rhea that the British had sent them two battery cannon, and if the fort did not surrender immediately the fort would be blown apart and the garrison massacred. Stickney told them to *"fire their Quaker Guns and be gone."*

The Potawatomi Indians, aware that General Harrison with a relief force of 2,500 men was less than a day's march from Fort Wayne, tried once again to over-run the fort. This time when they withdrew, the Indians burned all of the out buildings, farms, animals, and crops that they could not take with them.

Lt. Curtis and Lt. Ostrander astounded at the behavior of Captain Rhea during a time of war, filed charges with General Harrison against their commander. Their accusations coupled with Indian Agent Stickney's testimony caused Captain Rhea to be placed under arrest. After hearing the charges against Captain Rhea, General Harrison was in favor of a court martial. However, because of his past service and young family, Rhea was allowed to resign.

Benjamin Franklin Stickney

With the past experience firmly entrenched in his memory, Stickney would later write[12] to Lewis Cass[13], the Michigan Territorial Governor in 1815. Stickney reiterated the difficulties experienced with the military and the offices of Indian Agent. The powers of the Military and those of Agent should be made clear, and that the Indian Agent should have a military rank similar to the British agents. The Indians recognize military rank, thus giving them a concept they can relate to.

In recognition of his service at the beginning of the siege in informing Major Stickney [14] of the impending attack against the fort, and his declaration of loyalty in the Officer's Mess with Winamac, Bondie was appointed *issuing agent* at Fort Wayne with sufficient pay to enable him to support his family. Later Bondie would be appointed captain of the Indian scouts operating from Fort Wayne.

Towards the end of September British regulars equipped with artillery and their usual Indian allies reached Fort Defiance on their way to take Fort Wayne. Coupled with this advance down the Maumee was an effort to salvage as much corn as possible from the vast fields that lined both sides of the river. The cornfields were also sought by the Americans from Fort Wayne under Winchester.

As Major Muir of the British Army proceeded down the Maumee River, he received intelligence reports that a vastly superior American Army under the command of Major Winchester was marching for Detroit. Facing what he expected was a superior force; Muir ordered their artillery and heavy equipment dumped into the Maumee River, and prepared to withdraw the British troops back to Detroit.

With strategically placed British troops, and Indians using hit and run tactics, Winchester did not reach the ruins of Fort Defiance till the 1st of October and with the difficulties they encountered in erecting Fort Winchester "... *Detroit by Christmas*" was in serious doubt. Winchester decided to send 900 troops under the command of General Tupper[15] with orders to proceed down the Maumee to the Foot of the Rapids.

Expecting serious Indian opposition Tupper decided to make an end run from Fort Defiance to Fort McArthur [16], and then to follow Hull's route to the Rapids. Almost a month had past before the 650[17] troops under Tupper's command peered across the Maumee at present day Perrysburg. Five hundred Indians and fifty British regulars were loading the much needed corn that they had harvested as they retreated along the Maumee River into two gunboats, six large canoes, and a schooner.

Deciding on a pre-dawn surprise attack on the British forces, the first faint rays of the sun found Tupper's men drowning in large numbers as they attempted to cross the ice-cold Maumee. Altered to the attack by the cries of the drowning men, the Indians maneuvered across the river and chased the ill-equipped Americans almost back to Fort McArthur.

In an effort to regain the Foot of the Rapids after Tupper's disastrous exploit, Harrison ordered Winchester to the Rapids to erect a supply depot. After trudging through deep snow and ill-suited weather, Winchester arrived at the Foot of the Rapids on the 10th of January. Harrison's critics said that it only took the army four months to reach the proposed Ohio base to drive the British out of Fort Malden.

Some thirty-one miles north of the rapids, the residents of Frenchtown appealed to Winchester to protect them from the British and their deadly Indians. Formulating a plan of action, Winchester ordered Colonel Lewis and Colonel Allen and a force of six or seven hundred men to cross the Raisin River and engage the British. Finding the enemy where the residents of Frenchtown said they would be, the American assault defeated the combined British force on the 18th. Informed of their victory Winchester and 250 more men rushed to press the advantage and take the retreating British at Fort Malden.

Benjamin Franklin Stickney

During the cover of darkness, the British led by Proctor were able to move cannon, supplies, and men across the frozen Detroit River the 18 miles from Fort Malden to Frenchtown. Loaded with grapeshot, the British cannon rained destruction on Winchester's entire command cutting them to pieces. Surrounded and with no supplies or reinforcements forthcoming, Winchester surrendered. Unable to control the barbarity of their Indian allies, the British watched as Winchester's force of approximately a thousand were reduced to three hundred killed, and 600 wounded. Only thirty-three managed to escape.

General Harrison and Winchester's reinforcements received intelligence of the massacre before they left Rapids on the Maumee. Conferring with his officers, Harrison decided to return with about seven hundred men to the hastily built supply depot. General Harrison was so worried that General Proctor would follow them to the Rapids that they burned the supply depot and retreated some 18 miles to the Portage River for the winter.

It was during this time that Harrison reassigned Stickney to the Wyandot Indians at Upper Sandusky. While assigned at Upper Sandusky, Stickney's assistant John Shaw objected to the war that was sweeping across the northwest, and as a protest resigned his commission on the 31st of March 1813. Having worked for both John Johnston and Stickney at various agencies Shaw was well versed in the workings of the agency and would be difficult to replace.

John Armstrong[18] replaced William Eustis in 1813 as President Monroe's Secretary of War, and issued new orders to Harrison that would decree that the entire Ohio Theater of operations would become a second front and supplied as such. Harrison's efforts in the northwest would be strictly defensive. Much of the blame for Winchester's utter defeat on the River Raisin campaign came to rest on Harrison, whether warranted or not.

Benjamin Franklin Stickney

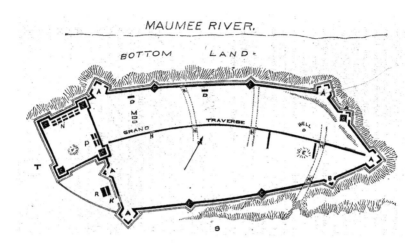

Layout of Fort Meigs from *Fort Meigs a Condensed History by James P. Averill, 1886.*

Adhering to his new political and military situation General Harrison ordered a new fort to be built at the Foot of the Rapids across the Maumee River from Wayne's success at Fallen Timbers. Named Fort Meigs after Ohio's governor Return Jonathan Meigs and designed by Captain Eleazer Derby Wood, the defensive structure became the forward point for American men and material in the Maumee Valley. Located almost at cross-angles from the British Fort Miami on the Maumee River, Fort Meigs quickly foiled any British attempts on the interior from Detroit. Constructed with a circumference of over a mile and a half, the fort was protected with a wooden barricade twelve feet high, eight blockhouses, four artillery batteries, and earthen mounds that traversed the length of the fort in all compass directions. Fort Meigs was a brilliant design that would become an absolute impediment to the British plans for the American interior.

Ten years after Ohio became a State of the Union, the British under General Proctor and the Indians led by Tecumseh began their blatant siege of Fort Meigs on Saturday May 1st, 1813. The British used long range cannon fire from across the Maumee River[19] in Maumee, Ohio, to soften Harrison's Army and their will to resist. Actually, the bombardment of Fort Meigs had little effect because of the earthen mounds that deflected or absorbed the incoming cannon balls.

Fort Meigs as viewed from the north side of the Maumee River. Excerpted from James Averill's *Fort Meigs,* 1886. Author's collection.

General Harrison, embarrassed by the lack of cannon balls for return fire, followed a suggestion by Magazine Keeper Lt. Thomas L. Hawkins [20] of Kentucky. Hawkins suggested that a gill[21] of whiskey be offered to any soldier who recovered a British cannonball suitable for the American guns. Over a thousand gills of whiskey were distributed to the American soldiers in the next eight days.

When asked to surrender the fort or suffer the casualties of war by British General Isaac Brock, General Harrison replied *"... it will be in a manner calculated to do him more honor ... than any capitulation could possibly do."*

Benjamin Franklin Stickney

The siege ended more or less on the 5th of May 1813 without the British breeching the walls of Fort Meigs or exploding Fort Meigs powder supply.[22] The Canadian farmers that made up the majority of the militia were already behind schedule and were eager to return home for the spring planting. Additionally, Tecumseh's warriors were also growing restless and bored with Proctor's siege tactics, and had started to drift away from Fort Meigs in growing numbers. Any thought of continuing the siege ended with the arrival of the 1,200 Kentucky volunteers under General Green Clay. With his Canadian militia and Indians slowly abandoning the siege of Fort Meigs, General Henry Proctor and his British regulars vanished with the darkness down the Maumee River to the security of Fort Malden.

The second siege of Fort Meigs started on the 25th of July 1813 when British General Proctor[23] returned to the old position on the Maumee opposite Fort Meigs with twenty-five hundred regulars and militia, and a like number of Indians under Tecumseh. Not wanting to endure another siege, Tecumseh devised a ruse to lure the fort's defenders into the open. Quite simple in its plan and execution, Tecumseh and his warriors devised a sham attack on a bogus American relief column heading for Fort Meigs. Firing live ammunition over each others heads, Tecumseh's Indians dressed as Americans from the relief column hurried for the fort, while Indians from the thick woods fired at the relief column. As the deceptive relief column got within sight of the Fort's main gate, General Clay refused to open the fort's gates. Within minutes it was obvious that the relief column and attack was a charade when both Indians and sham soldiers melted into the safety of the dense forest. When their travesty failed General Proctor and Tecumseh turned their attention to present day Fremont, Ohio or as it was known then, Fort Stephenson.

General Harrison, who was at Camp Seneca[24] on the Sandusky River in 1813, was apprised of the planned attack on Fort Stephenson, ordered Major George Croghan[25] to burn the post and destroy the supplies that they could not carry, and retreat up the Sandusky River to join with his forces at Camp Seneca.

Benjamin Franklin Stickney

Croghan replied *"... we have determined to hold this place, and by heavens we can."* Croghan who had served with Harrison since Tippecanoe was ordered to explain himself. Croghan said that his response was a ruse in case the message fell into enemy hands, but if Harrison would give him half a chance he could carry out the defense.

Major George Croghan. *Picturesque Northwestern Ohio by VanTassel 1913.*

The blockade of Fort Stephenson began with British gunboats on the Sandusky River and hundreds of troops in the woods surrounding the fort. Fort Stephenson was designed with a palisade of wooden tree trunks and a moat eight feet deep and wide and one six-pound artillery piece[26]. Undermanned and outgunned, the fort's defenders met with the British under a flag of truce. The British officers recalled the memory of the River Raisin massacre and suggested that they could not control the Indians after they had breached the fort's defenses. The haughty British calculated that a total massacre was inevitable, and their conclusion was that Croghan should surrender at once. Croghan responded that if the Indians could take the fort *"... there would be no one left alive to massacre."*

The barrage started on the 1st of August in 1813 as the British under of flag of truce returned to their lines. Using their six-pounder effectively and moving it frequently, the Americans convinced the British that they had more cannon and men than they expected.

Fort Stephenson's Old Betsy. *Picturesque Northwestern Ohio by VanTassel 1913.*

The next morning General Proctor unleashed an all-out assault that had the troops and warriors reaching the water filled moat. As the British forces hesitated, the Americans would counter each wave of the assault with grapeshot from their six-pounder, that they named *old Betsy,* that would rip down the length of the moat cutting the British forces to pieces. Each round of buckshot would rid the living and the dead from the reddish tinged mud of the moat. The crippling grapeshot convinced the Indian warriors to retreat to the safety of the woods. General Proctor's siege without his Indians faltered, leaving Fort Stephenson in the hands of the Americans.

Tecumseh was furious with Proctor and issued his most remembered quote of the war. Tecumseh told Proctor that he was unfit for command and should *"... go and put on petticoats."* Proctor quickly laid the blame with Tecumseh and his warriors saying that they were the ones that urged the attack and that they were the ones that left the attack unfinished.

Within a few days after the successful defense of Fort Stephenson, a group of fourteen families staked out claims to farms around the fort and began to clear the land. Complaining to their Indian Agent, Benjamin Franklin Stickney, a delegation of Wyandot Indians said that the squatters had no right to the land and wanted them removed.

As Stickney arrived to confront the settlers, they had already constructed temporary shelters and were clearing the trees and scrubs. Gathering the farmers together, Stickney told them that they would have to leave or the military would escort them off the land. General John S. Gano[27], who had been left in charge of Fort Stephenson, told the squatters that they were permitted to stay and build their cabins, and that he had no authority to remove them. Stickney, following the law written in the land treaties, wrote to Governor Meigs for relief. A later petition to Ohio's Governor Meigs[28] resulted in the settlers being granted the right to establish a permanent settlement on the Wyandot's land.

Harrison's long anticipated naval action by Commodore Perry against the British forces that roamed across the Great Lakes at will, finally came to fruition on the 10th of September 1813. Perry's simple message to Harrison *"We have met the enemy, and they are ours,"* meant that the Americans now controlled the

Benjamin Franklin Stickney

supply lines that the British so dearly depended on. With no supplies, and over the protests of Tecumseh, Proctor and the remaining British Army made ready to leave Fort Malden for the safety of eastern Canada.

Using the same naval vessels that had defeated the British on Lake Erie, Commodore Perry transported General Harrison's men, cannon, wagons, and supplies to the Canadian shore. When the Americans caught the retreating British at the Battle of Thames on the 5th of October 1813 *"Remember the Raisin"* was the cry that echoed from the Kentuckians as they rode through the British lines leaving death and destruction in their wake. The death of Tecumseh was the final skirmish that broke the spirit of the Indian resistance and the elimination of an Indian Confederacy. With fewer than one hundred troops and warriors on both sides killed, American dominance over the *old northwest* was established as the British presence and influence came to an end.

In the closing months of 1813 two events within weeks of each other, emerged that would affect Benjamin Franklin Stickney and his impact on the Maumee Valley. …. Captain John Whistler[29] after his release as a British prisoner of war was appointed commander of Fort Wayne, and Lewis Cass[30] who was highly critical of General Hull's surrender of Detroit, was appointed by President Monroe as Michigan's Territorial Governor.

Benjamin Franklin Stickney

End Notes from Chapter Seven
fort wayne, war & whistler's grandfather

[1] What General Hull did not know, but might have suspected, was the capture of his ship *Cuyahoga*. The *Cuyahoga* loaded with wounded, supplies, and General Hull's personal trunk was ordered to sail from the Maumee to Detroit past the guns of British Fort Malden. Soon after her departure she was captured by the British. Hull's trunk containing personal papers, latest instructions and orders, and the United States detailed plans to carry-out the war were delivered to General Brock. One of his comments was that "... I had no idea that General Hull was advancing with such a large force. ..."

[2] William Hull displayed bravery in the Revolutionary War and was commended by Washington and was advanced to rank of lieutenant colonel. Afterwards he practiced law in Newton, Mass. On March 22, 1805 he was appointed governor of the newly created Michigan Territory. Hull's land cessions from the Indians formed the basis of their discontent. In the spring of 1812 he was persuaded to accept a commission as brigadier general in the army designed to defend the Michigan Territory and attack Upper Canada. Instead Hull surrendered to General Proctor at Detroit. Severely censured for his activities in Detroit Hull was tried for treason and sentenced to be shot. President Madison approved the sentence but remanded his sentence at the last moment because of his service in the Revolution.

[3] Stickney believed that the position of Indian Agent derived its authority directly from the Secretary of War, thus independent of Harrison the Territorial Governor of Indiana. Stickney would later have the same difficulty with Whistler, commander of Fort Wayne.

[4] Captain Rhea was from New Jersey and joined the army as a Lieutenant in 1791, and was promoted to Captain in 1807. Promoted to captain in 1807, Rhea married Polly Forsyth, the daughter of James Forsyth a wealthy Detroit merchant. While a lieutenant, Rhea served as commander of Fort Industry. Rhea took command of Fort Wayne in 1810 succeeding Nathaniel Heald who was transferred to Fort Dearborn {Chicago]. Rhea was accused of drunkenness during the siege of Fort Wayne, and Harrison permitted him to resign rather than face a court martial on December 31, 1812.

[5] Zachary Taylor was a soldier and the twelfth president of the United States. He was transferred to Fort Harrison with his company of fifty men, and successfully defended the fort against an attack of 400 Indians

Benjamin Franklin Stickney

on September 4, 1812, and as a result of his actions was promoted to the rank of major.

[6] From the character of Rhea's letters it was evident that he had changed his mind concerning Bondie's warning.

[7] Lt. Daniel Curtis was a school master from New Hampshire that eventually married Major Whistler's daughter and was posted to Fort Michilimackinac. The last item that I was able to find concerning his career was a magazine article for WESTERN PORTRAITURE written in 1852 extolling the delights of Mackinac.

[8] Letter from General Harrison to the Secretary of War, June 26, 1810. "Chief Winamac assured me that the Prophet not long since proposed to the young men of the tribe to murder the principal chiefs of all the tribes; observing that their hands would never be untied until this was effected; that these were the men who had sold their lands, and who would prevent them from opposing the encroachments of the white people."
An example of the Prophet's power occurred on the 1st of June 1810 when he declared Leatherlips [Two Equal Clouds], who was Wyandot supporter of the Americans, a witch. Roundhead who was also a Wyandot and fought with the British at Fort Wayne and Fort Meigs killed Leatherlips and five of his followers near present day Columbus, Ohio.
Winamac was a celebrated Pottawatomie chief.

[9] Letter, October 4, 1812, from Lieutenant Daniel Curtis to Cullen describing the siege of Fort Wayne. "A Mr. Johnston an express to Piqua, Ohio, was killed on the evening of the 28th (August) before he had gone a half mile from the post. He was shot through the body, tomahawked, scalped, stabbed in 23 places, and beaten and bruised in the most cruel and barbarous manner."

[10] William Oliver was from Virginia, and at the time of the siege of Fort Wayne he was acting as the fort's sutler. While he was in Cincinnati purchasing supplies for Fort Wayne and hearing of the siege of Fort Wayne, Oliver volunteers to bring news of Harrison's relief Army that was approaching Fort Wayne. Oliver left Cincinnati on September 1 and reached the fort bringing news of the relief army. According to BFS: ▯.... William Oliver, though a private citizen, was the most efficient man in the Fort after his return. ..." Later in Toledo, he built the Oliver House.

[11] Actually Harrison's force had just arrived at Piqua, Ohio. Another source indicates that William Oliver arrived with thirty Shawnees, while Lt. Curtis's account of the siege does not mention William Oliver at all.

[12] Letter from Benjamin Franklin Stickney, Indian Agent Fort Wayne to Lewis Cass Michigan Territorial Governor, September 27th, 1815.

Benjamin Franklin Stickney

[13] Lewis Cass was born and educated in Exeter, New Hampshire, in 1782, seven years after the birth of Benjamin Franklin Stickney. Cass moved to Marietta, Ohio, and studied law under Governor Meigs, and set up a law practice in 1802. Married Elizabeth Spencer, the daughter of Revolutionary war General Spencer, and elected to the Ohio legislature at the age of twenty-four.

Colonel Cass was with Gen. William Hull when he surrendered and broke his sword rather than surrender it to the British. Was extremely critical of Hull, and during his parole in Washington was named a colonel in the regular army and Major-General of the Volunteers. Was with William Henry Harrison at the Battle of Thames, and led the pursuit of General Proctor. At the end of the war he was left in command of Michigan, with headquarters at Detroit.

Before the month was out he was named Governor of the Territory of Michigan in October of 1813, which he held till July, 1831. The shake up in President Jackson's cabinet caused by the Eaton affair brought Cass into the War Department in 1831. After a five year tenure he left the cabinet because of ill health, but was promptly sent to France as Minister in October of 1836. His political career reached its climax as Secretary of State for the Buchanan administration.

Cass also served as Grand Master of Masons in Ohio and Michigan.

[14] This was the first instance where Benjamin Franklin Stickney was referred to as Major.

[15] General Tupper

[16] Fort McArthur was located near the Scioto River, three miles southwest of Kenton, Ohio.

[17] Desertion, sickness, and other errors would account for the difference.

[18] John Armstrong diplomat and career soldier suggested in the *Newburgh Letters* that if Congress would not pay the army that the officers should take matters into their own hands. His term as Secretary of War contained many mistakes concerning the northern frontier and the capture of Washington and subsequent burning by the British. Resigned from government service in 1814.

[19] River at the present site of the Presbyterian and Methodist churches

[20] After the siege of Fort Meigs and the Battle of the Thames River, Lt. Tom Hawkins was appointed custodian of government property at Fort Stephenson, Lower Sandusky (Fremont). All the British property from the Battle of the Thames and that belonged to the captured British officers and General Proctor was brought to Fort Stephenson. Bragging rights at Israel Harrington's tavern in Fremont belonged to Tom Hawkins as he would describe in great detail General Proctor's

coach. He was especially fond of hitching a team of oxen to the General's coach and riding around Fort Stephenson.

Lt. Thomas Hawkins had an eccentric personality and this was evident in his outward appearance. Lt. Hawkins refused to tie his shoe laces, and as he tells the story this practice saved him from the devil. *"As I was dressing one morning, the devil appeared and said "Come along with me." "I replied that I would as soon as I finished lacing my boots. To this the devil agreed, and that's why my boots are untied."*

Hawkins also appeared in the Log Cabin Campaign at Fort Meigs along with Rev. Badger. Together they rode the wagon with the replica of Harrison's cabin to Columbus.

[21] A gill was defined as between 1/4 to 1/2 of a liquid pint, or 4 to 8 ounces.

[22] The powder magazine was one of the weakest points of a Fort's defenses, because without powder they could not return cannon fire or even small arms fire. Originally the powder was stored in portable wagons adjacent to the trenches, but it became a necessity that a suitable underground cellar with a reinforced roof be built as soon as possible. Construction was begun at night and finished within a couple of days.

[23] . General Brock was killed in a fight at Queenstown Heights on the Niagara River in October of 1812.

[24] Camp or Fort Seneca was erected by Harrison in 1813 bewteen Lower Sandusky [Fremont] and Franklinton [Columbus]

[25] Major George Croghan was the nephew of famed George Rogers Clark.

[26] The six-pounder was nicknamed "old Betsy."

[27] General John S. Gano, son of Baptist minister Rev. John Gano, served as Brigade Chaplain in the Army of the Revolution. One of the original settlers of Columbia, Ohio in 1788. He made his living a a biographical engineer. Gano commanded an advance survey party for General St. Clair's march into Indian Territory. Gano was appointed Major General of the Ohio Militia in 1804 by Governor Tiffin. In early 1813 Gano was Governor of the Michigan Territory and Superintendent of Indian Affairs. He ended his career as Clerk of the Ohio Supreme Court in 1818. Gano was also commander of the Ohio Militia at Fort Stephenson after Croghan left.

[28] Return Jonathan Meigs, fourth Governor of Ohio, Senator, and Postmaster General was born 1764 in Conn. largely through his efforts 1,200 state militiamen were recruited and equipped in time to meet up with Hull in Dayton. In March of 1814 he resigned as governor to accept

Benjamin Franklin Stickney

the position of postmaster general, an appointment that was in recognition of his wartime support.

[29] Major John Whistler, United States Army, was made a prisoner of war at the surrender of Detroit by Hull, August 16, 1812, and was regularly exchanged, holding the rank of captain at the time, September, 1813. He was in command at Mackinac in 1833-34, and at Fort Gratiot and Detroit, and other stations in Michigan.

While building the first Fort Wayne his son George Washington Whistler was born in 1800. George Washington Whistler served in the topographical department of the Government and died in Russia in 1849 while superintending the construction of the Moscow to St.Petersburg railroad. His son and also Major Whistler's grandson, James Abbott McNeil Whistler became a famous artist. His most renowned canvas was "Whistler's Mother."

[30] Lewis Cass was born in 1782 and schooled in Exeter, New Hampshire, his classmates included Daniel Webster and Edward Everett. Cass moved to Ohio, served in the Ohio House of Representatives even though he was under age. He wrote a resolution during the Burr Conspiracy affirming Ohio's loyalty to the Union, for which he was rewarded with appointment as U. S. Marshall for Ohio. At the outbreak of the War of 1812 he held the rank of general in the Ohio Militia. Served with General Hull and was highly critical of General Hull's conduct. Lewis Cass was appointed by President Monroe as Governor of the Michigan Territory possibly because of those vigorous attacks directed at Hull's conduct.

Benjamin Franklin Stickney

PROCLAMATION

By the Supervisor and Justices of the Peace of the town of Ypsilanti.

Whereas, it appears that the Asiatic Cholera now exists in the City of Detroit, and that it is expedient and desirable to use every precaution to prevent its introduction into this village, (Ypsilanti,) Therefore, by virtue of the power in us vested, (contained in an act of the Legislative Council, approved June 29, 1832,) we do order and direct, that from and after the publication of this Proclamation, no person or persons coming directly from Detroit, or any city, town or place, where the disease aforesaid is known to prevail, shall enter the township of Ypsilanti, until such person or persons shall have been visited and examined by a Health Officer or Officers, and a certificate given; and the citizens of Ypsilanti are respectfully requested to aid and assist in carrying the objects of this Proclamation into full effect.

In witness whereof, we have hereunto subscribed our names, and caused our seals to be affixed, this ninth day of July, eighteen hundred and thirty-two.

                        JOB GORDON, *Supervisor.*

SOLOMON CHAMPION,
JOSEPH H. PECK,
ANDREW CORNISH,
CHARLES H. KELLOGG,
        Justices of the Peace.

Handbill for Cholera Epidemic for the greater Detroit area on June 29, 1832 to be posted in Ypsilanti. Courtesy of the Toledo Lucas County Public Library.

Benjamin Franklin Stickney

upper sandusky, whisky, & doubt
chapter eight

With Commodore Perry's mastery of the Great Lakes in September of 1813 coupled with Tecumseh's death in the twenty minute Battle of the Thames a month later, the pro-British Indian threat was all but removed from the Maumee Valley. For the Wyandot Indians the everyday living conditions of hunting and gathering around Upper Sandusky were beginning to return.

While he was posted at Upper Sandusky, Stickney reflected on the time he had spent away from his own family and the changing times. Lewis and Clark had left St. Louis on their Journey of Discovery almost a year after One had been born, and returned a year after Louisa came into the world. As Stickney read Quaker Gerald T. Hopkins' Journal, Stickney probably realized that Hopkins knew more about the Wyandot Indians in 1804 than Stickney did almost ten years and a war later. *"....The town [Brownstown] had a civilized appearance. Its residents lived in log houses with bark roofs, erected fences around their fields, cultivated corn, wheat, oats, and fruit, and raised cattle, hogs, and horses. ...."* [1] The scientific discoveries of the expanding west were leaving Stickney behind, and for the first time in his life he wondered just what role he was destined to play?

After the Fort Stephenson land incident[2] Stickney was tarred by the Wyandot Indians with the same brush as General Gano, but with the passage of time the Wyandot began to separate Stickney from the military officers of the day. Stickney began to use his time as Indian Agent to travel extensively through the Maumee Valley. Many times Stickney would remind the Indians of John Hunt[3], a five-year old boy, who had traveled unafraid in 1803 through the Maumee Valley with his parents learning everything that he could about his surroundings from the valley's caretakers.

"We[4] left Detroit in fifty Montreal bateaux, and though sixty-three years have passed --- I being then but five years old, I recollect distinctly entering the mouth of Swan Creek near Fort Industry. The sergeant in the bow of the boat in which the family were, shot at some ducks, and the gun bursting tore off one of his

Benjamin Franklin Stickney

thumbs, and lacerated his hand. We passed up the Maumee River, then called the Miami of the Lake Erie, the men wading and hauling the boats over the rapids ...." [5]

Any insecurity that Stickney may have had with his stance on whisky among the Indians was removed by the Wyandot leader Between-the-Logs. Initially they met on other matters in 1814, but with each visit trust built upon their friendship. Within one moon the discussions between them returned to the time before the war on the Miami of the Lake or the Maumee River. They would often return to the occasions when the missionaries from the east spread throughout the Maumee Valley. Between-the-Logs would later become an ordained Methodist minister, and with his fellow minister and traveling companion, Monocue, they would lecture to large audiences in the eastern cities.[6]

Between-the-Logs. Courtesy of Picturesque Northwestern Ohio, Van Tassel

Monocue. Courtesy of Picturesque Northwestern Ohio, Van Tassel

Between-the-Log's thoughts on Christianity
"Our fathers used to worship with feasts, sacrifices, dances, and rattles .... The French sent us the good book by a Roman Priest. He taught us that we must confess our sins, that we must

Benjamin Franklin Stickney

upper sandusky, whisky, & doubt
chapter eight

worship Lady Mary, and do penance. He told us, also, it was wrong to drink whisky. But we found out he would drink it himself. ...."

Father Marquette on the Mississippi River, Courtesy of Michigan as a Province Territory and State, 1906

Father Marquette, a Jesuit missionary, on the Mississippi River from a painting by William Lamprecht. The painting was used by the United States Post Office for the one cent postage stamp for the Trans-Mississippi Exposition of 1898 held in Omaha, Nebraska.

Benjamin Franklin Stickney

Stickney found out the Jesuit *Black Robes* were not the only religious influence that had followed the early trappers and traders into Maumee Valley. When the ice had left the lakes and rivers, the Reverend Daniel Bacon with the blessing of the Connecticut Missionary Society left Detroit in 1802 to convert the unbelievers[7] to Christianity.

After a five-day canoe journey, the Reverend Bacon and his interpreter William Dragoo arrived at the mouth of the Maumee River, and found most of the Indians drunk on the white-man's whisky. Arrangements were made to meet with Ne-gig[8], or Little Otter the next day.

Returning at the arranged time, Reverend Bacon's small party had learned that an Indian child had died and as a result of the village's grief and sorrow they were all drunk. Dragoo was instructed to camp about five miles from the mouth of the Maumee near their *dancing ground* [9] and wait till they were called for. On Friday, the 14th of May, 1802 sixteen days after leaving Detroit, the Reverend Bacon addressed the Ottawas.

"....Supposing that they might want to know why we had not sent them I minister before, since we were so urgent to have them receive one then. I informed them we had been prevented by wars, by a want of ministers, and by their living at such a great distance from us, but that we had sent ministers to the other Indian Nations who lived nearer to us.

Having heard of the four objections which I supposed they stood ready to offer, I brought them up and answered them. The first objection was, that our religion was not designed for Indians.

..... The second objection that I noticed was, that our religion was not good for them. .... The third objection was that by listening to me they would expose themselves to the fate of the poor Moravians. .... The fourth objection I thought to be much the most important, and the most difficult to answer. That they could not live together so as to receive any instructions on

Benjamin Franklin Stickney

account of their fighting and killing one another when intoxicated. ......"

When the sun reached the zenith of the following day Ne-gig, or Little Otter of the Ottawas and son of Pontiac, turned to Reverend Bacon and said:

"Brother, we listened to you yesterday, and heard all you had to say to us. ... Brother, if you and your great black-gowns and Chiefs want to help us and make us happy, why don't you stop your people from settling so near us?. If you would do this, we might have game enough and do very well. Brother, we know that it is all true what you say about the stuff the white people make, which we like so well. We know that it makes us foolish and quarrelsome, and poor, and that it destroys us, and has greatly diminished our number; that we used to be much happier before it came among us, and that it would be much better for us to be entirely without it. ...... if your people did not make it and bring it to us, we should not have it. .... But when we get a taste of it, we like it so well we do not know how to stop drinking. Brother, since it is so, why do you not stop your people from bringing it among us. … But until this liquor is stopped, ... you will not be able to do anything with us."

In August of 1804 Constantin Volney wrote about his travels and observations through the Northwest Territory in his just published book "*View of the Climate and Soil of the United States of America.*"

"From early in the morning both men and women roam about the streets, for no other purpose but to procure themselves rum: and for this they first dispose of the produce of their chase, then of their toys, next to their clothes, and at last they go begging for it, never ceasing to drink, till they are absolutely senseless. Sometimes this gives occasion to ridiculous scenes; they will lift up their cup to drink with both hands like apes, then raise up their heads with bursts of laughter, and gargle themselves with their beloved but fatal liquor; to enjoy the pleasure of tasting it the longer; hand the cup from one to another with noisy

invitations; call to one only they steps off as loud as they can bawl; take hold of their wives by the head and pour the rum down their throats with course caresses, and all the ridiculous gestures of alehouse sots. Sometimes distressing scenes ensue, as the loss of all sense and reason, becoming mad or stupid, or falling down dead drunk in the dust or mud, there to sleep till the next day. I could not go out in the morning without finding them by the dozens in the streets or paths about the village, literally wallowing in the dirt with the pigs. It was a very fortunate circumstance if a day passed without a quarrel, or a battle with knives or tomahawks, by which ten men on an average lose their lives yearly. On the 9 th of August, at four o'clock in the afternoon, a savage stabbed his wife in four places with a knife within twenty steps of me. A fortnight before a similar circumstance took place, and five such the year preceding. For this vengeance is immediately taken, or dissembled until a proper opportunity offers, by the relations, which produces fresh causes for waylaying and assassination.
..... „10
.....

In the Summer of 1805 Reverend Cram, from the Boston Missionary Society, gathered together a number of the principal chiefs and warriors from the Five Nations at Buffalo Creek, New York. The following is excerpted from the reply by Seneca Chief Red Jacket (Sagoyewatha) who had little empathy with the way in which the customs and practices of the white population were being forced upon the Indians.

Brother listen to what we say. There was a time when our forefathers owned this great island. Their seats extending from the rising sun to the setting sun. .... But an evil day came upon us. Your forefathers crossed the great water and landed on this island. Their numbers were small. They found friends and not enemies. They told us they had fled from their own country for fear of wicked men and had come here to enjoy their religion.
.....
    They called us brothers. We believed them and gave them a larger seat. At length their numbers had greatly increased. They wanted more land; they wanted our country. .....

Benjamin Franklin Stickney

wars took place. Indians were hired to fight against Indians, and many of our people were destroyed. They also brought strong liquor amongst us. It was strong and powerful and has slain thousands. ......

You say that you are sent to instruct us how to worship the Great Spirit...... you say that you are right and we are wrong. ...... We understand that your religion is written in a book. If it was intended for us as well as you, why has not the Great Spirit given to us, and not only to us, but why did He not give it our forefathers the knowledge of that book, with the means of understanding it rightly?

..... If there is but one religion, why do you white people differ so much about it? Why not all agreed, as you can all read the book?

.....We never quarrel about religion." [11]

Considering Stickney's limited exposure and experience with the Indians at Fort Wayne, and his continuing education with the Wyandot at Upper Sandusky, Stickney began to realize the devastating effect that whisky had on the fabric of life that held the Indians together.

The year of 1814 left the Maumee Valley adrift as recognized regional Indian leadership conflicted with the cross purposes of the Indian Agents. John Johnston, the agent at Piqua, wrote to General Harrison his views concerning the Indians: *"... with a view of increasing their [the Indians] wants and distresses and thereby rendering them more harmless, I have permitted all traders to sell as much liquor as they thought proper, this in a political point of view at this time is of more effect than many would suppose. .."*[12] Another quote of Johnston stated that *"... liquor is sometimes sold to the Indians at this post yet no notice has been taken of it. Many white people treat this Law with great contempt; many alleging the sooner the Indians are destroyed the better, and scarcely care by what means this is affected."*[13]

Fort Meigs, with the Maumee Valley's lessening need for protection, was left in charge of Lt. Almon Gibbs and a detachment of forty regular soldiers. Along with his regular duties at Fort Meigs, Gibbs was appointed postmaster for the Maumee/Perrysburg region. Stickney left Upper Sandusky for a Fourth of July celebration with the men who defended Fort Wayne at the start of the War of 1812. Stickney considered this one of his greatest triumphs.

As Stickney arrived he found that Fort Wayne's new commander, Major John Whistler had arrived along with his widowed family. When Whistler's wife died the previous April in Newport, Kentucky Whistler complained to any one who would listen that his children, Harriet and Eliza, were forced to walk a great part of the 19 day journey to Fort Wayne.

As the Fourth of July celebration commenced, Stickney against all military protocol offered the first toast. With all the glasses charged, Stickney proposed: *May the Union never fall from the colors she now bears up,* and Stickney's comrades in time of battle emptied their glasses. Stickney usurped Whistler's position as commander of the fort when he proposed a toast to the assembled garrison that should have been the purview of the Fort's commander and from that point on there was hell to pay.

In early September of 1814 Stickney learned that John Johnston had refused to council with the Indians that had brutally murdered his brother, Stephen, during the siege of Fort Wayne. Johnston's refusal caused him to resign in the midst of raising a contingency of Wyandot for a mounted expedition. Since William Henry Harrison resigned in May of 1814, Stickney turned to Lewis Cass, the Territorial Governor of Michigan, and Duncan MacArthur[14], Harrison's replacement for assistance.

1st of September 1814: A number of the Indians who went from Greenville to Detroit with you, have returned here, and demand of me pay for their services. I have no information whether they have been paid or not: nor have I any power to pay them if they are not paid. And what is worse I am ordered to call out the Indians again and nothing is fair about compensation. And the Indians demand as a condition of their turning out an express

Benjamin Franklin Stickney

stipulation of the terms. Mr. Johnston has relieved himself of the difficulty by resigning; of which he notified me day before yesterday. Of course I am left alone to meet the difficulty. I have called upon the Indians to embody at St. Mary's on the 20th next. I shall go there [St. Marys] in ten or twelve days. I have no interpreter suitable for the Wyandottes in the contemplated expedition. It would be a convenience if you can spare John Walker, if you can, will you be obliging as to divert him to St. Mary's.

The mounted expedition of Wyandot Indians that Stickney refers to cannot be fully explained. According to several sources Stickney was in charge of an Indian detachment on the left flank of General Andrew Jackson's Army in the Battle of New Orleans. Still, another source says that Stickney was singled out for his bravery. [15]

However, letters written from St. Mary's, Ohio by Stickney to John H. Piatt and Secretary of State James Monroe that were dated the 30th of December 1814 and another written on the 1st of February 1815 from St. Mary's, Ohio makes it highly unlikely that Stickney was in New Orleans.

John Johnston must have reconsidered his resignation because on the 1st of February 1815 Johnston recommended to James Monroe, the current Secretary of War that Stickney be returned to Fort Wayne as its Indian Agent. Major Whistler, who lived in a constant fear for his life, believed that Fort Wayne was in constant danger of an Indian attack. To protect them, Whistler in January of 1815, ordered the arrest of the Potawatomi leader White Pigeon[16]. Whistler also wrote to Stickney on the 21st of February 1815 that he had intelligence reports from reliable sources that pro-British Indian forces have been gathering about sixty miles north of Fort Winchester [Defiance].

Stickney returned to Fort Wayne sometime during the Spring of 1815 and learned that White Pigeon had escaped, and that Major Whistler received permission to rebuild the fort but not the Agency.

Benjamin Franklin Stickney

Disillusioned with past practices by the Indians, Stickney's letters indicated that the Indians would sell themselves to the British more often than to the Americans, and at the greatest advantage to themselves. Stickney would later write an article entitled *"The Condition of the FRONTIER"* for Hezekiah Lord Hosmer that reflected accurately on his war years in the northwest.

"The British authorities saw they might possibly make something out of predatory incursions by the Indian upon the partially protected frontier, as they had much the largest number of Indians who adhered to them. The Indians committed some depredations upon the scattered settlements. This produced a very uneasy state of mind among the inhabitants of Ohio and Indiana. Some hundreds of families broke and run. In this state of things, General Harrison ordered the two principal Indian Agents, John Johnston. Esq., and myself, to head quarters at Cincinnati, to consult upon ways and means of protecting the frontier. We made a written report to the General, the substance of which was, that as the Indians had their settlements scattered along the frontier, to confine them there, by feeding them daily, at their proper places of residence and no other, and to inform them that they must be responsible for the safety of the frontier; that if they suffered the British Indians to kill the white people over their heads, the white people would retaliate by killing them, as often as opportunity offered. This answered a tolerable protection; but the frontier inhabitants were yet in a very feverish state -- hundreds fled -- the friendly Indians were great objects of fear -- the Agents, who doing all they could to protect them, were suspected of intentions to let the Indians loose, and were thus placed between two fires. The Indians grew impatient of restraint and made several efforts to escape, which were thwarted by the vigilance of the Agents.[17]*"*

On the last day of April 1815 Stickney writing from Fort Wayne informed the Secretary of War, James Monroe that *"From all accounts I receive runners who have come in lately in that the British agents are acting in the same part they did after the Treaty of 1783. They are using their utmost exertions to excite the Indians of the north to harass our frontier. ... If it is your pleasure that the Agency be reestablished here the buildings will again be necessary."*

On Monday, May 29th, 1815 Major Whistler received his orders from Alexander J. Dallas [18], acting Secretary of War: *"Immediately to place the works at Fort Wayne in proper condition for maintaining his position and for affording protection for the country."*

There was no mention of the Indian Agency and Whistler obeyed his orders to the letter.

End Notes from Chapter Eight
upper sandusky, whisky, & doubt

---

[1] Joseph E. Walker, ed., Plowshares and Pruning Hooks for the Miami and Pottawatomie: The Journal of Gerald T. Hopkins, 1804, Ohio History, Vol. 88 (1979): 401-2.

[2] See Chapter 7, page 100.

[3] Colonel Thomas Hunt was ordered to St. Louis in 1803 and took his son, the future General John E. Hunt, who was five years old at the time with him.

[4] . Col. Thomas Hunt and family.

[5] Notes on the Maumee Valley, Dunlap, p 8-9.

[6] In the Summer of 1826 Between-the-Logs and Monocue lectured in Buffalo, New York, Philadelphia, Baltimore, and Washington City.

[7] The actual terms used were either heathens or savages.

[8] Pontiac's third wife, Ken-tuck-e-gun had five sons of which Ne-gig was the oldest. At that time they were living in the Ottawa Village Presque Isle, the site of Toledo's present day CSX coal docks.

[9] The Ottawa Indian dancing ground was believed to have been located at the intersection of Elm and Erie streets in Toledo's present day north end. From Reverend Bacon's journal: *"found upon a beautiful bluff on the bank of the river. The turf has been removed from the dancing ground, which was an area about 20' by 40' in size.*

Benjamin Franklin Stickney

[10] For further explanation, and a first hand account read *Young Jim* by Dresden Howard in the Northwest Ohio Quarterly. Vol. 23, N1, p46.

[11] Red Jacket or Sagoyewatha, a Seneca Chief, in reply to an address by Reverend Cram. From *A LIBRARY of AMERICAN LITERATURE*, Edmund C. Stedman and Ellen M. Hutchinson, eds. Volume 4, pages 36-38, New York 1889.

[12] Letter Book of the Indian Agency at Fort Wayne, edited by Gayle Thornbrough, Indiana Historical Society, p208n.

[13] Life of Elijah Tyson, B. Lundy, 1825, page 65; John Johnston, Memorandum for the Committee of Friends from Baltimore. At the Headwaters of the Maumee, Paul Woehrman, Indiana Historical Society, 1971, pg 138 No.63.

[14] Congressman and Governor of Ohio Duncan MacArthur was born in New York 1772. Took a noteworthy part in Hull's Campaign as a Colonel in the Ohio Militia. He urged Hull to attack Malden at once, and led a raid that penetrated some thirty miles into Canada. He was later a principal witness against Hull at Hull's court-martial. Elected to congress in the fall of 1812, MacArthur raised volunteers for Harrison's regular army. He then undertook the defense of Fort Meigs. Upon Harrison's resignation he was appointed commander. In 1830 he was elected governor of Ohio in a narrow victory over Robert Lucas. In 1832 he chose to run for congress but was defeated by a single vote by William Allen, who later married his daughter Effie.

[15] Taken from a biographical sketch of Stickney by genealogist Howard Parker Moore author of Life of General John Stark of New Hampshire, 1949.

[16] White Pigeon was reported by Sugden in his book *Tecumseh* as traversing the Illinois and upper Mississippi Rivers calling on the villagers to take arms from the British, and his village was on the headwaters of the St. Joseph River.

[17] Taken from H. L. Hosmer's "Early History Of The Maumee Valley."

[18] Dallas, originally from England, migrated to the United States on April 10, 1783 and was required to wait the two years before he could practice law. Dallas was a close friend of Albert Gallatin, and when Gallatin resigned from the United States Treasury, Dallas was appointed Secretary of the Treasury after George Campbell on October 6, 1814. Because of President Monroe's illness, Dallas took it upon himself the duties of Secretary of War on March 15, 1815.

Benjamin Franklin Stickney

whistler, richardville, & politics
chapter nine

With the threat of war removed from the frontier, the newly minted states of Ohio, Indiana, and the Territory of Michigan eagerly awaited the flood of expected immigrants from the poverty and crop failures that had gripped the eastern states. The fresh faces of farmers, merchants, and tradesmen that sailed Lake Erie from Buffalo to the Detroit and Maumee Rivers had psychologically moved the Indian threat to the ever changing westward frontier.

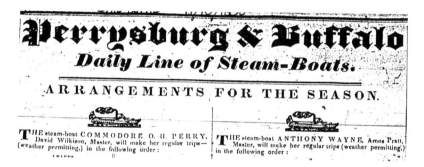

Captain David Wilkison of the *Commodore Perry*. From the Ohio Whig newspaper of November 10th, 1838.

Land transportation into Ohio and Indiana had always been impeded by the Black Swamp, which caused many of the immigrants to turn to lake transportation. Early Perrysburg claimed many of the pioneer captains, crews, and vessels that rose to meet the demand. David Wilkison[1] was fifteen when the lake finally cleared of ice in May of 1815 when he sailed up the Maumee with his uncle Captain Jacob Wilkison on the schooner *Black Snake*. On board were many of the families, baggage, livestock, and expectations that were destined for the fertile ground of the Maumee Valley and the River Raisin. One of the pioneering eastern families on board was the Monhollens, and they would make their mark on the region some twenty years later.

As the years and the need for lakes transportation progressed, Captain David Wilkison had the schooner *Commodore Perry* constructed by master ship carpenter F. N. Jones at his Swan

Creek shipyard. Promising to pay his investors back in one season, many of Wilkison's Perrysburg friends and neighbors were stockholders. William Hodge wrote about one the owners. "... *Among those that had taken stock in the Commodore Perry was one Joe or Joseph Langford, a colored man who had been cook on the EAGLE, and afterwards had the same position on the PERRY. His wife, a colored woman, was one of the most lady-like and stylish women in Perrysburg. During one of the steamboat's trips, after nearly all the passengers had eaten their dinner and none were left at the table, Langford sat down and was eating, when he was interrupted by a passenger who chanced to be late for dinner. This person seeing Langford at the table said, "I am not going to eat with a nigger." Langford felt quite indignant at the remark and curtly observed, "I should like to know who has a better right to eat his dinner aboard this boat than one of the owners."* [2]

Just below the high ground of Maumee's Presque Isle near the Rapids of the Maumee River, where John Carter and John Race had built their rough cabin; the river was slowly reclaiming the flatboats that General Winchester used to bring supplies to Fort Meigs. During the summer months, Amos Spafford and the other settlers of Orleans of the North or Perrysburg, lacking the initial use of a saw-mill used whatever wood they could find to build the sturdy cabins needed to winter in the valley. Working together Spafford and his neighbors dismantled the flatboats for their usable logs, lumber, and nails.

Lt. Almon Gibbs and his small detachment of soldiers made daily patrols, but with Fort Meigs closing, the settlers soon learned that they would have to rely on each other for protection. Most of the government property at Fort Meigs had already found its way to Detroit when in late summer of 1815 the fort's cannons, guns, and ammunition were loaded aboard the *Black Snake* for Detroit.

By the 1st of July Major Whistler's soldiers were actively cutting timber for the required palisades that would surround the rebuilt Fort Wayne. Stickney had already questioned the competence

Benjamin Franklin Stickney

of Whistler when Stickney asked for the Agency's inventory and it could not be found. According to Stickney Whistler was openly laughed at and called unflattering names by the rank and file soldiers, and with his officers he often traded curses. Stickney would later cite an officer's statement that called into question Whistler's aptitude for the job. *"... that his officers considered disobeying his orders and risking a court martial to decide Whistler's competency."*

Throughout his career as an Indian Agent, Stickney was always having difficulty with the bookkeeping of his inventory of goods and accounts. Control over the Agency's inventory and money was an impossible task considering the number of officers that were able to delve into Stickney's trade goods without his knowledge or permission.

When called to task, Stickney offered the following summation to Secretary of War William Crawford [3] in his defense. Stickney to Secretary of War Crawford, October 1st, 1815.

"Goods shipped to Fort Wayne prior to the War of 1812 were sent to a warehouse in Dayton for safe keeping. A detachment of Kentucky militia marching through Dayton to relieve the siege at Fort Wayne helped themselves to the goods. During the siege of the Fort, goods were lost, burned, or turned over to the soldiers. With the arrival of General William Henry Harrison, Stickney was ordered to turn over to the Commanders of regiments all such goods, as were suited to the necessities of the army. Also annuities due the Indians during the war were given to those Indians friendly to the United States. Further, stores were given to the Indians by the fort officers and not reported to the Agent."

But for a month or so Whistler was going to be someone else's problem, as Stickney made his way to New Hampshire to gather his family, possessions, and other goods necessary for the trek to Fort Wayne.

Benjamin Franklin Stickney

whistler, richardville, & politics
chapter nine

The following is a compilation of historical truths from a play that described Mary [Stark] Stickney's travel from Bow, New Hampshire to Fort Wayne in 1817.[History Center, Allen County Historical Society, Fort Wayne, In.]

I stayed to keep our homeplace and raise our young-ens for the brief time we thought Benjamin would have to be away from us. A few months became a few years, the loneliness interrupted only by letters carrying news of a remote land and unfamiliar people. While he was gone my closest sister Elizabeth died, a little more than a year later, my mother passed on. The years without Benjamin were long.

When Benjamin did return the occasion arose to leave my beloved New Hampshire and accompany him west to Fort Wayne. Great sadness prolonged my decision, but the need to unite as a family once more put us on our journey.

As we walked, Benjamin talked at length about the Indians and the settlers I would meet, the life within the fort and the hope that Major Whistler would have our house ready upon our arrival. If the house was not quite completed, we would be welcomed and comfortable in the spacious Officer's Quarters with Lt. Daniel Curtis, a former schoolmaster also from New Hampshire, who was engaged to marry the Major's daughter Eliza.

We traveled the highway which ran from Boston to Albany, crossed the expansive Hudson River, and wended our way along the lush Mohawk Valley in the State of New York. At [Pennsylvania] Presque Isle[4] Benjamin made arrangements to transfer our meager possessions to a Pirogue. The land from that point being swampy and inaccessible to cart and oxen.

We were one month on the water, coming in the last three days on sea biscuits and berries, having given the last of our provisions to a small band of less than cordial Indians. I eagerly watched for the flag Benjamin said flew high above the stockade and anxiously longed for the safety of our new home.

Benjamin Franklin Stickney

Our arrival was one of celebration, salted with disappointment. The timbers Benjamin had left behind had been taken into the fort, and the cellar had been filled in. No house awaited.

We are now living inside the fort, in the Officer's Quarters. Benjamin is happy with his small, but serviceable office on the first floor. We have lovely sleeping quarters just above it, and the young-uns sleep snug and warm on the third floor. We are thankful to be together, and are grateful for the Major's hospitality. We are comfortable, but the children are not used to quite as strict confinement as we must regulate to. They can no longer run freely through the rolling meadows, nor laugh and play tumble in the kitchen. But Benjamin takes the boys along occasionally on his frequent sojourns to the Indian villages. Mary, who is eight this year, is content to sit with me and learn her letters and her stitches, while One and Two are gone.

Sixty years later Mary[5] [Stickney] Green wrote of her travels with her mother, father, and family to Fort Wayne after being approached by the Toledo BLADE. Mrs. Green's account appeared on Saturday, February 23, 1867.

My father's family and attendants, which consisted, of himself, my mother and three children, an Englishman (a deserter from the British Army) and three Frenchmen, arrived in a perogue, (most of our pioneers will remember the name of a boat made of a single log, about thirty feet long and three wide) at Presque Isle[6] about midnight, on the third day of July, 1815. And without pitching a tent, we laid ourselves down with only bed clothes to protect us from the dew, with the sand for our feather bed, and the blue sky for our canopy, to count the stars until we slept, which if I remember right, was very soon, until the dawn of our glorious Independence.

After breakfast, we rowed up the river, and landed on the spot where the city of Toledo now stands. After examining the charred remains of the old British Fort, and other objects of interest, my mother was so pleased with the place that she expressed a desire to live and die there. But destiny forced us

Benjamin Franklin Stickney

onward. There were no houses there at this time, and but one habitation composed of two arks, drawn out of the water, turned up edgewise, with a blanket for a door and a chimney built of sticks and clay, on the outside. The family consisted of a man and wife, and child, which was born there, and my childish eyes were delighted with a very curious cradle made of an Indian blanket, tied at both ends with a rope made of bark swung across the corner of the cabin, in which the little one slept as quietly as though it had been lulled to sleep in rosewood or mahogany, and pillows of down, - that is my first memory of Toledo.

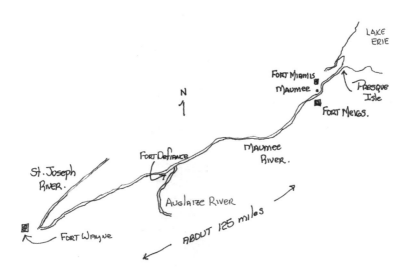

Mary [Stickney] Green's travels from Presque Isle to Fort Wayne on the Maumee River. From the author's collection.

Again we embarked for Fort Meigs, where we arrived a little after noon, and found no accommodations outside the fort. There was no garrison there at that time. We spent a week with Captain David Hull; and there I saw the first Indian belonging to my father's agency. They were Shawnees, and were delighted to see "Appasesab," as they called my father, and his papooses. We were all obliged to shake hands with them.

Benjamin Franklin Stickney

After spending a week in providing supplies, we bade good bye to Captain Hull, and his sisters, who had so kindly entertained us. My father and the Frenchmen were very despondent at the low state of the water, and could not conceive how we were to get the boat over the rapids; but landing at Reash Deveau (now Waterville) we found a pair of twin brothers by the name of Gunn, with very numerous families, and father employed one of them to take our load past the rapids. By the way, I should say something about the way in which these people were commencing a settlement. They had a yoke of oxen, a wagon and a cart, both of which were covered with canvass, and as they had been there but a few days the wagon was their only covering. And here again I saw a novel cradle, a blanket tied together at each end, tied between two trees and the baby in it, swinging back and forth in great comfort. After loading our goods into the cart, we resumed our journey, the family following on foot; while the Frenchmen pushed and poled the pirogue over the shallow water as best they could. We were to meet at night on the bank of the river and all camp together, the boatmen having most of the camp equipment, which we accordingly did. There being no road but an Indian trail, when we came to deep ravines, of which we found many, they had to strike out into the woods with the cart to get around them. With so many obstacles to surmount it took us several days to get eighteen miles on our journey. On the second day out, about five o'clock, we came to a very deep gully, with an Indian trail winding through it. The cart set out to go around, while mother thought to lead us across. We had left our shoes in the cart it being so very warm, and we soon found ourselves in the midst of a bed of nettles; and you may very well believe there was some loud crying. In the midst of the noise mother espied the boat, and called to the men to take us little ones on board, which they did leaving her to follow the cart. We were now parted from our mother, for an indefinite time, but we enjoyed hanging our feet in the water, counting the small fish, and seeing the men wade in the water to push and pull the boat through the narrow places. We camped that night according to appointment, and awaited the arrival of the cart and

Benjamin Franklin Stickney

our parents, but they failed to come. We traveled all the next day, and camped the next night, but still found no mother.

Dear Reader, you may imagine the feelings of two children, one seven and the other five years of age, left with four rough men, all of them strangers, in a howling wilderness, infested with hostile savages and wild beasts, parted from our mother for two days and nights, thinking we should never see her again. You may guess our joy was equal to our sorrow, when we came around a point near the head of the rapids, and spied our dear mother upon the high banks of the river, cooking by a good fire, accompanied by my father, brother, Mr. Gunn, and several Indians. It did not take us long to scramble up the bank and join them. When we were seated on the ground, an Indian came and placed between us a dish, formed of bark, containing some delicious honey, and my mother gave us some of the cakes that she had baked before the fire; and that night we feasted sumptuously. After dark we saw lights moving over the water, and my father told us that it was Indians, hunting deer. They brought us some of the venison next morning, for which we had to pay dearly out of our own provisions.

Some days elapsed without any particular incidents, until we arrived at old Fort Defiance, which we found evacuated. Here we found one white man, the only one between Fort Meigs and Fort Wayne.

After leaving Defiance, the second day out we had a storm which lasted all night; so hard a wind that the men found it impossible to pitch the tents; and after building a roaring fire, they stuck the poles into the ground on which they fastened a coverlet, slanting, under which my mother sat with one of us children on either side watching the eyes of the wolves all around us. We could see their teeth and hear the sticks crack under their feet. The next morning we were very wet, but the sun rose clear and bright, and we had all day to dry in. During the remainder of our journey we had very pleasant weather, and nothing remarkable happened to us, with the exception of meeting a party of Indians, who begged the most of our

Benjamin Franklin Stickney

provisions, and we had to sustain on five sea biscuits for three days. We arrived in old Fort Wayne on the third day of our fasting, it being the 4 th day of August, just one month to the day from Presque Isle.
                           Mary Green, Formerly Stickney.

A month after the Stickney family arrived at Fort Wayne, Levi Hull[7] would be the last settler killed by Indians in the Maumee Valley. Hull's body was found near the First Methodist Church on Perrysburg's Second Street.

As 1815 drew the snow and cold of winter around its shoulders, the Potawatomi and Wyandot were complaining to Stickney that the land surveyors were running the boundary lines from the last Michigan land purchase without a representative of the tribes present. Both blockhouses and three of the barrack's buildings of the rebuilt Fort Wayne had been completed, necessitating the use of the logs that were reserved for the agency buildings. Amos Spafford, representing twenty-three of his neighbors, successfully processed their claims for four thousand dollars in damages from the last war against the United States. And lastly, while still living in Fort Wayne's Officer's quarters, Stickney estimated that there were around 2,600 Indians living in the Maumee Valley. This included the 450 Ottawas living at Presque Isle near the present day CSX railroad docks on the Maumee Bay.

As December's full moon developed the horns of January the year 1816 soon became known as *"1800 & Froze to Death."* 1816 brought one of the coldest years ever recorded.[8] At the dawn of 1815, twelve months earlier, at least six almanacs forecast unusual weather for the coming year, and the *Old New England Farmer's Almanac & Register* had forecast snow storms during the month of July. Along with Columbus being named the capital of Ohio, May brought deep snow and sleet on more than half the days of the month. Thinking that June would bring a change in the frigid conditions, the nearly 500,000 residents of Ohio faced 19 inches of snow during the first ten days. Ponds and rivers froze every month during the summer,

Benjamin Franklin Stickney

and no crops grew north of the Ohio River. In the spring of 1817, seed corn was selling for ten dollars a bushel, if you could find some available. [9]

Of the coldest year on record, January found Whistler sending his troops three miles for suitable logs to complete the fort and its buildings.[10] Using the Indian Agency's team of oxen to haul the logs, Whistler had improved the fort's building schedule, but Stickney still bristled at having to receive Indians in the same room where his family lived. Towards the end of June, Whistler finally received the order from the War Department to rebuild the Indian Agency.

Major Whistler, Fort Wayne's military commander, had fostered the concept that Stickney's Indian Agency was under his command, and of course Stickney never recognized the major's authority. Their latest difficulties arose from the issue of provisions to the visiting Indians. Whistler maintained, for a ticket to be valid it must contain his signature. As a result the clash between the two men escalated.

In his spare time, Stickney and his sons had been rebuilding the foundation for the Indian Agency when Lt. Curtis and several enlisted men took the required tools by force claiming that the tools belonged to the garrison and Stickney had no right to them.

The removal of the tools necessary to rebuild the Indian Agency appeared to have been the last straw in the Stickney/Whistler dispute, and prompted Stickney to write to his friend Lewis Cass who was now Michigan's Territorial Governor.

"Major Whistler appears to have conceived an idea from this order (War Department May 7, 1816[11]) that the Indian Agency is put under his control and that he may give or withhold aid as caprice may dictate, and otherwise regulate the Agency. ..... Added to this, that my compensation is not adequate to my support. I shall be compelled to resign as soon as I can obtain the settlement of my accounts."

Benjamin Franklin Stickney

Major Whistler appears to be displeased and to make me feel the effects of his displeasure he has taken from me the labourers who were employed in building a house for my accomodation ...... Until within a few days, I have generally been furnished with a waiter as has been usual for Agents. And he is taken away likewise.[12]

The real unrest at the fort was coming from Whistler's son-in-law, Lt. Daniel Curtis[13], and Dr. William Turner[14]. A letter from Stickney to the Secretary of War Crawford over Major Whistler issuing tickets for provisions has caused Lewis Cass, Territorial Governor of Michigan, to summon Lt. Daniel Curtis to Detroit to explain a charge of improper conduct in relation to the Indian Department.[15]

Stickney would write to Lewis Cass on the 27th of July explaining the cause of the bad feelings. "*I believe there would be no difficulty with Major Whistler if it were not for his Son in Law and a Dr. Turner*[16] *who are the conductors of the mischief (you know that the Major Whistler has never been very strong in intellect, and of course grows weaker by old age.) I think I now may venture to believe that Mr. Johnson is acting a double part not with standing his professions of friendship. To crown all, I am informed that Mr. Curtis says that* [Indian Agent] *Mr. John Johnson wrote him in his last express offering him the Agency.*

In addition to your advice by letter to go immediately to Washington..... But for a variety of reasons both public and private it is not possible to leave for ten or twelve days. .... Lieutenant Saunders sets out from here tomorrow for Washington.[17] *He has resigned through the intrigues of Lieut. Curtis and Doctor Turner. By their conduct he was led to make unguarded expressions, which was made a ground for his arrest. ..... Mr. Saunders is a family friend of Mr. Monroe and will deliver my letter in person. .... Mr. Monroe will certainly lay the matter before the President, to whom I am not a stranger. This with your letter to the Secretary of War, upon the subject, I think must preclude the necessity of my repairing to Washington, if anything can.*[18] [19]

Benjamin Franklin Stickney

When Stickney returned from Washington, he was furious to find that Whistler had repaired the failed foundation for the Indian Agents quarters, and blamed Stickney for not using mortar in the failed foundation. With all the accusations of petty impropriety between Whistler and Stickney, the first hint of real difficulty was contained in a letter of the 22nd of October that John Johnston wrote to the War Department. Part of the letter described the difficulties that Jean Baptiste Richardville[20], a Miami, has had in his past dealings with Stickney at Fort Wayne. What was not mentioned was Richardville's history with the British, which Stickney had documented as far back as 1811[21] by John Shaw, a sub-agent of Stickney.

Indian Agent John Johnston. Excerpted from Howe's Historical Collection, Howe, 1896

Benjamin Franklin Stickney

Major Whistler mentioned in early September while Stickney was in Washington *"... that Richardville had purchased a house within two or three hundred yards from the Garrison for the purpose of trading, but coming to my knowledge put a stop thereto as knowing him to be a British Subject and holding a Commission under that Government. This is the same Richardville who endeavored to make the Indians believe that the English had not made peace with the United States."* [22]

By this time Major Whistler and Agent Stickney are so displeased with each other, that instead of talking to each other they are writing letters to each other from the opposite sides of the Fort. In a last ditch effort to have Stickney replaced, Lt. Curtis and Dr. Turner preferred charges that were sent to the War Department against Stickney.

The charges that Lt. Curtis and Dr. Turner alleged were contained in a letter from Secretary of War Isaac Shelby to Lewis Cass on January 23, 1817.

No.1   *That a trading license was given to a known British subject. No name was included with the charge.*[23]

No.2   *Converted trade goods to his own purpose.*

No.3   *Gave presents to various Indian women in return for [sexual] favors.*

No.4 ... *and the worst charge was that Stickney did not believe in God.*[24]

In his defense, a letter writing campaign, supporting Stickney, was initiated by the residents of Fort Wayne,[25] and Stickney's interpreters. Stickney also wrote to Lewis Cass, Michigan's Territorial Governor, and demanded a hearing to clear him of the charges. Cass appointed Michigan's Attorney General Charles Larned[26], to conduct a thorough inquiry into all the charges against Stickney.

After a systematic and methodical examination, Larned declared Curtis's letter of accusations completely false, and dismissed all charges against Stickney. The aftermath of the Curtis letter was quite profound. Major Whistler was appointed military storekeeper in St. Louis, Lt. Daniel Curtis was posted to Fort Mackinac, and lastly Stickney's daughter, Indiana, was born at Fort Wayne.

Lewis Cass sent the complete proceedings to George Grahm[27] Clerk of the War Department, in an effort to suggest to the military that a complete investigation into Curtis's statements should be initiated.

Jean Baptiste de Richardville, or Peshewa, 1761-1841. An extremely wealthy Miami who used the laws to further the Miami Nation's position. Courtesy of Wikipedia.

Another incident occurred a little more than a year later on Wednesday, May 6th, 1818 in which Stickney runs head long into difficulty. Richardville was caught selling whiskey to the Indians and settlers from his cabin or trading post just outside Fort Wayne. Stickney described his actions in a letter to Michigan Territorial Governor Cass: *"Yesterday I was under the necessity of having 7 barrels of whiskey destroyed belonging to him. I had permitted 8 barrels to be sold to him here upon the express Condition that it should not be moved or disposed of without my permission ---- Sometime afterwards he came and asked my permission to move it off, of the reserve, which I refused, & he plainly told me he would remove it without my consent, he carried it over the line, into the Indian Land where he believed I could not lawfully touch him: and in defiance established a store solely for the sale of whiskey, having obtained a larger quantity from down the St. Mary's river. I had called the Miamis here to receive their annuity, and to council with them. Part of them came, and the rest he kept back with the whiskey. It appeared very evident to me that in addition to his desire to make money, he wished to render abortive, all attempts to confer with the Indians."*

It was not long before Richardville wrote letters to his influential friends in the United States about his inability to sell whiskey to the Indians and demanded Stickney's removal.

Lewis Cass, Territorial Governor of Michigan, would write Indian Agent John Johnston in June of 1818 in defense of his friend Stickney.

"I do not consider his [Stickney's] quarrel with Richardville will destroy his ability there. The circumstances which I can collect from him and from others warrant the belief that some decisive step was necessary to enforce his authority and that had nothing been done he would have become a mere cipher at his post useless to the Government and contemptible to the Indians. You and I would not differ in our estimate of Mr. Stickney. I think him a very worthy man and felt anxious to relieve him from the embarrassment occasioned by the legislative abstraction of his office."[28]

Benjamin Franklin Stickney

But less than nine months later on the 12th of September Stickney was offered and accepted the position of Sub-Agent to the Wyandot at Upper Sandusky and Dr. William Turner was appointed sub-agent at Fort Wayne. All this occurred after Stickney's difficulty with Richardville over the sale of whiskey. Lewis Cass would later write to Calhoun regarding Stickney's service at Fort Wayne. "... *Circumstances have occurred at Fort Wayne, with the detail of which it is unnecessary to trouble you, which have had a tendency to injure the usefulness of Mr. Stickney there. On a full examination of the facts he is in my opinion exculpated from all censure. I fully agree with him in proceeding respecting the whiskey, although subsequent events made it prudent to pay* [for the United States to pay for the whisky as property destroyed] *for it.*"

On Tuesday, April 19, 1819, in pursuance of orders by the Secretary of War, Fort Wayne was turned over to the civilian authorities. The civilian authorities, represented by Major Stickney, Indian Agent, took possession of the fort buildings and quarters, which were then leased to the pioneer families and individuals who desired them. Less than three years old, Fort Wayne ceased to function as a Government outpost *"eighty miles from white civilization."*

End Notes from Chapter Nine
whistler, richardville, & politics

---

[1] **Captain David Wilkison was master of the** *Black Snake, Pilot, Saucy Jane, Prudent, Superior, Guerriere, Eagle, and the Commodore Perry* **each ship larger and faster than the one that came before.**

[2] **Early Navigation on the Great Lakes, William Hodge, Buffalo, 1883.**

[3] **William Henry Crawford was a senator, cabinet member, and presidential candidate. William was accepted as Minister to France in 1813, and resigned this post to become Secretary of War in 1815 by President Madison. Was seriously considered as a candidate to oppose President Monroe. Crawford declined and continued to serve as Secretary of the Treasury under both Monroe terms.**

Benjamin Franklin Stickney

[4] Presque Isle, Pennsylvania on Lake Erie.
[5] Benjamin Franklin and Mary Stickney's daughter, Mary.
[6] This Presque Isle could be located at the mouth of the Maumee River near the Ottawa village of Ken-tuck-e-gun.
[7] Levi Hull was found shot and scalped near where the First Methodist Church now stands on Second Street in Perrysburg, Ohio.
[8] The cold weather was not just limited to the United States, this world wide change in climate was attributed to volcanic eruptions in Indonesia. The Tambora volcano on the island of Sumbawa in the Lesser Sundra Islands exploded in May of 1815 sending millions of tons of debris into the atmosphere severely reducing the sunlight in 1816.
[9] . Robert Evans, *Blast from the Past,* Smithsonian, July 2002, pg52-57.
[10] The pickets are five feet in the ground and twelve and a half feet above the ground, and by April the stockade was completed except for the last fifty feet that surrounded the Indian Agency's buildings, and a store house for the Agency's goods was finished.
[11] The order that Stickney refers to concerns the issue of rations to the Indians. The excessive number of rations has required that new checks and balances be instituted to prevent fraud. To this end, it is directed that all abstracts for issues to the Indians shall be signed and certified by the Officer commanding the post.

[12] Excerpts from the *"Letter Book of the Indian Agency at Fort Wayne 1809-1815,"* edited by Gayle Thornbrough, Indiana Historical Society, 1961, page 243-4.
[13] Lt. Daniel Curtis was a school master from New Hampshire who married Major Whistler's daughter and was posted to Fort Michilimackinac. The last item that I was able to find concerning his career was a magazine article for WESTERN PORTRAITURE written in 1852 extolling the delights of Mackinac.
[14] Dr. William Turner's driving ambition was to become the Indian Agent at Fort Wayne. To this end he engaged in ruthless campaign of misinformation and half truths against Benjamin Stickney. He succeeded in becoming secretary to the Commissioners who negotiated the Treaty of St. Mary's in the Fall of 1818, and he occupied William Well's former post of subagent for the Miami from March 1819 to May 1820, when he was discharged for unsatisfactory conduct. Although Turner was a drunkard, his dismissal was actually caused by his ill-advised deposit of Government annuities in a Cincinnati bank that failed.
It should also be mentioned that he married Ann Wells, the second daughter of Captain William Wells.

The following is taken from the *Biographical Field Notes of Dr. Lyman Draper* as printed in the NWOQ V5:N4:p1 *"General Hunt bought of Benac a pair of rifle-barrel pistols taken from (Capt.) Wells after he was slain, and marked with his initials W. W. and sent them to Well's son-in-law Dr. Turner of the U. S. Army.*

[15] Letter from Stickney to Sec of War Crawford on July 15, 1816.

[16] Dr. Turner later married Ann Wells, or Ahpezzahquah, the daughter of William Wells by his first marriage. Dr. Turner enlisted as a Surgeon's Mate in Maryland in 1812, and resigned January 31, 1815.

[17] Sunday, July 28, 1816.
[18] Letter from Stickney to Lewis Cass, July 27, 1816.
[19] In a letter from Governor Lewis Cass to the Secretary of War on Tuesday, July 30, 1816 Cass recommends Stickney as the Indian Agent for Fort Wayne, and another letter on the 27th of August Governor Cass makes the same recommendation.
[20] *(Mentioned in letter from Lewis Cass, Michigan Territory, to Indian Agent John Johnston: dated June 15, 1818.)*

Jean Baptiste de Richardville, Peshewa, a Miami Chief, was to succeed his uncle, Little Turtle, in 1812. Possibly the earliest record of Richardville appears in the Journal of Henry Hay: *There are two villages at this place one on this side the (St. Joseph) River & one on the other - the former belongs to the Gree (Le Gris) - the other to Paccan who's now in Illinois, but in his absence is commanded by his nephew one Mr. Jean Baptist Richardville, son to one Mr. (Drouet de) Richardville of Three Rivers in Canada by an Indian women - This young man is a trader here - his father has wrote for him to go to him which he means to do next spring. His mother is now gone into the Indian Country ... to trade; She lives with him when she's here - the young man is so bashful that he never speaks in Council, his mother who is very clever is obliged to do it for him.*

Richardville's mother, Tacumwah, was a sister of Little Turtle and a daughter of Aquenochquah. She is credited with prompting her son to save the life of an American tied to the stake for torture; he made himself a hero in the eyes of the savages and became a chief. Hers, also, was the plan to control traffic over the Maumee-Wabash portage which made Richardville the wealthiest Indian in the Midwest.

Benjamin Franklin Stickney

Peshewa, at the time of his death, was believed to have been the most wealthy man of the native race in America, the estimate of his property exceeding half a million dollars. A large part of this was in the best selected lands, reserved out of the original cessions of his tribe, and other real estate. He left nearly $200,000 in specie. This is the chief of whom it was said, on the occasion of the government feeling the general pressure for coin to meet its Indian annuities in 1837-8, that he offered to loan the disbursing agent the amount required for his tribe at a moderate interest.

In tribal affairs Richardville, Peshewa, was judicious and painstaking, adjusting all matters of business appertaining to them with the most exact discrimination and prudence. John Tipton said of him, *He was the ablest diplomat of whom I have any knowledge. If he had been born and educated in France he would have been the equal of Talleyrand.* He was a signer of four important treaties. On August 13, 1841, he died at the family home on the St. Mary's River.

[21] Wednesday, September 4, 1811

[22] September 7, 1816, Whistler to Cass.

[23] It was common knowledge around Fort Wayne that the license was issued to Jean Baptiste Richardville. Richardville wasn't named because he had powerful friends in Washington.

[24] . Gayle Thornbrough, Letter Book of the Indian Agency at Fort Wayne, Indiana Historical Society, 1961, page 248.

[25] Mrs. Suttenfield's recollections of Major B. F. Stickney, "... *who often sat at the same table with them, are still quite fresh. Mr. Stickney was a sterling pioneer and soldier, and did much for the alleviation of his country during its infant struggles in the west, ever attentive to the wants and sufferings of the red children of this locality, ... who, in many instances, came to sad destitution and debasement through the use of intoxicating liquors, ... "*

[26] Charles Larned was Attorney General of Michigan under Porter, studied law in Kentucky with Henry Clay. While a student with Clay he enlisted in Col. Owen's regiment, which came to the relief of General Harrison at Fort Wayne. Rose to the rank of major, and was in the Battle of the Thames. At the close of the war he engaged in the practice of law in Detroit. He died in August of 1834.

[27] Chief Clerk of the War Department, he temporarily filled the position as President Madison's Secretary of War between the appointments of Isaac Shelby and J. C. Calhoun.

[28] Written by Lewis Cass Territorial Governor of Michigan to John Johnston Agent for Indian Affairs on June 15th, 1818. Copies to U.S. Commissioners, Governor Jennings of Indiana, and Judge Parker also of Indiana.

Large elm tree on the bluff overlooking the Maumee River opposite Fort Meigs from which Indian sharpshooters would fire on the soldiers. From the author's collection.

Benjamin Franklin Stickney

Squeezed between the treaties that they signed and the immigrant land owners, the Potawatomi and Wyandot Indians demanded through their Indian Agent, Benjamin Franklin Stickney, to know the exact location of what was theirs, and the land that belonged to Ohio and Indiana. This time the Indians read the treaty carefully, and they were entitled to accompany the surveyors when they ran the boundaries. Twelve years before when Ohio became a state, the north and west boundaries were defined in so many words, but with the Indian difficulties on the frontier and the War of 1812, the actual boundary lines were not surveyed. Peace on the western frontier blurred the paper words, and like a torrential rain the immigrants spread across the land. The need for physical landmarks that separated the Nations and defined their boundaries was long overdue.

When Stickney wrote Lewis Cass, Michigan's Territorial Governor on Wednesday, September 27th, 1815 he included several thoughts of his on the state's boundary.

"... I have been informed that there are arrangements made for running the northern and western lines of the State of Ohio. If so, we shall know whether Fort Wayne is in Ohio or Indiana Territory. I have no doubt it is in the State of Ohio. Indeed, I wish it may be so, in that case there can be no doubt of the propriety of my being under your superintendence, which as we have observed, I think highly necessary. ..."

Not all inquiries about boundary lines were the subject of contention, especially when United States Comptroller of the Treasury, Josiah Meigs[1] wrote to Amos Spafford[2] on April 12th, 1816 fifteen days before Congress officially passed the land act. *"... As you will have a town on the Miami of Erie, it will be well to think of the name it is to bear.[3] ... I will barely suggest to you that, if it would be named Perryville, or Perrytown -- or in some other form, which may always remind us of the victory of Erie ... We ought to make the best profit we can of the blood of our countrymen, which has been shed for the confirmation of our Independence. ... If it were left to me to name the town at Lower*

Benjamin Franklin Stickney

Sandusky, I should name it in honor of the gallant youth, Col. Croghan, -- and would say it should be CROGHANVILLE. I believe it is in your power to give the names...." [4]

Peace also brought communication and a free flow of ideas through the Maumee Valley and throughout the United States. Friends since being assigned to Fort Wayne, Amos Spafford wrote to Stickney concerning the safe arrival of Stickney's family and the difficulties he had in obtaining a suitable wine on December 23, 1816.

"... I received five letters from you by an unknown hand about two weeks ago, was happy to hear of your safe return to your family, & also of your good success while absent. The information concerning the running of the State Line was very pleasing as that will put an end to all difficulties. & I hope will be the means of making a strong settlement on the north & west line of our state. --- with respect to the wine, I had no opportunity of sending to Cleveland until it was too late to procure that which was good. I therefore can only send you three and a half gallons of my own..."

With the Treaty of 1817 safely negotiated, the Federal Government acquired title to Indian Lands stretching from the Sandusky Bay to Fort Wayne, and from the Treaty of Greenville Line to the north bank of the Maumee River. Along with the additional land came a shout from the newspapers and speculators for an accurate description of the land that had just been added to the United States.

Rising to the occasion, the newest member of Cincinnati's Western Immigration Society[5], Stickney wrote a twenty-nine page article in 1818 for the *WESTERN SPY*[6]. Inducted as an honorary member, Stickney was more than qualified to describe the land for the speculators. Stickney's article carried his convictions of possible canal traffic [7] from New York City to New Orleans. Stickney described how the six mile difference between the Maumee and Wabash Rivers could be connected by a simple canal.

Benjamin Franklin Stickney

"... The Miami River of the Lake [Maumee River] is formed by the junction of the St. Mary's and St. Joseph's rivers at Fort Wayne; pursues a general course northeast with its meanderings about 170 miles, discharging into the Maumee Bay. The river is navigable for vessels drawing five to six feet of water to Fort Meigs, sixteen miles from its mouth, and for smaller craft to its head. Although it is not, large, yet, in connection with the Wabash, the importance of its navigation will not be exceeded by any discharging into the northern lakes or the Ohio River. The Wabash pursues a diametrically opposite course to its junction with the Ohio. At the highest waters of these rivers, their waters are united at the dividing ridge, and you may pass with craft from one river to the other. There is a wet prairie or swamp, covered with grass, that extends from the headwaters of the Wabash to the St. Mary's, and discharges its water into both rivers, about seven miles from one to the other. At low water this swamp is six to ten feet above the waters in the rivers. It is composed of soft mud that can be penetrated twenty feet with a pole. Of course it would be a small expense of labor to connect the waters of these two rivers by a canal that would be passable at the lowest water. Those rivers will be the great thoroughfare between the lakes and the Mississippi; and, of course, will constitute an uninterrupted navigation from the Bay of St. Lawrence to the Gulf of Mexico, except for the short portage at the Falls of Niagara. ..."[8]

A copy of the Western Spy was sent to the Governor of New York, DeWitt Clinton, and in the correspondence that flowed between the two men Clinton was reported to have said *"I have shown you a way into Lake Erie, and you have shown me a way out of it. You have extended my project by 600 miles."* Without a doubt, Stickney's vision was the additional vision needed to influence and finally convince the bankers of the plausibility of DeWitt Clinton's [9] New York and Erie Canal.

While stationed at Fort Wayne as the Indian Agent, Stickney was one of the first to recognize the importance of the Maumee and Wabash Rivers in promoting commerce. Stickney was

Benjamin Franklin Stickney

visibly impressed with the six mile swampy plain that existed between the two rivers. Intermittently dry and impassibly saturated, Stickney marveled at how Jean Baptiste de Richardville of the Miamis made quite a good living by providing the workers that carried the goods between the rivers. Also, Stickney concluded correctly that with very little expense a canal with one or two locks could be built that would join the two rivers. Citing immigration and farm production from a political point of view, Indiana soon became the canal's leading proponent. For the residents of Indiana the Wabash and Erie Canal gave them access to the eastern markets at a reasonable financial cost.

Stickney's next step was to get the support of Jonathan Jennings[10], governor of the State of Indiana. Stickney visited Governor Jennings at Corydon[11], the capital of Indiana, and showed him the correspondence with DeWitt Clinton. *"The project of a Canal,"* said Stickney, *"electrified him. ... After several days discussion on the subject, and agreeing, upon the most profound secrecy, we fixed upon Gov. Cass, Gov. Jennings, and Judge Park as Commissioners for the contemplated treaty. I returned to Fort Wayne to prepare the Indians, and in April of 1818 reported to the War Department the probable practicability of the extinguishment of the Indian title to the lands of the Indians."* [12]

By October a series of four treaties had been held in St. Mary's, Ohio, by which the United States obtained title to all the Wabash Lands held by the Potawatomi, Wea, Delaware, and the Miami. Stickney went on to say that the most important topic of conversation at St. Mary's was about the canals, not the Indians.

All of these negotiations were carried on, said Stickney, with the most profound secrecy. *"What we most feared was, that if the state of Ohio supposed there was any such matter seriously contemplated, they would oppose it."*[13] The point was, of course, that the Wabash-Maumee Canal would be a rival of the Ohio system and might divert too much trade from the Cleveland Portsmouth interests. Moreover, a new commercial center might arise in Ohio eclipsing even Cincinnati. *"The southern and eastern parts of Ohio, only, were, at this time, inhabited – and the inhabitants of these portions opposed everything that promised to lead to a speedy settlement of the northwest part of the State, from a spirit of rivalry. Opposition from this source had been forseen by the original movers of the canal project. …. There was at this time one member of the Ohio Legislature of great political influence, … Many years before he had consulted with me in relation to the canal. He saw through the whole matter, … This was Micajah T. Williams. …"* [14]

Under the provisions of the Treaty of Greenville, sixteen reservations of land were given to the United States for the white settlers in the area. Located at the foot of the Maumee Rapids, the decayed Fort Miami was one of the reservations. Other reservations that were mentioned included the mouth of Swan Creek and a portion of the present site of Toledo. The lands were surveyed and sold at public auction at Wooster, Ohio on February 17, 1817. A group of Cincinnati speculators[15], who saw the possibilities of expansion in a canal link between their city and the Wabash-Erie Canal, had already bought 400 acres at the mouth of Swan Creek[16], and laid out a town which they called Port Lawrence.[17] Two other land companies, the Baum Company and the Piatt Company, purchased tracts 1, 2, 3, and 4 in the United States Reserve at the foot of the Rapids of the Miami, and also Nos. 86 and 87 on the east side of the river, opposite the mouth of Swan Creek at an average price of $48.125 per acre.

Discounting the valuable properties that the port of Toledo offered for a moment, it was possible that the founding of Toledo was part of a speculative movement originating in Indiana and was not favorably viewed by eastern and central Ohio.[18] This narrow view completely overlooked the Indiana farm immigrants coming from New York via Lake Erie through the fertile farm lands of the Maumee Valley to Fort Wayne.

The speculators laid out the town of Port Lawrence and advertised the sale of lots to take place on September 20, 1817. With an intimate knowledge of the area, Stickney realized that

Benjamin Franklin Stickney

the natural outlet for the canal into the Maumee River was at Swan Creek, and at the September land auction at Fort Meigs, Stickney was one the largest land purchasers.

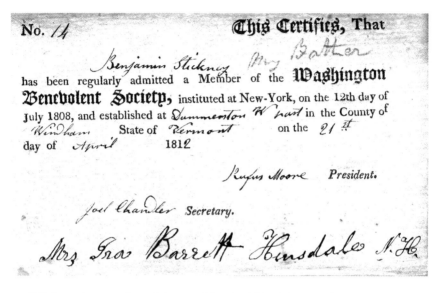

Stickney's membership card in the Washington Benevolent Society. Courtesy of the author.

Letters flooded the Indian Agents and government officials of the area asking for descriptions of the lands that were being offered for sale. Some of the first written or published descriptions of the Maumee Valley were a result of this correspondence, and are included as they were written.

Recollection of the Maumee Valley in the Spring of 1817, by George Clark[19] of Ecorse, Michigan. *"In the Spring of 1817, I visited Maumee, then claimed by the Territory of Michigan. There I found the country inhabited by half breeds, French, and a few immigrants from the States.*

Mr. Hunt, Mr. Conant, and a few others, principally engaged in the fur trade. The people lived almost entirely upon game, fish, and corn. There being no mills in the country, to prepare the corn for food, round holes were burnt in the ends of logs; these were set on end, and the corn crushed by means of a pounder attached to a spring pole thirty or forty feet long. From this crushed corn their bread was made. On still, calm evenings the Indian war drums and the hammers could be distinctly heard up and down the river. The country was heavily timbered, the woods, marshes, rivers, creeks, ponds, and the whole country, both land and water, was teeming with animal life. There were collected hundreds of Indians, with their families, and the people from the surrounding country, to catch, smoke, and dry their season's supply of fish.

..... Where Toledo now stands there were but two small houses, located on the flats at the mouth of Swan Creek. The eagle's nests, one on Eagle Point and one on a sycamore tree on Delaware Island, were prominent landmarks on the river. There was Fort Meigs on the opposite bank from Maumee and the British fort three miles below at Miami.

An Indian carried the mail on his back once or twice a week from Sandusky to the Rapids. Following the blind trail through the Black swamp, he was obliged to wade through water, mud, and ice, and camp out nights. About this time I took passage on the BLACK SNAKE, one of the small vessels running between Cleveland and Maumee. The vessel was a government bateau, built up with deck boards, which in heavy seas would break loose, almost crushing her sides in. She was commanded by Jacob Wilkison, of Cleveland. ...."[20]

Another letter from Benjamin Rathburn[21] in 1870 to David E. Merrill[22] described the land sales and the area: "*I was once where Toledo now is. It was in the Spring of 1817, while a portion of it was being surveyed for Village lots. I then took up the first lot ever sold in Toledo as a village lot. The title of the Company failing for non-payment of their purchase, of course I lost my lot. I have never been at Toledo since I left in August, 1818. At that time there was not a dwelling house there. A man by the name of Henderson built a log and stone house on the*

Benjamin Franklin Stickney

bank and partly over the water, just below what was then know as Swan Creek; and there was a French cabin on the "flats" near Swan Creek, for the Indians to get rum in. These were all the buildings Toledo could boast of in 1818. My own family, consisting of Mrs. Rathburn and one son, and Major Keeler's family, occupied Henderson's log and stone warehouse while we were there."

Seventy-nine lots were sold realizing almost $900.00 for the land companies. The year with no summer created what was commonly called by the newspapers *Ohio Fever, and the extraordinary crush of New Englander's that migrated to the western frontier in 1817.*

Western land sales were made possible by the rising prices of cotton, cattle, and grain sales experienced in the United States. With just a little credit, immigrants from poverty stricken eastern states could afford the land purchased from the speculators. Couple the land sales with a tightening eastern credit market, and the crisis that was brewing in the West was only minutes away. The failure of the western land sales was nothing compared to the Panic of 1819. The syndicates failed to make their land payments, and most of the land reverted back to the government. This time, desperate for "hard" money, the land was sold at $2 per acre on time, or $1.25 cash.

In early 1817 Stickney was encouraged by his good friend, DeWitt Clinton, to correspond with one of the leading experts in the scientific method of discovery in the country, Dr. Samuel Latham Mitchell.

"I had the gratification, a few days since, of receiving yours of the 26 th February, and I am much pleased to see that such rapid progress is making in the knowledge of the surface of this portion of the new continent. And I am very glad that you still have health, strength, and inclination to support the leading part you take in this great work. Only a very few persons who have passed over, or who reside in the neighborhood of those great bodies of water, have paid any considerable attention to the

Benjamin Franklin Stickney

evidences of past changes, or even the changes taking place before their eyes. To this few you have assigned the task of determining where the mound stood that raised the waters to such a height as to cover the island of Michilimackinac. For myself I can only say, I have glanced my eye upon those waters from the mouth of the St. Lawrence to Lake St. Clair, and I have seen no place that has presented a shadow of probability of having been the place where a mound existed of sufficient height to raise the water over the island of Michilimackinac except at the straight of Niagara, and the evidence there appears to be conclusive. But the barrier itself must have been of secondary formation, for the perfectly horizontal strata of calcareous stone, containing some shells with every other evidence of being formed by deposition, is to be seen down to the water's edge; but what restrained the water from flowing into the Mississippi does not so distinctly appear. However, if we surmount this difficulty, what shall we do when we come to examine the range of the Alleghany Mountains, and find them likewise to be of secondary formation?

Whenever I have crossed them I have observed the superior strata of sandstone, the second bituminous shale, the third coal, and the lake clay of various degrees of indurations. But the immersion of the country between the Lakes and the Mississippi appears to have been of much more recent date.

This level alluvial country at the dividing of the water discharging into the Gulf of Mexico and Bay of St. Lawrence is truly an interesting tract. The extreme richness of the alluvia affords a luxuriance and variety of vegetation superior perhaps to any other on the surface of the globe, and almost entirely unexplored by the botanist. And I am inclined to believe a very considerable part of the plants, and some trees, remain undisturbed, some of which would be of great value to medicine and the arts, if proper inquiries were made. But I have paid no attention to botany. There is one small plant, with the root of which the Indians dye the most beautiful and permanent scarlet. It is the most permanent dye I ever saw. Exposure to the rays of the sun has no effect other than to change a bright scarlet to blood red, and

Benjamin Franklin Stickney

this is affected but by very long exposure. With the bark of a large tree, resembling the ash, they dye a fine blue. The process of dying with both are very simple. The scarlet dye of cochineal, and the blue of indigo, require so much skill in conducting the process, that our infant manufactories are scarcely advanced to a degree of perfection sufficient to afford favorable results from such delicate materials, particularly cochineal.

I have been five years with the tribes of Indians northwest of the Ohio as Agent for Indian Affairs. This has afforded an opportunity of doing something toward analyzing the character of the original Americans and determining its affinities, - to learn their traditions in relation to their own origin and other events, of races of animals who have existed and are now extinct, and the little knowledge they profess in medicine, surgery, and the arts. Although their knowledge is enveloped in much mystery and superstition, yet some interesting matter may be culled from the mass. More upon this subject at a moment when I have more leisure. With salutations of much respect, I am yours, B. F. Stickney."

Further examples of intellectual life are found in a letter to Thomas L. McKenney[23], Superintendent of Aborigine Affairs, Washington, August 27, 1817, from Stickney, Agent to the Miamis and Potawatomi Indians at Fort Wayne.

"I shall pay every attention to the subject of your letter, developing the exalted views of philanthropy of the Kentucky Baptist Society for Propagating the Gospel among the Heathen. The civilization of the Aborigines is not a new subject to me. I have been, between five and six years, in the habit of daily and hourly intercourse with the Aborigines northwest of Ohio, and the great question of the practicability of civilizing them ever before me. That I might have an opportunity of casting in my mite to the bettering of the condition of these uncivilized human beings, and the pleasure of observing the change that might be produced on them, were the principal inducements to my surrendering the comforts of civilized society.

Benjamin Franklin Stickney

Upon my entering on my duties, I soon found that my speculative opinions were not reducible to practice. What I had viewed at a distance as flying clouds, proved upon my nearer approach to be impassable mountains. Notwithstanding these discouraging circumstances, I am ready to aid your views by all proper means within my power; and in so doing believe I embrace the views of the United States Government of which I am Agent .... It will be proper for me to be more particular, and give you something of my ideas of the nature and extent of the obstacles to be met.

Firstly. The great, and I fear insurmountable, obstacle is the insatiable thirst for intoxicating liquors that appears to be born with all the yellow-skinned inhabitants of America; and the thirst for gain of some of the citizens of the United States appears to be capable of eluding all the vigilance of the Government to stop the distribution of liquor among them. When the Aborigines cannot obtain the means of intoxication within their own limits, they will travel any distance to obtain it. There is no fatigue, risk, or expense, that is to great to obtain it. In some cases it appears to be valued higher than life itself. If a change in habit in this can be effected, all other obstacles may yield. But if the white people can not be restrained from furnishing them spirituous liquors, nor they from the use of them, I fear all efforts to extend to them the benefits of civilization will prove fruitless. The knowledge of letter serves as the medium of entering into secret arrangements with white people to supply the means of their own destruction, and, within the limits of my intercourse, the principal use of the knowledge of letters or civilized language has been for them to obtain liquor for themselves and others.

Secondly. The general aversion to the habits, manners, customs, and dress of civilized people; and, in many cases, an Aborigine is an object of jealousy for being acquainted with a civilized language, and it is made use of as a subject of reproach against him.

Thirdly. General indolence, connected with a firm conviction that the life of a civilized man is that of slavery, and that the savage life is manhood, ease and independence.

Benjamin Franklin Stickney

Fourthly. The unfavorable light in which they view the character of the citizens of the United States - believing that their minds are so occupied in trade and speculation, that they never act from any other motive. .... Their opinion of the Government of the United States is, in some degree, more favorable, but secretly they view all white people as their enemies, and are extremely suspicious of everything coming from them.

All the Miamis, and Eel River Miamis, are under my charge, about one thousand four hundred in number; and there are something more than two thousand Pottawotamis who come within my agency. The proportion of children cannot be ascertained, but it must be less than among the white inhabitants of the United States. They have had no schools or missionaries among them since the time of the French Jesuits.[24]

They have places that are commonly called villages, but perhaps not correctly, as they have no uniform place of residence. During the fall, winter, or part of the spring, they are scattered in the woods, hunting. The respective bands assemble in the spring at their several ordinary places of resort, where some have rude cabins made of small logs covered with bark; but more commonly some poles stuck in the ground and tied together with pliant slips of bark, and covered with large sheets of bark, or a kind of mat made of flags. Near these places of resort they plant some corn. There are eleven of these places of resort within my agency. The Miami and Eel River Miamis reside principally by the Wabash, Mississinewa, and Eel River, and at the head of White River. The Pottawotamis reside on the Tippecanoe, Kankakee, Iroquois, Yellow River, St.Joseph of Lake Michigan, the Elkhart, Miami of the Lake (the Maumee) and by the St.Joseph and the St.Mary emptying into it.

They all believe in God as a creator and governor, but have no idea of His will being communicated to a man, except as it appears in the creation, or as it appears occasionally from his providential government. Some of them had been told of other communications having been made to the white people a long time since, and that it was written and printed; but they neither

Benjamin Franklin Stickney

have conception nor belief in relation to it. Their belief in a future existence is a kind of transubstantiation – a removal from this existence to one more happy, with similar appetites and enjoyments. They talk of a bad spirit, but never express any apprehensions of his troubling them in their future existence."[25]

With all the treaties that had been negotiated with the various Indian Tribes, the *Treaty of the Foot of the Rapids of the Miami* was perhaps attended by over seven maybe eight thousand Indians, and an account was found in the *John Hunt Memoirs: Early Years of the Maumee Basin, 1812-1835.*

"The House became so famous that in May 1817, Genl Cass than Governor of Michigan and Superintendent of Indian Affairs wrote to us to know if we could furnish a table for seventy five persons and accommodations for the commissioners (Cass and McCarther) with their (suit) sweete and requiring of us to build a Council House in which to hold a treaty with all the North Western tribes of Indians, our reply to him was that we would do the best we could do to accommodate them. I think it was about the first of September 1817 when the Indians began to concentrate from all quarters and about the 15 th of the same month the Commissioners made their appearance with their sweete of about twenty gentlemen from Detroit, about sun down of the same day, the Commissioners and myself were standing in the front yard when Genl. Macomb and his staff (who had been to escort President Monroe to Cleveland) rode up the hill to the house and after shaking hands with the Genl wanted to know if we could not keep them all night......"

".... we had a jolly time of it with the five hundred white men and seven or eight thousand Indians to take care of. The whole valley for miles on each side of the River was lined with Indian camps...."

"....It was upwards of seven weeks before the treaty was finally concluded and the Commissioners succeeded in buying the northern part of Ohio, the southern part of Michigan and a part of Indiana.."

Benjamin Franklin Stickney

"The Commissioners distributed to the Indians probably one hundred thousand dollars worth of goods, and as soon as they left any number of whiskey boats made their appearance, to trade for goods and money, and it may be better imagined than described the noise and confusion made by Seven thousand Indians nearly all drunk....."

Not all that attended the treaty conference were in agreement with the new concessions made by the tribes. The following account of *Mashkeman* was also found in the *Hunt Memoirs.*

"There was an Indian present whose name was Mashkeman, who was a great warrior, and prided himself on being a British subject. He had been bribed to oppose the treaty. When he found the Indians giving way to Cass and MacArthur, it made him very angry. He said in his speech that the palefaces had cheated the Redman, from their first` landing on this continent. The first that came said they wanted enough land to put a foot on. They gave the Indians a beef, and were to have so much land as the hide would cover. The palefaces cut that hide into strings, and got enough land for a fort. The next time they wanted more land they brought a great pile of goods, which they offered for land. The red men took the goods, and the palefaces were to have for them so much land as a horse would travel round in day. They cheated the red man again by having a relay of horses to travel at their utmost speed. In that way they succeeded. Now, you Cass, pointing his finger and shaking his tomahawk over Cass's head, Now you Cass, come here to cheat us again. Thus closing he sat down. Cass replied: My friends, I am much pleased to find among you so great a man as Mashkeman. I am glad to see that you have an orator, a man who understands how much you have been cheated by the white people, and who is fully able to cope with them --- those scoundrels who have cheated you so outrageously. Tis true what he has said, every word true. And the first white man was your French father. The second white man was your English father you seem to think so much of.

Benjamin Franklin Stickney

Now you have a Father, the President, who does not want to cheat you, but wants to give you more land west of the Mississippi than you have here, and to build mills for you, and help you till the soil.

At which Mashkeman raved and frothed at the mouth. He came up to General Cass, struck him on the breast with the back of his hand, raising his tomahawk with the other hand, saying, Cass, you lie; you lie!

Cass turned to Knaggs, who was one of the interpreters, and said: Take that women away and put a petticoat on her; no man would talk that way in council." [26]

Another incident of note occurred at the signing of the Treaty of the Rapids which was recorded by the Indian Agent, John Johnston.

I never saw the celebrated Ottawa Chief Pontiac, he passed away with the war which ended in 1763, his surviving sister was with us at the Treaty of Miami Rapids, September 1, 1817, and signed that Treaty much against her will, because said she no women ever done such a thing, the interpreters and other residents among the Indians took it into their heads that she must sign the Treaty, brought her forward, held her hand until she made her mark, it appeared to distress her, she must have been at the time above 60 years old. [27]

However, the same incident is recalled by Maumee Valley pioneer Peter Navarre in a conversation that he had with noted historian Dr. Lyman C. Draper[28] in his Maumee Valley home on Thursday, October 4, 1866.

Kap-pesh-kum-o-qua was greatly revered by the Ottawas - and she signed the Treaty of 1817. .... O-tus-sown said to have been Pontiac's son, as Navarre is positive, and I think he is right from O-tus-sown's high character among his people, and from the great reverence shown to his mother - she being called by the whites in her old age Mother Pontiac. [29]

Benjamin Franklin Stickney

letters from home
chapter ten

Peter Navarre as he appeared in Henry Howe's Historical Collections of Ohio, Vol 2, 1896, pg 152.

The last account was from an event that was celebrated throughout the northwest during the long War of 1812 that cut swaths of destruction up and down the Maumee Valley. The poem written by Army Captain Henry Whiting[30] celebrated the removal of one of the sailor's remains killed in the *Battle of Lake Erie* from Put-In-Bay to Fort Shelby. Called *Too Long on a lonely isle neglected*, Whiting's poem was published during the month of November in 1817 in the *Detroit Gazette* on the 5th Anniversary of Perry's Victory.

Benjamin Franklin Stickney

Too long on a lonely isle neglected,
Marked by no stone, thy dust has slept,
By humble turf alone protected,
O'er which rude Time each year has swept.

Ere many summers there has reveled,
Decking thy grave with wild flowers fair,
The timid earth, depressed and leveled,
Had left no index vistige there.

Still had the wave, around that dashes --
Scene of thy fate -- the story told,
And, against the isle that held thy ashes,
In seeming fondless ceaseless roll'd.

But now with kindered heros lying
Thou shalt repose on martial ground
Thy Country's banners o'er thee flying
Her castles and her camps around.

And friendship there shall leave its token,
And beauty there in tears may melt,
For still the charm may rest unbroken,
So many tender hearts have felt.

Then rest, lamented youth, in honor,
Erie shall still preserve thy name,
For those who fell 'neath Perry's banner,
Must still survive in Perry's fame.

Benjamin Franklin Stickney

Endnotes from Chapter Ten
letters from home

[1] Josiah Meigs was the United States Comptroller of the Treasury in 1816. Brother to Return J. Meigs who would become Governor of Ohio in 1810. Josiah in 1812 was Commissioner of the General Land Office after being Surveyor General of the United States.

[2] Major Amos Spafford was "Collector of the Port of Miami" and commissioned as "Deputy Post Master of Miami in Erie District State of Ohio" was involved in the naming the fledgling village of Perrysburg.

[3] The act referred to by Meigs was passed by Congress on the 27th of April, 1816 and provided for a survey of a 12 mile square reserve for the United States which was set aside by the Treaty of Greenville in 1795. Land Agent Bourne and surveyors Joseph Wampler and William Brookfield examined both sides of the Maumee from Toledo to Waterville and concluded that Perrysburg was the best site for the reserve.

[4] The letter from Meigs to Spafford appeared in *Early History of the Maumee Valley*, by H.L.Hosmer & W. H. Hosmer, page 26.

[5] The Western Immigration Society was a Cincinnati based group of moneyed land speculators that were promoting the West.

[6] It was first published in 1799 as the *Western Spy & Hamilton Gazette* in Cincinnati by Joseph Carpenter. Carpenter strived to make the four page paper " .... *open to all communications, if the language is not scurrilous and personal. Such will be studiously avoided."* Carpenter further stated, *"that no exertion on his part shall be spared to make the SPY an interesting and intelligent paper."*
The *WESTERN SPY* is best known for its 1817 stand against imprisonment for debt and for public schools.

[7] It should be noted that Captain Robert B. McAfee in his "History of the Late War in the Western Country," published 1816, said, *"The Miami (Maumee) is navigable for boats from this place (Fort Wayne) to the Lakes. The portage to the nearest navigable branch of the Wabash is but seven or eight miles, through a low, marshy prairie, from which the water runs both to the Wabash and St. Mary's."* I should be noted that the St. Mary's is a head stream of the Maumee.

[8] Excerpt from Stickney's 29 page article that appeared in the Western Spy in 1818. Some sources claim that it was only twenty pages in length.

Benjamin Franklin Stickney

[9] DeWitt Clinton graduated from Columbia College he carried forward a program of study under the guidance of Professors S. L. Mitchell (known to correspond with Stickney) and David Hosack of Columbia, but still found time to oppose the administration of President Adams. On the resignation of John Armstrong from the United States Senate, Clinton was appointed, February 19, 1802, to be his successor. Resigned the office of Senator to become Mayor of New York in October of 1803. While Mayor he was a state senator (1806-11) and then lieutenant governor (1811-13). Appointed one of the Canal Commissioners in 1810, and journeyed across the state to Buffalo to satisfy himself that the canal could be built.

[10] Jonathan Jennings first Governor of Indiana was from either New Jersey or Virginia. Dissatisfied with his law practice in Ohio, he traveled to Vincennes, Indiana, where he found employment in the territorial land office under Nathaniel Ewing. In 1809 he became a territorial representative to congress on the platform of "no slavery in Indiana." He was elected governor of Indiana against Thomas Posey. In 1818 along with Lewis Cass and Benjamin Parke, he negotiated the St. Mary's Treaties.

[11] The state capitol.
[12] *The Autobiography of Stickney*, appeared in the Toledo City Directory for 1858, pages 52-70.
[13] *The Autobiography of Stickney*, appeared in the Toledo City Directory for 1858, pages 52-70.
[14] *The Autobiography of Stickney*, appeared in the Toledo City Directory for 1858, pages 52-70.
[15] Micajah T. Williams, William Oliver, and Martin Baum.
[16] Summit Street located on the hog's back between the Maumee River and the old stream bed of Swan Creek. Louis W. Campbell in his book "BIRDS OF LUCAS COUNTY" stated: "At the present time Swan Creek enters the Maumee River at the foot of Monroe street, but the old channel terminating at Bay View Park can be traced through North Toledo terminating in Detwiler Marsh. .... The original channel of Swan Creek, first identified by J. E. Carman of Ohio State University, extends from Elm and Utica streets to the Maumee Bay." The greater part of Detwiler Marsh is now the Detwiler Golf Course.

[17] "The Ohio Union kept two large, wampum alliance council grounds in the west. One stood along the Auglaize River near Wapakoneta. The other

was located at the confluence of Blue Heron [now Swan] Creek and the Miami of the Lake, in modern day downtown Toledo. From *Land of the Three Miamis*, by Barbara Alice Mann, University of Toledo Urban Affairs Center Press, 2006.

[18] A cynic might look at the period described and say that like today if the idea did not benefit one or all of the three "C's" Ohio would be interested.

[19] George Clark's Recollections cover the period from 1817 to 1876.

[20] Michigan Pioneer Collections, Volume One, Lansing, 1877, page 501-2.

[21] In 1870 Benjamin Rathbun was the owner of the Broadway Hotel in New York City, he was formerly an important business man in Buffalo, New York.

[22] David E. Merrill.

[23] Thomas McKenney, Author and Administrator of Indian affairs, is probably best known for his narrative *Tour To The Lakes* written in 1827, when he accompanied Lewis Cass to negotiate the treaty of August 11, 1827 at Butte des Morts on the Fox River. In 1816 he was appointed Superintendent of Indian Trade by President Madison. Widely praised for a $10,000 appropriation for the education of the Indian children through the missionary schools. During reorganization he was placed in charge of the Bureau of Indian Affairs under the auspices of the War Department.

[24] Major Stickney overlooked the efforts of the Society of Friends by Little River in 1804 and afterward.

[25] The following views are written by the author, Charles Slocum, about B.F.Stickney's letter to McKenney. *"It is obvious that the mind of the Aborigines has never seriously occupied itself with any of the higher themes of thought. The beings of its belief are not impersonations of the forces of nature, the courses of human destiny, or the movements of human intellect, will and passion. In the midst of nature, the Aborigine knew nothing of her laws. His perpetual reference of her phenomena to occult agencies, forestalled inquiry and precluded inductive reasoning. For example if the wind blew with violence, it was because the water lizard, which makes the*

wind, had crawled out of his pool; if a blight fell upon the corn, it was because the Corn Spirit was angry; and if the beavers were shy and difficult to catch, it was because they had taken offense at seeing the bones of one of their race thrown to a dog. Well, and even highly developed in a few instances - I allude especially to the Iroquois - with respect to certain points of material concernment, the mind of the Aborigine in other respects was and is almost hopelessly stagnant. The very traits that raise him above the servile races are hostile to the kind and degree of civilization which those races have attained. His intractable spirit of independence and the pride which forbids him to be an imitator, reinforce butt too strongly that savage lethargy of mind from which it is so hard to rouse him. No race perhaps, ever presented greater difficulties to those laboring for its improvement.

To sum up the results of this examination, this primitive man was as savage in his religion as in his life. He was divided between fetish worship and that next degree of religious development which consists in the worship of deities embodied in the human form. His conception of their attributes was such as might have been expected. His gods were no whit better than himself. Even when he borrows from Christianity the idea of a Supreme and Universal Spirit, his tendency is to reduce Him to a local habitation and a bodily shape; and this tendency disappears only in tribes that have been in long contact with civilized white men. The lives of the American Aborigines fully illustrate the great power of heredity and early environment in the formation of habit (character) that longest endures - and the lower in the scale of barbarism and savagery was the tribe, the more difficult it was to effect improvement toward civilization."

[26] Excerpted from PIONEER SCRAP BOOK by Charles W. Evers, Bowling Green, Ohio, 1910, page 14.

[27] Letter from John Johnston to Dr. Lyman C. Draper, August 21, 1847. From the book "John Johnston and the Indians," page 100

[28] Dr. Lyman Draper's widowed mother lived at 191 Lagrange Street in 1872.

[29] *Biographical Field Notes of Dr. Lyman C. Draper* as reported on the NWOQ, V5:N4:81-82, October, 1933. Pontiac, by his first wife had a daughter named Meck-ke-sic-ko-qua, and with his second wife Pontiac had no children. Before his second wife died, she asked if Pontiac would marry her twelve year old sister, Kap-pesh-kum-o-qua (Women's Camp). Other historians have named the sister that Pontiac married Kantuk-kegun (Women Canoe Paddler). They were married in 1764. Their union produced a son named Au-tus-sown or O-tus-sown in 1768.

Benjamin Franklin Stickney

[30] Henry Whiting was in the Army's Quartermaster's Corp posted in Detroit. More later on this largely forgotten author.

ONTWA,

THE

SON OF THE FOREST.

A POEM.

"Il parle ainsi au bruit de l'onde, et au milieu de toute la solitude." *Chateaubriand*.

NEW-YORK:
WILEY AND HALSTED,
Office of the Literary and Scientific Repository.

M DCCC XXII.

Written by Henry Whiting in 1822 while he was in the Army's Quartermaster Corps

Benjamin Franklin Stickney

Fort Wayne had become one of the last outposts of the frontier that had a modicum of civilization and Mrs. Mary Stickney wanted her husband Benjamin Franklin Stickney to be transferred to Upper Sandusky. Mrs. Stickney was quoted "… this [Fort Wayne] is not a place to raise a family." Mrs. Stickney would use the deterioration of Fort Wayne as a subtle ruse to move closer to the property that her husband bought last September. With all of their money tied to land speculation at the mouth of the Swan Creek and the Maumee River, it would be difficult to oversee the promotion and possible sale of the seventy-nine parcels of property from Fort Wayne.

Stickney following his wife's lead echoed her comments about Fort Wayne in a letter to Lewis Cass the Territorial Governor of Michigan written on the last day of 1817.

"At present this (Fort Wayne) is a resort for discharged soldiers and others of the refuse of the human race. … As soon as it is understood here that there is no law or none but the state laws of Indiana to act upon the traders here, some of them at least will take advantage of these circumstances, and the drunkenness and other irregularities of the Indians proceeding from the unrestrained conduct of the traders will render this place a very uncomfortable residence."

However, for the time being, Stickney remained at Fort Wayne as the Indian Agent, and received the approval of Lewis Cass and even Piqua's Indian Agent John Johnston. Johnston wanted the agencies at Piqua and Fort Wayne combined, with Stickney as the subordinate agent at Fort Wayne. When the Secretary of War agreed with Johnston, Stickney wrote that he could not continue as sub-agent at Fort Wayne for $500/year, one third of what he was earning several days ago. Seeming to agree, John Johnston wrote to Secretary of War Calhoun[1] suggesting that Stickney be appointed Agent to the Wyandot at Upper Sandusky.

The times finally caught up with Jean Baptiste Richardville for his pro-British support and attitude. At the Treaty of St. Mary's in

Benjamin Franklin Stickney

late 1818, the Miami Indians under Richardville were punished for not supporting the United States and were forced to give up most of central Indiana. The lands included the lucrative portage between the Wabash and Maumee Rivers, an area of more than seven million acres. Lurking just beneath the surface was Richardville's objection to the canal project. The canal would ruin his profitable control over the transfer of goods between the Wabash and Maumee Rivers. Coupled with his overt support of the British, Richardville's political friends in Congress[2] quietly deserted him when they were shown the possibility of immense profits that accompanied the proposed canal.

Less than a month later, John Johnston wrote to J. C. Calhoun, Secretary of War, that the Miami Indians, under Richardville, would not accept Stickney as their Indian Agent at Fort Wayne. When informed of the Miami's displeasure Stickney in an unfortunate choice of words refused to deliver *"... no man's speech to them, not even that of the United States President."*[3]

With Stickney's reply to Richardville circulating through the political circles of Washington, Anne Well's[4] husband, Dr. William Turner[5], finally received the appointment as sub-agent for Fort Wayne. Rescued by his friend Lewis Cass, Benjamin Franklin Stickney, who was the Indian Agent for Fort Wayne, was ordered to function under the auspices of Lewis Cass the Territorial Governor of Michigan.

Finally on the 24th of November 1820 Secretary of War J. C. Calhoun agreed with Lewis Cass's recommendations concerning Benjamin Franklin Stickney.

"Agreebly to your recommendation, I enclose an appointment for Mr. Stickney as sub agent, accompanied by a letter which explains to him the condition upon which it is made. You will designate his station, and give him the instructions necessary to direct him in the discharge of his duty."

Benjamin Franklin Stickney

a disputed territory, redemption, & expeditions
chapter eleven

Lewis Cass would write his good friend Benjamin Franklin Stickney on the 16th of December that everything they had planned for had been achieved.

"Accompanying this I have the pleasure to transmit to you an appointment of Sub Agent for the Ottawas. The provision respecting the pay between the period of your declining the former office and your acceptance of this, is one which was inserted in the report, which I made upon the subject, at the request of the Secretary of War. It appears to me to be perfectly equitable. But it will now be so far departed from, that your pay will commence from the time, when you assumed the execution of the duties at Fort Wayne. ... After that you will take a position, such as may appear to you best calculated to affect the object. I need scarcely say, that nothing in my power will be wanting to render the execution of your duties, as pleasant as possible. The arrangements shall be in every respect the same as though you were a principal Agent."

While the disputed boundary line was on everyone's mind, it did not stop or prevent the crush of settlers streaming out of the eastern states in search of reasonable land and a fresh start. Following the lead of the Indian Agents, even Lewis Cass was writing to prospective settlers. Cass' letters recommended the best localities and settling their fears of hostile Indians. Later in 1818 Cass and a group of Detroit's leading citizens and business men formed a committee to provide information to prospective immigrants. Advertisements were sent to various eastern newspapers. The following is from the Salem, Massachusetts, *REGISTER* of June 10, 1818.

"The opportunity now offered to industrious and enterprising men, to lay the foundation of moderate fortunes does not often occur, and ought not to be neglected."

Before any action could be taken over the disputed boundary line between the Territory of Michigan and the State of Ohio, President Monroe announced that the Michigan lands were open to sale, and the first sale would be held July 6th. By 1821 more

Benjamin Franklin Stickney

than two and one half million acres of land in Michigan were sold at prices ranging from $2 to forty dollars per acre.

Sketch of the *Walk-In-The-Water* that appeared in the Toledo BLADE. Courtesy of the Toledo BLADE.

As an indication of changing times, Noah Brown who had constructed Commodore Perry's fleet of ships during the War of 1812 was building a new ship at Black Rock, New York. Christened the *Walk-In-The-Water*[6], she was launched on Thursday, the 28th of May 1818 at the foot of Auburn Street at Black Rock on the Niagara River. Powered by steam her engines were not powerful enough, to the dismay of the spectators, to defeat the Niagara River. Using the *horned breeze*[7] to pull her into Lake Erie, her captain Jacob Fish[8] was quite pleased with such a fine vessel.

For an initial fare of twenty dollars, the *Walk-In-The-Water* with a full load of passengers and freight left Black Rock[9] for the three hundred mile trip to Detroit on August 25th. The throng of spectators that crowded the waterfront cheered when the *Walk-In-The-Water* used her four pound mounted cannon to announce her arrival at Detroit on the 27th.

Benjamin Franklin Stickney

a disputed territory, redemption, & expeditions 165
chapter eleven

Not all of her planned voyages were as successful. The *Walk-In-The-Water* was financed by a group of eastern money men that had also purchased large tracts of land on the Maumee River above the planned city of Perrysburg, hoping to create an *Orleans of the North*. The 340-ton steamer on its first trip against the Maumee River's swift current could not get any further than Swan Creek. With what seemed like a natural barrier to further transportation up the river, the Port Lawrence group was extremely pleased.

Intellectual exploits in the Territory of Michigan were moving at a fast pace in an effort to describe and catalog the natural resources that were available to entrepreneurs. Henry Schoolcraft's tome *A View to the Lead Mines of Missouri* was published with the approval of Dr. Samuel Mitchell. Schoolcraft lost no time in sending copies to those he considered would help him with his explorations and his ultimate goal of Superintendent of Mines for the United States. Copies of his monograph were sent to such scientific notables as: Mitchell, David Hosack[10], and Benjamin Silliman[11]. On the political side copies were also sent to: Dewitt Clinton, Vice President Daniel Thompkins, President Monroe, Secretary of War Calhoun, Treasury Secretary Crawford, Senator Thomas, and Commissioner of the General Land Office, Josiah Meigs.

Secretary of War, John C. Calhoun was extremely pleased with Schoolcraft's work and wanted to meet with him. At the time of the meeting the Secretary of War was preparing the instructions for the expedition to the Lake Superior-Upper Mississippi area. The expedition was to be under the command of Michigan's Territorial Governor Lewis Cass. So impressed was Calhoun with Schoolcraft that he offered him the position of mineralogist to the expedition, which Schoolcraft readily accepted.

Preparations made, the *Expedition of Exploration* left Detroit on the 24th of May 1820. Lewis Cass, Henry Rowe Schoolcraft, Major Robert A. Forsyth[12], James Duane Doty[13], Charles C. Trowbridge[14], Alexander Ralston Chase[15], Captain David Bates

Benjamin Franklin Stickney

Douglass[16], Dr. Alexander Wolcott[17], and others entered the Detroit River in three large birch bark canoes made by the Saginaw Indians[18] especially for the exploration of Lake Superior and the northwest region. Headwinds prevented them from making much distance the first day, and they spent the night at Grosse Pointe, where they remained until Friday the 26th. The Expedition was welcomed by the army troops at Fort Gratiot (Port Huron) on the 29th.

Lewis Cass and Henry Rowe Schoolcraft.
Courtesy of the Michigan History, 1906.

Traveling through the upper reaches of the Lake Superior region and Michigan, the expedition reached Fort Dearborn[19] near present day Chicago on the 29th of August. The expedition had taken 122 days and traveled over four thousand miles in birch bark canoes. Rather than return by canoe, Cass elected to return to Detroit overland. One of the little known aspects of the expedition was that Lewis Cass, with the permission of J. C. Calhoun, purchased land at Sault Ste. Marie for a military post to

a disputed territory, redemption, & expeditions
chapter eleven

counter the perceived British influence in the country encompassing the St. Mary's River. The real reason was to control the portage between Lake Superior and the St. Mary's River and the lower lakes.

Stickney on one of his many travels from Fort Wayne to Swan Creek was intercepted by land speculator James Riley on his return down the Maumee. Riley had been on a land investigation expedition to determine where the best lands were located for a possible farm. Riley would later write of his travels on the 28th of November 1819 in a Letter to the Editor for the Philadelphia UNION which was published on the 21st of January 1820.

"We left Fort Defiance on the 27 th, at an early hour, forded the Miami at the foot of the 9 mile Rapids, just above the Fort, and proceeded along the left bank of the River to Camp Number three, 6 miles, where three of four families have squatted on the public lands. ...... Pursuing our journey with diligence, we reached the head of the Lower Rapids (4 miles by computation) at dusk, where we found shelter with a Mr. Menard, all this day. The gentlemen in company, Mr. Stickney, Mr. Dennison, a Frenchman of Detroit, and myself were delighted with the country we traveled over, ... Twelve miles below Fort Meigs, the left bank of the river, at the mouth of the Swan Creek, a town is laid out, bearing the name of Port Lawrence, situated on the margin of the river and the left bank of the creek. Its site appears to be well chosen, standing partly on bottom land and partly on an elevated plain, and has an excellent view of the river for many miles, on Miami Bay, and part of Lake Erie.

At this place, I was informed by B. F. Stickney, Esq. And other gentlemen of respectability, that contrary to the general impression the tides flow and ebb twice in 24 hours,[20] .... Philosophers may, if they can, explain this phenomenon. What has come within my own knowledge strengthens the opinion I had before formed, viz: that through the channels of the Miami and Wabash rivers will soon be opened the shortest and best natural route between Buffalo and the Mississippi rivers. That canals uniting these rivers will shortly be prosecuted and

Benjamin Franklin Stickney

finished, and that this will prove an immense thoroughfare for supplying much of the vast and fertile interior of the states of Ohio, Indiana, and Illinois, with goods and commodities from the Atlantic states; and that returns will be made through the same channels, in the productions of those luxuriant regions, through the great western canal, to the City of New York, and thence to any part of the globe. ... ."

The Harris Line which was ordered to be run in 1812 to define Ohio's northern boundary was not surveyed till 1817, because of the turmoil caused by the War of 1812. Edward Tiffin[21], who was Surveyor General of the United States and incidentally Ohio's first governor, ordered William Harris to follow the Ohio's amended legal description; that is, from the southern tip of Lake Michigan to the northern tip of the Maumee Bay. With the Harris Line, Toledo was included in Ohio. A year later when Lewis Cass, Territorial Governor of Michigan cried foul, the Fulton Line was run. This boundary followed the exact legal description; that is, due east from the southern tip of Lake Michigan. This time Toledo was placed in Michigan.

Following the Harris Line of 1817, Ohio injected itself into the affairs of the Maumee Valley by creating Wood County in 1820. Wood County had jurisdiction across the *Great Black Swamp* and across the Maumee River to the disputed Ohio Michigan boundary. *"A disputed jurisdiction is one of the greatest evils that can happen to a country."* wrote the Territorial Governor of Michigan, Lewis Cass in late 1817 to Ohio's first governor Edward Tiffin, now the United States Surveyor General.

Using the Harris Line to define the northern boundary of Ohio, Ohio's Wood County tax assessors immediately appeared to prepare the way for including the area in Ohio's property tax system. To this, the land-poor Stickney strongly objected, and he undertook a campaign which eventually stopped the Wood County officials. Benjamin Franklin Stickney became a Justice of the Peace for Monroe County on May, 16th, 1820 in and for the Territory of Michigan. Stickney in his reply of June 13th to acting Territorial Governor William Woodbridge[22] said: *"I consented to*

Benjamin Franklin Stickney

accept an appointment of justice of the peace to give such resistance as we might be able to make; or as the small number here might consent to make."

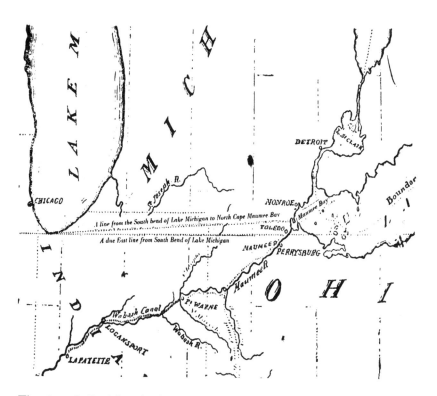

The top dotted line is the Harris Line and the bottom dotted line is the Fulton Line. Courtesy of the Maumee Valley Historical Society, *The Ohio-Michigan War, by B. F. Stickney*, Northwest Ohio Quarterly, August 1935.

A letter to Woodbridge on the 13th of June outlined Stickney's apprehension over his legal jurisdiction concerning the residents of Port Lawrence by his appointment as Justice of the Peace for Michigan.

Benjamin Franklin Stickney

The fancy that the people of Ohio entertain of their northern boundaries extending to the north cape of Miami Bay is likely to give us some trouble here. I perceive that you have made the necessary exertions in Congress for putting the question beyond all disputes. But I have not seen that any decision took place. The State of Ohio have formed a county and named it Wood and extended its limits to the north cape of the bay. The Officers of this county have commissioned their proceedings to levy and collect taxes from us; and they say that they shall proceed to final judgment and execution. And I now begin to think they will be unwise enough to do so. As I presume you are now the acting governor and this is a question affecting the Territory, it will not be improper to ask of you your advice and discretion in the case. Beside, we have every confidence that you are more conversant with the question than any other person. However clear it may be, that we do not belong to the State of Ohio, yet, resistance may cost more, than submission to pay taxes at home, and to the State of Ohio for years. But, we conceive, that we are entitled to support and defense from the U.S. against encroachments of Ohio...."[23]

Michigan's acting Territorial Governor William Woodbridge wrote to John Quincy Adams, Secretary of State, for President James Monroe. The contents of this letter strongly urged to strengthen Michigan by giving her the natural harbor at Toledo. Additionally, Woodbridge argued that the *Black Swamp* was Ohio's natural northern boundary, and that the Territory of Michigan was being used as a buffer between hostile Indians and the political power of British Canada and the citizens of Ohio.

"... Ohio began to see the importance of this disputed piece of land between the two lines, they being about eight miles apart on the shore of Lake Erie. It was evident that where the united canals, which traversed the two richest valleys in the west, terminated, a great commercial city must arise. The idea that Michigan should control this location -- this great distributing office of commerce of the west, was not to be endured. Ohio wanted it, to develop it, Michigan wanted it, to prevent its

Benjamin Franklin Stickney

development. She was aware that if properly improved, it would injure Detroit and ruin Monroe. ..."[24]

When asked about the inconsistency when Stickney would later change his allegiance to Ohio, Stickney said *that it was in his best interest to be for Michigan in 1820 and for Ohio in 1835.*[25]

End Notes from Chapter Eleven
a disputed territory, redemption, & expeditions

[1] J. C. Calhoun was the Secretary of War for President James Monroe, Vice President during the term of John Q. Adams and during the first term of Andrew Jackson, Secretary of State for John Tyler in 1844, and political advisor. In 1818 as Secretary of War, Calhoun had censured the capture of Spanish posts by Jackson during his campaign against the Seminoles. This produced a severe breach between the two men during Andrew Jackson's first term. This breach can be attributed to Mrs. Calhoun and her snub of Secretary of War Eaton's wife.

[2] These were the same friends that were able to transfer Stickney when he destroyed Richardville's liquor supplies.

[3] Letter from John Johnston to Noble. Thursday, December 24, 1818.

[4] Anne Wells was the daughter of William Wells long time friend of John Johnston.

[5] Money for the Fort Wayne agency was to be deposited at the United States Branch at Cincinnati. Soon after Turner's appointment Calhoun wrote him that a check for $17,900 had been issued for the Miami and Eel River annuities. Turner was pleased with these arrangements offering to post bond at Cincinnati when he picked up the annuity money. On September 1, 1819, Calhoun wrote Turner that he understood that he had

sold the $17,900 note to the Farmer's and Mechanics Bank of Cincinnati and that the bank had failed. Calhoun rebuked Turner for the delay in paying the annuities and ordered him to obtain the money or face the Secretary's recommendation to the President for Turner's dismissal. In May, 1820, Turner was removed for unsatisfactory conduct.

[6] The Cleveland HERALD, in July, 1853, said: The WALK-IN-THE-WATER, the first steamboat on the lakes, was built at Buffalo, in 1818, for Dr. Stewart, and was named after a Wyandot Chief, who lived at Maguaga, on the Detroit River. Dr. Stewart told B.F. Stickney, of Toledo, at that time, that, including what he paid Fulton and Livingston for their patent, the boat cost him $70,000.

[7] A horned breeze was a team of oxen that were used to pull the boats against the powerful current of the Niagara River.

[8] Jacob Fish was an engineer with the firm Fulton, Livingston & Co. The Fulton was of course Robert Fulton the man who invented the steam engine.

[9] Black Rock was later to become Buffalo, New York.

[10] Dr. David Hosack, 1769-1835, medical degree from the College of Philadelphia and furthered his education in Scotland and England returning to New York in 1794. Appointed professor of Natural History for Columbia in 1795. Hosack studied botany as his medical career advanced towards obstetrics and surgery. Was renowned for his medical dissertations, and the founding along with his good friend Dr. John Francis the *American Medical and Philosophical Monthly*. Several years before his death he wrote *The Memoirs of Dewitt Clinton.*

[11] Benjamin Silliman, 1779-1864, a Yale professor of chemistry by vocation. Silliman was looked upon as an expert in his field by his contemporaries. In 1818, Silliman, founded and edited the first American scientific journal *The American Journal of Science and Arts.*

[12] Appointed to West Point in 1814, and was rewarded in 1817 as Cass's Aide de Camp, later becoming his personal secretary.

[13] The twenty year old youth moved to Detroit in 1818 and was admitted to practice law before the Supreme Court of the Michigan Territory one year later. He later became clerk of the court. He was appointed official journalist to the expedition. Later to become Territorial Governor of Wisconsin and Utah.

Benjamin Franklin Stickney

[14] Came to Detroit in his late teens in 1819. Contributed to the Michigan and Wisconsin Historical Societies. Cass assigned him the task of assistant to the topographer, Captain Douglass.

[15] Came from a prominent glass making family, and was given the position of commissary to the expedition. He later becomes a successful merchant in Ohio.

[16] Having heard of the expedition while teaching at West Point, he applies to the expedition for some position as an engineer. In the Summer of 1819 he served as a topographer to the Boundary Commission under Major Delafield, which sealed his employment as Topographer.

[17] Serving as Cass's Indian Agent in Chicago, he was appointed surgeon for the expedition.

[18] Known as *Big Belly* to the Saginaw Indians, Cass quickly became friends with the Indians and ordered the canoes especially built for the coming expedition.

[19] Chicago at the bottom of Lake Michigan.

[20] For those readers with a Masonic background will readily recognize the assertion that the Masonic Fraternity has established itself in the Maumee Valley. Masonry made its way into the Maumee Valley with Army Lodge No. 24 that traveled with General Harrison to Fort Meigs. Lt. Almon Gibbs was the first Worshipful Master of Maumee's Northern Light Lodge No. 40 on March 5th, 1817.

[21] Edward Tiffin was the first Governor of Ohio in 1803, and was born in England in 1766. Studied medicine in England, and later Jefferson Medical College in Philadelphia. Married Mary, the daughter of Thomas Worthington, a wealthy land owner. In 1812, Madison without consulting Tiffin appointed him Commissioner of the General Land Office. When the British invaded Washington, he had previously removed all the land records to a place of safety. In 1814 with the consent of President Madison he exchanged offices and duties with Josiah Meigs and became Surveyor General of the Northwest Territory.

[22] Woodbridge was Governor of Michigan, United States Senator, and was born in Conn. in 1780. His long career of political office began in Ohio with eight years of service in various offices culminating as state senator. Influenced by his advocacy of the War of 1812 and the strong

recommendation of Lewis Cass, President Madison appointments him in 1814 Secretary of the Michigan Territory and Collector of Customs at Detroit. Continued in this capacity till 1824. Became extremely active in the quest for Michigan statehood. In 1819 the Territory of Michigan was allowed a delegate in Congress and in that position he secured government aid to build the roads from Detroit to Chicago (now U.S. route 12) and from Detroit through the black swamp to the Miami River (Maumee River). Died in 1861

[23] Stickney's reply to Woodbridge is contained in the collection of the Burton Historical Collection, at the Detroit Public Library.

[24] *The Autobiography of Benjamin Franklin Stickney,* appeared in the Toledo City Directory of 1858, pages 52-70.

[25] *The Autobiography of Benjamin Franklin Stickney* appeared in the Toledo City Directory of 1858, pages 52-70.

the boundary, settlers, & a task unfinished
chapter twelve

Late in his life Benjamin Franklin Stickney wrote a selective autobiography in longhand, which was transcribed and printed in the 1858 Toledo City Directory. The following describes in Stickney's own words the foundation for the Toledo War or the Ohio – Michigan Boundary dispute.[1]

"By the Ordinance of 1787, it is provided that the territory northwest of the Ohio should be divided into not less than three States, nor more than four; that the Eastern State (Ohio) might be extended north so far as to take in a part or whole of the territory, to the British boundary, if Congress should see fit; but, in case of only making three States, the northern line of the eastern State should be drawn due east, from the southern boundary of Lake Michigan, until it should strike the Miami Bay or Lake Erie.

When the territory had been permitted to form a constitution in conformity to this line, and become a State, and the Convention had assembled at Chillicothe for the purpose of making the Constitution, there happened to be there a man by the name of Wells, who had long been a prisoner with the Indians residing in this region, who told the members that Lake Michigan would be found to be much farther south than was supposed. This induced the Convention to introduce a provision into their constitution, to the effect that, if a line drawn due east from the southern bend of Lake Michigan should strike the Maumee River or Bay before it should strike Lake Erie, then, and in that case, it should be so run, that a line drawn from the southern extreme of Lake Michigan should strike the North Cape of Maumee Bay.

Provision was made for surveying the lines between Ohio and Indiana, so far as they had not been run, and between Ohio and Michigan. Leave was necessarily asked of the Indians, as the lines must be run through their Territory, which could not be done during the war. Gov. Cass ordered me to obtain the consent of the Indians, and I did so, by assembling them in 1816, for that purpose, and reported the same to the General Land Office. Soon after this, a Mr. Harris was sent out, as Deputy Surveyor, to run the remaining part of the western and

Benjamin Franklin Stickney

northern lines of Ohio. He was sent to me to learn his starting points and to be furnished with Indian guides, & c. He showed me his instructions, and I reported the tenor of them to Gov. Cass. When Mr. Harris had completed his survey, he went to Detroit, and by request showed Gov. Cass the instructions he had received from Surveyor General Tiffin. Gov. Cass perceived that the Surveyor General had taken the Constitution of Ohio for his guide, in framing his instructions, instead of the Ordinance of 1787. He immediately made complaint to the President. President Monroe gave the Surveyor General a rap over the knuckles, and ordered him to send another deputy to run a line due east from the southern extreme of Lake Michigan, according to the views of Gov. Cass. The next year, a Deputy Surveyor by the name of Fulton, was sent to run a line due east. This laid the foundation of what has been called the "Toledo War".

The question as to which of those lines was to be considered the true one to divide the territory was not much mooted for a number of years. A few letters passed between the Governor of Ohio and the Governor of Michigan upon the subject. Several times it was introduced in Congress, but it was a question they were unwilling to agitate, and no decision was had."

Prior to Statehood the Ohio Legislature while meeting in 1802 in Chillicothe relied on noted cartographer John Mitchell's map of the northwest to determine the northern boundary of Ohio. Drawn in the year 1750[2], Mitchell's map located Lake Michigan further north than it actually was. When this was pointed out to the legislative body by an old trapper by the name of Wells, they thought to remedy the situation by adding a clause that essentially described the northern boundary of Ohio as "...*from the southern tip of Lake Michigan to the north tip of the Maumee Bay.* ..."

Another significant factor in the boundary dispute was the belief that Port Lawrence and Vistula later to be known as Toledo would become the leading city of the Northwest, surpassing both Detroit and Chicago. This estimate of Toledo's greatness was not based on population, but rather on potential. Situated on the

Benjamin Franklin Stickney

western end of Lake Erie, Toledo linked the commerce of the eastern Great Lakes with the promising wealth of the mid-west. Further, Toledo's location on the Maumee River and the proposed canal system gave it the potential of trade from the eastern cities to the Mississippi.

So important was Toledo that Michigan risked war for it in 1835, and as a result was denied statehood till 1837. Once the border question became tied to statehood, the question was no longer in doubt. The power belonged to the state, not the territory, which could deliver the electoral vote in the 1836 presidential election. However, Michigan did not give up easily. President Jackson's Secretary of War was Lewis Cass, Michigan's Territorial Governor, and Michigan's Legislative Council named nine of the state's southwestern counties in honor of President Jackson and his cabinet. Another interesting aspect of this whole mess was that both of the governors in the coming conflict; Stevens Mason[3] and Robert Lucas[4] were stubborn Virginia Democrats.

With the boundary dispute almost two decades away from a legal or political solution many of the Maumee Valley's pioneer families were beginning to make their way into the disputed territory, and by 1821 one of the Valley's most prolific chroniclers was Dresden W. Howard.

Young Howard[5] was six years old when, in the company of his father's extended family, crossed Lake Erie from Buffalo, New York and entered the mouth of the Maumee River on June 17, 1821. Dresden thought that the dark color of the Maumee River water was in strange contrast with the shadowy green of Lake Erie that they had encountered. Dresden was also delighted with the great number of fish that he could see stacked like cord wood slowly moving in the dark water.

The Shawnee Indian name for the Maumee River was Ot-ta-wa Sepe or Ottawa River, and referred to the Indians that lived on its banks and inland. The French explorers that came to the Maumee Valley as early as the 1600s' understood the name of

Benjamin Franklin Stickney

the Miami Indians to be Me-au-me, which they recorded in French as Miami. Following the War of 1812, the influx of settlers would take on the local pronunciation of Maumee, and before long it was spelled the same way.

FUNERAL OF COL. HOWARD

LAID TO REST IN A TOMB FASHIONED BY HIMSELF.

Impressive Services at the Old Homestead—The Colonel's Last Christmas Gifts.

Staff Correspondence of The Blade.

Winameg, O., Nov. 13.—A few miles back from Delta, Fulton county, among the picturesque hills that border upon the Michigan state line, in a grave fashioned by himself, was laid to rest yesterday one of the sturdy pioneers of Northwestern Ohio—Hon. Dresden W. H. Howard. It is a beautiful spot, shaded by the famous old Council Oak, where old Chief Winameg first met the man who now sleeps at his side. At the top of the hill, which is skirted by tall evergreens and spruce pines, some of which are over 100 feet in height, and all of which were planted by the hand that now lies in the palsy of death, is an old-fashioned colonial residence, built 47 years ago. This was the summer home of Col. Howard and his aged companion, and of late years they had been accustomed to moving into their snug cottage in Wauseon for the winter. The house reminds one of the old wartime mansions of the Virginias, in style of architecture.

Obituary of Dresden Howard, November 13, 1897. Courtesy of the BLADE.

Benjamin Franklin Stickney

the boundary, settlers, & a task unfinished
chapter twelve

The dreaded and sometimes impassable swamps which drained the surrounding Maumee Valley contained waters that were stained with tannic acid from the bark and rotting wood. From this debris the Maumee River would take on a dark almost black color. From these and other references which also stated that the Maumee was a clear stream, it appeared that the Maumee's water was similar to the present day Tahquamenon River in Michigan's Upper Peninsula.

Some of the Maumee Valley's earliest recollections were from its youngest immigrants. Captain David Wilkison's daughter Amelia, who was then 12, related her remembrances of the meeting of the First Presbyterian Church of Christ in 1821: *".. our home in Orleans was the most pretentious and was built square, with two stories, two rooms above and two below. .... The audience would occupy both rooms below and the minister used the staircase for pulpit. ..."* The congregation that gathered together from the area surrounding the abandoned and crumbling Fort Meigs had no pastor or permanent church, and would meet in the two story home of Captain Wilkison.

Newspapers in the Maumee Valley were in short supply and when a copy of the *Detroit Gazette* would appear in Port Lawrence, Maumee, or Perrysburg it would be read from cover to cover and passed to the next eager reader. So when the February 9th, 1821 issue of the *Detroit Gazette* announced that explorer Henry Rowe Schoolcraft was going to publish a book about his exploits with last year's Governor Cass' *Expedition of Exploration*, several of the Maumee Valley's merchants had numerous copies available for purchase.

With his position as Indian Agent[6] to the Ottawas at Port Lawrence finally confirmed by the Secretary of War, Benjamin Franklin Stickney moved his family from Fort Wayne[7] to the site of the old British Fort Miami[8] in present day Maumee, Ohio.

Even though Stickney had purchased a considerable amount of land at Swan Creek and the Maumee River, he lost the property when the company that he purchased it from could not afford to

Benjamin Franklin Stickney

pay the government in 1819. Stickney would later write about this financial setback in his *Autobiography*:

".. A company of Cincinnati men purchased at the sale two tracts, making about 400 acres, at the mouth of Swan Creek - laid out a few town lots, and called it Port Lawrence. They offered a part of their lots for sale at auction in September, 1817, at the Indian treaty at Fort Meigs. I was the purchaser of a greater number of lots than any other person. I then conceived that this property was to constitute a part of the future commercial city.... The company had purchased these lands of the United States upon the conditions of paying one-fourth in hand, and the remainder in three equal annual payments, and had sold on the same terms. After the first payment, in consequence of the revulsion of money affairs, they found themselves unable to pay the other installments, they having agreed to pay for the Port Lawrence tract seventy-six dollars and six cents per acre. Congress passed a law for their relief, known as the "Relief Law," by which they were allowed to relinquish a part to the United States and to apply the amount to the quarter payment upon the three installments upon the tract they chose to retain. Under this provision, the Port Lawrence tract was entirely relinquished. All the lots that had been sold were surrendered to the United States. I prosecuted the company on their contract with me, and obtained a compromise. Before the surrender, I had made brick to build a dwelling on the lots I had purchased. These I now removed on a large tract adjoining, which I had purchased some years before, and built a house[9] there, and commenced making a farm, determined to live by farming until the canal should be made. ..." [10]

Not letting this initial delay deter his earlier ambitions, over time Stickney continued to expand his land holdings in the Maumee Valley, Stickney received five patent land deeds from the United States under the Congressional Act *Making Further Provision for sale of Public Lands*. The act reduced the minimum purchase and price to eighty acres at $1.25 an acre, and Stickney increased his land holdings by almost 355 acres for less than four hundred and thirty dollars. [11]

Benjamin Franklin Stickney

Adding to his greatly expanding knowledge of the Indians in the Old Northwest Territories was almost a never ending quest for Governor Cass. In a letter to Capt. David Douglas[12] of West Point, Cass described the information about the various tribes that he was looking for. To further the inquiry to a wider audience than just Captain Douglas, a 64-page circular letter was being printed[13] for distribution to all of the Indian Agents of the Northwest. Cass also talked about his further travels and a wish that Douglas would save the seeds from fresh fruit and send them to his office in Detroit.

"... If I can get my queries answered in season, I will contribute something towards the joint work we all talked about by Mr. Schoolcraft and yourself. I do not yet understand precisely the whole plan, nor do I know when you expect it to appear. But Mr. Schoolcraft will probably be here in a few days and I shall be able to learn all the necessary details. I expect he will go as Secretary to the Chicago Treaty, and my intention now is to descend the Wabash and ascend the Illinois which will give him a favorable opportunity of exploring an interesting section of the country. .... I will next week send to you copies of all my letters to the War Dept. on the subject of the expedition. Make such use of these as you think proper period. Before publication, it would however be desirous to obtain the consent of the War Dept. .... You will much oblige me by eating fresh choice plums, followed by cherries, apricots and #### peaches in this year, and by saving the seeds and stones for me."[14]

On the day before Independence Day in 1821 Schoolcraft arrived in Detroit at the break of dawn, and several hours later the Cass expedition left for the *West*. Traveling by canoe, they followed the Detroit River south to the western shore of Lake Erie, where they spent the night at the mouth of the Maumee River with their mutual friend Benjamin Franklin Stickney. The next day they followed the Maumee River to Fort Winchester[15], near present day Defiance, Ohio where they departed the Maumee and traveled through the country to Fort Wayne.

Benjamin Franklin Stickney

While they were in Fort Wayne, Cass held numerous meetings with the local Indian Agent, and visited the Reverend Isaac McCoy of the Baptist Indian School. They then left Fort Wayne for a Potawatomi village near the head waters of the Wabash River. Schoolcraft, relying on past experience and the stories told around the campfires, was astonished to observe that the Indians of the Maumee and Wabash rivers lived in log houses, raised livestock, and cultivated large gardens or fields of corn, pumpkins, beans, and squash. Adding to his disbelief, Schoolcraft and Cass were served by their Potawatomi hosts supper and breakfast on plates, with knives forks and spoons.

Several days later news reached them from the Reverend James McCoy, a Methodist Indian Agent for the Senecas, that two Seneca women had been killed after being accused of being witches. The reverend further stated that unless this useless murder was stopped at once, the guilty would be subject to *"white man's"* justice.

Most of the postal service to the Maumee Valley was postmarked through the station at Fort Meigs with Almon Gibbs as its first postmaster.[16] It was not till October of 1821 that the postal route of Sandusky to Fort Meigs down the river to Port Lawrence and then to the River Raisin and Detroit was changed. The conversation between William Woodbridge, Secretary of the Michigan Territory, and Stickney was directed at establishing another postal station that would give them better access to the mails and a faster delivery schedule. According to their thinking the mail would come directly to Port Lawrence from Sandusky on its way to Detroit instead of Fort Meigs. The mail to Fort Meigs [Maumee & Perrysburg] would be a sub-route from Port Lawrence.

With a constant stream of letters touting the advantages of this new postal route, the change was accomplished around December of 1823 with the creation of the Depot Station at Port Lawrence with Stickney becoming the appointed postmaster. Depot Station would become Port Lawrence Station less than two years later.

Benjamin Franklin Stickney

the boundary, settlers, & a task unfinished
chapter twelve

Several letters from Stickney to Lewis Cass that were written from the new station of *Depot* to each other still exist.[17] According to George Ball[18], the Depot Station was located three miles west from the Stickney Farm on the Maumee River, at the intersection of the old Territorial Road[19] and the U. S. Reserve Turnpike[20], near the intersection of Toledo's Collingwood and Detroit Avenues.

When the Ottawa Indians gathered at Port Lawrence for the distribution of government annuities, many of the established Christian religions in the Nation's east thought this would be the perfect time to convert the Indians to their established religions. Several of the religious orders had written to Stickney for assistance. However not all of them thought that they had received the assistance that they had paid for or were entitled to.

"You mention having received the answer of the Indians to your propositions, with Mr. Law's[21] notes. I gave you the answer in substance as I received it. But, I could plainly perceive that their answer was not the result of their unbiased opinion and Mr. Law was satisfied of this. I think it was instigated by a family of French people who have much influence over them, residing at the mouth of the river, and of catholic religion as far as they have any. ...."[22]

Furthering their cause, the Reverends Law and Swift had paid Stickney eighteen dollars to arrange for runners and provisions for the assembly of Ottawas that they expected to attend their meeting, and another two dollars for Mr. Carass to convert their remarks to the Ottawa language.

After paying Stickney to arrange for the meeting, the Reverends Swift and Law were concerned that the Indians attending the Council were not getting a correct translation of their thoughts and words. *".... As the interview proceeded.... repeated bursts of laughter ran around the assembled circle. At length it was more than suspected that we (Swift and Law) were not being understood."*

Benjamin Franklin Stickney

To which Stickney replied, "The Indians received their communication with respect but with evident caution, having had their minds prejudiced by some profligate traders, who dreaded the introduction of the gospel among them. [23]

Wayosemigoyun, geevhikoong aibeyun.
Universal father, in heaven dwelling.
Gaitshe gitshe twahwaindahgwuk ke dezhenokahzowin.
Greatly revered be thy name.
Ahpaidush nah taibainemeong.
Thy rule be over us.
Aizhe minwaindamun izzhewaybud ohomau akkeeng gya ishpimming.
Thy will be done on earth as it is in heaven.
Meezhishinaum noongum geezhiguk kay meedjeyong.
Give us this day our food.
Ahbwayaynemishinaum kah mudjee dodumahngin, gya neenowind aizheahbwayaynemungidwau owweeth kah mudgee dodahweyunjidgin, kaigo kuggway debainemishekahngain.
Forgive us our evil deeds, as we forgive those who have done evil to us.
Ikkoonawowishenaum kukkinnuh myonauduk.
Do not put a trial before us.
Minze gaigo keen keedebaidahn, neebwakauwin, taibwaywin, mushkowizziwin kukkinnuh keen oonjee muggud.
Put away from us, that which is bad. For thine are all things - wisdom, truth, and strength.
Kaugegaikummig, gunnahgaikunnah.
Ever, So be it.

Translated by Henry Schoolcraft as found in the *Notes* of Henry Whiting's poem *SANNILLAC* which was published in 1831.

The Presbyterians were also concerned that they were not getting their message of redemption through to the Ottawa Indians either as evidenced by this letter.

"..... to the proposals made by the committee to the Ottawa Indians was received .... and is very disheartening, ... They say the Great Spirit made them, and he made the white people, that to each he gave all that was necessary to know and whatever the white people know more than the Ottawa Indians was given to answer a purpose which to them was not needed. This is no doubt the suggestion of the wicked French traders with which

Benjamin Franklin Stickney

they are surrounded that they may be keeping the Indians in ignorance the better to cheat and take advantage in dealing with them."[24]

The missionaries complained that they were not making progress with the various tribes that they were working with. However, the Lord's Prayer was translated into the Ojibwa language and found in Schoolcraft's notes for *Sannillac A Poem*.[25]

1821 closed with discontent among the Indians in the Maumee Valley concerning their previous land treaties or sales, and as Indian Agent for the Ottawa's Stickney was placed in the middle of this ongoing dispute. Verification of the Indian's discontent was confirmed by the following letters to Governor Cass from Stickney written late in 1821.

"They mention, that either Knaggs desired them not to sign, to go to Detroit for the money, and he would give them saddles bridles and other things. McKay sent his son here for the Indians to go to Detroit, as, his son came, I do not particularly know that he was sent. I can, however, persuade very c####ly in my conferences with the Indians that Detroit(?) is writing such a part towards the Indians as to keep them in a state perturbation and impress them with a belief that they disavowed out of a part of the annuity. Among other things the Indians say, he told them, that you retained a $100 for your own private use. Probably there is not proof of those things that would be received in a court of law, but, from combining circumstances, equally as satisfying. The Indians now say that when he [Knaggs] speaks they will put they hands on their ears.[20]"

"Neowash the speaker of the Ottaways has spoken to me several times about a horse and bridle that you promised to him among the chiefs at the Treaty at St. Mary's. That the other chiefs had received theirs at Detroit, but he, not being present at the time, did not receive his. He has asked me to write you upon the subject …. At the time of delivering the annuity to the Ottaways, they had a long and pretty sharp talk, about the

Benjamin Franklin Stickney

dimensions of their reservation on the south side of the mouth of this river. They say it was interpreted to them by Knaggs that it was to lay 34 miles on the river that it would extend from the mouth to a point above Roche DeBoe [Boeuf]. I could affirm them nothing of that kind was said by you, and that the treaty was translated in English in that manner. I read to them the treaty and explained what 34 sections by marking out distances on paper. But they insisted that they had been cheated, and that it made no difference to them whether it had been done by the Commissioners, or their Interpreter.[27]"

Friend of Stickney, Schoolcraft, and Gov. Cass Capt. Henry Whiting was appointed Assistant Quartermaster of the United States Army and posted to the Federal Arsenal in Detroit. Whiting was no stranger to the area, and in the summer of 1818 had accompanied General Macomb[28] to the military forts in Sault Ste. Marie, Mackinac, and Chicago to make an assessment of their defenses. Whiting also wrote a series of articles published in the *Detroit Gazette* describing the trip and natural characteristics of the land that they were passing through.

In 1822, Whiting published his first book, *Ontwa, the Son of the Forest*, a 136, page fictional narrative of the demise of the Erie Indians at the hands of the Iroquois Indians.[29] The *Detroit Gazette* highly praised *Ontwa, the Son of the Forest*, and published Whiting's *Review of Schoolcraft's Narrative Journal* which also appeared in the *North American Review*. This literary achievement demonstrated that Whiting had obtained a recognized position in American Literature, and a friendship that would last their lifetimes.

1822 arrived with the Ottawa Indians concerned with land negotiations, and with Captain Henry Whiting assigned to the Michigan Territory in Detroit. Whiting would establish the historical foundation for the later generations. Three men, Lewis Cass, Henry Schoolcraft, and Henry Whiting, would be credited with the creation of the written historical record that has been retained about many of the tribes that resided in the *old northwest territory*.

Benjamin Franklin Stickney

Disturbed with the possibility that the Indians of the *old Northwest Territories,* like the tribal entities of the eastern United States, had already vanished from the American consciousness. Schoolcraft and Whiting urged Gov. Cass to recognize that the Indians of the *old Northwest Territories* regardless of tribal affiliation could be gone within one more generation. Their way of life was rapidly disappearing from the plains, valleys, rivers, and woods. Before the Indian way of life passed from the historical narration, Cass decided to have all the Indian Agents under his control obtain all the native accounts of their oral traditions. To that end, Cass had a sixty-four page booklet printed by Sheldon & Reed in 1823.

INQUIRIES
RESPECTING THE
HISTORY, TRADITIONS, LANGUAGES, MANNERS,
CUSTOMS, RELIGION, &c.
OF THE
INDIANS
LIVING WITHIN THE UNITED STATES

On Friday, the 4th of January 1822, without the benefit of the booklet, Stickney had started to work on the task that his friend Gov. Cass had presented, and to his astonishment he was making progress as noted in Stickney's letter to Cass.

"Day by day pouring over the knotty task you have assigned me, I make progress, but that of a snail. I am now upon the language of the Wyandots, which I conceive to be the most difficult part. And from every days work, I find abundant reason to acknowledge my errors in conceiving that the Wyandotte language was wanting in capacity to express ideas. I find no deficiency in veracity of well known forms. The great number of syntactical rules, is all I think we have any reason to complain of.... I find some extraordinary anomalies. One is, in their degrees of comparison They have a positive, relative, and three superlatives. They say, good, better, or degree better than the preceding two, still better, and the end of all good. An other is

they personify cold and heat, by the masculine and feminine gender. In this way, (page two), they make cold positive and heat negative. They make use of those ideas, to form many metaphors. They represent cold in a very masculine character and having complete command. They say, that when he, cold, comes forward, and takes command, she heat retires. And when he, from condescension gives way, she, heat, comes forward. …. In some cases, they confirm in a single word, and article, or noun, or an adjective, or preposition, and as an adverb. Each can be expressed singly, except the article. By taking a part of each, and combining them together in conformity to the rules of the language, they make serving in the number of sounds. …. I have found ten articles, and I do not know that these are all. They are never used singly, but, proceed a noun, making always the first syllable of the word. The article made use of, shows to what class of objects the noun belongs. As, two articles used for the animal kingdom!.

It must be a work of years to give a full amount of those languages, so complex (page three), as form, and differing from all others. …. If you desired me to name other subjects of inquiry in relation to the knowledge of the Indians, if others occurred to me. I would suggest, in addition to the ones mentioned,, Zoology, Ornithology, Ichthyology and Botany. This knowledge in relation to is very minute; and not much if any also, in relation to birds and fishes. And they have some knowledge as to plants. They are well known and named, in the county they inhabit; and same shaped. ……." [30]

On the surface Cass' proposal was two-faced and hypocritical; the entire Indian problem was a direct result of one culture colliding with another, and the resulting land policies of the victor. Individually the Americans idolized the *Noble Redman*, but were terrified of their brutal violence. With the land of the eastern states expensive, and employment scarce, the western movement coveted the Indian's ancestral land. The United States' solution to the dilemma they created was to have the Indians fade westward into oblivion.

Benjamin Franklin Stickney

Endnotes from Chapter Twelve
the boundary, settlers, & a task unfinished

[1] Parts of the autobiography have been excerpted in the Quarterly Bulletin of the Historical Society of Northwestern Ohio. The July 1935, Vol.7 No.3, issue *Centennial of the Ohio-Michigan War 1835-1935*, contains a part of Benjamin Franklin Stickney's autobiography from the 1858 Toledo City Directory.

[2] Mitchell's map while drawn in 1750 was corrected and improved, and published in 1755. John Mitchell was a Virginia physician and botanist and a fellow of the Royal Society. Mitchell's prestige was so great that the map was accepted without question and used in locating the *Proclamation Line of 1763, and the Peace Commission of 1782*. Thomas Hutchins, Geographer General to the United States endorsed Mitchell's map in 1778.

[3] First governor of the State of Michigan, and Territorial Governor of Michigan during the Ohio Michigan Boundary dispute. President Jackson appointed his father John Mason as Secretary of the Michigan Territory, and father and son arrived in Detroit in 1830. One year later his father resigned and set out for Texas and Mexico, supposedly on private business, but in reality on a secret mission for the President, who without hesitation named Stevens Thompson Mason to the position of secretary. Various writers have described John Mason's dwindling financial base and attribute his trip to Texas to exchange Revolutionary War land claims for interest in a land company that was developing a vast tract on the Red River. Others attribute the trip to a secret diplomacy mission to induce Texas to become part of the United States by President Jackson.

Ignoring the furor over his appointment, 19 year old Mason conducted himself discreetly and always asked the advice of those that surrounded him. During the period 1831-1836 he was acting Governor during the Ohio Michigan boundary dispute. Became an embarrassment to President Jackson and was relieved of office. Elected governor in 1836 when Michigan became a state.

[4] Governor of Ohio and Territorial Governor of Iowa was born in Virginia in 1781. A staunch supporter of Jackson he became well known in Ohio, ran for governor in 1830, defeated, ran again in 1832 and was elected. Lucas would serve two terms as governor of Ohio. After two years of retirement, in 1838, Van Buren appointed him Territorial

Governor of Iowa. Interestingly Iowa and Missouri had a boundary dispute in which he used the tactics of Mason to win the property for Iowa.

[5] Arrived at Fort Meigs with his parents Edward Howard and their extended family on June 17, 1821, from New York. Coming to the Maumee Valley as a six year old child, Dresden learned the Indian languages and was in demand as an interpreter. Kept a valuable written record of the Indian way of life in the Maumee Valley.

[6] While Stickney was sometimes listed as a sub-agent to the Ottawa's, it was always known through Cass, Calhoun, and Stickney that Stickney was the agent in charge of the Ottawa's and his pay reflected his position. See letter from Cass to Stickney dated 12.16.1820.

[7] It should be noted that a school has just been established for the children at Fort Wayne in February of 1821.

[8] On the south side of River Road across from Koral hamburger in Maumee.

[9] This is the brick home or mansion that has been referred to earlier at the corner of what is now Summit and Bush Streets on the Maumee River.

[10] *The Autobiography of Benjamin Franklin Stickney,* contained in the 1858 Toledo City Directory, pgs 52-70.

[11] Certificate No.32 *The fraction of Section number 31, of Township number 9 south, in Range number 8 east in the District of Detroit Michigan Territory, containing one hundred and forty nine and eighty five hundredths acres.* Signed by President Monroe Saturday, November 10, 1821.

Certificate No. 33 *The SE fraction of Section number 36, of Township number 9 south, in Range number 7 east, in the District of Detroit Michigan Territory, containing 64.47 acres.*

Certificate No.56 *The west half of the southeast quarter of Section number 30, of Township number 9, south in Range number 8 East in the District of Detroit Michigan Territory, containing eighty acres.* Signed by President James Monroe Saturday, November 10, 1821.

Certificate No.57 *The East 1/2, NE 1/4 of Section No. 36,of Township number 9 South, in Range number 7 East in the District of Detroit Michigan Territory, containing 80.00 acres.*

Certificate No. 69 *The West 1/2, SW 1/4 of Section Number 14, of Township Number 9 South, Range 7 East in the District of Detroit Michigan Territory, containing 80.00 acres.*

Benjamin Franklin Stickney

[12] Capt. David B. Douglas was the Professor of Mathematics at West Point, New York University, and Hobart College. As an engineer Douglas planned and designed the Croton Water System for New York city, and taught science and engineering.

[13] The printed circular letter was in reality a 64 page booklet of questions that Cass wanted his Indian Agents to ask of learned elders of the tribes they represented. 1823

[14] Letter excerpts from Lewis Cass to Capt. Douglas West Point, Detroit June 7, 1821.

[15] Fort Winchester was built during the War of 1812 near the present site of General Anthony Wayne's Fort Defiance. Defiance, Ohio, at the confluence of the AuGlaize and Maumee Rivers

[16] M. T. was understood to stand for Michigan Territory.

[17] The first recorded letter postmarked Depot, M. T. was on December 1, 1823 with Benjamin Franklin Stickney as postmaster.

[18] Ball, an avid postal history collector wrote: *The Toledo Strip.*

[19] Collingwood Avenue.

[20] Detroit Avenue.

[21] The Reverend Michael Law as mentioned in a letter from Stickney to the Reverend E. Swift. Excerpted from Marjorie Barnhart, *Prisoners of Hope: A Search for Mission.*, Presbyterian Historical Society, 1980.

[22] Letter from Benjamin Franklin Stickney to Reverend E. Swift, September 3, 1821. Excerpted from Marjorie Barnhart, *Prisoners of Hope: A Search for Mission.*, Presbyterian Historical Society, 1980.

[23] Excerpted from the book MACURDY by David Elliot. Page 141.

[24] Excerpted from Marjorie Barnhart, *PRISONERS OF HOPE,* Published by Presbyterian Historical Society 1980. Page 147-148.

[25] Wayosemigoyun, geevhikoong aibeyun.
Universal father, in heaven dwelling.
Gaitshe gitshe twahwaindahgwuk ke dezhenokahzowin.
Greatly revered be thy name.
Ahpaidush nah taibainemeong.
Thy rule be over us.
Aizhe minwaindamun izzhewaybud ohomau akkeeng gya ishpimming.
Thy will be done on earth as it is in heaven.
Meezhishinaum noongum geezhiguk kay meedjeyong.
Give us this day our food.

Benjamin Franklin Stickney

Ahbwayaynemishinaum kah mudjee dodumahngin, gya neenowind aizheahbwayaynemungidwau owwccth kah mudgee dodahweyunjidgin, kaigo kuggway debainemishekahngain.
Forgive us our evil deeds, as we forgive those who have done evil to us.
Ikkoonawowishenaum kukkinnuh myonauduk.
Do not put a trial before us.
Minze gaigo keen keedebaidahn, neebwakauwin, taibwaywin, mushkowizziwin kukkinnuh keen oonjee muggud.
Put away from us, that which is bad. For thine are all things - wisdom, truth, and strength.
Kaugegaikummig, gunnahgaikunnah.
Ever, So be it.

[26] Letter from Stickney to Cass November 5, 1821.
[27] Letter from Stickney to Cass December 16, 1821.
[28] On Christmas Day, 1820, Henry Whiting married Eliza Macomb daughter of William Macomb, and niece of his superior General Alex Macomb.

[29] *Ontwa* was followed in 1831 by *Sannillac A Poem* with notes by Cass and Schoolcraft.
[30] Letter from Stickney to Cass, January 4, 1822.

Benjamin Franklin Stickney

tradition, canals, & manhattan
chapter thirteen

With the heavy snow that had settled over the Maumee Valley, Benjamin Franklin Stickney finally found the solitude to confront the thorny dilemmas Michigan Territorial Governor Lewis Cass had left on his Indian Agency: tribal histories, missionaries, and boundaries.

Weeks of meetings with the Wyandot tribal elders were needed to simply gather the material that was needed. The comprehensive review of the Wyandot at Upper Sandusky would take months, not the couple of days Cass proposed.

"... I have had several meetings of the Wyandotte chiefs to collect from them all that was possible, it has taken considerable time to convince them of the advantages that would be derived from the undertaking, and particularly to themselves. They have at length entered upon the business with some zeal. But, they have asked for some time to refresh each other's memories, and arrange and digest their tradition." [1]

Stickney, fluent in the Wyandot language, needed assistance with the Ottawa tongue. In a letter of June 3, 1823 Stickney continued to have difficulty in finding a suitable interpreter of the Ottawa language to check his analysis.[2]

"There is no person speaking Ottaway in this vicinity in whom I have much confidence, as an interpreter. ... I can hardly hope to go even as far in the analysis of the Ottaways as of the Wyandotte language. Nor do I think the Ottaway language, in itself, as perfect as the Wyandotte. A thorough investigation would be opening an extensive field for the exercise of intellect. I think it would be giving to the learned world, an inventive new mode of arranging sounds to convey ideas, which, would be no less than an inquiry concerning the human mind. And as you have so justly observed, "would be one of the most profound subjects ever offered to human investigation."

Meeting with the elders and gathering the material on the Wyandot and Ottawa Indians, Stickney was still working on a biography of Pontiac for Gov. Cass[3], when he received an inquiry from Cass regarding Stickney's lack of progress. Frustrated with the immensity of the investigation, and Cass' impatience, Stickney responded:

"... I have not forgotten the inquiry to be made respecting Pontiac. There are none of the family of Pontiac[4] who are, or have been at their village since you wrote me upon the subject. ... As soon as an opportunity shall present, the subject shall be attended to. I wish that the inquiry should not be a partial one."[5]

"Are there not several chiefs who have figured more recently, who would be worthy of some notice. Such as Little Turtle[6], Crane[7], Walk in the water[8], Five Medals[9], etc. ... After I had sent you my observations upon Indian antiquities, I observed that there was one point I had not noticed, that I had marked for that purpose when I passed over Mr. Atwater's[10] work. It is what he calls his parallel walls connected at both ends. Resigned as he is in discovering the use to which everything has been applied, this appears to stagger him. Had he have asked any Indian or Indian wise white man: They would have solved the difficulty for him at once. By showing him, that it was for the purpose of great national dances. And this is an additional evidence of identity between the ancient and modern Indians. The moderns make such now. With this difference only, that, they now do not raise the earth more than from one to two feet. I have been present at many of those dances. I think I have seen one thousand persons in motion at once performing the circuit of the dance, in single file, between those walls. The two ends of the center wall occupied as the orchestra: Between the two bands of music, were many fires. And hanging over them kettles containing food cooking. At those fires they offer up "sweet incense" to the great Spirit before they commence dancing. ... It is not surprising that the ancients should raise walls of earth high enough to protect the dancers in the night, when they danced about fires, when they were so much engaged in war as to require walled towns for their common security. I have often seen temporary dancing ground, prepared by removing the surface only in the form described by Mr. Atwater. Leaving a strip of ground in the inside

Benjamin Franklin Stickney

on its rough state, for the musicians and cooking. The earth removed from the dancing ground is laid in a small row round the outside margin, with great regularity. When there are but a small number to dance, they are made in an oval form period. Some, near or ###le, thousands of those temporary preparations for dancing may be seen through the Indian country."[11]

Inherent and supplemented with the Ottawa traditions, Stickney was also gathering the necessary tribal biography of Pontiac. The Ottawa Village on the east side of the Maumee River at Presque Isle near present day Oregon, Ohio was traditionally the home of Pontiac and his third wife Ken-Tuck-ee-gun. The discussions in 1825 were with Chief Tussan[12], whom Stickney would at first call Pontiac's nephew, and later would identify him as Pontiac's son.

"I have at length, the chief Tus-saw engaged in the biography of his uncle Pontiac. To give me this, he communes with the earliest traditions of the Ottaways. For it appears that Pontiac, has been a name existent with the tribe or nation. That there was no power, civil or military, except that emanated from him. The creation of standing war-chiefs has been of recent date. To show what Pontiac was, it is necessary to give a detailed account of all the transactions of the nation. I have been engaged two days in the detail. My traditionist makes the best story of any Indians I have had under examination. He had disclosed a number of new points. Particularly, the leading incidents of a bloody war waged between the Flat Heads (who now reside along the coast side of the Rocky Mountains) on one side: and the Ottaways Chippewas and the Potawattomis on the other. When the war commenced, the Flat Heads occupied this river in its whole extent. This was the most sanguinary war the Ottaways, Potawattomis, and Chippewas have ever been engaged. The details of its commencement are not less intensive than that between the Wyandottes and the Six Nations."[13]

Benjamin Franklin Stickney

The intellectual landscape of the frontier was slowly changing, and in less than three months after the series of interviews with Pontiac's son, the first issue of the Monroe, Michigan's *SENTINEL* appeared. Taking its place along with the Detroit *GAZETTE,* the western frontier received the news from the Michigan point of view.

With the historical insight provided by his friends Henry Schoolcraft and Henry Whiting, Gov. Cass mandated that all the Indian Agents under his sphere of influence would collect the data as required and specified in his *INQUIRIES*. In recognition of the governor's *".... considerable knowledge, manners, customs, and languages of the Aborigines of this Country.."* Gov. Cass was nominated for membership in the American Philosophical Society by historians Pierre DuPonceau[14] and Charles J. Ingersoll[15]. *".... He [Cass] has collected ample materials of information on these subjects, which he is preparing for publication,"* [16] as found in Cass': *Inquiries Respecting the History, Traditions, Languages, Manners, Customs, Religion & of the Indians Living Within the United States, Sheldon & Reed, Detroit 1823.*

With communication and newspapers came elections for the various governmental functions that were associated with growth. Stickney was chosen over Dr. Horatio Conant as one of 18 members elected to the Legislative Council of the Territory of Michigan from Monroe County in 1823 by a margin of just 47 votes. The vote range was from 1185 for doctor and previous member of the Ohio Legislature Abraham Edwards[17] to Maumee, Ohio resident and doctor Harry (Horatio) Conant[18] with 503 votes.

1823 closed with Conant's letter of December 20th to Ohio Senator Ethan Brown concerning Ohio's northern boundary.

"The inhabitants in this vicinity have lately expressed considerable solicitude respecting the northern line of the State; and several of them have requested me to write to your honor upon the subject. It seems to have been taken for granted, more

Benjamin Franklin Stickney

from inadvertence, possibly, than for any good reason, that the southern line is the correct one. The jurisdiction of the territory of Michigan is extended to the territory between the two lines with the decided approbation of the inhabitants of the disputed ground, which makes it impossible for the State officers of Ohio to interfere without exciting disturbance ..... Almost any line that could be run would be preferred to the present, cutting off, as it does, the bay and mouth of the river. The line to the north cape of the bay is probably the only one that could be expected, other than the one now established, and would be the most agreeable to us."

The Miami & Erie Canal along with the Wabash & Erie Canal coupled with the northern boundary of Ohio had become so intertwined as to be viewed as almost one topic. So it came as no surprise that the topic of conversation in 1825 was centered on the boundary of Ohio and Michigan. Before the canal could be built the boundary dispute between Ohio and Michigan had to be settled. If the terminus of the Wabash & Erie Canal from Indiana was to be at Toledo, then Ohio must have control of the disputed territory. If the terminus was to be at Maumee, then Ohio did not need the disputed tract. Also if Maumee were chosen as the canal's eastern terminus, the State Canal Commission in 1825 recommended the building of a dam across the Maumee River to raise the river level deep enough to receive lake shipping into the towns of Maumee and Perrysburg.

The political leadership of Port Lawrence and the fledgling Stickney based Vistula[19] were convinced that the tremendous cost of the dam and ship lock would lead Ohio to terminate the canal at Vistula. Located east of Port Lawrence near the mouth of the Maumee River, Vistula was platted in 1832. Therefore it was Stickney's view that every citizen of the disputed territory should make every effort to become annexed to Ohio. In an effort to make his choice known throughout the region, Stickney resigned as Justice of the Peace for Monroe County, and was replaced by his friend John Baldwin a respected businessman of early Toledo area.

Benjamin Franklin Stickney

In a letter written for W. V. Way [20], on February 9, 1867, Thomas W. Powell [21] recalled some of the significant events in the history of the Maumee Valley.[22] The following illustrates and perhaps explains Stickney's reversal in allegiance.

"...... In the meantime a very serious and interesting question arose in the affairs of the Maumee Valley. Under the authority of the State of Ohio, a survey had been made for a canal along the valley, and the great question was where that canal should terminate. Judge Gaddis, of New York, who had been employed as Civil Engineer for Ohio, had reconnoitered the valley and determined that the canal should terminate at the foot of the rapids --- that a dam with a ship lock should be placed on Knagg's Bar, just below Maumee City and Perrysburg, and the river from there down, to be improved for ship navigation. When this matter was so ascertained, Major Stickney called another meeting of the citizens of Swan Creek, and to them he know represented that they had committed a great error in seceding from Ohio, and going over to Michigan, that while they belonged to Michigan, they could not expect that the State of Ohio would construct the canal to Swan Creek. They must go back to Ohio. They must secede from Michigan and go back to Ohio again. They must undo their former secession and rebellion, or they could not expect to secure the canal. Thereupon all sorts of resolutions were adopted, to the effect, that they were, and of right should be part and parcel of the State of Ohio; that Ohio was a great and glorious state, and that they would maintain their position, if necessary, at the point of a bayonet.

Throughout the ensuing contest, Maumee and Perrysburg supported the Michigan cause in the boundary question because the Wabash & Erie Canal would force Ohio to build the dam and lock across the Maumee River, thus ensuring their growth and survival. Adding impetus to the question was the opening of New York Governor DeWitt Clinton's Erie Canal on Wednesday, the 26th of October 1825. This canal across the broad expanse of New York opened a water way that connected the farmland of northern Ohio and Indiana with the port of New York.

Benjamin Franklin Stickney

tradition, canals, & manhattan
chapter thirteen

While the inhabitants of the Maumee Valley wrestled with the boundary issue, the other residents of northern Ohio and southern Michigan continued to make the most of their part of the northwest.

Rescued from obscurity at Fort Meigs by his exploits at Fort Stephenson, Lt. Tom Hawkins and his partner Elisha Howland on Monday, the 6th of May 1822 launched a vessel at Lower Sandusky, now recognized as Fremont, called the *PEGASUS*. She was designed to carry freight from Lake Erie's Sandusky on the Sandusky River to Fremont and was powered by four horses walking on a treadmill that powered a paddle wheel. The *PEGASUS* had the appearance of two canoes with a treadmill for the horses mounted between them. The odd looking contraption made three scheduled round trips a week between Sandusky and Fremont carrying passengers and freight.

Just two days after the successful launch of the PEGASUS, Henry Rowe Schoolcraft was confirmed as the Indian Agent for Sault Ste. Marie by the United States Senate. At the desperate urgings of Governor Cass, Secretary of War Calhoun successfully lobbied President James Monroe for Schoolcraft's appointment. Schoolcraft reported directly to Detroit and Gov. Cass in June of 1822. Schoolcraft's official instructions for his agency at Sault Ste. Marie were conveyed to him along with a commission as Justice of the Peace, so that he could deal with the civilian population at the Sault.

With everyone invited, the entire Maumee Valley celebrated when Almon Gibbs[23] married the twice widowed Chloe Spafford Gilbert Hecox, daughter of Amos Spafford. Their new home was to be in Maumee, on the north side of the Maumee River from Orleans [Perrysburg]. Chloe's first husband, Stephen Gilbert, drowned in a Lake Erie shipwreck off Cleveland. Her second husband, Ambrose Hecox blew himself up firing a cannon to celebrate Independence Day.

Benjamin Franklin Stickney

Almon Gibbs. Courtesy of Perrysburg Historian Judith Justus.

Almon Gibbs, along with being postmaster, was Justice of the Peace and in one of the first instances of slavery touching the Maumee Valley, Gibbs found himself the judge.

In 1820 there was a despicable tavern keeper by the name of Isaac Richardson. Richardson and two others[24] faced a charge of kidnapping a free Negro with the name of Patrick and trying to sell him back to the south. During the trial Richardson had violently berated the court calling Gibbs a "damm rascally court." Gibbs, a staunch abolitionist, during the ensuing shouting match with the defendant Isaac Richardson, passed out. After regaining consciousness, Gibbs found Richardson guilty of kidnapping and levied a huge fine for his lack of courtroom manners. Within days Almon Gibbs died from a sudden stroke.[25]

After Gibb's death and with the money secured from his land investments and leasing the tavern business, Chloe and her sons built a fine home in Maumee at 209 West Harrison which still stands today. As Historian Eleanor Crosby used to say, "Chloe had a terrible time keeping a husband alive."

Liquor once again raised its head when Schoolcraft as the Indian Agent at the Sault said to Governor Cass in a letter from March of 1823:

"I have to remark, that the provision of the Act of Congress for the exclusion from the Indian Country of spirituous liquors is imperative, and I think it should be so when we reflect upon the facility, with which any exception to it may be violated. It appears to me that licensed traders passing your agency should leave behind them all the liquors that they may have ..."[26]

Three months later, in June of 1823, Governor Cass reversed his position when the American Fur Company complained that they were at a disadvantage to the Hudson Bay Company. Sensitive to the ever present British influence the Hudson Bay Company had over the Indians, Cass allowed the traders to purchase whiskey for their use only. Knowing full well that the traders would resume business as usual, and liquor would once again be used in the trade practices.

With the death of the Reverend Michael Law at his Ashland, Ohio home in October of 1822, the Reverend Elisha Swift redoubled his efforts in getting a mission established on the Maumee and had asked for Stickney's assistance in obtaining a suitable site. Eager to assist Stickney replied:

"I hope you will succeed in the obtaining the grant of land from the U. S.. But in the event of a failure you can be accommodated with a situation that I think will answer. Although, not immediately on the bank of the River (at present) at a low price: not near the minimum price of the U. S. The lots immediately in

Benjamin Franklin Stickney

the rear of the river lots, on this side of the river are unsold, and can be had at the $125 per acre. I am still of the opinion that the place viewed by us in company with Mr. Shane [27] on the other side of the river, is much the best place. And if you cannot obtain a grant: I do not think there would be a great risk in commencing on it. It will probably be for sale the ensuing summer or fall. There would be but few, who would be disposed to attempt to purchase, after you had set down upon it: if they should wish under other circumstances to obtain it. ... In relation to the land near the Wolf Rapids: should you wish to make an establishment near that place I can only say. That I should think the most suitable place (off the Indian Reservation) would be on the southeast side of the river opposite the Indian Reservation. This is not yet offered for sale.[28]"

News of the proposed mission along the Maumee traveled fast among the neighbors of the Maumee Valley, and it was not long before others were asking the Reverend Swift to include eastern purchases of goods along with the shipment of their own material.

An example of multiple shipments was made in March of 1822 in a letter from Horatio Conant at Fort Meigs to Elisha Swift.

"I learned from Mr. Stickney a few days since, that you had offered to furnish him with glass, nails, ### ## manufacturers of Pittsburgh, on conditions much better to the purchasers, than they can be had here. .... I am building a small house and should it be convenient for you to extend the same privilege to me, although it is but little I should save in expense, I should prefer saving it, to throwing it away..... 100 feet of 9 by 7 glass and 100 pounds of amounted nails will probably be as many as I shall make use of, but should you wish to consign more to my care I have no doubt of making a useful disposal of them."[29]

Dr. Horatio Conant not only wanted supplies to accompany the missions to the Maumee Valley, but he was genuinely interested in obtaining a minister that would schedule regular services for the community along with his other tasks. Conant also offered to

Benjamin Franklin Stickney

Swift that the Indians at Wolf's Rapids were *"... better disposed to the purposes of the WMS[30] Society and particularly to our government than those at the mouth of the river, where many of them are much under the British influence. ... Wolf Rapids is less exposed to the influence of unprincipled characters that prowl around the lake shore, and of the French residents, most of whom are a small grade above the Indians in civilization, but their inferiors in morality.*[31]

"It was agreed that Swift and Law should ride upstream to consult with Peter Manor, a Frenchman named Pierre Menard, also called Peter Minor, formerly employed by the Northwest Fur Company. He had been adopted by Ottawa Chief Tontogany and given the name of Sawendebans (Yellow Hair). ..... Swift and Law easily found Peter Manor. ..... He lived near Tontogany Village on the 960 acres at Wolf Rapids which had been given to him in the Treaty of 1817. ..... Manor could give little hope the Chief Nawash, who was away in Chicago, would give either land or approval for a school at Tontogany Village. Swift and Law were directed to consult other Ottawas who had a thirty-four square mile reservation (McCarty's Village) near Port Lawrence. ...... As soon as possible, the two preachers set out. Nightfall came and they found shelter in the upper part of a rude cabin used as a trading post ..... A considerable number of the chiefs and other Indians were nearby. The proprietor returned to his family for the night, leaving Swift and Law to sleep in the loft. .... Soon a gentle tap was heard at the door. This was followed by several loud taps. Then there were voices calling out "feskey, feskey."[32] *It was the Indians demanding the firewater these profligate traders were in the habit of giving them. .... The Indians crowded into the store. Swift and Law attempted to put them out but to no purpose. Threats were freely interchanged and the confusion soon became terrible. .... They were apprehensive that the morning's light would reveal nothing of the cabin and themselves but a heap of smoking ruins."* [33]

Benjamin Franklin Stickney

VanTassel's Mission School on the banks of the Maumee near Volmar's Park. Excerpted from VanTassel's Picturesque Northwestern Ohio.

An associate of Swift with the Western Missionary Society was Alvan Coe, who had been teaching at their school at Lower Sandusky [Fremont] under the direction of the Reverend Joseph Badger. Coe was rather concerned that if the Mission at Wolf Rapids was established any later in the year, that their garden would not be sufficient for the winter.

Also a letter from *"a white husband of an Indian Women.."* arrived at Lower Sandusky addressed to Alvan Coe[34]

" ..... If you remove to the Maumee River or at Sandusky I think the Indians will be more willing to send their young Indians. Where you have .... kept your school, it has been some distance. The Indians are unwilling to let their young children go very far from home. .... Now it is a well known fact in the history

of Indian Nations, that they always begin to emigrate or to melt away soon after the white settlers go among them." [35]

On Sunday, October 27, 1822 the Reverend Isaac VanTassel[36] arrived at the Presbyterian Mission, about nine miles above Fort Meigs, at the mouth of the Tontogany Creek and the Maumee River. The reverend was accompanied by his wife of a month, Lucia B. VanTassel. Mrs. VanTassel was the daughter of the Reverend Joseph Badger, General Harrison's chaplain during the siege of Fort Meigs.

Stickney relayed to Alvan Coe that it was imperative that the VanTassels learn the Ottawa language as soon as possible to ease their everyday activities with the Indians. Dresden H. Howard would later write.

"... I had a long acquaintance with these good missionary people and have no words but kindness for them. While they may have accomplished but little in Christianizing the Indians, they did the best they could for them and with the best intentions. Their work was one of great difficulty; white men and half breeds sold whiskey to the Indians, used all efforts against their patronizing the institution, and hired Indians to keep their children from school...." [37]

Success at the Missionary School was measured in small increments and one of those milestones was written about during the last days of 1825 by the Reverend VanTassel, and published in the *Missionary Herald at Home and Abroad:*

"....These specimens (of writing) will give you a more correct idea of their (the students) improvement than I could by writing a volume.

""December 16, 1825 A steady minded person and wise person do not talk so much as tattlers do. A tattler always makes some difficulty among neighbors, and now friends do not be tattlers, it is not necessary to tell all that we know. Once I had a friend, and always talk very prettily before me, and next thing I

know he was talking bad about me. What is become of that friend? O he is wandering in the wilderness. Sally Holmes[38]."

Like the dark storm clouds that were building over the Maumee Valley from the missionary work among the Ottawa Indians, the seemingly simple task of rerouting the Valley's postal schedule had become an immense quandary that had found its way to Washington within a few months.

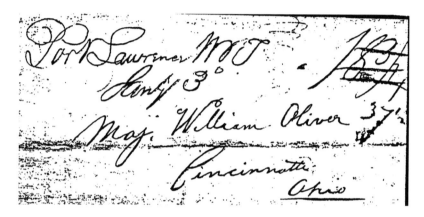

Letter from Port Lawrence, Michigan Territory. Courtesy of the State Library of Ohio as it was reproduced in *The Toledo Strip* by George J. Ball

Dr. Horatio Conant [39] had written from Fort Meigs in 1822 to United States Senator Ethan A. Brown. [40]

"I understand it is in contemplation to so alter the route of the great Eastern mail to Detroit, that it shall not pass this place, but go by Port Lawrence, nine miles below, on the Maumee River. ..... Respecting Port Lawrence, there is not, nor has there been for years, nor is there likely to be, more than three English families, including all within three miles of the place; and whatever public business is done there, must be done by one man (B.F. Stickney), who is already Indian Agent and Justice of the Peace for Michigan."

Benjamin Franklin Stickney

tradition, canals, & manhattan
chapter thirteen

Regardless of Conant's objections, Stickney's application for the changes in routes and post offices won the day. The post office at Depot, Michigan Territory which had operated since 1823 became Port Lawrence. The name Port Lawrence and its postmaster Benjamin Franklin Stickney remained in place until January of 1834. Possibly in protest, Austin E. Wing [41] resigned as Sheriff of Wayne County, Michigan Territory on October 14 just two days later.

Salmon Keeney was the postmaster for Erie, Michigan and Platt Card was Stickney's son-in-law. From the author's collection.

In a simplistic view of the Indian Lands in 1826, all the land at the mouth of the Maumee River belonged to the Indian Chief, Ottokee[42]. The late Judge Francis L. Nichols, who came to the Valley when the Indians were in power, told Toledoan John E. Gunckel, that Ottokee represented the tribes who claimed ownership of the land. Ottokee was also one of the signers of the deed that sold eight hundred acres of land at the mouth of the Maumee River to a Buffalo, New York, syndicate in 1826, for $15 an acre. This large purchase of land at the mouth of the Maumee River would later be known as Manhattan.

Sophisticated in the inner workings of the New York financial markets, Stickney knew that the Ohio Canal system would be in

Benjamin Franklin Stickney

need of their banking services. The bonds that paid for the huge statewide developments provided an opportunity for men with vision to make a considerable amount of money. With the canal terminating in Manhattan, Stickney made it almost impossible for Ohio to resist Toledo and the disputed strip. Privy to the same information, several of the same money men involved in the financial bond market were poised to make a considerable amount of money with their land speculation in the eight hundred acres of land at the mouth of the Maumee River.

End Notes from Chapter Thirteen
tradition, canals, & manhattan

[1] Letter from Stickney to Cass on Saturday, January 19th, 1822.

[2] Letter Stickney to Cass, June 3, 1823.

[3] Lewis Cass was planning in 1821 to write a life of Pontiac, but apparently did not proceed beyond the state of gathering material. Nor must I omit Chief Tus-saw, a descendant of Pontiac, who was reported in 1825 to be dictating a biography of his forbear. .... Whoever Tus-saw was, he was engaged in dictating a biography of his celebrated ancestor to Stickney for Cass. *PONTIAC and the INDIAN UPRISING*, Howard H. Peckham, 1947. According to Willard Carl Klunder in his book, *Lewis Cass and the Politics of Moderation*, 1996: *In 1821, the governor distributed a detailed questionnaire seeking information on various topics including tribal traditions, religion, government, and peculiar societies. .... and he (Cass) provided notes for Schoolcraft's Narrative and Henry Whiting's Ontwa and Sannillac and research material for several of Francis Parkman's works.*

[4] The Ottawa's migration from the Michigan Peninsula resulted in all probability from Pontiac's unsuccessful Rebellion, and there is no reason not to believe that Pontiac's relatives were scattered among the various bands.

[5] Thursday, March 31st, 1825 letter from Stickney to Lewis Cass.

[6] Strongly pro-American Miami chief residing in the Fort Wayne area.

[7] Tarhe the Crane a pro-British Wyandot chief

[8] A pro-America Wyandot chief who offered his services to General Harrison.

[9] Potawatomi chief whose village was on the St. Joseph River in Indiana.

[10] . Ohio lawyer and historian who supported highways and canals. Social and intellectual pioneer of Ohio, and one of the first to support forest conservation and to support the rail system.

[11] Thursday, March 31st, 1825 letter from Stickney to Lewis Cass.

[12] Could be Ottusson, or Otussa, or Watusson.

[13] Letter from Stickney to Cass, June 6, 1825.

[14] Born in France and served with VonSteuben and Greene in the American Revolution. Admitted to the bar in 1785 and became an expert and author of many valuable early works on Indian history.

[15] Lawyer, legislator, and congressman was the author of many unpopular works which created discussion on both sides of an issue. Wrote *Inchiquin, the Jesuit's Letters 1810* which was a declaration of our literary, social, and moral independence.

[16] For further information regarding the questions concerning the manners, customs, etc of the Indians under Territorial Governor Lewis Cass's charge, I would suggest the following: INQUIRIES Respecting the History, Traditions, Languages, Manners, Customs, Religion, &c of the INDIANS Living Within the United States by Lewis Cass. Published by Sheldon & Reed, Detroit 1823.

[17] President of the Michigan Territorial Council from 1824 to 1832 was born in Springfield, New York, in 1781. Became a physician in 1803 and an army surgeon in 1804, serving in Ohio and Indiana. Was a member of the Ohio legislature in 1811, and was ordered to Detroit in 1812 where he took charge of the medical department of the army. Was an aid of General Cass in 1823 with the rank of colonel. In 1831 became U.S. Register of the land office of western Michigan and held it till 1849.

[18] Dr. Conant was one of the first doctors to come into the Maumee Valley in 1816. General Cass, being personally acquainted with Dr. Conant, and Governor of the Michigan Territory, sent him a commission as justice of the peace in the County of Erie, Territory of Michigan. In 1819, Seneca Allen, residing on the south side of the river near Fort Meigs, was an acting justice of the peace for Waynesfield Township, State of Ohio. In an earlier meeting Allen requested that Conant never act under his commission regarding it as illegal. In December of 1819, Seneca Allen was called upon to officiate at a wedding in Maumee, because of the running

river full of ice, it was impossible to cross. Allen called upon Conant to officiate under his commission from Cass. Conant married the couple and received a jack-knife as his payment. Later, the two justices met and Allen made the following proposal: He would exercise control of the territory south of the river, and Conant would exercise control on the north side.

[19] Revealed in an article by George A. Chase which appeared in the *Friday, April 9, 1909, issue of the TOLEDO DAILY BLADE:* "*Stickney named his town Vistula, the name of an important river in Central Europe, that flows into the Baltic Sea, and navigable for 550 miles. It is connected by canals with the Dneiper, the Oder, and the Niemen rivers.*"

[20] Endowed the present Way Public Library in Perrysburg.

[21] Thomas W. Powell came to Wood County in the Fall of 1820 to practice law, and left Perrysburg in December of 1830, for Delaware. Interestingly, when Ohio held its second Constitutional Convention on May 14, 1873, he was the oldest delegate present and was named temporary chairman.

[22] The reminiscences first appeared in the Perrysburg Weekly *Journal* on March 13, 1868, and later in the Defiance *Democrat*, May 2, 1868.

[23] Almon Gibbs is also credited as being the first Worshipful Master of Northern Light Masonic Lodge in Maumee.

[24] James Thompson and William Griffin

[25] Charles Evers in his WOOD COUNTY HISTORY says that Gibbs experienced ".... death from trouble bred by his defense to the Negro (Patrick) whom he rescued from neighbors, who wished to carry him South (and into slavery)."

[26] Letter from Governor Cass in Detroit to Indian Agent Henry Schoolcraft in Sault Ste. Marie on Wednesday, March 12, 1823.

[27] Anthony Shane of the Shawnee tribe was a guide and scout for Harrison's regiment in their advance on Malden. Son of French-Shawnee half-breed Antoine Chesne. His father founded Shane's Crossing on the St. Mary's River in Mercer County. Later Anthony Shane platted Shane's Crossing as Shanesville June 23, 1820. Later to be known as Rockford, Ohio. Did much harm to the Americans prior to the Treaty of 1795, and much good after the treaty. Mrs. Shane, a Delaware Indian, was baptized at Shane's Crossing on the St. Mary's River, while her husband served as interpreter.

Benjamin Franklin Stickney

Specifically mentioned in the Treaty of 1817:

> "To Anthony Shane (Chesne) a half blood Ottawa Aborigine one section of land to contain six hundred and forty acres on the east side of the River St. Mary and to begin opposite the house in which Shane now lives, thence up the river with the meanders one hundred and sixty poles, and from the beginning down the river with the meanders one hundred and sixty poles, and from the extremity of the said lines, east for quantity."

[28] Friday, March 15, 1822 letter from Benjamin Franklin Stickney to Reverend E. Swift from Port Lawrence.

[29] Saturday, March 30, 1822 letter from Horatio Conant at Fort Meigs to the Reverend Elisha Swift

[30] Western Missionary Society.

[31] Letter from Dr. Horatio Conant to Rev Swift, Saturday, April 16th, 1822.

[32] Whiskey, whiskey.

[33] Excerpted from Marjorie Barnhart *PRISONERS OF HOPE* by, published by the Presbyterian Historical Society 1980. Page 140-141.

[34] Alvan Coe was western Missionary Society teacher of Indians. Coe had practiced law in the East for three years before migrating to Ohio in 1809. Teaching at the Western Missionary School at Lower Sandusky (Fremont) under the direction of the Reverend Joseph Badger, Coe had learned the Wyandotte language and eventually become fairly proficient.

[35] Saturday, June 8, 1822 letter from a white husband of an Indian women to Alvan Coe.

[36] Isaac VanTassel was of the Catskills of New York, the region made famous by Washington Irving in the "Legend of Sleepy Hollow," which involved characters Katrina VanTassel and Ichabod Crane. He arrived in Ashtabula, Ohio, in 1821 and was appointed to the Maumee Mission. In September of 1822 he married Miss Lucia Badger, daughter of early Maumee Valley missionary Reverend Joseph Badger. (See letter by Indian Agent James Jackson August 29, 1833).

[37] Dresden H. Howard papers and manuscripts Toledo Lucas County Public Library and the Maumee Valley Historical Society.

[38] There is another letter written by Eliza Holmes on the 18th of December that was included by Reverend Isaac VanTassel in his report to the *MISSIONARY HERALD*. Under speculation, I would suggest that both Sally and Eliza were related to John Holmes, who was the son of

Wassaonoquette. Wausenoquet was the grandson of Pontiac through his father O-tusa.

[39] Dr. Conant was born and trained in Connecticut with further study in New York before coming to Detroit in 1815. Opened a mercantile with Gibbs in Maumee in 1816. Pro-Ohio in nature held numerous positions.

[40] Established a law practice in Cincinnati in 1804, and in 1810 was appointed by the legislature to the Ohio Supreme Court. He resigned in December of 1818 to accept the Ohio governorship which he won against James Dunlap. In 1819 he addressed the legislature with the following: "Roads and canals are veins and arteries to the body politic that diffuse supplies, health, vigor, and animation to the whole system." The canals were dug and Brown became to Ohio what DeWitt Clinton was to New York. Reelected-governor in 1820 Brown resigned in 1822 in order to fill the unexpired senatorial term of William A. Trimble, deceased. His previous activity in canals now obtained for Brown the chairmanship of the Committee on Roads and Canals. Defeated in the Senate race Brown held the post of Ohio Canal Commissioner from 1825-1830.

[41] Austin E. Wing was born in 1791 in Massachusetts. Graduated from Williams College with honors in 1814, and moved to Detroit, Michigan the same year. He was for a number of years sheriff of the Territory of Michigan, studied and practiced the profession of law and was also a farmer. With two other partners; Musgrove Evans, and Joseph Brown they founded and developed Tecumseh, but Austin continued to live in Monroe. Austin Wing had political ambitions, and is credited with the following remark: *"If we go into milling and farming, and establish a mill, settlers will know that I'm interested and will vote to send me to Congress. If I am elected, with the aid of General Jacob Brown (Commander in chief, U. S. Army), you can be appointed government surveyor."* Wing and Evans decided to go back to New York and interest Joseph W. Brown (a brother of General Brown) who was both a miller and a farmer to settle in the area. Evans and Joseph Brown were brothers-in-law. Austin was a elected a delegate to Congress from the Michigan Territory from 1825-1829 and 1831to 1833. After admission of Michigan as a state he was appointed United States Marshall under Polk. Later moved to Cleveland where he died in 1849.

[42] Wausenoquet, Ottokee, Wassonquette, and Notino were the sons of Pontiac's son O-tusa.

Benjamin Franklin Stickney

boundaries, canal talk, & development
chapter fourteen

1827 was a year of legislative action designed to advance the population expansion of the *Old Northwest Territories,* which would provide added incentive for the pioneers to move into the area. And as a consequence, the purchase of available government lands would greatly benefit the depleted treasury of the United States.

On a tour designed to promote the government land in the Old Northwest, Thomas L. McKenney Superintendent for Indian Affairs, published his book *Sketches of a Tour To The Lakes* in 1827. After his journey across Lake Erie from Buffalo onboard the HENRY CLAY from Buffalo, McKenney described his arrival in Detroit, Michigan Territory. After a dinner meeting with Governor Cass and his secretary, Major Robert A. Forsyth[1], and Col. and Mrs. Henry Whiting[2] at the Governor's residence, McKenney's bed for the evening was at Major Biddle's residence[3]. McKenney continued his narrative on Saturday, June 17, 1826 by describing the residence of the Governor of the Michigan Territory.[4] Located adjacent to the Detroit River near the Springwell Road, the home's log construction was covered with clapboards with a long covered porch, and the governor took great delight in showing the bullet and arrowhead marks from Pontiac's Rebellion.

The United States House of Representatives Committee on Territories reported in 1827 that the intent of the writers of the Northwest Territory Ordinance of 1787 was to give every state that would be created equal access to the Great Lakes. This ruling supported Indiana's claim to an outlet on Lake Michigan, and Ohio's claim to the Maumee Bay. With this achievement completed, Congress took no further action to resolve the Ohio and Michigan boundary dispute. To add further confusion to the matter, President John Quincy Adams approved the Congressional Act that granted land in the disputed strip to the State of Indiana to build a canal from Lake Erie to the Wabash River at Fort Wayne.[5] At the same time that Ohio was trying to exercise control over the disputed lands, Michigan's Monroe County created Port Lawrence Township in the land between Ohio and Michigan.

Benjamin Franklin Stickney

Above, a map of the old northwest territory from 1915 showing the location of the future state and lakes. Below shows the Harris and Fulton Lines that follow the intent and actual legal line. From the author's collection.

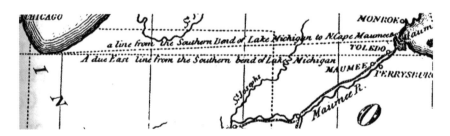

Note that the line drawn due east from the southern tip of Lake Michigan intersects the Maumee River at about Ewing Island.

In the disputed territory the natural channel for the Maumee River entered the Maumee Bay on the north side of Turtle Island and continued with two major turns, till it finally arrived on the south side of the mouth of the Maumee River adjacent to Presque Isle near present day Oregon or East Toledo. With an eye towards navigational aids and future commerce, Edward Bissell[6] of Lockport, New York purchased from the United States government the entire 6.68 acres of Turtle Island. Several years later Bissell would sell the island back to the United States for a lighthouse at the western end of Lake Erie.

Benjamin Franklin Stickney

In what appeared to be an event of no consequence in 1827, Indian Agent Benjamin Franklin Stickney wrote to Gov. Cass in late October and said that: "...*An Indian Chief has died and the relatives have mounted a British flag over his grave. The whites have said considerable about it. The Indians have come to me to make excuses for making use of a British flag, saying they had no other; and requesting me to give them an American one. Having none, I told them I would ask one of you for them. If you have them, and think it proper to send two, it may be convenient to have one spare one....*"[7]

This request for a flag by Stickney occurred at about the same time that Otussa, Pontiac's son, died at Presque Isle. Otussa was poisoned by Oquanoxa[8] (Oquinoxey) who was a village chief of the Ottawa settlement on the Auglaize River above present day Defiance, Ohio. The poisoning was in revenge for having been removed as a council chief. "*I know the man who has poisoned me*," Otussa is reputed to have said before he died several days later without naming the man responsible. Otussa's grave could have been the one referred to by Stickney and noted historian Dr. Lyman Draper in his *Field Notes [89]*.

"*Mr. Hall also showed me a somewhat smaller British Silver Medal which once belonged to Pontiac - struck in the reign of George III- with his images - with a legend on the reverse side representing a church and steeple and the insignia of Christianity and civilization guarded by a lion - and at the back a gaunt Indian cur evidently feebly attempting to protect the Indian wilderness in his rear from the advance of civilization. This medal was worn by Pontiac's widow, and by his son Otussa, in whose grave it was buried, and from which obtained by some of the old French settlers long since the Ottawa migrated to the west.*"[9]

Mary Stark, Benjamin Franklin Stickney's faithful wife, companion, and business partner of 25 years died on January 13, 1828 of typhoid fever complicated with influenza. At a loss for words, Stickney described his marriage in a letter to his good friend Gov. Cass several days later.

"The accompanying report of the wishes of the Indians ought to have been made on the 4th last. But Mrs. Stickney was then sick and had been for about a month. From that time her illness became extreme; until last Sunday morning -- when her existence terminated. I had not a moment to devote to any thing else, night or day, while life lasted. I several times attempted to write, but found it impossible. It has been the first time in my life that I have been <u>sensible</u> of my nerves being affected. Almost without sleep, was the principal cause. It has left a monstrous blank that probably will never be filled. Yet, no just cause of complaint; for we have lived very comfortably together 25 years: being more than the common period of such connections. And it was not at a very early period of her life. She was 54." [10]

Mourned and buried by the friends that knew Mary Stickney, life continued throughout the Maumee Valley. The progress of the Mission School was described in a letter dated October 1, 1828 by the Rev. VanTassel to the *Missionary Herald at Home and Abroad*.

"The Ottawas, the Indians for whose benefit this mission was specially designed, though children from other tribes are admitted to the school, reside on small reservations, lying at intervals on the Maumee River, from its mouth 60 miles into the interior. These Indians, surrounded by white men, are brought in a great degree under their influence, and, as is commonly the fact, with Indians in such circumstances, are poor, indolent, and addicted to intoxication to a lamentable degree. A desire to have their children educated seems to be, on the whole, prevailing, and some individuals have of late been hopefully converted by the labors of the mission family. .....

We have received six new scholars from the mouth of the Portage River, and have them bound for five years. ..... Our school now contains 18 scholars. ...... A number more have applied, some of whom we expect shortly.

Benjamin Franklin Stickney

> As it respects the state of religion, I have nothing particularly gratifying to communicate. We are much pleased with worldly cares, and I fear spiritual concerns are too much neglected. ...."

Dresden Howard came to the Maumee Valley as a six year old boy with his parents in 1821, and established an intimate friendship with the Indians of the Maumee Valley as he played and attended school with them. From journals and memories Howard supplied another depiction of the Mission School from a thirteen year old boy's point of view.

> "It is easy, I think for any one to appreciate the difficulty of establishing a school among these wild fierce people, these boys and girls who have never been restrained of their freedom of abridged in the least. There were altogether one or two hundred boys and girls of all ages from six or seven to twenty years of age. It was no easy task to ask them to come in out of the free woods. To cease their sports of hunting, fishing, paddling their canoes, riding horse back, running races and other pastimes was of course requiring great effort on the part of these young savages. After a few days in the classroom, with all its attendant restraints, it cannot be wondered that many of them took the trail back to their villages having had enough of civilization. I had the same experience and have not forgotten to this day."[11]

Along with religious questions regarding the missions, Ohio and Indiana were still struggling over the canal question, and to further complicate matters another form of transportation was starting to transform the United States east of the Allegheny Mountains. Coming to the aid of New York State's established canal system Governor Martin VanBuren's[12] depicted in a letter to President Andrew Jackson his attitude in 1829 towards the spread of railroad transportation.

> "The canal system of this country is being threatened by the spread of a new form of transportation known as "railroads". The federal government must preserve the canals for the following

Benjamin Franklin Stickney

reasons: One. If canal boats are supplanted by "railroads" serious unemployment will result. Captains, cooks, drivers, hostlers, repairmen, and lock tenders will be left without means of livelihood, not to mention the numerous farmers now employed in growing hay for the horses. Two. Boat builders would suffer and tow line, whip and harness makers would be left destitute. Three. Canal boats are absolutely essential to the defense of the United States. In the event of the expected trouble with England, the Erie Canal would be the only means by which we could move the supplies so vital to waging modern war.

For the above mentioned reasons the government should create an Interstate Commerce Commission to protect the American people from the evils of "railroads" and to preserve the canals for posterity.

As you may well know, Mr. President, "railroad" carriages are pulled at the enormous speed of 15 miles per hour by engines which, in addition to endangering life and limb of passengers, roar and snort their way through the countryside, setting fire to crops, scaring the livestock and frightening women and children. The Almighty certainly never intended that people should travel at such breakneck speed."

Facing increased pressure for their land from the influx of immigrants into the Old Northwest Territories, coupled with several years of devastating farm yields and extremely poor hunting in the surrounding forests, the Ottawa Indian leaders were forced to ask for help from the Federal Government to feed their families. They also asked for land that would provide them with a better standard living, and a land that was not bothered by unscrupulous whiskey traders.

"When we look around us and see our children cry with hunger, and can find no game wherewith to satisfy our wants - and where we see, on the other land, that wicked white men are constantly bringing spirituous liquor into our country, we are led to inquire where we can find a better country? Two of the undersigned have been through a section of country west of the Mississippi and with pleasure anticipate the time when we, with

Benjamin Franklin Stickney

our families shall inhabit that country. Will you have the goodness to intercede for us with the President for a donation of land for ourselves and nation, and also for necessary traveling expenses to that place whenever we, or our nation shall concede to go. Signed with the marks of Ottawa Indian Chiefs: Gosa, Wesaugone, Mikoubas, Ming gukik, I obe quum, Nawash, Kosh Konequet to Samuel Lykins. [13]

The early voices that had whispered for the removal of the Indians in the Maumee Valley were now shouting their expectations. Port Lawrence's leading residents had signed a petition for Governor Cass to remove the Ottawa Indians west of the Mississippi River under the provisions of President Jackson's Indian Removal Act. Even the merchants, who for the most part had fleeced the Indians of their yearly annuity, wanted the Indians removed. The ground swell of support was so great for their removal, that Cass was actively looking for a tract of land to temporally place the Ottawas. The only condition was that the land was out of the way of the *"white"* population.[14]

With all the turmoil swirling through the Maumee Valley, even the Ottawas were subjected not only to the removal of their lands, but the theft of their annuity.

"There is three thousand six hundred dollars payable to us annually at Detroit for our lands we have sold. We have requested you as a favor to give this money to our father to bring to us, and deliver it here in the same way you have given the money to the man from Kentucky to bring here. It is true he brought some money, but we didn't receive the whole amount. We do not know the whole sum that was taken, for he would not permit us to have any person count for us as our father Stickney had always done. This year, by insisting very strong about having it counted and by the aid of some friends we obtained leave to have it counted. When the whole sum that was brought was thrown out on a table and he (Lloyd) said it was all, on counting it we found that it was five hundred and eighty two dollars lacking; some of it being in boxes and some in bags. We observed that the bags had been opened after being sealed at

Benjamin Franklin Stickney

the bank and one of the boxes was not full. He then said the bank had not counted it right. We protested and insisted that it should be put up again in the boxes and bags and sent back to the bank, and he refused to do it. He then took up what he called twelve hundred dollars from the table and carried it away from this place where the payments have always been made, to Wood County, in the State of Ohio, where we followed him. ….. While our old father Stickney delivered our money to us, it was not counted wrong at the Bank, the bags and boxes did not get broken open by the way and the money lost, and we always had it counted before us and were permitted to count it ourselves, and to have it counted. We Indians do not like such things, and I think you do not, my father, and I think our great Father, the President, does not. But he appears to think he has the right to do with our money as he pleases: to put it in his pocket or to give it to whom he pleases: he acted very foolish with it. … Father, hear me. Take pity on me. I am very poor -- help me to take this burden off that is pressing me so bad, and I hope you will not suffer me to entirely loose the money that has been taken from me. [15]*"* This letter was probably written by someone that the Ottawas trusted …. Benjamin Franklin Stickney.

Contained in a subsequent letter from Indian Agent L. L. Lloyd to Lewis Cass on November 7, 1830 Lloyd tried to explain the missing funds.

" … I am very glad to perceive from its tone that you are not disposed to act against me without giving me notice. I have many enemies who have been watching for an opportunity to injure me. Some of these enemies, unfortunately, are too influential with the Indians and use them as instruments to accomplish their design, which is to get me out of Office…. My enemies, most of them, were originally political, but thence became personally hostile to me. Other enemies I have who became so from being disappointed in getting office, removed officers, whiskey sellers &c &c. … If the Indians are laboring under any real grievances I am perfectly willing to redress it, if it lies within my power. The only grievance of which they can complain with the least shadow of justice is the deficiency in

Benjamin Franklin Stickney

their annuity. This, I conceived, I had once settled with them. The occurrence is extremely unfortunate upon me, but the Indians will lose nothing by it, for they positively agreed to pay the debts of the dec'd Indians with the amount of the deficiency.

As the Ottawa Indians had expected, their annuity had been opened to their creditors by Lloyd to pay the trader's claims against deceased tribal members.

Even with the attention that was directed at the Ottawa Indian population, the problems and tribulations which followed the mounting population of immigrants were not left behind. The first tavern in what was to become Wood County was opened by Isaac Richardson on the Dodd homestead in 1816 near the Roche de Beouf [Bout] landmark. Richardson employed George Porter a black Mohican Indian, as a carpenter and laborer after he found his own construction skills in tune with serving whiskey. The tavern and hotel eventually consisted of a double ended log cabin, followed by an ill conceived dam across the Maumee River. The dam provided enough pressure to power a flour and wood mill. However, Richardson considered Porter nothing more than an escaped slave, and would continually taunt Porter with his inability to collect wages.

Porter, after years of begging for his wages, found Richardson on the tavern's front porch and shot him dead with number nine pellets from a well aimed shotgun. Several patrons that stood near Richardson were also wounded. The jury, while despising Richardson for his history of double dealings, and sympathizing with Porter, nevertheless found Porter guilty of murder and hanged him in 1830 near the south end of the Maumee Perrysburg Bridge.[16]

Michigan's Monroe County was not immune from the mayhem that tended to follow mass migration. Following Porter, S. G. Simmons received the death penalty for the murder of his wife. Convicted by the testimony of his children, Simmons was hanged on Friday, the 24th of September in Detroit. While

Simmons was the last to be executed, Michigan still had the whip.

On Sunday, almost six months after the public hanging of Simmons, a Mr. Dillon was sentenced to receive 15 lashes on his bare back. Col. Peter P. Perry, Justice of the Peace for the Territory of Michigan, said that whipping was a proper penalty because so few people had money to pay the appropriate fine. With the public assembled in Monroe's Public Square, the lashes were administered by either John Mulhollen or Miles Thorp. According to the sources at the time, Dillon left the Monroe area immediately after being publicly disgraced.[17]

Even with all the problems facing the Old Northwest Territories land speculators were still roaming over the lands looking for sites for speculation. Judge D. Higgins[18] recalled his first visit to the Maumee Valley in the Spring of 1830.

"....Our company consisted of Rodolphus Dickinson, J. C. Spink, Count Coffinberry, myself, and a countryman, whose name I forget. The voyage was a dismal one to Defiance, through an unsettled wilderness of some sixty miles. Its loneliness was only broken by the intervening Indian settlement at Ottawa Village, where we were hailed and cheered lustily by the Tahwa Indians, as would be a foreign war-ship in the port of New York. From Defiance we descended the Maumee to Perrysburg, where we found all well. In descending the Maumee, we came near running into the rapids, where we should probably have been swamped had we not been hailed from the shore and warned of our danger. ....."[19]

With the end of 1830 approaching, President Jackson in his message to Congress announced that coupled with the western expansion of the United States was the difficulty of obtaining title to the Indian lands. With Jackson's policy of Indian Removal to lands west of the Mississippi, came the direct purchase of the Indian Lands by the Federal Government. With just several strokes of his pen, President Jackson had removed the conflict

Benjamin Franklin Stickney

of the responsibility of the States and the Indians, and placed it squarely within the realm of the Federal Government.[20]

Canals were still the favored mode of cheap transportation when Indiana decided that the building of the Wabash & Erie Canal could mesh with the Ohio Canal project[21]. Following a petition to Congress that was signed by sixty-eight residents of the disputed territory, Indiana proposed that Ohio should build its part of the canal system from the Ohio/Indiana State boundary to Lake Erie. The compensation that was offered to Indiana from the Federal Government earlier concerning Ohio lands would now be offered to Ohio. The Federal Government, as well as the two States, agreed to the transfer, and Ohio came into possession of 292,224 additional acres of land for sale. To facilitate the sale of the combined 500,000 acres, land offices were established at Tiffin and Piqua.

Canal fever rekindled the fires of opposition in certain counties not directly benefited by the canals. The St. Clairsville *National Historian*[22] declared that Ohio was already amply in debt. Ohio's thoughts of transportation should be curved towards railroads not canals. Early in 1830 seven members of the Ohio House of Representatives protested against further funding of the Miami Canal. Ohio's House of Representatives rejected their attempt, but a large public meeting at Steubenville confirmed the grass roots opposition. Ohio actually delayed the beginning of the work on the Miami extension to Cincinnati and the Ohio River, because of the legal interests of Michigan concerning the disputed ownership of the canal's terminus on the Maumee Bay.

In consequence of such an expansion in Ohio and Indiana's transportation system, the whole Maumee Valley experienced a wave of real estate speculation and rising prices that ended with the Panic of 1837.[23]

On the national front the Michigan Territory and the resulting Ohio Michigan Boundary dispute was far from the mind of President Andrew Jackson. President Andrew Jackson with the decade of 1830 barely five months old, appointed William T.

Benjamin Franklin Stickney

Barry[24], a political supporter of Jackson in the 1828 campaign, Postmaster General of the United States. Firmly entrenched in his office, Barry convinced the President that his good friend John Mason[25] would be an excellent choice in replacing James Witherell as Secretary of the Michigan Territory.

Almost two months later John Mason and his teenage son Stevens Thomson Mason gazed at Detroit. The task of bringing the Mason family to the Michigan wilderness was left to Stevens T. Mason; and by October the family carriage, two wagons of household goods, his mother, grandmother, six sisters, and three family servants had successfully made the overland journey.

Within days of President Jackson's appointment of Gov. Cass as Secretary of War in July of 1831, Stevens T. Mason signed his commission as Secretary of the Michigan Territory and replaced his father as Michigan's Territorial secretary. [26]

As Gov. Cass assumed the mantle of Secretary of War, one of the first items on his agenda was to put an end to the Army's liquor ration, and to ban the sale of whisky and all such beverages at any military installation. At about the same time as Sec. Cass was banning liquor from the military forts, a fugitive slave by the name of Tice Davids was following one of Ohio's escape routes from Ripley on the Ohio River to Sandusky, Ohio. Instead of looking for a boat to cross the Ohio River, Davids saved precious time over the slave catchers by swimming the river. When the slave catchers finally secured passage across the river, Davids had disappeared into the adjoining dense forests that lined the Ohio River. The Kentucky slave catchers, dumfounded at their inability to apprehend Davids, was said to have uttered *"That nigger must have gone off on an underground road."* [27] Dresden Howard would later detail the Underground Railroad's routes through Ohio, the Maumee Valley, and eventually through to Canada.

"I think that the period of operation is fairly described by the years 1816 to 1835 or 40. I think the main and principal route

Benjamin Franklin Stickney

crossed the Ohio River near the Northbend; thence on as direct a line as possible (following the streams practicable) to the upper Auglaize, and the Blanchard's fork of the Auglaize, passing near the Shawnee village where is now the city of Wapakoneta, and to Ocquenesis town on the Blanchard, where is now the village of Ottawa; thence to the Grand Rapids of the Maumee (where the river could easily be forded most of the year), and at the Ottawa Village of Chief Kinjeino where all were friendly, and the poor slave was treated kindly; thence by a plain trail north to Malden, Canada.

Ten miles below the rapids at Roche Teboult or Standing Rock, lived one Richardson, a Kentuckian, who made his living by catching slaves. At one time my father, Edward Howard, was piloting a party of slaves north, and the trail passed only three miles west of Richardson's. In order to avoid being surprised by this man it was necessary to keep a close lookout; and for greater safety the trip north from my father's was always performed in the night. We had a whisper from an Indian friend that this party, which we had kept concealed in the thick swampy forest near our cabin for some time, was being watched and would be ambushed on the way. The night they moved out on the trail, we (I was then but a boy, but often accompanied my father) took a circuitous route, hoping to elude pursuit. After veering to our right and re-entering the old trail, my father left a boy to guard and bring up the rear. We had not advanced more than three miles, when we plainly heard the beat of horse's hoofs behind us; the guard was posted near the trail with orders to shoot the horse, if necessary; in a few minutes two horsemen approached the ambuscade and in a second more, the sharp crack of a rifle echoed through the forest, and the horse with a groan plunged to the ground. This checked the pursuing party and gave stimulus and speed to the feet of the fugitives. The slave catchers were now afraid to advance, and retreated over the trail, and the fugitives, though badly frightened, were permitted to continue their march to freedom unmolested."[28]

Finally, by early 1831 Ohio and Michigan were beginning to have serious discussions about their disputed boundary. Michigan's Legislative Council authorized Governor Cass to

Benjamin Franklin Stickney

enter into negotiations with Duncan MacArthur, Governor of Ohio, whereby Michigan would trade land east of the Maumee River for the land west of the river. The subtle implication was that the middle of the mouth of the Maumee River would be the joint boundary.

The response from the Ohio Legislature was to send a letter to Congress reviewing Ohio's position and requesting that either Congress approve the boundary to the northernmost cape of the Maumee Bay, or that the United States appoint boundary commissioners to settle the matter.

The Territory of Michigan, with ex-governor Cass working behind closed doors for Michigan, responded in 1831 by saying that the southern boundary of Michigan should follow the Ordinance of 1787. However, they were willing to let Congress decide whether or not the area north of the Lower Peninsula (Upper Peninsula)[29] and east of a line extended north from the middle of Lake Michigan should be part of the new territory (Wisconsin) or of Michigan. Gov. Cass remembered the immense natural resources of the Upper Peninsula that were available to fund Michigan's future for a simple concession in the boundary dispute.

Michigan's Legislative Council's major point of contention was that the boundary created by the Ordinance of 1787 could be changed only by mutual consent, but boundaries established by Congress in creating territories could be altered at the will of Congress. Congress had previously changed territorial boundaries in other areas. The Territory of Michigan's final position was that the southern boundary of a line due east of the southern end of Lake Michigan was unbreakable because it was provided in the Ordinance of 1787.

And the last thoughts concerning the condition of the Maumee Valley in 1831 were voiced by the Rev. Isaac VanTassel[30] and Miss Newell[31] in letters to the Missionary Herald at Home and Abroad.

Benjamin Franklin Stickney

boundaries, canal talk, & development
chapter fourteen

Rev. Isaac VanTassel *"... I have of late spent most of my time among the Indians that are scattered in the wilderness, and I have seen the fruits of human depravity exhibited in a great variety of ways. I have also seen wretchedness and poverty enough. The Indians are generally debased by their intercourse with a certain class of whites, who get there living, such as it is, out of the Indians; and they are impoverished by the free use of ardent spirits which is constantly brought among them. ..."*

"The prospect of doing good at this place was soon after blighted by an attempt to purchase their land, and induce the Indians to remove to a country west of the Mississippi River. The agent[32], who was commissioned to conduct this negotiation, after rehearsing to the Shawnees the fate of the Cherokees, and stating that these were the last proposals the government of the United States would ever make to them, and presenting other motives, at last obtained their assent to the proposed treaty. Miss Newel, who was present at the council, and witnessed all the proceedings, gives the following account of the distressing despondency manifested by the headmen." [33]

Miss Newell *"One of the chiefs said it was tough, hard case, to give his people up to come under state laws without being permitted to vote, or having their civil oaths regarded before a magistrate; it would be as bad as to give themselves up to have their throats cut: for he could easily conceive of their being driven to desperation and immediately committing outrage that would bring them to the gallows; and it was a tough, hard case, to decide to go, but as there was no alternative, they had better be reconciled to go. ....*

The old men sat in council looking each other in the face, and mourning over their fate from Monday morning until Tuesday night. They sat and talked all night long, and parted with no better state of feeling than when they came together. They think their prospect of earthly good is blasted forever. They say they have nothing to hope for here, or beyond the Mississippi either. They had thought for years past, that there would be no hope for them; only by their conduct pleasing the white people so well, that they would not wish them to move

Benjamin Franklin Stickney

away. This they had endeavored to do, had made up their minds to encourage schools, attend to agriculture and examine the religion of the bible; but they now saw it would all be in vain. Those Indians that had learning, and had received the religion of white people, were all hated and despised alike, and were now invited to take up their lot together. ......"

Almost immediately after the signing of the Treaty of 1831 concerning land concessions in the twelve mile Indian reserve at the mouth of the river, Major Stickney the leading land owner in the Maumee Valley offered his services to Indian Agent James B. Gardner[34] in assisting and preparing for the removal of the *Ottawa of Michigan*. Gardner wanted to *".... and offered to take a deputation of the Ottawa of Michigan to the Mississippi, for the purpose of exploration, with a view to removal."* According to early pioneer Dresden Howard by 1832, the Maumee Valley had been *"overrun by speculators more or less."*

Not only were the Ottawa Indians, who had lived along the Maumee River for hundreds of years, being removed to lands in the west ...... The Ottawa Indians faced one final degradation as they witnessed a final display of the permanence of the "white" settlement on the traditional Indian lands. The Maumee Valley's first recognized cemetery[35] was established by a gift of two acres by Dexter Fisher at Madison Avenue & 17th Street near Toledo's present day Hillcrest Hotel. While the Ottawas, who according to their religious beliefs continued to enjoy the forests and streams of the Maumee Valley after death, were forced to abandon the ancient burial grounds of their ancestors.

Endnotes of Chapter Fourteen
boundaries, canal talk, & development

---

[1] A graduate of West Point and Governor Cass's secretary.

[2] Colonel Whiting, of the United States Quartermaster Corp was stationed in Detroit and took an active interest in Detroit's intellectual community. Colonel Whiting makes reference to the *Chinese looking* part

Benjamin Franklin Stickney

of the Governor's mansion in a poem *The Age of Steam* which was read to a Fourth of July celebration on board the steamer HENRY CLAY in the Detroit River in 1830.

[3] According to Thomas McKenney in his book *Sketches of a Tour to the Lakes, The most commanding, and in all respects, the best looking building is that which is owned and occupied by Major Biddle. It was built I believe, by the unfortunate Hull.*

[4] *It is not exactly in, nor entirely out of the city - I mean its settled parts; but stands by itself on the bank of the river, with the road-way from the city towards Spring Wells*[4] *..... The house is of cedar logs, and weather boarded, one story, with a high sharp roof, out of which, and near the centre, comes a short stone chimney of enormous thickness, and on which the roof leans, being a little sunk around it. Before the front door, which is nearly in the centre of the building, the building being some fifty feet front, is a porch that, being a little out of its perpendicular position, inclines north. Its figure is as nearly that of a square as of any other figure, with a sharp Chinese looking top, that shoots up some three feet above the eaves of the house, and seems to have in no one place the least connection with the building. I told the Governor that my puzzle was to decide which was built first, the porch or the house. He acknowledged his inability to decide the question, but added, "the house itself is anterior to the time of Pontiac's war, there being on it now the marks of bullets that were shot into it then." I learned afterwards that the porch had once ornamented the garden as a summer house; but had been advanced from its retirement to grace the front of the residence of the executive of the Michigan territory."* Thomas McKenney, see no. 3

[5] Followers of the United States Constitution wondered how the President of the United States could grant to one state the power to build a canal across the state lands of another? This questionable action would be delt with at a later date.

[6] Bissell is credited with the first use of steam power in Toledo in 1834. He operated a steam powered sawmill near the foot of Elm Street. Summit and Elm or Elm and the Maumee River.

[7] Wednesday, October 17, 1827 letter from B. F. Stickney to Lewis Cass.

[8] Oquanoxa was village chief of the settlement called Charloe on the Auglaize River near present day Defiance, Ohio. He has been described as a cruel and wicked savage who had previously killed three of his wives. He is also reputed to have killed O-tusa by using witchcraft.

Benjamin Franklin Stickney

[9] Dr. Lyman Draper notes as reprinted in the 1933 NWOQ.

[10] Wednesday, January 16, 1828 letter from B. F. Stickney to Lewis Cass.

[11] *An Experiment in Christianity: The Presbyterian Mission on the Maumee*, Dresden Howard, Edited by E. S. Muttart, Northwest Ohio Quarterly, Vol.21, No.1

[12] At the time January 31, 1829, Martin VanBuren was Governor of New York and Andrew Jackson was President of the United States. VanBuren's point of view could have been to protect the newly opened New York canal from competition. Letter to Pres. Jackson, 01.31.1829

[13] Letter written probably by Stickney expressing the Ottawa Chief's words to Samuel Lykins, Thursday February 5, 1829.

[14] Monday August 2, 1830, Port Lawrence Residents to Lewis Cass.

[15] Letter from the Ottawas at the Mouth of the Miami River to Lewis Cass, October the 12, 1830.

[16] Simon Thomas, a boot black for Toledo's Island House and minister to Perrysburg's African Methodist Episcopal Church on 3rd Street was erroneously said to have claimed Porter's body and buried it in the old graveyard located off Perrysburg's Indiana Avenue. The Rev. Thomas would have been two years old at the time of the murder in 1830. However it was rumored that Porter was placed with his feet facing towards his home in the south.

[17] Monroe's Public Square was near where the Presbyterian Church now stands. Also whipping was abolished in 1838 in Michigan.

[18] Elected by Ohio's General Assembly to Judge of the Second Judicial Circuit of Ohio. The counties that composed the second circuit were as follows: Huron, Richland, Delaware, Sandusky, Seneca, Crawford, Marion, Wood, Hancock, Henry, Williams, Putman, Paulding, and VanWert.

[19] History of the Maumee Valley, H. S. Knapp, Toledo 1877, page 279-280

[20] This policy was later upheld by the Supreme Court in the case of *Cherokee Nation vs State of Georgia*, however, in a later ruling, Chief Justice John Marshall ruled with the court in *Worcester vs Georgia* that the Indians retained certain rights in their own lands. President Jackson is reported to have said, *"John Marshall has made his decision, now let him enforce it."*

[21] Lee Newcomer, Construction of the Wabash & Erie Canal, O.S.A.H. Quarterly XLVI 199-208.

Benjamin Franklin Stickney

[22] St. Clairsville (Ohio) National Historian, February 6, May 15, 1830.

[23] The Panic of 1837 was a direct consequence of President Andrew Jackson's *Specie Circular* which directed all government payments must be made in gold and silver. This action crippled land payments and speculation.

[24] Barry was a leader of the Democratic Party in Kentucky and was elected Lt. Governor in 1821. Barry supported Andrew Jackson in his presidential campaigns and was rewarded with Postmaster General for 1830. Barry denounced a Congressional investigation of the postal services as political in nature and resigns in 1835. President Jackson then appoints him Minister to Spain. Barry dies enroute to Madrid.

[25] Well known in Kentucky's political circles John T. Mason had dismal success in financial matters. The substantial land holdings that had been accumulated by his father Senator Mason of Virginia had been depleted and his investments had been unreliable. His son Stevens Thomson Mason had been forced to withdraw from Transylvania University to help with the family's income. John was forced to apply to his old time friend President Andrew Jackson for a governmental appointment.

[26] John T. Mason had inherited his father's Revolutionary War land claims which he was able to trade for a substantial interest in a vast tract of land along the Red River in Texas. There has always been a belief that John T. Mason's mission to Mexico and Texas was more than the promotion of the Red River Land Company. President Jackson was extremely interested in the annexation of Texas and was willing to use open and covert diplomacy to achieve those ends. It has always been considered a distinct possibility that an arrangement was made between Mason and the President which allowed for his son to assume his father's position as Territorial Secretary, thus assuring a continued income for the family, while the father continued his and President Jackson's annexation efforts in Texas. Stevens T. Mason would later describe his father's travels to Texas as *"a long and hazardous journey in a precarious climate."*

[27] That phrase remained in popular usage till around 1835 when it was changed to Underground Railroad. From the Ohio Archaeological and Historical Society, Vol.4, *The Underground Railroad in Ohio*, Prof. Wilbur H. Siebert, A. M., pg 57.

[28] From the Ohio Archaeological and Historical Society, Volume 4 (1895), contained in the article *The Underground Railroad in Ohio*, by Prof. Wilbur H. Siebert, A. M., page 60-61.

Benjamin Franklin Stickney

[29] Working behind the scenes in Washington, Cass proposed that as a compromise Michigan be admitted as a state, that she surrender the Ohio strip, and accept as recompense that area north of the Straits of Mackinac, now known as Michigan's Upper Peninsula. It was the land that he and Schoolcraft explored; he knew its timber and mineral riches. Schoolcraft was privy to this plan and came to Washington to advocate it. He told a Senate Committee that the region would be *found of far greater value and importance to the state than the seven mile strip surrendered.*

[30] Maumee Mission School first on June 10th and later on June 29th.

[31] Excerpts from Miss Newell's letter of June 29, 1831, which was printed in the *"Missionary Herald at Home and Abroad"* in which she described the Ottawa Council that was convened to hear Mr. Gardner.

[32] The Indian Agent in question is James B. Gardner.

[33] Excerpted from the *MISSIONARY HERALD at HOME and ABROAD*, Indians in Ohio, Isaac VanTassel, Vol. 27, pgs 387-8, 1831)

[34] The Indian Agent from Columbus was charged with misrepresenting the terms of the Treaty of 1831 with the Shawnees. When the Shawnees found out they had been deceived they appealed to the Quakers. A Committee of Friends went to Washington and presented their case to Congress, showing that the Shawnees were to receive $115,000 less than was represented to them. After a delay of twenty years the amount received was increased by $96,000.

According to Carl Klopfenstein *".... He (Gardiner) conceitedly told the Indians (Shawnees) to listen to the advice of the whites as they were wiser than the Redmen as the latter were wiser than the blacks. The following morning, Wayweleapy, a noted chief and orator of the Shawnees, acting as spokesman, replied to Gardiner. Chiding the commissioner for his racial prejudices, the chief declared the Great Spirit had created all men equal. Furthermore if the Great Spirit had made one race superior to all others, he undoubtedly gave the Redmen more sense than the whites."* Removal of the Indians from Ohio 1820-1843, Western Reserve University, 1955, page 100.

[35] Dexter Fisher owned eighty acres in 1830 in the center of what is now Toledo. Dexter sold two acres for a cemetery centered around Toledo's Madison and 17th Streets. The cemetery was discontinued in 1840 and the number of burials was never recorded.

Benjamin Franklin Stickney

vistula, boundaries, & preparations
chapter fifteen

In 1831 when Michigan's Territorial Governor Lewis Cass was appointed Secretary of War, President Andrew Jackson selected George D. Porter[1] as Governor of the Territory of Michigan. Having unfinished business in Pennsylvania, Porter was forced to leave the political and business necessities of the Michigan Territory in the questionable hands of Stevens T. Mason, the Territory's nineteen year old secretary. Mason arrived in Detroit on Sunday the 24th of July, and on Monday met with five members of committee[2] that were circulating a petition to have him removed from office. Using impeccable manners and flawless logic, Mason acknowledged that his age and lack of experience could be a hindrance, but since President Jackson appointed him, the President must have faith in his capabilities.

Stevens T. Mason. Courtesy of Michigan History, 4 volume, Publishing Society of Michigan, 1906.

During one of Governor Porter's absences, while walking down Detroit's Jefferson Avenue, Mason had a chance meeting with George Corsellius, editor of Ann Arbor's newspaper the *Western Immigrant.* The newspaper was the leading critic of Mason, and the most fervent voice of the Anti-Freemasonry movement in the Territory of Michigan which was sweeping across the United States. From most accounts their meeting was rather lively and energetic. Their conversation remained civil until Mr. Corsellius made several disparaging remarks about Mason's father. As the conversation deteriorated to insults, it reached a point were the newspaper editor received from Mason "..*a severe cuffing, which from all accounts warmed his ears.*"[3] From the streets of Detroit to the other towns and villages of any consequence on the western end of Lake Erie, the *Old Northwest* was a civilization in transition.

Named in 1833, Toledo's birth was the result of two bickering communities that at first had nothing but contempt for each other. As the villages grew and matured they realized that their future was so intertwined as to make them indistinguishable. It was at this point that Port Lawrence and Vistula combined into Toledo.

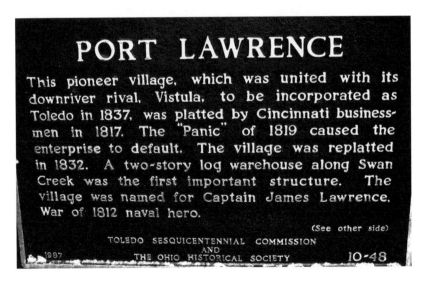

The Ohio Historical Society's marker for Port Lawrence.

Benjamin Franklin Stickney

vistula, boundaries, & preparations
chapter fifteen

Named after Commodore Oliver Hazard Perry's Captain James Lawrence, Port Lawrence was one of the oldest population centers in the Maumee Valley. Located at the confluence of Swan Creek and the Maumee River, Port Lawrence was the touchstone for the other river developments.

Vistula came into being when Benjamin Franklin Stickney pulled out of the Port Lawrence area, and purchased all the land on the north side of the Maumee River from what is now Cherry and Summit Streets to Suder and Summit Streets. *"... In 1832, seeing no prospect that Baum and Oliver would make any advances in improvement on their grounds at the mouth of Swan Creek, I closed with an offer made to me by Mr. Samuel Allen, of Lockport, New York, by which improvements were to be commenced on my land. ..."* [4] When Stickney left the Port Lawrence enterprise, the only thing he was able to recover from his failed land speculation was the Detroit building bricks for his planned family home. The Stickney brick home was built about in the middle of his beloved Vistula, on the northern bluffs overlooking the Maumee River. [5]

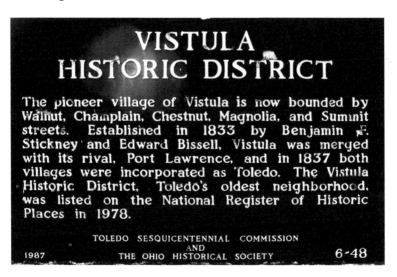

Ohio Historical Society's marker for Vistula. Located at the corner of Summit and Lagrange Streets.

Benjamin Franklin Stickney

vistula, boundaries, & preparations
chapter fifteen

The naming of Vistula has several credible parents in its genealogy. The name Vistula was claimed by the early inhabitants to be from a lone immigrant hunter/trapper from Poland named Wenzislaus. Wenzislaus had his cabin on the banks of the Maumee River in the vicinity of Cherry & Walnut along Summit Street. Noting the similarities between the largest river in Poland, the Wisla, and the Maumee River, he named the area Vistula.[6]

Another version of the origin of Vistula can be traced to another early pioneer of the Maumee Valley, Lewis Goddard[7] and follows several familiar lines. Goddard was one of the early store keepers in the village of Vistula. According to Randolph Downes in his book, *The Conquest*, *"It was Goddard's son, Alonzo, who dreamed up the name Vistula. He was studying his geography lessons during a meeting of the town planners in Detroit when the men asked him to find a name for the new town. He suggested the Latin name of the Polish River in eastern Europe, Wisla - Vistula."*

Giles Bryan Slocum would later write in his Journal for 1831 the following description not only of the developing area but that of Benjamin Franklin Stickney.

"...... and I put up for the night with Maj. Benjamin F. Stickney, a direct descendent of the celebrated Dr. Benjamin Franklin whose name he bears; and I would here remark, that Stickney bore a strong resemblance to the common portraits of Franklin which are to be found all over the country. Stickney prided himself in being of lineage to the great philosopher, and in the eccentricities of his manners sought to imitate in some degree that great man. Stickney I found ever kind and generous to me, and would receive no pay for stopping with him for several days. Stickney having lost his wife, a Mr. Parker and family ran the house (a good two-story brick mansion) for him very agreeably. Maj. Stickney had formerly been Indian Agent at Fort Wayne seven years, and I believe originally had charge of the construction of that fort. Having now four hundred acres well

Benjamin Franklin Stickney

situated on the northwest bank of the Maumee River, and with a view of entering the lists of the competitors for the "Big Town on the Maumee" he made an arrangement or conditional sale with one Samuel Allen, of Lockport, State of New York, of one hundred acres of land off the upper end of his tract, which was about to be laid off into city or village lots and offered for sale. About this time I made the acquaintance of Lewis Goddard, of Detroit, formerly of Lockport, a man of daring enterprise, restless ambition, and particularly calculated by his volubility of language and sanguine expectations, to unhinge any ordinary young man from the pursuit of plodding industry, and beget instead, notions and visions of acquiring sudden wealth by projects of speculation. I soon learned that Goddard had already contemplated interesting himself in the new town of Stickney and Allen, ... All hands agreed that a ball should come off on New Years evening, at Baldwin's old log storehouse, at or near the mouth of Swan Creek, the garret or upper story affording the best accommodations for a dance of any place to be obtained; and it did very well, without being lathed and plastered. Everybody turned out from the immediate neighborhood, and quite a number from Perrysburg, among whom were Capt. David Wilkinson and lady, who at that time sailed the schooner EAGLE, owned by the Hollisters, I think."[8]

"The Ball being over, all hands turned out to assist or to witness the commencement of laying out the new town, January 2nd, 1832, which about this time assumed the name of Vistula, and the old plat of the Ohio Company retained the name of Port Lawrence. Among the advantages of the old town, the mouth and deep channel of Swan Creek, as a safe place for vessels in the winter and spring from the effects of ice were considered paramount. There soon sprang up considerable rivalry between the upper town of Port Lawrence and the lower town of Vistula, ... Samuel Allen having previously sent a messenger to Maumee City to secure the services of Judge Rice to survey the new town, who declined for fear of displeasing Gen. Hunt, as was supposed, who was the principal citizen of Maumee at that time, and said to be the principal owner. Although, a family by the name of Forsyth were doing a heavy business of storage

Benjamin Franklin Stickney

and trade -- General Hunt being a brother-law of General Cass was supposed to possess advantages of influence excelled by none on the Maumee River. At all events, General Hunt did not visit the new town during the winter, and therefore did not incur the charge of being jealous of the new town. But occasionally some of the leading citizens of Maumee would put in an appearance, and affect to ridicule the new project of building up the new town on the Maumee. Monroe being a pretty smart place at this time, and in some measure presumed to rival Detroit, but from that date soon fell far in the rear. Myself, having opened a store, went to work cutting brush, carrying chain, and driving stakes and assisting generally in laying out the new town of Vistula. I had forgotten to say that upon being disappointed in getting Judge Rice, Seneca Allen, of Monroe was procured to take charge of surveying the new town, who proved to be competent for the task. My object in assisting the work was to get a practical knowledge of surveying, as I had a theoretical knowledge from books on surveying. I received seventy-five cents per day, and boarded myself, for my services. After things started sufficiently, Samuel Allen took in a man from Lockport, New York by the name of Otis Hathaway to take charge of the docking at the foot of Lagrange Street, which was the first point docked out on the plat of Vistula. I took the contract for furnishing timber which I procured on the south shore of the river at one half of one cent per foot standing, flattened it on two sides, hauled it to the river, drove in an iron wedge in one end and hitched a pony to the wedge, mounted a boy, and away went the sticks of timber over the smooth ice to the foot of Lagrange Street, and were immediately put into dock by Hathaway and his workmen. I think I furnished the timber, big white oak of the best kind, for three cents per foot, running measure delivered. I also took the job from Philo Bennett to furnish the hewn frame for a two story house or store on the south-east corner of Lagrange and Summit Streets, which was the first frame building on the new plat of Vistula. ...[9]"

Another early pioneer, Sanford L. Collins who came to Port Lawrence in December of 1831 would later write of that time in Toledo's history.

Benjamin Franklin Stickney

vistula, boundaries, & preparations
chapter fifteen

"Vistula was laid off and platted in 1832, and the clearing of the plat of brush and timber commenced; also the putting in of a long line of docking in the front of the property at the foot of Lagrange Street, extending down toward Elm Street some forty rods, or thereabouts. This line of docking was built upon the ice, and notwithstanding its great weight, it being some nine feet high, it did not break through until the ice began to give way in the spring; and of course while kept up by the ice it presented a very formidable appearance, so much so that it attracted the attention of our enterprising neighbors of Perrysburg who came down upon the ice with a large party to pay their respects to the new proprietors and witness the new mode of building docks without piling. After examining carefully they said it looked very well, but they thought it would disappear with ice in the spring, and perhaps the same might be the case with many of the new inhabitants in the coming months of July and August with fevers and agues which they most assuredly would have. The Spring came and, contrary to the predictions of our Perrysburg neighbors, the dock did not disappear, but it became greatly displaced; and so it was with the new settlers, they did not disappear, but had a great amount of shaking." [10]

One of the best descriptions of Port Lawrence and Vistula comes from the pen of Mrs. Samuel Allen.

"When my husband, Captain Allen[11], visited the Maumee Valley in October, 1831, the principal Ottawa Indian Village was located on the west or Manhattan side of the river near the bay and where the government made its payments to the tribe. Their hunting grounds were on the other side of the river. I remember well the beautiful road leading from Vistula to the Indian village. It was winding, and shaded by magnificent trees. We frequently rode thither with Major Stickney in his one horse wagon; and as we passed through the village, the little Indians would run out calling him – "Father! Father!" which would please Mr. Stickney greatly. What is now (1872) chiefly the track of Summit Street, formed then a charming ride through a delightful forest. The banks of the river, at some sections, were bold, high bluffs, and

Benjamin Franklin Stickney

graceful little fawns and flocks of wild turkeys, in season, often crossed our path as we were riding, and would disappear in the deep woods back from the river."

"The Vistula section of the town was surveyed by Seneca Allen[12]. The streets bear the names originally given them - myself naming LaGrange[13] in memory of the home, in France, of Lafayette. Major Stickney gave Summit Street its name; and Captain Allen suggested the names of all the others. During the Autumn of 1831 our family returned to Lockport, and in the winter following Captain Allen re-appeared with a force of hands and built the first wharf in the new town (Vistula) at the foot of LaGrange Street. After the opening of Lake Navigation in the spring of 1832, our whole family removed to Vistula. At Buffalo my husband chartered a steamboat, the PIONEER and freighted her with the family, servants, workmen, goods, and provisions; and on the last day of May, 1832, passengers and goods were landed at Vistula."

"The Indians were uniformly kind and hospitable. Their title was extinguished by treaty made on the part of the United States by the Territorial Governor of Michigan, in 1833. The Canadian French suggestions regarding the diseases then peculiar to the country, and means to avoid them, were ascertained to be valuable." [14]

With the lumber provided by Slocum, Cornelius G. Shaw[15] a carpenter and joiner by trade, built the first frame house in Vistula at the corner of Summit and Locust Streets. Shaw would later build the first jail for Lucas County at the corner of Summit and Cherry. [16]

When the ice melted across Lake Erie and the Maumee River, an attempt was made on the part of the business owners and land owners spearheaded by Mr. Lewis Goddard[17] to make an arrangement with several of the passenger boats loaded with immigrants running from Buffalo to Detroit, to make Vistula a regularly scheduled stop on their scheduled run.

Benjamin Franklin Stickney

Mr. Goddard was able to come to terms with the master of the steamer *PIONEER*[18] to run between here and Sandusky. The *PIONEER* would then meet the regularly scheduled boats at Sandusky[19], transfer the immigrants and their belongings, and bring them directly to the docks at the foot of Vistula's Lagrange Street. To further facilitate the immigrants travel arrangements, Stickney sent his son Two Stickney to Buffalo to aid the settlers in their travel west. And of course, to direct them to Vistula with the assurance that a boat would be waiting for them in Sandusky to facilitate their journey.

This is the only known picture of Two Stickney. Courtesy of the Toledo Lucas County Public Library.

An example of this arrangement with the steamer *PIONEER* and the developing settlement of Vistula was found in the Journal of B. J. Harvey.

"June 4th: At 7 o'clock this morning we left this place for Vistula we had a strong fair wind and moved very rapidly. About 1 in the afternoon when 15 miles from Vistula one of the shafts of our

boat broke, and in such manner the steam could not be applied, but fortunately the wind being fair, by means of a sail we reached Vistula about 5 P.M. …. This is a newly laid out town on the left bank of the Maumee three miles from its mouth, has a fine harbor, the river here being a half mile in width, the town is to be built on a high piece of table land commanding a fine view of the river. This will eventually be a place of importance as it will accommodate the Territory of Michigan better than any other port on Lake Erie being some miles farther west than Munroe or Detroit. …" [20]

From the June, 1832 issue of the *The Ohio and Michigan Register and Emigrant's Guide*[21] published by Jesup W. Scott, Perrysburg was described by a correspondent D. B. who said: "… that the town had an indifferent courthouse, two taverns, one store, and forty or fifty dwellings and shops. Land could be had in the neighborhood at from $1.25 to $10.00 per acre. The outlet of the Miami & Erie Canal was then supposed to lie between Perrysburg and Maumee City, the towns below those points then being understood as probably belonging to Michigan."

Continuing in his description of the Perrysburg area correspondent D. B. spoke about the village of Vistula:

"The new town, Vistula, just being born, and mentioned in your last, makes a great noise, and attracts much attention from the numerous immigrants who are seeking the most eligible site for a town on the Maumee. A considerable number of lots, according to the information obtained from Maj. B. F. Stickney, one of the proprietors, had been sold in the course of the spring and summer, and improvements of a permanent character and on a large scale engaged to be made. This nascent village is handsomely situated on the left bank of the Maumee River, about three miles from its mouth, and immediately below the site of Port Lawrence. These places will probably some day grow together and become one, provided my opinion shall turn out to be correct, that the great town of the Maumee shall be situated there." [22]

Benjamin Franklin Stickney

vistula, boundaries, & preparations
chapter fifteen

Jesup Scott visited Vistula and Port Lawrence in 1832, and would later write his *Recollection* of the trip starting as an installment article in 1844 and finishing in 1857. In Scott's first installment he writes:

"In June, 1832, I visited the country at the mouth of the Maumee. My residence was then temporarily at Florence, then in Huron, now Erie County, Ohio. Although I had for years held in high estimation some indefinite good place for a city on the harbor formed by the entrance of the Maumee into the lake, I had not taken the trouble to visit it, until I read in the National Intelligencer, an article from the pen of Maj. Benjamin F. Stickney, in which it was stated that the plan of a town - indeed of a city - had been laid out by some enterprising gentlemen from the State of New York, and setting forth the advantages of its position. This called up the desire to see the site of a city that might one day be great; and I accordingly mounted my horse, and, passing through Milan, then one of the largest places in Northern Ohio, Lower Sandusky (now Fremont, and then a place of some promise, and some 300 or 400 people), and thence along the thirty-one miles of road through the swamp to Perrysburg, thence crossing, by ford, the Maumee, above the old town of the same name, I, with some difficulty found my way along the Monroe Turnpike, and thence from Section 16, T.3, U.S.R., by a rude path through the openings and woods to the mouth of the Swan Creek, and thence down along the river bank, mostly through the forest, to the new town of Vistula; and below to the residence of Major Stickney..... A few board shanties had been put up on Summit Street near Lagrange, and some men were at work grading down what is now the foot of Lagrange Street, preparing a wharf for the landing of vessels. At the gate of the brick house now standing (1844) - I overtook Major Stickney and Samuel Allen (known as Captain Allen), the Major's associate in laying out the new town. The Major received my address in his own courteous, grave manner, and Mr. Allen in that prompt business style, and with an air that might have become one of the solid men of Boston, accustomed to shake State Street by his stately tread. I told them my errand was to see where the mighty city site of the Maumee should be, and to

Benjamin Franklin Stickney

write about it - perhaps to make some purchase, if I should be satisfied that this was the right spot. Mr. Allen kept, as a boarding house, temporarily, the residence of the Major for the accommodation of the persons coming to settle or purchase in the new plat, or in the neighborhood. There I domiciled myself for a few days to look about." [23]

On an inspection tour of his property[24] that he purchased in 1832, Jesup Scott and J. Austin Scott became lost in the Mud Creek swamp near what is now the corner of Huron and Adams Streets. Only the whistle of a steamboat passing by on the Maumee River guided them back to familiar ground.

The forced migration of the area's Indians came to the forefront with rumors of the Black Hawk Indian War in Illinois reaching the Maumee Valley. Residents were so frightened of their Indian neighbors that the alarm traveled from neighbor to neighbor throughout the Maumee Valley of possible Indian reprisals. Traveling unspoken with the alarm was the need to remove the Ottawa Indians to the West of the Mississippi River.[25]

Black Hawk. Courtesy of Michigan History, 4 volumes, Publishing Society of Michigan, 1906.

Benjamin Franklin Stickney

The Ottawas' in preparation of their removal from the Maumee Valley wanted to be vaccinated against the smallpox which was rumored to be spreading through the west. Bowing to their request, they were inoculated against smallpox by Dr. Oscar White[26] who was paid for each vaccination[27].

Realizing that the plight of the Ottawas was inevitable, the Rev. Isaac Van Tassel wrote:

"In my last, I wrote you that some of the Indians had agreed to go west of the Mississippi. I think now they will settle down with the others, and remain till the rest of their land is taken from them. They are more willing to receive instruction."

Within days of meeting with the Ottawa delegation, Michigan's Territorial Governor George Porter wrote to Secretary of War Cass and informed him that the Michigan Ottawas' did not want to go west, but instead they had considered Ontario's Walpole Island. Shortly after he wrote Sec. Cass about the possibility Canada's Walpole Island Governor Porter died after a four day illness in Detroit[28].

"I have no hesitation in saying, that this tribe are desirous of selling their land, but from all I can learn, they do not wish to remove west to the Mississippi. They are rather inclined to go to Canada, or somewhere in our vicinity." [29]

Dresden Howard who was employed as an interpreter for the Ottawas would later write in *Recollections of Old Winameg* the following: *"I may be censured for my sympathy for these poor wandering people driven from place to place and finally exterminated. But I still say, It would have been better to give them homes and make friends of them, than to rob and starve and alienate them, as we did."*

The Ottawa Indians still demanded that the shortage of almost six hundred dollars in last year's annuity given to them by Lloyd, be corrected to their advantage in their conversations with

James Jackson[30] their new agent. On the other hand, Governor Porter before he died recalled the incident in a September of 1832 memorandum.

"... If they had anything to complain of, they must do it to him. This was the first time he had heard of their complaint against Lloyd. He was Dead. They had given him their receipt for the money, & on the papers all appears right. ..... They also complained of being cheated in their bargain with the whites. If they were cheated, it was because they drank too much whiskey, & did not know what they were about. If we wanted to get their land for nothing, when we were making a bargain for it, we would give them plenty of whiskey. ..."[31]

Even the land that they considered the Ottawa *Burying Ground* had been turned over to the Government with the Treaty of 1833. With the treaty duly signed and witnessed and on its way to Washington, the words of Forsyth, Peter Menard, and She-wu-naw, as conveyed through agent Jackson, would have little effect on the treaty's outcome. As a last effort to remain on their ancestral land they offered to follow the *white man's* example and farm the land. The Ottawas had offered to pay the asking price for title to a hundred acres *to kindle a fire and pray for their dead.* But by this time no one was listening. The last council fires of the Ottawa Indians in the Maumee Valley had been extinguished, and would only be remembered by the tribal elders.

In one of his last letters from the mission, the Rev. VanTassel in 1833 wrote to the *Missionary Herald at Home and Abroad:*

"Last Fall the Ottawa Indians residing on the Maumee River sold the only tract of land remaining in their possession to the United States; by which act this unhappy remnant, embracing 600 or 700 persons, are left wholly destitute of country or home, except a few small reservations retained by the principal men. They still persist in refusing to accept a country west of the Mississippi river, and though strongly urged to remove thither, very few have consented. At the suggestion of Mr. VanTassel the Committee

authorized him to offer them the use of a portion of the mission lands, which amount to 600 or 700 acres, provided they would erect buildings and open fields upon them, abandon their unsettled mode of life and the use of intoxicating liquors, and would avail themselves of the advantages offered for obtaining religious instruction and educating their children.

They have, however, with the exception of ten or twelve families, treated this offer with much indifference. Their present condition, with no fixed place of residence, and exposed to almost every species of temptation from the surrounding white settlers, who are pressing in upon them, is nearly as unfavorable as possible to their improvement in any respect. Should no favorable change take place before the ensuing spring, it will probably be expedient to discontinue the mission."

Meanwhile, Stickney withdrew from the Port Lawrence land syndicate, to devote his efforts to the development of Vistula. As a consequence, William Oliver[32] resurrected the village of Port Lawrence with a land swap with the University of Michigan. The University of Michigan's land grants came from an 1804 Congressional grant of one section of township land for a learning seminary, and in 1826 they chose river tracts one and two. Three additional sections were granted by the Indians at the Treaty of Fort Meigs, and the four sections of land were within the village of Port Lawrence which at one time was thought to be in the Territory of Michigan. As Ohio's canal plans advanced William Oliver approached the University's trustees in 1831 and traded other land tracts that he owned to get back the two river tracts.

This land speculation enabled the partners to gain possession of the two river tracts[33] they wanted. Centered on Swan Creek and the Maumee River, Oliver surveyed the land into residential lots and sold the first one on July 13th of 1833. At the eastern end of Port Lawrence, Vistula's first lot, number 958, was sold to Erie Long for $75 in late December of the same year. The new partnership along with their current land holdings were filed with the recorder in Port Lawrence Township, Monroe County, Territory of Michigan.

Benjamin Franklin Stickney

Stickney, similar to the New Years of 1832, welcomed all his friends and neighbors to a 1833 Grand New Year's Ball. Held in the second floor of John Baldwin's Port Lawrence warehouse, they celebrated the one year anniversary of Stickney's new town of Vistula.

With the warm winds of spring beginning to flow across the Maumee River, Benjamin Franklin Stickney had used the winter months to confer with the men of vision that resided in the Maumee Valley. They had spent their winter months huddled around fireplaces talking about the new form of transportation that was transforming the east. In 1828 the Baltimore & Ohio Railroad was vastly becoming Baltimore's cheapest way to transit western goods to their door. Railroads were superior to canals in freight cost, time in transit, and year round transportation regardless of the weather. The railroads were becoming the investment that could not fail. They named the proposed railroad on April 22, 1833 the Erie & Kalamazoo Railroad, and applied for a charter from the State of Ohio[34].

With the Maumee Valley's success in transportation and commerce, Indian tribulations were still on everyone's mind. A little over two months later, sub-Indian Agent James Jackson needlessly alarmed Ohio and Michigan about rumors of an intended Indian uprising in the Maumee Valley.

"Yesterday we had a report of an intended uprising of several tribes of Indians in this place shortly. The information came by an old Ottawa named Su Sa, stating that a few days ago 4 Pottawattomys with ####### Wampum Belt took counsel with the Ottawas in which number was Was-y-on-Quit [35] who received the Wampum Belt to wage war with the Government of America. The people towards the Rapids were in great alarm, being informed that 4 or 5 tribes were bound together in this business. In consequence of the information I sent for Was y on Quit who stated before Mr. R. A. Forsyth and others that a Council was held to take into consideration their moving west of the Mississippi, and that they expected fighting with the Indians

on the new hunting ground. Wanted the Ottawas to join them in Battle if necessary...."[36]

With all the talk in the Maumee Valley centered on railroads as the wave of the transportation future, Austin E. Wing[37] of Monroe County continued to promote the River Raisin ship canal to General Gratiot[38] in October of 1833.

The Ohio Legislature in March of 1834 finally authorized the construction of the canal from the mouth of the Maumee River to the Indiana state line. With the completion in 1833 of the Ohio Canal from Portsmouth to Cleveland, the tolls for the Ohio canal were expected to rival those of the Erie Canal in New York. Actually Ohio had a hidden agenda for waiting. The national debt of the United States was almost extinguished in 1834, and the surplus in the Treasury was expected to be returned to the States. Therefore, the money for the construction of one of the last legs of the Ohio Canal system would now be in place. Another aspect of this inquiry was that Ohio had received from Congress in 1828 a grant of Federal lands of 438,301 acres for extending the Miami Canal from Dayton to the Maumee River, and another grant of 500,000 acres for general canal building purposes.

This action by the Ohio Legislature was a clear signal to the population of the disputed Toledo Strip that Ohio was serious in its intentions to develop the area. B. F. Stickney correctly believed that if Michigan continued its possession of the disputed territory it would block the completion of the proposed canal. This action on the part of Michigan would promote the commercial development of Monroe and its main terminal of Detroit.

Stickney would later write in his autobiography: *"... It was evident that where the united canals, which traversed the two richest valleys in the west, terminated, a great commercial city must arise. The idea that Michigan should control this location -- this great distributing office of the commerce of the west, was not to be endured. Ohio wanted to develop it -- Michigan wanted*

Benjamin Franklin Stickney

to prevent its development. She was aware that if properly improved, it would injure Detroit and ruin Monroe. ..."

Another worry that faced Ohio was Washington City's public opinion. If Ohio took the disputed strip from Michigan by force it would have the appearance of a Biblical David and Goliath confrontation, and the public's sentiment would side with Michigan. Also if the *disputed or Toledo Strip* was resolved by law, the Courts would side with Michigan.

Therefore the one essential item in Stickney's plan to gain control of the *Toledo Strip* was that Michigan had to be branded the regional aggressor. Stickney in an exceptionally brilliant plan to gain control of the disputed territory known as the Toledo Strip, urged the Territory of Michigan into adopting and passing the *Bill of Pains & Penalties Act*[39]. In his own words from Stickney's autobiography he explained the trickery:

"In the fall of 1833, I determined to attend the ensuing session of Congress, to do what might be in my power to urge on a decision of the important question. The session of the Ohio Legislature, of the Legislative Council of Michigan and of Congress met about the same time. Through the aid of a confidential friend, and for the purpose of getting up what I conceived to be the necessary excitement, I caused a suggestion to be made to several of the members of the Legislative Council, to the effect that they might derive great benefit from the passage of a law, inflicting heavy pains and penalties upon any who should acknowledge any other authority, than such as should be derived from the territory, within her limits. Soon after my arrival at Washington, I was informed that the plan had taken well, and that a bill of a very strong character, was drawn and passed, with one of two dissenting votes. There was in the Legislative Council, Daniel S. Bacon[40]*, a man of more coolness and forecast than the rest, who saw the effect that would be likely to follow. He prevailed upon the Council to re-consider or lay on the table. Bacon wrote his views of the matter to Austin E. Wing, who was then at Washington as an Agent for the territory. Wing consulted Gen.*

Benjamin Franklin Stickney

Cass, then Secretary of War. They agreed with Bacon, and Wing, with the assistance of Cass, wrote Bacon a very able letter, denouncing the bill of Pains and Penalties. This was shown to the Council and it put the bill to rest. Bacon wrote Wing another letter, extolling his services very highly for having written so fine a letter. Proud of his performance, and not being aware of my plans and views, wing read to me the entire correspondence. Lucius Lyon[41] was then a delegate in Congress from the territory. He was a man of warm, impetuous temperament and moderate forecast. The Governor and a majority of the Legislative Council of Michigan were of the same pattern. Lyon had much more influence with them than such men as Wing and Bacon. I requested three members of Congress, friends of mine, to have a conversation with Lyon, and make the impression upon him, that some immediate and decisive action was necessary on the part of Michigan, to determine Congress to decide the boundary question in their favor. Lyon took the bait, and wrote immediately to the Council at Detroit, urging them to pass the bill of Pains and Penalties. It was passed, with no other opposition than that of Bacon."

Supplementing his explanation, Stickney continued:

"The Legislature of Ohio, being now in session, as soon as the mail could carry the proceedings of the Michigan Council to Columbus, it kindled a fire as violent as any of us could have desired. It worked even better than we had anticipated. The Legislature authorized the Governor to call out ten-thousand militia; placed between the two and three hundred thousand dollars at his command to defray the expenses; authorized him to appoint Commissioners to re-mark the Harris Line, appoint executive officers, and organize government on the disputed territory, &c. The fire soon reached Washington. A warm correspondence ensued between the Secretary of State and the Governor of Ohio. A young hotspur by the name of Mason[42] was the acting Governor of Michigan. He showed but little disposition to be under the control of the general Government."

Benjamin Franklin Stickney

J. Baron Davis a tenant of Vistula's *Bachelor's Hall* judged the resident's of the Toledo Strip correctly when he stated:

"...... *Well it doesn't matter which survey is correct; we claim that the Northerly line is the boundary between Ohio and Territory of Michigan. It has been in Congress for a number of years, and they have done nothing with it, and they never will till there is a fuss; and the only thing that we can do to settle the question, is for us of Port Lawrence and Vistula to declare ourselves under the authority of Ohio, elect our judicial officers, which will arouse Michigan, and there will be war, and we'll get up a stir and interest sufficient to have Congress settle the boundary question. Ohio has thirteen members of Congress, Michigan is a Territory with little representation, and as Congress is strongly Democratic, we can make it a political question, and shove the thing right through. ....*"[43]

When Michigan started to enforce Stickney's premeditated *Bill of Pains & Penalties Act,* the well planned and executed understanding to decide the Ohio Michigan boundary dispute, the Toledo War ... was just minutes from execution.

Endnotes from Chapter Fifteen
vistula, boundaries, & preparations

[1] Porter was a lawyer from Pennsylvania that came to Cass's attention when he served as the United States Marshall for the eastern district of Pennsylvania.

[2] After obtaining a copy of the petition against him, Mason determined that over 142 of the 162 signatures were members of the Anti-masonic Party and supporters of Henry Clay.

[3] Thursday, October 13, 1831.

[4] *The Autobiography of Benjamin Franklin Stickney,* the 1858 Toledo City Directory, pgs 52-70.

[5] The location would be in the middle of Summit Street near the intersection of Bush Street. Stickney's home included the defunct Riverside Hospital to the Maumee River.

[6] Vistula is the Latinized version of the polish Wisla.

Benjamin Franklin Stickney

[7] Sanford L. Collins operated a small mercantile store in Vistula in 1828 near the corner of Summit and Lagrange streets under the firm of Goddard & Briggs.

[8] Excerpted from *"The 1831 Narrative of Giles Bryan Slocum."* The reminiscence was written in 1875. Toledo Lucas County Public Library.

[9] Excerpted from *"The 1831 Narrative of Giles Bryan Slocum."* The reminiscence was written in 1875. Toledo Lucas County Public Library.

[10] History of the Maumee Valley, H.S.Knapp, Toledo, 1877.

[11] Entered into various developments with Stickney, brought his family to Toledo 1831.

[12] Seneca Allen was born in Vermont and was a surveyor by trade. He moved to Monroe, Michigan in 1827 and taught school during the winter months. He platted and laid out the village of Vistula (Ohio) in early 1832, also the towns of Trenton and Flat Rock, Michigan Territory. In the Fall of 1829 he opened a dry goods store where Manhattan, Ohio was located with Dan Miller as a partner. The store was designed to trade with the Indians. He was also a Justice of the Peace for the south side of the Maumee River. Opened a trading post with the Indians at Roche de Bout, where Isaac Richardson had a mill. Was elected first Worshipful Master of Monroe's Masonic lodge on Wednesday, October 29, 1824.

[13] An opposing thought is brought forth by George A. Chase in an article which appeared in the April 9, 1909 issue of the *TOLEDO DAILY BLADE*: *"Stickney named his principal street Lagrange, after Joseph Louis Lagrange, a mathematician of the highest rank, born in Turin, Italy, in 1736. In the advancement of almost every branch of pure mathematics Lagrange took a conspicuous part."*

[14] History of the Maumee Valley, H.S.Knapp, Toledo, 1877.

[15] Shaw and family left their first cabin in Stony Point, north of Monroe, and traveled by row boat with all their possessions to Vistula. He was Sheriff Munson H. Daniel's deputy in 1836, and was elected Sheriff of Lucas County in 1837 and 1839.

[16] Some historians have erroneously claimed or hinted that the jail was located at the corner of Water and Cherry Streets.

[17] Lewis Goddard was in partnership with Sanford L. Collins in a mercantile store at Summit and Lagrange.

[18] The *Pioneer* was a steamer with a paddle wheel on both sides of its hull. Reports would later indicate that they *Pioneer* made very few runs between Sandusky and Vistula before being discontinued.

[19] Before settling on its present name Sandusky was first referred to as Portland, and later by Ogontz Place. The use of the name Portland probably came from the Portland House, an early hotel, which was located at the present site of the SANDUSKY REGISTER building. The stage coach, which provided basic land transportation, left from this hotel for points east and west.

[20] The Journal of B. J. Harvey, Historical Society of Northwestern Ohio, July 1934.

[21] Published as a monthly periodical at Florence, Huron [now Erie] County in 1831 by Jesup W. Scott.

[22] June, 1832 issue of the *The Ohio and Michigan Register and Emigrant's Guide*

[23] Toledo Lucas County Public Library.

[24] Jesup Scott purchased seventy acres of land in what is now considered downtown Toledo. Which included the present sites of the Lucas County Courthouse and the Toledo Lucas County Public Library.

[25] An interesting sidelight was that the steamer *Henry Clay* was destined for Chicago with 370 troops on board for the Black Hawk War. The steamer docked at Detroit overnight. One of the soldiers died of cholera and in the resulting panic Cholera was dispersed throughout the Detroit area by the ship's deserters. For further information I would suggest Captain Henry Whiting's accounts of the Cholera epidemic.

[26] Dr. Oscar White was the doctor who inoculated the Indians. The Indians thought that the vaccination was a plot for their extermination. Dr. White was saved from death by the arrival of his interpreter who explained the concept to the Ottawas. White came to the Maumee Valley from New Hampshire in 1829 and formed a partnership with Dr. Conant. White's mother was the grand-daughter of General Israel Putnam. White would later marry Miss Anna Maria Jackson, the daughter of James Jackson, the sub-Indian Agent for the Ottawas in 1832.

[27] Various accounts place the number at around 800 vaccinations.

[28] July 6, 1834.

[29] Letter from Governor Porter to Lewis Cass Wednesday, July 4th, 1832.

[30] James Jackson was from Tennessee and was a first cousin of President Andrew Jackson. He was the third Collector of Customs for the Ports of

Maumee and Perrysburg. He was succeeded in that office in 1835 by Charles C. P. Hunt. He followed Lemuel Lloyd in 1831 as Sub-Agent for the Ottaways. In 1836 James Jackson and James H. Forsyth plotted the village of Swanton. James Jackson while living in the Port Lawrence/Vistula vicinity organized the first Methodist Class in his home on "the Point" over on Broadway Street. It has been alluded to by several authors on President Andrew Jackson that James Jackson was Andrew's step brother; however the reality was that James was his first cousin.

[31] Friday, September 21, 1832, Memorandum of a Talk with the Ottawas held by George Porter.

[32] Major William Oliver originally from Cincinnati, fought under Harrison at Fort Meigs and in the War of 1812. After the War with other speculators formed the Baum Company and purchased some of the first land in the Toledo area from the sale held in Wooster, Ohio. Oliver and Baum built the log house (warehouse) at the foot of Monroe Street. Major Oliver started building the landmark Oliver House hotel in 1853. His son in law, James Hall, continued building the hotel after Oliver died.

[33] The plat was bounded by present day Jefferson Avenue, Swan Creek, Superior Street and the Maumee River.

[34] The original incorporators of the Erie & Kalamazoo Railroad were: Stevens B. Comstock, Benjamin Franklin Stickney, David White, Caius C. Robinson, Darius Comstock, Asahel Finch, E. Conant Winter, Seth Dunham, Silas Holbrook, Stephen Vickery, and Edwin H. Lathrop.

Later after the initial investment of $50,000 had been met, other prominent businessmen bought stock. They were: David S. Bacon, Jacob A. Baker, Edward Bissell, Joseph Chittenden, Addison J. Comstock, George Crane, William P. Daniels, Joseph Gibbon, Dr. Caleb Ormsby, and Andrew Palmer.

[35] Was-se-on-o-quet, *"fair Sky,"* was considered the ruling chief of the Maumee Valley Ottawas, and grandson of Pontiac.
Maumee Valley Indian Sub-Agent, James Jackson, in a January 24, 1834, letter to Gov. Porter describes Was-se-on-o-quet as follows: *".... It is but right you should know that he is a most notorious drunkard, gambler, and squanderer of everything he can get a hold of. So that if he gets any but his own the poor Indians will never see one cent."*

[36] Letter from Jackson to Gov. Porter on Wednesday, July 24th, 1833.
[37] Austin Wing came to Detroit in 1814 but soon moved to Monroe. For a number of years he was a sheriff for the Michigan Territory, a farmer,

and lawyer. Formed the present government of Michigan and was instrumental in Michigan becoming a state.

[38] One of four French youths appointed by President Jefferson to West Point after the Louisiana Purchase. Graduated as an engineer; in 1819-29 planned and erected the defenses of Hampton Roads, including fortress Monroe, and from 1828 to 1838 was chief engineer of the army with the rank of Brigadier General.

[39] *The Bill of Pains & Penalties Act* was designed by Stickney acting as a friend of Michigan, designed the bill to extend harsh fines and prison terms to any Ohio resident who sought to extend Ohio control over Michigan territory. In other words a person who favored Ohio that lived in the Toledo Strip could not do anything favoring Ohio over Michigan in control over the disputed area.

[40] One of the most popular men from Monroe County. From New York, Bacon taught school on the River Raisin and became a partner of Levi Humphrey in business. Bacon became a lawyer and later a judge. President of the Bank of Monroe and a director of the Michigan Southern Railroad, Bacon will probably be remembered most for his daughter Elizabeth. Elizabeth or Libby married General George Armstrong Custer.

[41] Never married, Lyons was a Territorial delegate to Congress from 1832 to 1835, a United States Senator from the State of Michigan from 1835-1840. A surveyor by profession he was appointed Surveyor General of Ohio, Indiana, and Michigan in 1845. Lived primarily in Detroit.

[42] Stevens T. Mason was the Secretary of the Territory of Michigan and in George Porter's absence would fill in for him. Porter died in Detroit on Sunday, July 6th, 1834. Although widely reported, Porter's death after an illness of just four days was not caused by Cholera. [*Democratic Free Press, July 9th, 1834*] This left Stevens T. Mason as acting Governor of the Territory of Michigan. Mason read for the law during Porter's time as Governor of the Michigan Territory, and after attending a series of lectures at Detroit's Steamboat Hotel was admitted to the bar on December 11, 1833.

[43] History of the City of Toledo and Lucas County Ohio, Clark Waggoner, Munsell & Co. 1888, page 292.

Benjamin Franklin Stickney

war fever, robins, & prison
chapter sixteen

The disputed territory or Toledo strip which was located between the Harris survey and the Fulton survey contained the port of Toledo. Access to the Great Lakes was so important to Michigan that in 1835 she almost went to war with her southern neighbor, Ohio.

United States Surveyor General Edward Tiffin. Courtesy of Howe's Historical Collections of Ohio, 1896.

Surveyor William Harris received Instructions from the United States Surveyor General Edward Tiffin in 1817 to mark the northern boundary of the State of Ohio. Tiffin, who was a past governor of Ohio, instructed that the boundary would be run from the southern tip of Lake Michigan to the northern tip of the Maumee Bay. When surveyor John A. Fulton remarked Ohio's northern boundary in 1818 due east from the southern tip of Lake Michigan the surveyors found that the Harris line

Benjamin Franklin Stickney

intersected Lake Erie a little over seven and one half miles to the north from where it should have been. This discrepancy placed the port of Toledo in the territory of Michigan.

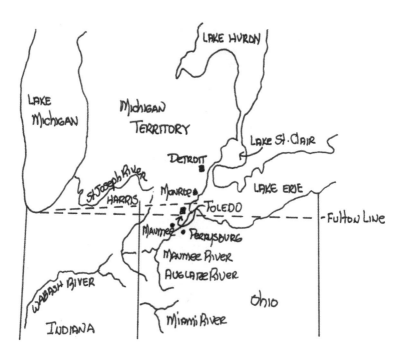

The Harris Line is top most dotted line, and the dotted Fulton Line is located just blow the Harris Line. The Toledo Strip is the land between the two dotted lines and the eastern boundary of the State of Indiana.

Both of the protagonists of the *Toledo War*; Ohio's Governor Robert Lucas and Michigan's Territorial Governor Stevens T. Mason[1] were both stubborn Virginia Democrats. Robert Lucas, a long time friend of President Andrew Jackson, was named Chairman of the Democratic Party's first nominating convention[2] in Baltimore, Maryland. During the ensuing election campaign the Jackson-VanBuren ticket carried Ohio, and with President

war fever, robins, & prison
chapter sixteen

Jackson's prestige Robert Lucas defeated his opponent Darius Lyman for governor of Ohio by over 8,000 votes. The steady hand of Governor Robert Lucas[3] coupled with the stable and covert influence of Benjamin Franklin Stickney would guide the State of Ohio through the tenuous months of *the Toledo War.*

Governor Robert Lucas. Courtesy of the Toledo Lucas County Public Library.

The active agitation for Michigan statehood began as early as 1831. There had been earlier false starts such as an editorial in the Detroit *Gazette* on October 8, 1824, that had put forth the view that with the present progress in population and settlement, Michigan would be eligible for statehood in 1826. Also the Detroit *Free Press* of September 8, 1831, forecast a sufficient population *"in a year or so,"* so that vote for statehood could take place in 1832. A favorable vote on statehood was taken in 1832, but the total voter turnout was not sufficient for Congressional requirements. [4]

Benjamin Franklin Stickney

war fever, robins, & prison
chapter sixteen

With the 1836 presidential election in the offing, once the politicians connected the border question to statehood the question was no longer in doubt. The power belonged to the state, not the territory that could deliver the electoral vote in the 1836 presidential election. One of the consequences of Michigan's actions at the hands of Mason was that the Michigan Territory would be denied Statehood for another two years.

Michigan Territorial Governor Stevens T. Mason. Courtesy of the Toledo Lucas County Public Library.

The first issue of the Port Lawrence *HERALD* [5] on the 15th of April 1834 followed the dictates of Ohio's Democratic Governor and Legislature. The *HERALD's* editor was Andrew Palmer, and the publisher was James Browne. An ardent Democrat for Ohio's territorial rights, Palmer soon began to reprint many of the articles contained in the Columbus Democratic newspaper, the *WESTERN HEMISPHERE*.

Palmer's offices along with J. Baron Davis were in the Vistula building called the Bachelor's Hall, on Summit Street between Locust and Walnut. The Hall was noted by Vistula's residents as the headquarters of the pro-Ohio faction.

Benjamin Franklin Stickney

war fever, robins, & prison
chapter sixteen

Dr. Jacob Clark who came into the area in early 1834 also resided at the Bachelor's Hall. Dr. Clark's opinion of the canal's location echoed that of the canal's engineer. The Maumee River, between Maumee and Toledo, was not suitable for the lake vessels that would be necessary to carry the canal trade to the eastern markets.

At a public meeting held in Toledo in November of 1834 some of the Port Lawrence and Vistula's early residents repeated the sentiments of Captain Samuel Allen. *".... the geographical position of Toledo identified it in interest with and made it properly a part of Michigan. The Black Swamp, lying at the east and south, practically cut off Toledo from Ohio, with which for many years there could be but little communication. On the other hand, the town lay immediately on the border of the most improved portion of Michigan, with which it was already in direct communication by water, by railroad and otherwise. In Michigan, Toledo would become the "pet" of the Territory."* After both sides expressed their thoughts and feelings on the subject the prevailing opinion of those that lived in Vistula and Port Lawrence, later known as Toledo, was that their destiny and financial wellbeing was with Ohio. While Stickney developed the political strategy, J. Baron. Davis and others would provide the substantial gust of wind needed for the political solution.

Tactics and strategy devised by Stickney and implemented by men like Davis were the real master minds behind Ohio's struggle for the Toledo Strip. Stickney, one of the areas largest land holders, would skillfully guide Ohio's response to any action by Michigan. It was Stickney's idea to make the residents of Michigan act as the aggressors, and by urging restraint on Ohio's part; Ohio would gain the support of the President and Congress. Stickney correctly believed that the dispute would be settled politically, not judicially.

Progress in the construction of the Miami and Erie Canal was exceptionally slow, and when the Ohio Canal was completed in 1833 different plans were conceived to avoid the Ohio Michigan

Benjamin Franklin Stickney

Boundary issue. The concept of Ohio constructing a canal that would channel the trade from the interior, and then having this business terminate in a Michigan port (Toledo) was intolerable. While Ohio and Michigan kept their war of words at a fever pitch, others were working on a solution that neither State would appreciate.

If Toledo could not reach an agreement others could. Several residents of Sandusky, Ohio, formed the Sandusky Bay Navigation Company to pursue for itself the terminus of the Miami and Erie Canal. Oran Follet and others reasoned that the Maumee and Sandusky Bays could be joined by using Mud Creek, the Portage River, and a short canal of two miles in length. If such a canal and terminus came to fruition, the Lake voyage to the East could be reduced by 70 miles.

Land speculation was never far from the surface, and the arrival of 1835 brought major changes to the Maumee Valley. The Port Lawrence Company was dissolved, and the eleven stock holders divided their holdings into separate land ownership. Two lots were set aside for school buildings, two more for churches, five acres for county purposes, and lot 335 for one dollar was voted to be given to Mrs. Harriet Daniels, wife of Munson Daniels. *"As a complimentary present on the occasion of her being the first marriage at Toledo,"* Mr. & Mrs. William Oliver graciously paid the dollar.

Expecting Toledo and the canal's terminus to be in Michigan, Secretary of War Lewis Cass and several leading men of the State of New York[6], generally known as the Cass Company, purchased the lands on the south side of the River Raisin. Expecting windfall profits, Austin E. Wing said that the land included the entire river front at, or near, the head of navigation on both sides of the Raisin adjacent to the Lake Erie shipping.

Responding to Mason's offer of mediation, Governor Lucas in a February 6, 1835 message to the legislature, urged passage of an act extending the boundaries of Ohio's northern counties to the Harris Line of 1817. Accompanying this legislation was the

Benjamin Franklin Stickney

war fever, robins, & prison
chapter sixteen

order that the northern counties enforce the laws of Ohio to their proper border, as defined by the Harris line.

Just six days later on Thursday, February 12, 1835 the Michigan Territorial Legislature passed the *Bill of Pains and Penalties*. This was exactly what Stickney and three trusted Michigan legislators had planned for.[7] This legislation was clearly aimed at any attempt by Ohio to act jurisdictionally in the Toledo Strip. Michigan had been duped, because any attempt by Ohio to enforce its laws would have to be stopped by force. And this force would be the Michigan militia not the local authorities.

The crux of the whole problem was that both Ohio and Michigan wanted the Maumee Bay for their port on Lake Erie. President Jackson tried to keep out of the fight on the grounds it was a Congressional problem. That was, until the presidential election loomed on the horizon.

Just as Stickney intended, two weeks after Lucas ordered officials in the border counties to enforce Ohio law's to the Harris line, on February 19, 1835, Michigan's Territorial Governor Mason[8], authorized General Joseph W. Brown[9] to take the necessary measures to prevent Ohio officials from enforcing the law in the *Toledo Strip*. General Brown was urged to take a conciliatory policy, but he was to enforce the *Pains and Penalties Act* even if he had to call out the Michigan militia.

PUBLIC NOTICE

The citizens of that part of Ohio, lying north of an east and west line drawn through the southern extreme or bend of Lake Michigan, and which has heretofore been under the temporary jurisdiction of the Territorial Government of Michigan, are requested to meet at the new building of the Messrs. Collins, in Tremainsville, on Saturday next, the 28th February instant, at 3 o'clock P.M. to take into consideration the recent Legislative enactments, affecting their rights as citizens of a free, sovereign and independent state of the Union. A general attendance of the people is required.

Benjamin Franklin Stickney

Charles Blivens would later write about the meeting at Tremainsville: *"Very cold. Left for Tremainsville and found a large concourse of people assembled; the meeting was opened and resolutions passed concurring with the Legislature of Ohio as to the disputed ground. A good deal of feeling was shown on the occasion."* [10]

The next day Andrew Palmer wrote Governor Lucas advising him of the meeting and its activities. *"... which had heretofore been under the temporary jurisdiction of the Territorial Government of Michigan. The purpose of the meeting was to spread the news among the people that the State of Ohio was extending its jurisdiction over the territory. A delegation from Michigan was also present, headed by Generals Brown and Humphrey, whose real purpose was to divide the meeting, and report which citizens were backing the Ohio plan."*

Dr. Conant also attended the Tremainsville meeting, however his report was directed to Territorial Governor Mason. *"Your committee were pleased to recognize among those present, many of their old acquaintances, and to learn that the spirit of opposition to the claims of Michigan which had hitherto manifested itself in that section of the country was in a great degree confined to those residing in the disputed territory who have staked their property and fortunes upon the hope the disputed boundary set off to Ohio. .... One of those speakers, Andrew Palmer, in the course of his remarks, gravely attempted to show that the claims of Ohio to the lands in dispute were legal. .... General White, of Whiteford, manfully and ably combated their arguments, and utterly demolished the fabric they had raised........ At this stage of the meeting an effort was made by General Brown to read his instructions from the acting Governor of Michigan, but the meeting refused to hear him; the question was called for and carried for Ohio by a large vote, the meeting then adjourned. When another attempt was made to read the General's instructions, and after much dispute they agreed to hear them. ...... In conclusion, they express their firm conviction that a large portion of the inhabitants on the disputed*

Benjamin Franklin Stickney

ground are fully prepared and determined to resist the further operation of our laws in that district. H. Conant, Ch'n."

With all the letters flying back and forth between the governors describing the situation in the *Toledo Strip,* a simple action by Sanford L. Collins[11] best described the attitude of the Vistula residents. Collins, a Captain in the Ohio Militia, purchased a double barreled shotgun *"the better to repel the forces of Michigan."*

Almost as an after thought, Governor Mason sent a letter on the 9th of March to President Andrew Jackson in which he stated that *".... A collision between Ohio and Michigan is inevitable, ..."* and *"... the military movements of our adversary, ... without waiting for an order from the Secretary of War, so soon as Ohio is properly in the field. ..."*

A Mr. "J" writing in Toledo's newspaper, the *GAZETTE,* declared that it was well known that Michigan had *"for some years exercised forcible jurisdiction over a small strip of country included in the constitutional limits of the State of Ohio."* Mr. "J" continues *"However, now that Ohio had definite plans to build the canal, the news of which caused thousands of eastern immigrants to come into the area, Michigan should give control to Ohio, and stop trying to block the canal for the betterment of Monroe and Detroit. If this did not occur, there was ever reason to resist Michigan's jurisdiction and welcome Ohio's rightful domain over the area."*

On March 21, 1835, Attorney General Benjamin Butler[12], responded to a request from President Jackson, after he had received Mason's letter, as to what options were legally available in the rapidly escalating mess. Butler advised the President that although the final decision about the boundary belonged to the congressional or judicial branch, the President had the duty to see that the federal laws were faithfully enforced. Further, in Butler's opinion Congress had acted legally in postponing the decision of the Ohio boundary, and further, Congress had the right to change the boundary; however, until

Congress acted, the disputed area must be part of the Michigan Territory. Since only Congress could annul legislation passed by the Michigan Territory, the Michigan act of February 12, 1834, was legal and any attempt by Ohio to increase her jurisdiction without congressional or judicial approval was illegal. Additionally, Butler was of the opinion that Ohio's remarking of the Harris Line was not in itself an overt show of force.

Almost as an after thought, Butler told the President that territorial governors served at the pleasure of the President. And if the President desired, Mason could be removed from office as Michigan's territorial governor.

At almost the same time that the attorney general's advice had reached the President, another event was taking place in Detroit on the 21st of February that would have severe consequences. A letter had reached Henry Whiting[13], Quarter Master Detroit Federal Arsenal, from Stevens T. Mason.

"The Acting Governor of Michigan has made a most earnest request of me to issue 1,000 stand of muskets, with the proper equipments, and 75,000 ball cartridges, in order to enable him to maintain the integrity and laws of Michigan in the contest with Ohio, which must come to a crisis the 1st of next month..."

Not knowing the proper course of action to take, Whiting directed the request to Chief of Ordinance Col. Bomford[14], in Washington City.

The next day, Sunday the 22nd of February, President Jackson's Secretary of State, John Forsyth[15], wrote to Benjamin Howard[16] of Baltimore, asked him to serve as one of two *confidential & influential friends* to confer with the quarreling governors. The other commissioner was to be Richard Rush[17]. On March 23, 1835 Governor Mason asked Michigan's Senator John Norvell[18] to talk with President Jackson, and to emphasize how embarrassing this constant agitation was to the territory. Also, Territorial Governor Mason had written to Secretary of War Cass requesting permission to use arms from the United States arsenal in Detroit. Cass replied that the only help he could provide regarding the request for arms was to talk to President Jackson.

Meanwhile President Jackson, finding himself extremely annoyed and politically embarrassed, considering that both of the governors were Democrats, instructed Secretary of State Forsyth to suggest to the Governors of Ohio and the Michigan Territory, that under no circumstances would he send Federal troops to the disputed area. *"That under no circumstances, in any part of the country, can military force be justifiably used, except in the aid of the civil authority in executing civil process."* [19] Also they were to avoid a military conflict at all costs.

Governor Mason's letter contained the added suggestion from Secretary Forsyth that Congress might use its power over a territory to force a compromise with Ohio, if Michigan refused to bend on the enforcement of the *Pains & Penalties Act*. This letter so disturbed Mason that he asked President Jackson to remove him as governor if neither the President nor his administration could support him in the boundary dispute.

On March 31, 1835, Ohio Governor Lucas, accompanied by his staff and the boundary commissioners, arrived at Perrysburg on their way to run and re-mark the Harris Line. General John Bell, in command of the Seventeenth Division of the Ohio Militia, arrived at about the same time. The force went into camp at the Old Fort Miami. [20]

Two days earlier on the 29th Benjamin Howard wrote to his wife from Pittsburgh: *"... Tomorrow morning we must be off again to Cleveland where (I think) I asked you to write to me. How long we shall be there I have no idea as yet - whether one of more days or hours: for if the Governor of Ohio is not there we must go after him. ...."*

By April 1, 1835, Michigan citizens had elected their officials for the disputed territory in a meeting near Port Lawrence, and Ohio citizens had elected their officials for the disputed territory in Port

Lawrence, or Toledo as it was coming to be called for the last couple of years. Michigan's Governor Mason, was located in Monroe, and Ohio's Governor Lucas was in Perrysburg. Michigan (Mason) could now confront Ohio on two counts: first, the attempt to rerun the Harris Line and, second, the voting activities of April 6th.

Governor Mason, with General Brown and from 800 to 1,200 men, were camped just north of Toledo, ready to resist any intrusion of the Ohio authorities into the disputed territory. Governor Lucas with a like military force was camped near Maumee ready to enforce its rights. Primed to explode, the *Toledo strip* waited for the incident to spark the conflagration.

"As yet hostilities have not commenced, but there is great excitement on the side of the people of Michigan and we must hurry forward. ...." wrote Benjamin Howard from Cleveland, Ohio to his wife Jane. Continuing in his letter after dinner Howard wrote: *"... It is to take us to Perrysburg at the head of the Lake, about 40 or 50 miles south of Detroit and on the Miami River, where the Governor of Ohio is supposed to be at present. ...... From sundry papers and documents that we have seen, the Governor of Ohio seems resolutely bent upon carrying out the law of his State which embraces the disputed ground within Ohio. Now, if the other party is equally obstinate we shall have much difficulty in preventing collision; ..... We must say and do what we can and may have to pass and re-pass several times between the two Governors who are about 20 or 30 miles apart. In my next I can tell you what our prospects are of adjusting this matter."*

Governor Mason, who was usually portrayed as being irresponsible and impetuous, sent a letter to the governor Ohio pleading for the preservation of peace and a spirit of compromise to prevail over the current situation. Mason continued the correspondence with a flattering and courteous reference to Governor Lucas's service to the citizens of Michigan during the War of 1812. This conciliatory letter was sent in response to an earlier letter that he had received on the same day from Col. Bomford directed at Col. Henry Whiting.

"... the President directs that you apply to the Governor of Michigan to restore the arms and ammunition, which have been issued without the approval of the War Department, and contrary to the regulations." [21]

With the two forces within spitting distance of each other, Todd B. Galloway told an amusing incident of Governor Lucas's encampment. *"Frank Work and John G. Deshler, two men from Columbus, volunteered to work as aides to Governor Lucas. While in Camp at Fort Miami they set out one day, well supplied with whiskey, on a foraging expedition. While returning to camp with a large number of chickens they were apprehended by a small group of Michiganders. Deciding that diplomacy was the better part of valor, Work and Deshler proposed that they all join in the feast of foraged food and whiskey. Of course the two men drank very little of the whiskey, and when their captures were lulled into sleep, they made their escape and returned to Fort Miami."*

On Friday, April 3rd the United States Commissioners, the Hon. Richard Rush, of Philadelphia, and Colonel Howard of Baltimore, accompanied by Elisha Whittlesey of Ohio, arrived in Toledo from Washington. They would later write that neither governor fully accepted their mediation. Mason agreed to take no action if the Ohio officials stayed out of the disputed area, Lucas insisted that the Ohio or Harris Line was to be remarked. Rush and Howard informed Mason that the President did not want the Pains and Penalties Act enforced, and if he chose to enforce the Act it could lead to President Jackson removing Mason from office.

Toledo - at the mouth of the Miami River - 1 o'clock in the morning of Saturday April 4th. My Dearest Wife, ...for we must set off as soon as possible for Monroe a town about 20 miles north of this, where the Govr. Of Michigan is. ..... We are just in time. In a day or two (perhaps today, Saturday) some collision

Benjamin Franklin Stickney

might have taken place, for the Governor of Ohio arrived at his nearest town last night. We are mid way between the two Governors, and our difficulties are rather increased by the news we learn here; for the Govr. of Michigan has brought with him 1000 stand of arms and 15 kegs of cartridges. But I think we can keep him quiet.*[22]*

Confirming his disdain of Monroe, Howard said on April 5, 1835, *"... I am 2 miles outside of the world or, Monroe, ..."* and indicated that Lucas would carry out the wishes of the Ohio Legislature. Howard characterized Gov. Lucas as *"..He is very firm in his character, and though doing what nine tenths of the nation will here after pronounce wrong, yet will listen to no argument upon the point, because he says that his State has decided upon it and it is his duty to execute her laws."*

The Commissioners and Mr. Whittlesey had several conferences with both governors, and finally on the 7th of April 1835 they submitted the following propositions for the governor's approval. First, that the Harris Line should be run and re-marked pursuant to the Act of the last session of the Legislature of Ohio without interruption. Second, with regards to the civil elections under the laws of Ohio having taken place throughout the disputed territory, that the people residing upon it should be left to their own government, obeying the one jurisdiction or the other, as they may prefer, without molestation from the authorities of Ohio or Michigan until the close of the next session of Congress.

Fearing that their mission might not succeed, Rush and Howard told Mason the real reason for their visit. They had a personal message from the President. In it, President Jackson renewed his personal affection for Mason but warned him that he would have to surrender to Ohio unconditionally. President Jackson was a realist if nothing else. Ohio had 21 electoral votes and Indiana had fourteen, Michigan had none. He would follow Attorney General Butler's recommendation if Mason would not cease in his actions against Ohio, he would be replaced.

Benjamin Franklin Stickney

Governor Lucas accepted the terms at the urgent request of the commissioners and Mr. Whittlesey. Stunned at the message that was delivered by the peace envoys, Governor Mason refused to give either silent or passive approval to the stipulations or propositions. With the above thoughts on the matter at hand, Governor Lucas disbanded his force, and Governor Mason withdrew his forces to Monroe. Governor Lucas continued with his plans to re-mark the Harris Line, hopefully without interference from the authorities of the Territory of Michigan.

Toledo, Tuesday, April 7, 1835
.... our interview with the Governor of Ohio has terminated more favorably than I had anticipated and quite as much so as I hoped. We are now on our way back to Monroe to the other Governor .... I look upon our mission as almost certain to produce the result which the President and Forsyth wished ...[23]

On April 8, 1835, a posse led by the Monroe County Sheriff moved into Toledo and began arresting violators of the Pains & Penalties Act. The most publicized incident involved George McKay and Naaman Goodsell[24], friends of Benjamin Stickney. According to the newspaper accounts of the day the Monroe posse numbering 35 to 40 armed men, entered Stickney's house and drove his guests, McKay and Goodsell, out of their beds, after assaulting Stickney's daughter for sounding the alarm and choking her. The posse carried them to Monroe and after a mock trial two days later released them on bail.

Stickney responded with: *"We are driven from our homes for acting under the authority of Ohio; our houses broken open in the dead of night, citizens taken prisoners, bound hand and foot, and tied to wild fiery horses, gagged that they may not alarm the rest of the citizens; the females too in the same house are treated with violence by being held and prevented from going to alarm the neighbors; and all this for saying to an individual, he need not obey the laws of Michigan."* And to add insult to injury: *"They dishonored the Ohio flag by dragging it through the streets of Toledo on the tail of a horse."*

Benjamin Franklin Stickney

With a day for reflection, Stickney sent a letter to the Toledo *Gazette,* which they published with all of its lurid details.

"On the morning of the 9th, then on my return home, I was met by some gentlemen some 14 miles from Toledo, with the intelligence that a band of ruffians of 30 or more, had at dead of night come to my house from Monroe, and in a ferocious manner demolished the door leading to the principal avenue of my house and seized a gentleman, Mr. Naaman Goodsell[25], bore him off and treated his lady and daughter, the only females in the house, with brutish violence, notwithstanding I had exhorted all to exercise moderation. When my daughter gave out the cry of murder, she was seized by the throat and shaken with monstrous violence, and the prints of a man's hand in purple were strongly marked, with many other contusions. Mrs. Goodsell exhibited marks of violence also, the Michigan banditti proceeded likewise to the sleeping apartment of another gentleman, Mr. George McKay, burst in the door, seizing him in bed; and as the first salutation, one of the villains attempted to gouge out one of his eyes with a thumb. After two days of Court-mockery at Monroe, these gentlemen were admitted to bail.

"On the 10th, it was reported that an armed force was assembling under General Brown[26], to march to Toledo, and take prisoners such as accepted office under Ohio, about 12 men. On the 11th they arrived in force, about 200 strong, armed with muskets and bayonets. The Officers of Ohio having been lulled into security by assurances of the Commissioners of the United States, Rush and Howard, were not prepared for defense, and retired, giving them full space.[27]"

Another incident occurred about the same time that Stickney's house was ransacked. Cyrus Holloway, of Sylvania Township, one of the first commissioners of Lucas County, was elected Justice of the Peace, under the laws of Ohio in the last election. Justice of the Peace Holloway aware that the Michigan law officers were looking for him, vanished into the woods, hiding for several days in a sugar-camp shanty. Some of his religious friends reported that Providence had brought forth a miracle on

Benjamin Franklin Stickney

his behalf. They told the story that little robins went to his home every day, found food, and delivered it to Holloway in the woods. Many residents believed the story, and accepted it as proof of the justness of the claim of Ohio to the disputed Territory.[28]

One of the last letters that historians have from Benjamin Howard described the situation in Monroe on April 10th.

"... Men galloping about – guns getting ready – wagons being filled with people and hurrying off, and everybody in commotion. Since we got back here things have gotten dreadfully worse. The Court is sitting and has ordered some men in the disputed district to be arrested – and the Sheriff has gone out with his Posse Comitatus [meaning everybody he can pick up]. ..." [29]

The next day Governor Lucas with the Commissioners; Patterson, Seely, and Taylor selected Engineer Dodge who was engaged in the construction of the canal, to re-survey the Harris line. Dodge reported at once to Perrysburg and after looking over the situation wrote to Samuel Forrer, one of the Ohio Canal Commissioners.

"We shall start tomorrow for the northwestern corner of the state, and the next you hear from me, I shall probably inform you that I am in Monroe, the headquarters of General Brown. He was yesterday at Toledo, at the head of a sheriff's posse of 100 armed men. They came for the purpose of arresting those who have accepted office under the State of Ohio. He informed me that any attempt to run the line would be resisted by the whole force of the territory;... that they have 1,500 stand of arms taken from the United States arsenal at White Pigeon; ... The Governor of Ohio started on the 8th for Defiance and is entirely unprepared to meet the forces of Michigan. Our party consists of fifteen or twenty unarmed men; ... The governor has power to call out the militia, but has no funds to sustain them."

By Saturday, April 25, 1835, Dodge and the Ohio Survey party had marked thirty-eight and one half miles starting from the northwest corner of the state. Michigan authorities considered

Benjamin Franklin Stickney

this to be an infringement of the Pains and Penalties Act, and made arrangements to intercept and arrest the survey party. Justice Charles Hewitt of Tecumseh issued a warrant for the arrest of the Ohio survey party, and William McNair, the under sheriff of Lenawee County, organized an armed posse of over thirty men to carry out the judge's order.

Michigan's advance intelligence suggested that Ohio would have forty armed guards with the survey party. McNair along with General Brown left the posse behind and advanced to within shouting distance. They then ordered them to surrender.

According to General Brown, the Ohioans loaded their muskets and fled to a nearby log house. When asked to surrender a second time, the survey party bolted from the house towards the woods. However, a volley of musket fire over their heads convinced nine of the Ohio members to surrender. The three Ohio Commissioners who watched the action from another house escaped through the adjacent Cottonwood Swamp[30] and made their way back to Toledo. The captured men were taken to Tecumseh; two were released on their word, six were placed on bail, and one was jailed when he refused to post bond. The Michigan authorities decided to hold the chief of the engineers, J. E. Fletcher to test by law the validity of the arrest. Mr. Fletcher was allowed to be his own jailor, and when he desired exercise he would carefully lock the door behind him, stroll through the village, and lock himself back in his cell when finished. Michigan residents, their honor restored, enjoyed the resulting newspaper coverage showing and describing in great detail how the three Ohio Commissioners escaped through the swamp. This whole action became known as the *Battle of Phillip's Corners*.[31]

The best account of the *Battle of Phillip's Corners* from the reminiscences of Dr. Patterson[32] & Benjamin Baxter[33], of Tecumseh, Michigan

"... A Posse Comitatus of about twenty men was sworn in, and Sheriff James Patchin being ill, Deputy Sheriff Col. William McNair[34] was in command. General Brown, having been

Benjamin Franklin Stickney

appointed "Special assistant of the Territory of Michigan to watch the Ohio situation" went along to assist. It might have been a civilian operation, but it had a decidedly military bent."

From the diary of Benjamin Baxter: "*I was not yet of legal age to join the troops but ambitious of military glory, I ran away and joined them in Adrian. After a night of jollification which seemed to me (badly scared as I was) strangely out of place under the solemnities of the occasion, we started out on a Sabbath morning for the invaded territory. After being carried part way in wagons the roads gave out and we were then furnished with U.S. arms and ammunition. I remember I very foolishly took over 40 rounds to carry. We were then put on the line of march. About half were on horseback but the rest of us were on foot and we plodded on for about ten miles and arrived at the place about noon. It seems there were two cabins in which the Ohio invaders were spending their Sabbath and the mounted troops arrived there first.*"

From the diary of Dr. Patterson: "*Judge Blanchard and Colonel McNair entered the house which had been surrounded by the posse, and the judge politely informed the Ohioans, who were under a Colonel Hawkins[35], that they were under arrest. When they blustered and leveled their guns, he gave a signal to the men outside who gave a threatening shout, which took all the pluck out of the invaders. They made a dash for the door and took to their heels. As they were fleeing towards the woods a few guns were fired over their heads by the order of General Brown, which brought them to a halt.*"

From the diary of Benjamin Baxter: "*We, that is, some of us fool soldiers, had not yet arrived on the spot but were rapidly approaching the forest. Every musket reverberated through the tall trees and sounded like cannon. Stopping for a minute to consider how I could best find out which side I was on, I started for the battlefield, very excited and nearly on the run. William Hixon was with me, but our other three companions went as rapidly the other way and we saw no more of them until the call for supper. I think about 12 of the invaders were taken and about*

Benjamin Franklin Stickney

as many got away, running some 15 or 20 miles to Maumee, where they arrived in the night, very peculiarly and lightly clad, it is said, by reason of the prickly ash and blackberry bushes through which lay their line of retreat. Returning in triumph to Adrian about midnight and home the next day with our prisoners, it was concluded by the proper authorities to retain only the engineer, Colonel Fletcher, in nominal imprisonment to test the validity of their arrest. The rest of the men were permitted to return to their homes in Ohio. Soon after this came the celebrated Toledo War and, as in the meantime I had arrived at the Military age and was liable to be warned out with the rest, and, as my former march and experience had fully satisfied my ambition for military glory, I quietly took my gun and went for a three day hunt into the forest..... Our prisoner, Colonel Fletcher, remained with us for many months, a genial gentleman not suffering apparently from his term of incarceration, but sometimes subjecting us to the inconvenience of hunting him up when we had the occasion to use the jail for some counterfeiter or horse thief, as he was likely to be found out riding with one of the sheriffs lovely daughters, having taken the jails keys with him."

J. E. Fletcher seemed to be one of the forgotten men in the Battle of Phillip's Corners, and after ten days in jail Fletcher wrote to Governor Lucas for relief.

"Considering it my duty to inform the authorities of Ohio of my present situation, relative to my imprisonment in Michigan, I take the liberty to address your Excellency. I am at present incarcerated in jail - was committed yesterday. The Sheriff was influenced to change his course of treatment towards me by Governor Mason and General Brown - chiefly, I believe by Brown. I dined with General Brown yesterday. Governor Mason was there He (Mason) strongly urged me to give bail. .... Governor Mason expressed himself as being very anxious that the difficulties might be settled without further hostilities. General Brown was silent on this issue......Governor Mason expressed the determination to prevent the running of the line at all hazards. ...... On Saturday evening last, I received a

Benjamin Franklin Stickney

communication from the Commissioners, by Col. Green, in which they approve of the position which I had taken: and instructed me to abide by it. .... I will only add. That I shall remain as I am until further instructions, which I doubt not will be forwarded in due time."

On May 1, 1835, Governor Mason indicated a willingness to permit Lucas to rerun the Harris Line, if Ohio would do nothing to extend jurisdiction over the Toledo area. Lucas refused the peace offer. The intransigence of the Ohio Governor outraged Secretary of War Cass. He asked Mason to temper his actions and to delay the enforcement of the *Pains & Penalties Act*.

At Rush & Howard's urging, Lucas agreed to keep the peace if no prosecutions were made under the *Pains & Penalties Act*. The residents of the area could use either the law of Ohio or Michigan, and Ohio would be allowed to finish running the Harris Line. The Rush-Howard proposal was opposed to the desires of the President, who favored Ohio's withdrawal from the area until Congress established the boundary. The first week in May found Rush and Howard heading for Washington to confer with President Jackson.

May 2, 1835, the Ohio volunteer army was disbanded by Lucas, and tensions began to cool on both sides. Governor Lucas called a special session of the Ohio Legislature for early June. At his suggestion, Lucas County, with its seat at Toledo, was created from the northern part of Wood County. The Legislature also approved the Rush-Howard proposals on the condition that Michigan also agree to abide by them. On the other hand, they also approved three hundred thousand dollars to enforce the Laws of Ohio. Almost as an afterthought, the lawmakers directed the court of common pleas to hold session in Toledo the first Monday in September.

Anticipating the adverse effect that this set of actions would have on President Jackson, Lucas sent a three man delegation to speak with the President. William Allen[36], (later to become Ohio governor), Noah H. Swayne, (later Associate Justice of the

Benjamin Franklin Stickney

United States Supreme Court), and David T. Disney met with the President and he acceded to everything that Ohio wanted.

To further aggravate the situation, the Monroe County sheriff arrested Stickney and his second wife, Mary. The County authorities quickly determined that their jail was no place for Mrs. Stickney, and that she could spend her time in the hotel across the street. They also decided that Stickney would be placed in jail and be forced to post bond for his release. By posting bond Stickney was admitting Michigan's jurisdiction over the matter. What they had not counted on was the temperament of the man they were dealing with. The jailers placed him in the same room as an old, filthy Frenchman, who had been confined for non-payment of a debt. As Stickney peered through the layers of dirt and vermin, Stickney inquired what he was in jail for. The Frenchman replied *"Because I can't pay my debts."* Stickney's next question was, *"How much do you owe?" "Twenty dollars!"* Stickney quickly pulled a twenty dollar bill from his pocket and gave it to the old man. *"Well here's the twenty, take up your duds and cut dirt quick."*

History of the City of Toledo and Lucas County Ohio, Wagoner, 1884.

Benjamin Franklin Stickney

war fever, robins, & prison
chapter sixteen

The next day found Stickney writing to Governor Lucas from the Monroe jail. *"... peeping through the grates of a loathsome prison, for the monstrous crime of having acted as a judge in the last election ..."*[37]

Endnotes for Chapter Sixteen
war fever, robins, & prison

---

[1] First governor of the State of Michigan, and Territorial Governor of Michigan during the Ohio Michigan Boundary dispute. President Jackson appointed his father John Mason as Secretary of the Michigan Territory, and father and son arrived in Detroit in 1830. One year later his father resigned and set out for Texas and Mexico, supposedly on private business, but in reality on a secret mission for the President, who without hesitation named Stevens Thomson Mason to the position of secretary. Various writers have described John Mason's dwindling financial base and attribute his trip to Texas to exchange Revolutionary War land claims for interest in a land company that was developing a vast tract on the Red River. Others attribute the trip to a secret diplomacy mission to induce Texas to become part of the United States by President Jackson. Ignoring the furor over his appointment, 19 year old Mason conducted himself discreetly and always asked advice of those who surrounded him, and eventually gained their acceptance. During the period 1831-1836 he was acting Governor during the Ohio Michigan boundary dispute. Became an embarrassment to President Jackson and was relieved of office. Elected governor in 1836 when Michigan became a state.

[2] Through the chance illness of its chairman, Judge Overton of Tennessee.

[3] Governor of Ohio and Territorial Governor of Iowa was born in Virginia in 1781. A staunch supporter of Jackson he became well known in Ohio, ran for governor in 1830, defeated, ran again in 1832 and was elected. Served two terms as governor of Ohio. After two years of retirement, in 1838, Van Buren appointed him Territorial Governor of Iowa. Interestingly Iowa and Missouri had a boundary dispute in which he used the tactics of Mason to win the property for Iowa.

[4] Authors have said that the vote in 1818 and 1823 by the French-Canadians expressed a fear of an increase in taxes that swayed the strength of the negative vote. The small size of the favorable vote in 1832

probably indicated the extent of the distractions caused by the threat of Indian uprisings and the cholera epidemic.

[5] Would later become the Toledo *Gazette*.
[6] Judge John P. Cushman of Troy, Jacob D. Lansing of Lansingburg, Thomas W. Olcott of Albany, with some others
[7] This act stated that if a Michigan court convicted any official of acting other than by authority of either Michigan or the United States in any part of the Territory, such a person would be subject to a fine up to one thousand dollars and or imprisonment for up to five years.
[8] From Charles E. Bliven's Pioneer Address in September of 1880: "Palmer returned from Ohio and informed us that the Legislature of Ohio had conceded to take the disputed ground into their own hands." Whether this was Andrew Palmer, editor of the *HERALD* is open to speculation.

[9] Joseph Brown was born in 1793 of Quaker parents in Pennsylvania, the youngest of eleven children, and brother to U. S. Army Commander, General Jacob Brown. Joseph W. Brown is appointed Adjutant in the New York Regular Cavalry by Governor DeWitt Clinton in 1817. At the urging of his brother-in-law Musgrove Evans, he moves to Tecumseh in 1824, the village site having been bought by Brown, surveyor and engineer Musgrove Evans, and Austin E. Wing, friend of Governor Cass, of Monroe. He is appointed Chief Justice of the Michigan Territory and later a Colonel of the Michigan Militia by Lewis Cass.
Joseph Brown was a miller and farmer by trade and his partners required his skills to make the area profitable. They erected the first saw mill in 1825, and grist mill in 1826.
In 1832 he was a general in the Black Hawk War, and from 1833 to 1837 he was largely engaged in the staging route from Detroit to Chicago. After the Ohio Michigan Boundary dispute was largely over, President Jackson appointed him United States Registrar at the Ionia, Michigan Land Office. He was regent of the University of Michigan in 1839, and first judge of Lenawee County in 1826. Colonel in the 8 th Michigan militia 1829, and Commander of Michigan troops in the Toledo War. Died 1880.
After the Ohio Michigan conflict or the Toledo War, General Brown moved to Toledo and became one of its respected inhabitants and a neighbor of Judge Pratt. One of Joseph Brown's daughters married Henry Waite, son of Morrison R. Waite, Chief Justice of the United States.

Benjamin Franklin Stickney

It should be noted that Musgrove Evans, engineer and surveyor, and Joseph Brown were the agents of Count LeRay deChamount, a French gentleman of rank who came to this country with Lafayette, and who served as his aid in the War of the Revolution.

[10] *From Charles E. Bliven's Pioneer Address in September of 1880:*

[11] Interesting item concerning the Port Lawrence post office. It took the United States until June of 1837 to authorize Collins to use the "Ohio" postmark on the mail. Postmaster Collins of Tremainsville received a letter from the United States Post Office in June of 1837 expressing surprise to learn that his post office was located in Ohio.

[12] Benjamin Butler was a partner at Albany, New York, with Martin Van Buren for whom he retained a life long admiration and affection. Van Buren who was Andrew Jackson's Vice President urgently solicited Butler to enter Jackson's cabinet as Attorney General in the fall of 1833. Butler held the office of Attorney General for five years and added to his duties Secretary of War when Lewis Cass resigned to become Minister of France.

Charles Butler was the brother of President Jackson's Attorney General Benjamin Butler and partner in the law firm of VanBuren & Butler. He had huge speculative land holdings in the Toledo and Chicago area.

[13] Colonel Henry Whiting was in charge of the government arsenal at Dearborn, released one thousand stands of arms and five thousand rounds of ball ammunition to the Michigan patriots. Governor Lucas screamed foul and blamed Cass, accusing him of ordering the issue and siding with Michigan. This effort the Secretary of War Cass denied, but he admitted privately that *the state of affairs in Michigan has given me great uneasiness, both as a public officer and a private citizen.* He cautioned Mason that *the crisis is one for calm deliberation & not for rash action,* adding *that a just regard for the President called for moderation.*

Henry Whiting wrote a precursor to Longfellow's Hiawatha. They were called Ontwa and Sannillac. No book was considered authentic on the "West" unless it carried Cass's endorsement. Cass's notes were added to Schoolcraft's "Narrative" and Whiting's work. "A poem of great merit and by a native American is now printing in New York," Cass informed a Washington editor concerning Whiting's poem "Ontwa." "To show that the author adhered with fidelity to Indian usages, at his request, I furnished him with a body of notes which appended to the poem." He requested the editor to give "Ontwa" good notices.

It should be remembered that Cass in a review of British subject James Dunn Hunter, who claimed to have been kidnapped as a child and raised by the trans-Mississippi Indians, wrote a book of his adventures which received wide popularity in the East and England. The review which appeared in the columns of the North America Review, Cass proved that Hunter was an imposter and his story a fraud.

Whiting, along with Cass, Schoolcraft, Trowbridge, and Father Richard were the incorporators of the Michigan Historical Society in 1828.

[14]Col. George Bomford invented the howitzer in 1813 after being assigned to ordnance. Owned a large estate near Washington called, "Kalorama," which was a famous meeting place for diplomats and Government officials. Died in 1848.

[15]John Forsyth served as Jackson's Secretary of State from 1834-1841.

[16]The letter from Forsyth to Howard, March 22, 1835, is marked "Confidential" and indicates that Howard was chosen in the place of Mr. William Cabell Rives who had declined the mission.

Howard (1791-1872) was the son of Colonel John Eager Howard a distinguished Revolutionary officer from Baltimore and Margarita Oswald Chew of Philadelphia. Howard entered Princeton [the College of New Jersey] at fourteen, graduated in 1809, and received his Master's Degree three years later. Howard had an extremely lucrative law practice in Baltimore, and maintained his connections to the Maryland State Militia rising to the rank of Brigadier General. In 1818 he married Jane Grant Gilmor. Howard was a member of the committee that recommended the construction of a railroad between Baltimore and the Ohio River. In 1829 he was elected as a Democrat to the twenty-first Congress and then re-elected in 1831. President Jackson appointed him one of the Peace Commissioners for the Ohio Michigan Boundary dispute in 1835.

[17]Lawyer, diplomat, and statesman was born in Philadelphia in 1780. With President Monroe he served as Secretary of State till John Quincy Adams returned from Europe. In this position he negotiated with Britain the Rush-Bagot convention which prohibited naval armaments on the Great Lakes. Appointed minister to Great Britain on October 31, 1817. When John Quincy Adams became president in 1825 he was appointed

Secretary of the Treasury. In 1828 he ran as JQA's vice president and lost. Active in the Anti-Masonic movement and declined to run as their chosen candidate.

In the summer of 1836 he went to England to secure the Smithson bequest to the United States. James Smithson, an Englishman, had died without issue, and had left the whole of his estate, on the death of a nephew to the United States. In August of 1838 he brought back to the United States in English gold coins upwards of 104,000 pounds, which was used to establish the Smithsonian Institution.

President Polk made him minister to France.

[18] John Norvell, along with Lucius Lyon, were chosen as Michigan's first Senators, from 1835 to 1841. On the advice contained in a letter written by Thomas Jefferson, John learned a trade as a printer, at the same time studying law. Friend and correspondent of President Madison. In May, 1832, he came to Detroit having been appointed postmaster by Andrew Jackson. Leading member of Michigan's constitutional convention. Secured the mineral wealth of the upper peninsula. In 1845 was appointed U. S. District attorney of Michigan.

[19] Secretary of State Forsyth to Lucas, March 19, 1835

[20] The force consisted of five companies of the first regiment, second brigade of the seventeenth division of militia under the command of Colonel Mathias Van Fleet. The Captains of these companies were J. A. Scott, Stephen S. Gilbert, John Pettinger, Felton and Granville Jones, of the Lucas Guards, an independent company of Toledo.

[21] Col. Henry Whiting, Ordinance Officer for the Detroit Arsenal: *"The moment he [Mason] received the above letter, in which the issue was disapproved, he applied for their immediate restoration. Governor Mason said that the boxes had never been touched, and that they should be sent back with all practicable dispatch."* On the next day, the 30 th of April, the stores are reported as having been returned by the Acting Governor of Michigan. (Contained in a letter from Lewis Cass, Secretary of War to John Forsyth, Secretary of State, November 19, 1835)

[22] Letter from Benjamin Howard to his wife Jane, April 4, 1835.
[23] Rush writing to Howard, June 21, 1835, *My remembrances to our young friend and fellow traveler Charles Gilmore, Howard's eighteen year old brother in law. O the days of Toledo! Positively you or he must, one of these*

days, immortalize them in verse. I am no poet. What a character Captain Allen would make in the piece! The Indian chief, Ott-kee, and my rifle shot at the duck, might also come in. I'll leave it to the reader to decide the seriousness of political messengers Rush & Howard.

[24] The reason they were being pursued was for the violating the Act of February 12th in the following manner. According to papers filed by James Q. Adams, District Attorney, McKay and Goodsell had interfered with Deputy Smith in the arrest and transport of John Carr, Thomas Tracy, and Benjamin Feral to Monroe for trial. They informed the arrested men that Deputy Smith had no jurisdiction in the manner and advised them to escape from the custody of Deputy Smith, which they promptly did.

Interesting to note that John Carr was the same person that Stickney had given a lot to as the first child born in Vistula.

[25] Mr. Goodsell's comments on the evening: "My journey was rendered unpleasant by the insolence of some of the party, and my life jeopardized by being obliged to ride upon a horse without a bridle, which horse being urged from behind became frightened and ran with me till I jumped from him. I arrived at Monroe, and was detained there until the next day, as they refused me any bail from day to day. I was taken before the Grand Jury, then in session, and questioned concerning our meeting the officers, etc. During the second day a large military force, or posse, was raised, armed and started for Toledo. After they had gone nearly long enough to have reached Toledo, I was admitted to bail."

[26] Mr. Goodsell's narrative continued: "....passed the force on the road, and inquired of the Sheriff whether that was to be considered an armed force or a Sheriff's posse. He answered that he considered it a posse at that time, but it was also arranged that it might be either - as circumstances should require; that General Brown and aide were along, who would act in case they assumed a military force."

[27] Andrew Palmer or Stickney in the Toledo *GAZETTE*.

[28] The miraculous part of the story had a very slight foundation in the fact, that Mr. Holloway's children, who daily carried food to their father, had a pet robin, and usually took it with them on such visits; hence the robin story.

Benjamin Franklin Stickney

[29] *"With what anxious thoughts did we hang over the case, day and night, turning in our mind every possible expedient for a temporary compromise to ward off bloodshed threatening us every hour almost. But no matter; we did our duty as well as we could, knowing, seeing, all the embarrassments on the spot; and I venture to feel sure that when all that we wrote comes to seen, nobody will blame us, for who has been able to do better than we would have done?"*

[30] Starting at Sylvania, the Cottonwood Swamp is located west of the sand ridge that extends from Sylvania to Adrian, and north of Ten Mile Creek.

[31] Phillip's Corners was located about 18 miles west of Sylvania on the Sylvania-Metamora Road approximately where it presently intersects State Route 109. It is the present location of Seward, Ohio, two miles east of Lyons, Ohio.

[32] Dr. Michael A. Patterson was born in Easton, Pa., March 11, 1804, and was educated there till early manhood. Studied medicine at the University of Pennsylvania, and graduated from there at age 19 with honors. He practiced in western New York for four years, and settled in Tecumseh, Michigan, where he continued in practice until 1875. Representative in 1846, and Senator from Lenawee county in 1844-45. He was a regent of the University six years and held many local offices.

33. Was born at Sidney Plains, Delaware County, New York, on April 7, 1815. He came to Tecumseh in 1831 with his father, Hon. Levi Baxter. Attended and educated for three years at Dartmouth College in New Hampshire. In 1843 he took charge of the Tecumseh branch of the University of Michigan, while he studied law with Hon. Perley Bills. Later he became his law partner for twenty five years. He was regent of the State University from 1858 to 1864, and was Representative in the state Legislature from 1869 to 1870.

[34] Was born in Bucks County, Pennsylvania, in 1800. Came to Michigan in 1826, and became a merchant in Tecumseh, and afterwards a farmer. He was a representative in 1849.

[35] This is the magazine keeper at Fort Meigs of 1813, Lt. Thomas Hawkins, who now resides in Fremont. He is said to have been the lone Ohioan who confronted Sheriff McNair outside the log cabin with pistols drawn, and was one of the party who was confined in the Tecumseh jail.

Benjamin Franklin Stickney

[36] Interesting note on Allen's career was that in his first race for Congress, the Jacksonian Democrat, ran against General Duncan MacArthur, and won by one vote. He served one term in the house, 1833-1835, and in 1842 married General MacArthur's only daughter, Effie. Won the senate in 1837 in a race with Thomas Ewing. Towards the end of his life he made a political come back winning the race for Ohio governor in 1873.

[37] Letter from Stickney to Lucas, May 6, 1835.

William C. Holgate, author of the Holgate Journal of 1835 from which Louis A. Simonis wrote *MAUMEE VALLEY 1835*. Engraving from Knapp's *History of the Maumee Valley.*

Benjamin Franklin Stickney

a wedding, the stabbing, & a dead horse
chapter seventeen

Austin E. Wing in a letter to John Biddle[1], president of Michigan's Constitutional Convention, wrote the following explanation for the Toledo War.

"... a large, wealthy and influential land and town-site company organized in Cincinnati, had acquired very extensive land interests at the mouth of the Maumee River, where they proposed laying out a city, and to make there the terminus of the western Ohio and Indiana canal. Being an Ohio company and composed of citizens of the state, familiar with the public men and interests, they naturally preferred to build their city and harbor with their own state rather than in a territory with which they had no relation save the ownership of the property."

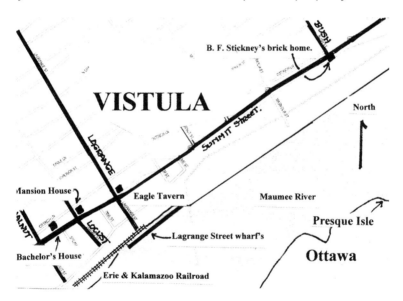

Map of the Vistula Area of 1835. From the author's collection. Even with the outcome of the *Toledo* Strip in question, travelers and immigrants were making their way to the Maumee Valley in droves. William C. Holgate[2] arrived in Vistula on the 27th of May 1835 after traveling from Buffalo down the length of Lake Erie on board the *Governor Marcy*[3]. Holgate noted in his journal that the Eagle Tavern[4] was located a short walk from the wharfs located at the foot of Lagrange Street.

Benjamin Franklin Stickney

Not liking the appearance of the Eagle Tavern, Holgate and his father made their way to Port Lawrence and the Toledo House[5] owned by Mr. William P. Daniels[6]. As they walked towards the crest of Summit Street, they passed the Mansion House near Locust and the Bachelor's Hall both operated by J. Baron Davis. The two story brick Toledo House was built in 1832 on the northwest corner of Summit and Perry streets, at the mouth of Swan Creek.

Another businessman from New York arrived in Vistula in June. Jacob A. Barker, 21 years of age represented his father's Buffalo freight and cartage-forwarding firm of Barker & Holt. Barker was one of twelve stockholders that included George and Platt Card,[7] Benjamin Franklin Stickney's son-in-law, for the new town of Manhattan on the left bank of the mouth of the Maumee River. Having assurances and advanced information from Platt Card, that the Wabash & Erie Canal would have its terminus on the northern bank of the mouth of the Maumee River, they set about to gather title to the appropriate land.

Platt Card had long wished to lay out a town at the mouth of the river, but had been deterred by the caution of his New York stockholders. At that time, stockholder J. T. Hudson was not counting on the canal coming out at Manhattan. Hudson wrote on June 19th, 1835: *"That old bed of the creek can be turned to good account if the canal terminates at Toledo with a little expense & if the canal terminates at Perrysburg or Maumee the nearer the City (Manhattan) is to the lake the better.*

Card even wrote to Manhattan shareholder Richard Sears, in Buffalo, and told him that he had sold out all of his land holdings in Toledo *"... to prepare for the change ..."* With plans inside of plans, Card purchased another 160 acres at the mouth of the Maumee from the Ottawa leader Wasaonoquette. What the others in the Manhattan plan were not aware of was that Card did not get rid of all his holdings[8] in Toledo.

Benjamin Franklin Stickney

What Platt Card did not know was that Barker also had other plans. Barker in early June of 1835, attempted to gain control of the Erie & Kalamazoo Railroad so that it would terminate at the projected town of Manhattan. His plan was for a friend[9] of his on the board of directors to have the railroad's stock expanded, whereupon, Barker would purchase enough of the stock to gain control. Through a narrow interpretation of the railroad's charter, Barker was advised that the charter permitted any railroad crossing the Erie & Kalamazoo to use it at the going standard rates. Therefore, all they had to do was build a small branch line from Manhattan to join the Erie & Kalamazoo Railroad. By late August of 1835, the group had succeeded in getting a Michigan charter for such a line, the Michigan Branch Railroad. Hedging their bets in 1837 they also obtained a charter for another branch line, the Manhattan & Harve Railroad. By this curious route they would be able to eventually connect Manhattan to Monroe.

Even five years later Daniel S. Bacon would write to Barker: *"We look upon the connection of Manhattan and Monroe by the railroad as certain, and as being the salvation of each place."*

William Allen. History of Ohio 1924.

Benjamin Franklin Stickney

Noah Swayne. Howe's Historical Collections of Ohio 1896.

By early July of 1835, a specific agreement was arranged, brokered by Noah Swayne[10], David Disney[11], and William Allen[12] between Governor Lucas and President Jackson that would give Ohio the disputed *Toledo Strip*. The conclusion was supported by a letter from President Jackson to Governor Lucas on July 4th. The contents were direct and to the point: *".... To avoid forcible hostile action. ..."*

It was not until 1874 that the full impact of the Whitehouse meeting with the Toledo delegation of Swayne, Disney, and Allen with President Jackson would become apparent. The following account of that meeting and what followed was excerpted from an address[13] by participant William Allen, reproduced in the 1874 issue of the Toledo COMMERCIAL.

"The question arose while I was in Congress, and we came very near having a war over it. Some people of Ohio apprehended a war. War between whom, Ohio and Michigan? Not at all. Such a war would not have lasted eight hours, for Ohio would have put her foot on Michigan and she would have ceased to exist. The

danger was between Ohio and the United States because Michigan was at that time organized under an act of Congress."

"A foolish Governor named Mason was appointed who took it into his head to be exceedingly patriotic. He wanted to be the first Governor, or Senator, or something else of that character. He had the audacity to take arms from the arsenal at Detroit to prevent the Ohio Commissioners from running the line. That made the Ohio people mad, and they pressed for an act appropriating $100,000 to sustain a call for military forces to prevent this Michigan invasion. The Legislature was called together and passed a bill, but a clause was put into the bill which provided for a suspension of the act until Governor Lucas could send a Board to Washington to present our case to President Jackson."

"A few days after this clause was put in the bill the Governor called me to go and see President Jackson about the impending war, and see if he would not prevent the conflict by an order to Mason. I told Lucas I thought Ohio was to big a thing for one man to represent, and he thought so too and named David S. Disney, and Noah Swayne, now Associate Justice of the Supreme Court of the United States and off we went to Washington".

"It was very hot weather at the time -- I believe in the later part of July --- but we traveled over the mountains, and arrived in Washington. We then called on Old Hickory and told him we had come there to see about the Michigander business. The old man got up, received us cordially, and putting out his pipe and placing it on the mantle-piece, said, "Well, what do you want me to do?" We explained the matter to him, and, after taking a few minutes, he said, "well, gentlemen, come to me to-morrow morning with what you want on paper." He then bowed us out and it was not long before we had all we wanted put down on a very small piece of paper. Calling the next morning we gave it to him. He was a great man in all his organs and parts, and one of God's noble men. Well, he rubbed up his specs, and reading over what we had written, handed it back saying: "Take that to

Benjamin Franklin Stickney

the Secretary of State, and tell him to copy it and put the seal of the United States upon it." We did so. It was copied, the seal put on it, and three and a half days thereafter, we were back in Columbus and the Ohio and Michigan boundary troubles were settled."

Northwest of Toledo, public sentiment from Sylvania and Whiteford favored Ohio's claim. David White[14] of Whiteford, one of the principal land owners in the area, anticipated a huge monetary gain when Ohio obtained the Toledo Strip. Michigan would then construct a road across southern Michigan from Sylvania to Monroe, thus giving his properties access to the Monroe-Detroit markets and the enlarged Lake Erie port at the Bay settlement (Erie, Michigan).

From Stickney's arrest and imprisonment in Monroe on the 6th of May 1835 through the months of June and the first week of July, Governors Mason and Lucas had quieted the war fever that was running rampant. If this peace continued, the disputed territory between Ohio and Michigan was headed for the Congressional hearing rooms or worse yet ... the Courts. Stickney's view of their solution would award Toledo to Michigan and that would devastate the value of his extensive land holdings and plans for the region. Stickney had to devise a confrontation between Ohio and Michigan that would cause Governor Mason to become the aggressor.

Such an event presented itself on the 11th of July 1835 when James H. Miller, a Monroe County constable, received legal authorization from the court in Monroe to collect a debt against Jeremiah Odel of Toledo in favor of Henry Clark also of Toledo. Since Odel did not have enough money to satisfy the debt, Sheriff Miller seized some of Odel's furniture and held it to satisfy the liability.

The highlights of the sheriff's sale which was set for Saturday, two days away, was Odel's furniture coupled with a fine set of carriage horses and a wagon that were seized earlier. When the auctioneer began his recognizable cadence, J. Baron Davis owner of Toledo's Mansion House, knocked the constable down, and with several other men drove the horses into the woods. By this time, the crowd of prospective buyers had grown into a multitude of Ohio supporters. They stormed the auction building, seized the key from Sheriff Miller, and liberated Odel's furniture. In the confusion that followed what was left of the auction, the sheriff was able to positively recognize two members of the rowdy audience, J. Baron Davis and Two Stickney.

With Two Stickney a possible target of Michigan law enforcement over an Ohio resident, the wedding of Benjamin Franklin Stickney to Mary Matilda Way,[15] on Sunday, formed the cover to perfect the overt act that would force Michigan Territorial Governor Mason to react.

On Wednesday the 15th of July, Deputy Sheriff Joseph Wood of Monroe received information that Davis and Stickney were seen at the Mansion House on Summit Street. Deputy Sheriff Wood and Lyman Hurd who were going to serve a Federal arrest warrant on George McKay, headed south for Toledo. When they opened the door to the Mansion House,[16] they saw J. Baron Davis, Two Stickney, and McKay sitting at a table playing cards. Walking up to the small wooden table; Hurd informed McKay that he was under arrest on a Federal warrant, and Wood said that he had an unrelated state arrest warrant for Two Stickney.

Mr. Hurd stumbled backward as McKay pushed violently away from the table, grabbed his chair, and threatened Hurd by saying *"...unless he desisted he would split him down."* Stunned by McKay's actions, Stickney refused to accept the warrant unless it was served under Ohio authority. With the rest of the tavern looking at the source of the commotion, Deputy Wood attempted to arrest Stickney.

Placing both of his hands on Two Stickney's shoulders, Deputy Wood quickly grabbed Two by the collar. Testing each other for a weakness as the scuffle started, and finding none, Two drew a small knife[17] from his pocket and stabbed Deputy Wood between the second and third rib on Wood's left side. Facing

Benjamin Franklin Stickney

each other after the scuffle which had stopped as fast as it had started, Two was heard to have said *"There, Damm you, you have got it now."* McKay followed Two's head long rush for the door and the freedom of the darkening forest.

Bewildered, Deputy Wood grabbed his left side and staggered towards the door. Hurd asked him if he had been stabbed and Wood answered very faintly, *"yes."* Hurd and Wood left Davis's tavern, summoned a doctor, and went to Ira Smith's tavern[18]. Dr. Jacob Clark[19], after a rather cursory examination, was of the opinion that the wound was fatal.[20]

Almost three hours after Dr. Clark applied a dressing to the four inch gash, and several liberal doses of whisky, Wood was astonished to learn that he was not dead. Several more doses of whisky, and Wood started to doubt the sincerity of a *"dammed Ohio doctor."* Almost six hours after the dreaded stabbing incident, Dr. Southworth[21] from Monroe, arrived at the Eagle Tavern for a second opinion.

After an extremely thorough examination of the wound, Dr. Southworth disagreed with Dr. Clark's diagnosis, and said that except for the hangover Sheriff Wood will be fine in the morning. Exhausted from his terrifying ordeal, Deputy Wood fortified with whisky, finally surrendered to sleep. With a rather large crowd[22] gathered outside the Eagle tavern, it was almost nine in the morning before Wood and Hurd mounted their horses and left for Monroe. As they mounted their horses, voices from the crowd told them to expect more of the same if any other Michigan lawmen tried to make any further illegal arrests.

According to Governor Mason, the actions of Wood and Stickney were civil actions that did not violate the Pains and Penalties Act. Governor Mason agreed to use a large armed posse rather than a militia unit to seize Two Stickney in Toledo. When the posse reached Stickney's brick home on Summit Street, none of the wanted men were to be found. However, after they searched Stickney's home, the posse found McKay and Andrew Palmer hiding in the cellar. These men, along with

Benjamin Franklin Stickney

several others, including Major Benjamin Stickney and his wife, were brought back to Monroe and promptly jailed for the second time.

On the way to Monroe, Major Stickney was totally uncooperative and fell off his horse on several occasions. The posse solved the situation by tying his legs together under the belly of the horse so that he could not fall off. After Two Stickney was indicted by a Grand Jury for attempted murder of a police officer, Governor Mason quickly offered a $500 reward for Two Stickney. On the 18th of July 1835 Governor Lucas refused Mason's request for extradition and said that Ohio had jurisdiction over the incident.

In spite of all the extradition talk or because of it, an armed delegation of 250 Michigan men visited Toledo, and made seven or eight arrests, chiefly for individual grievances. Arrests and prosecutions for holding office under the laws of Ohio were conducted with abandon. Throughout this time the people of Monroe County were kept busy as they served arrest warrants in the disputed territory. The instigation of one suit would lay the foundation for numerous others, and many personal grudges were settled against the settlers in the *Toledo Strip*.

The organized mob that fell upon Toledo on the 18th of July committed several blatant acts of violence. One of the worst was the damage to the newspaper office of Andrew Palmer[23]. Armed men demolished the front door of the Toledo *GAZETTE's* [24] office, and dumped the individual pieces of typeset all over the floor.[25] Palmer would later explain: *".. We have barely enough type and materials saved from outrages; we are about to relate, to lay the particulars before the public."*

An attempt was made by the authorities in Ohio to retaliate in kind; but for some reason or another, the accused would manage to escape into Michigan proper, or hide at home. Whenever the sheriff of Ohio's Wood County attempted to make an arrest, there would generally be spies who communicated the fact to the accused persons in time to hide, or make their escape. The town was kept in a great uproar as they watched the movements of the sheriffs and bailiffs of Monroe and Wood Counties.

BY STEVENS T. MASON,

SECRETARY AND ACTING GOVERNOR IN AND OVER THE TERRITORY OF MICHIGAN

A PROCLAMATION.

WHEREAS, I have been notified by the proper authorities of the County of Monroe, that in the execution of process issued from the court of said county Joseph Wood, a Deputy Sheriff of the same, has been forcibly resisted with arms, and dangerously, if not mortally, wounded, by a person by the name of

TWO STICKNEY,

at the village of Toledo, in the County of Monroe: And whereas, information has been received, that the said Stickney has fled from justice, and from the Territory

Now, therefore, I do hereby offer a reward of FIVE HUNDRED DOLLARS for the apprehension and delivery of the aforesaid TWO STICKNEY to the Sheriff of the County of Monroe: And I do further enjoin upon all good citizens and others, that they use all possible diligence and exertion to apprehend and secure the said culprit, so that he may be delivered over to the proper tribunal, to be dealt with according to law and justice.

In *testimony whereof,* I do hereunto affix my hand and seal, at the City of Detroit on the sixteenth day of July, in the year of our Lord eighteen hundred and thirty five.

STEVENS T. MASON

Arrest warrant handbill for the arrest of Two Stickney issued by the Territorial Governor Stevens T. Mason. Courtesy of the Toledo Lucas County Public Library.

Just two days after the outrages visited on Toledo by the Michiganders, Governor Lucas mindful of President Jackson's arrangement, took no official action regarding the Toledo incidents, and ordered the survey of the Harris Line resumed.

Benjamin Franklin Stickney

a wedding, the stabbing, & a dead horse
chapter seventeen

On Monday July 20th Perrysburg's Judge Higgins wrote Governor Lucas and said: " ... *that while ready to undertake such service, without regard to personal consequences, he still should feel acutely, as would every citizen of Ohio, the disgrace of capture and abduction by a Michigan mob, of a branch of the judiciary of the State, while actually engaged in the performance of judicial functions. ..."*

Robert E. Lee about thirty years apart. Courtesy of the Toledo Lucas County Public Library.

Following orders that were given in 1832 a third survey of the Ohio Michigan Boundary was underway. Under the auspices of the Army Engineers, Andrew Talcott[26] captain of the Army Engineers was commissioned to undertake the project, and the actual survey was run by Lieutenants Washington Hood[27] and Robert E. Lee[28]. Camped on Turtle Island, Lee and Hood had almost completed their survey on the 31st which would support the Fulton Line which favored Michigan. This was the same

Robert E. Lee who would command the southern forces in the Civil War.

"Turtle Island, Michigan, 31st, July 1835
Mon Ami

The country around Savors marvelously of Bilious Fevers, and seems to be productive of nothing more plentiful than of Moschitoes & Snakes. Of the good people in this Country, we have seen nothing. We hear about Toledo they speak hardly of us. ...... Hood & Myself are in high preparation for a trip up the Maumee River to make a survey ..... it is some 12 miles off, the Boat & men are ready, it is a long pull & we then have to establish ourselves for the night & among Enemies too.
Lt. Robert E. Lee."

Three days after Lt. Robert E. Lee wrote his letter from Turtle Island at the entrance to the Maumee River, General Brown informed Governor Mason that Governor Lucas was raising an armed force in Toledo to implement the government's September mandate to hold court. *"it appears that the game has changed, and that we shall have to meet our Ohio neighbors in a different manner,"* said General Brown.
On August 16, 1835 with letters from Secretary of War Cass and Secretary of State Forsyth threatening him with removal from office by President Jackson, Governor Mason decided he would not stand by and let Ohio take the territory. That action was against everything that Mason stood for as Governor of Michigan.

One day later Michigan's Legislative Council declined to accept the Rush-Howard proposal, and authorized Mason to borrow up to $310,000[29] to prevent further Ohio operations in Michigan Territory. On a side note, Mason was heard to proclaim that if the council rejected the Rush-Howard proposal he would resign. Mason did not resign and the Michigan Legislature reproached President Jackson for not applying the same firmness to Ohio as he had during the boundary dispute between South Carolina and North Carolina in 1764.

DETROIT *FREE PRESS*
August 26, 1835

"WAR!   WAR! - Orders have been issued for Volunteers to rendezvous at Mulhollen's[30] in the county of Monroe, on the 1st of September next, for the purpose of resisting the military encroachments of Ohio. The Territory, it is expected, will be on the alert, and we understand services will be accepted from all quarters."

Two days after the Detroit *Free Press* issued the proclamation of war; President Jackson carried out his previous warnings and relieved Stevens T. Mason as Governor of the Michigan Territory. Mason's immediate replacement, Judge Charles Shaler[31] of Pennsylvania, for obvious political reasons refused the assignment, which left Michigan without legal leadership during the critical month of September. President Jackson's second appointment, John S. (Little Jack) Horner[32] of Virginia was never really accepted by the people of Michigan. [33]

Dr. George G. Baker[34] wrote an interesting letter on the 1st of September 1835 immediately before the Toledo War. Dr. Baker was of the opinion that there would be money to be made in land speculation, and if there was a war Ohio would crush Michigan. ".... People here have an opinion that money will be scarce, but all who have credit are driving into speculation. The unsettled state of the Bound line has perhaps given a check to speculations at the Mouth of the Maumee River, but no where else. There are about 18,000 volunteers in Ohio ready to start when called on and Michigan has much, and is making great preparations to fight, and though you at East will probably [laugh] at all this, it is the belief here that blood will be shed unless the General Government quickly interferes. ...." [35]

Charles Blivens in an address given 55 years later to the Maumee Valley Historical Society, said that the residents of Toledo were greatly disturbed by four unknown steamboats that were tied to the wharfs along the Maumee River. The rumors were that the Michigan troops had arrived by water and were running rampant through Toledo. With no *Michiganders* sighted, Toledoans turned out in mass to watch an armed riflemen company of Ohio Militia strut through Toledo.

What the Toledoans did not know was that the Michigan volunteers on Saturday and Sunday had gathered in masse on Mulhollen's Monroe County farm about eight miles from the Maumee. The last of the Michigan troops pitched camp on Sunday as the rain fell in torrents making the fields of Samuel Mulhollen's[36] farm a muddy quagmire. General Brown, Governor Mason, and other officials expected to meet Lucas's force in warfare in the morning. Meanwhile they were dry and warm at Christian Hertzler's [37] Hotel at Vienna, near present day Erie, Michigan.

Expecting the Michigan forces to arrive just after daybreak on Monday morning, September 7th, Governor Lucas ordered the County Court to be held just after midnight of Monday morning. Governor Mason and the Michigan Militia under the command of General Joseph W. Brown were still at Mulhollen's farm when the letter of Secretary of War Cass expressing his condolences to the Governor for being dismissed along with the notice of his dismissal from President Jackson arrived at Detroit. A swift messenger delivered the letters to Governor Mason as the troops were passing in review Monday morning. Calling an orderly, Mason announced to the troops that were huddled around him that he was no longer their commander in chief. Realizing that he had been out of office for nine days at that point, Mason continued his address telling the volunteers that he had given command of the Michigan Brigade to General J. W. Brown, and urged them to follow his orders.

As Mason stepped aside, General Brown faced the volunteers and dealt with the hard choices that faced the Michigan troops: *"Our cause is just. We assemble to defend from invasion our constitutional privileges. The voice of law calls us to the field, and although young in history, Michigan must be placed by us in the proud attitude of seeking to do no wrong, and never shrinking to defend the honor of the country and the inviolability of her soil."*

After assembling one hundred volunteers[38], Colonel VanFleet, of the Ohio Militia, received a message stating that General Brown, with 1,200 volunteers were camped at Mulhollen's farm just north of Toledo. It was assumed that Colonel VanFleet upon hearing the latest report would not advance into Toledo to meet 1,200 volunteers with only 100 regulars, however VanFleet was reputed to have said to the assembled court officers, *"If you are women go home! If you are men, do your duty as judges of the court! I will do mine!"*

Dr. H. Conant. Courtesy of Knapp's History of the Maumee Valley.

As the time approached for the scheduled meeting of the Ohio Lucas Court; Adjutant General S. C. Andrews, Major General John Bell of Lower Sandusky (Fremont), Sheriff Junius Flagg, Clerk Dr. Horatio Conant, and the three associate judges

a wedding, the stabbing, & a dead horse
chapter seventeen

Jonathan H. Jerome, Baxter Bowman, and William Wilson huddled together just after midnight, in the ruins of Fort Miami, ready to move to Toledo under protection of Colonel VanFleet's thirty[39] regulars.

Colonel VanFleet, clerk, acting sheriff Junius Flagg, three associate judges, and thirty volunteers arrived in Toledo at 3 a. m. on the morning of September 7, 1835. The first Lucas County Court was held in a schoolhouse at the intersection of Washington Street and the proposed canal. The business of the court consisted of appointing John Baldwin, Robert Grower, and Cyrus Holloway as Lucas County commissioners, and to approve the county clerk's bond. The clerk of courts was one of the earliest residents of the area to be in favor of Ohio retaining jurisdiction, Dr. Horatio Conant of Maumee.[40]

The following account was gleaned from an address to the Raisin Valley (Michigan) Historical Society by Willard V. Way[41] of Perrysburg.

"After arriving at the school house on Washington Street near Erie Street at 2 A.M., the location previously agreed to for the court proceedings, they conducted the necessary business, and the proceedings of the court were written on loose pieces of paper and deposited in the hat band of one of the participants, Dr. Conant. When the court adjourned, the officers and escort went to the tavern to celebrate their good fortune. The tavern was kept by Munson H. Daniels, not to far from the American House. They registered their names and had a drink all around, while filling their glasses for the second round, someone gave an alarm that the Michigan troops were on their way, and the participants made their way post haste for the safety of Maumee. When they arrived at the top of the hill, near where the Oliver House[42] now stands, discovering that the Michiganders were not in pursuit, discovered that the clerk had lost his hat. VanFleet ordered the clerk and two guards to retrace their steps to find the errant hat and court records. The feeling of joy at recovering the papers was so great that Colonel VanFleet

Benjamin Franklin Stickney

ordered two salutes fired on the spot. Arriving back in Maumee at about 6 A.M."

When Mason's forces arrived in Toledo, just after daybreak on Monday morning, September 7th, not a single Ohio soldier was in sight. Disappointed and spoiling for a fight, some of the Michigan militia stayed in Toledo for three days, drinking, carousing, and plundering. In the eight months since Michigan passed the *Pains & Penalties Act,* many Michigan residents began to realize that Stickney was the architect behind its creation. When Governor Mason was goaded into the enforcement of the act, his actions created many of the confrontations that President Jackson wanted to avoid. As this information passed into the general population, Major Stickney and his property became the objects of the Wolverine's wrath. Since Stickney was not available to tar & feather, Stickney's brick mansion on Summit Street became their focus. Stickney's wine cellar was emptied of its contents and his vegetable garden was emptied of its produce. Private Abbey, a Michigan soldier, who was discovered in the act of pulling up potatoes, was asked what he was doing, Abbey replied, *" ..... drafting potato tops, to make the bottoms volunteer."*

Platt Card, Stickney's son-in-law, was also singled out for retribution. Michigan troops were ordered to surround Platt's weathered barn after hearing suspicious noises from the interior. After the required warnings were offered, the impatient soldiers that encircled the barn were ordered to fire their weapons. After the smoke cleared, the Michigan volunteers cautiously entered and found the only confirmed mortality of the war. The soldiers had managed to kill an old mare belonging to Lewis F. Bailey.[43]

With the urge to fight taken out of them and the hangovers that came with the liberation of Stickney's wine cellar, many of the Michigan volunteers embarked on the steamboat GENERAL BRADY for a voyage to Kelly's Island to commemorate the anniversary of Perry's Victory at Put-In-Bay. Finding Kelly's Island saloons hospitable to their failed mission, the citizen soldiers of Michigan drowned their disappointments in a series

Benjamin Franklin Stickney

of toasts to General Brown and Governor Mason. It was reputed that a toast was even offered to the fine wines and cider stored in Stickney's wine cellar.

At a mass meeting at Mulhollen's Farm less than a week after the conclusion of The Toledo War, as it was beginning to be called, ex-Governor Mason, surveyed the assembled Michigan volunteers and bid them a tearful farewell.

Trying to get in one of the last insults to the Ohio group that held court, Deputy Joseph Wood still smarting from the *stabbing incident,* led a group of volunteers to arrest the judge and the commissioners who held the night court. Historian Dr. Lyman Draper[44], noted historian and interviewer of the historical figures of the times, was visiting his parents Luke and Harriet Draper[45] at their grocery store[46] in Vistula when the alarm passed through their neighborhood. The following was from Dr. Draper's account.

"This time, probably because the marauding band was small, the Toledo citizens took umbrage and action. A militia captain called for a popular uprising, gathered those who heeded his call, and took off after the sheriff's band. Lyman Draper, witnessing a variety of border warfare went along. He was equipped for combat, for a man who had become ill on the way had turned over his gun and trappings to him. But there was no combat. A few shots were fired at random in the "Battle of Mud Creek," but the Michiganders escaped with their prisoners." [47]

During the *Battle of Mud Creek* Sheriff Wood was shot in the arm during the confrontation, but managed to get back to Monroe. Mason's successor, Governor Horner immediately went to Monroe and pardoned all the Ohio men arrested or even sought, with one exception. Michigan still wanted Two Stickney.[48]

Jonathon Fletcher, who had been in jail since the *Battle of Phillips Corners* in April for acting in the defense of Ohio, wrote to Governor Lucas asking for direction. *"... In pursuance of*

Benjamin Franklin Stickney

instructions, I proceeded, in July last, to Tecumseh, in Lenawee County, in the Territory of Michigan, and procured a writ of habeas corpus, returnable before his honor Judge Blanchard, for the body of Jonathan E. Fletcher, imprisoned in April last, for an alleged violation of the Territorial Law of February 12, 1835. …. His case was submitted to a jury upon the plea of not guilty. His Honor, Judge Fletcher, gave a very able and candid exposition of the law to the jury, who, after a short retirement, returned with a verdict of not guilty…. The mild and amiable deportment of Mr. Fletcher, as well as his firmness in maintaining, at the expense of his liberty, the rights of the State, have acquired for him many warm friends, even amongst those who contended most zealously for their rights of Michigan to the disputed territory.[49]

And last, but not in the least, was the case of Two Stickney who had been in hiding in Lower Sandusky since the infamous stabbing incident. Two wrote Governor Lucas on October 5, 1835 from Lower Sandusky.

Dear Sir: I look to you for advice. I therefore ask you to indulge my intrusion upon your Excellencies attention which I doubt not is fully occupied at this critical juncture…. Your age and experience in the vicissitudes of life I purpose has afforded your Excellency ample opportunity to sympathize or at least base with my impatience. Our situation appears bordering upon disparate. By your advice I have remained absent from my home and my business until I am reduced manly to this extremity of my means which were quite limited at the commencement of my exile. But be assured not only my pecuniary means but, my life also is devoted to the cause of principle. Should it appear consistent with your excellencies policy to gratify my impatience by communicating the period when the interests of the State will justify the setting aside exparte forbearance (if no other alternative will produce the desired effect) and permit us to share with your excellence the glorious legacy "Death rather than dishonor." T. Stickney

Benjamin Franklin Stickney

Michigan Territorial Governor John Horner wrote a report of his dealings with Two Stickney to President Jackson's Secretary of State.

"....I wrote a private note to Stickney, informing him that I should grant him a pardon, and therefore advised him against resistance to the process, which I knew to be the object desired by the Monroe party. ...... The District Attorney had the effrontery and timidity to say that "if he acted, the mob would throw him and myself into the river."

One of the last insults to Michigan occurred on December 23rd when Judge Daniel S. Bacon of Monroe wrote to United States Senator John Norvell of the Michigan Territory concerning the actions of Two Stickney.

"Dear Sir: Mr. Joseph Wood of this place, to whom Acting Governor Horner gave the requisition on Governor Lucas for the apprehension of Two Stickney; returned last evening from Columbus - I learn from Mr. Wood, that his Excellency did not recognize of our authorities, on the usual plea, that the act was committed within the Constitutional limits of the State of Ohio - his Excellency was kind enough to give Mr. Wood his objections in writing, which were sent to his lodgings. Mr Two. Stickney was the bearer, who it would appear, is in his Excellencies employ. .... The message and documents connected with the same, of Governor Lucas, needs no comment - I leave it with those who are injured to confute it."

Not only was the message delivered to Wood that Stickney would not be returned to Michigan, but Two was the one who delivered the message to Sheriff Wood. Two was said to have remarked who needs a pardon, when you have the governor on your side.

By March of 1836, it was generally acknowledged that for Michigan to enter the Union, she would have to cede to Ohio the "Toledo Strip" in exchange for the Upper Peninsula. On June 15, 1836 Congress passed an act admitting Michigan into the Union

Benjamin Franklin Stickney

once it surrendered the Toledo Strip for the Upper Peninsula. For the 49 delegates gathered in Ann Arbor there was really nothing to do but accept the plan. A presidential election was at hand, and if Michigan did not participate by its electoral vote it could hardly lay claim to the post-election patronage. Further, if Michigan was not a State by January 1, 1837, it could not have its share in the money from the sale of public lands. After 4 days of deliberations, the delegates turned down statehood by a vote of 28 to 21.

Senator Lucius Lyon expressed the feelings of Michigan in a letter to Dr. Zina Pitcher, a Detroit doctor.

"... All parties are courting the electoral votes of Ohio, Indiana, and Illinois and poor Michigan must be sacrificed. We shall probably be allowed to come into the Union if we surrender our rights, but the Union of gamblers and pickpockets, to a poor traveler who has just been robbed, is hardly to be desired...."

The border dispute of 1835 delayed Michigan's admission to the Union for over a year. However, this did not deter Michigan as it proceeded to act as if it were a state. In the fall of 1835, Michigan inaugurated their new government by electing Stevens T. Mason as Governor and by calling the legislature into session. The legislature elected John Norvell and Lucius Lyon as United States senators and Isaac Crary as representative. By this action, Michigan hoped to force Congress into seating the delegates when it met, as this would constitute a tacit recognition of the State of Michigan. Lyons, the most experienced of the delegates, was almost certain that it would fail because of the presidential election to take place in the fall of 1836. Lyons correctly deduced that President Jackson needed Ohio's electoral votes more than it needed Michigan.

After President Jackson and Governor Lucas had obviously arrived at a working agreement, and the matter had been referred to Congress for action, members of both parties assisted in a settlement. The Whigs wished to satisfy Ohio, and the Democrats feared to do otherwise. John Quincy Adams[50]

Massachusetts's congressman protested in the House and Missourian Thomas Hart Benton[51] in the Senate, but on June 15, 1836, Jackson signed the Clayton Bill "an act to establish the northern boundary of Ohio, and to provide for the admission of the State of Michigan upon the conditions therein expressed."[52]

The fact that there were twenty-nine congressmen in the House from Ohio, Indiana, and Illinois and thirty-five electoral votes from those states, which were all opposed to Michigan's interest, had been a highly important element in Ohio's favor.

The commercial interests of the state and especially the inhabitants of Toledo were happy at the outcome. With plans developing for the building of the Wabash & Erie Canal, it had become increasingly apparent that the canal ought to empty into Maumee Bay, rather than terminate at the town of Maumee. Persons interested in the development of Toledo naturally wanted it to be the terminus of the inland waterway. They preferred a political connection with a rapidly developing State, rather than with a territory just arriving at Statehood.

By the end of October another convention of assent was called for in Ann Arbor. The "Frost Bitten Convention" was underway. After two days of debate, Michigan's Territorial delegates voted 25 to 10 to join the United States, and on January 26, 1837 Michigan became the 26th state.

"... Gentlemen I have long looked for this day. I have sometimes thought that I would not live to see it; but I have lived to see justice, although tardy in her movements, at last triumphant. I came here twenty years ago, when there was nobody here but Indians, except Major Stickney. I used to wander along down by the bushes to meet him, when we would talk this subject over as a matter of diversion, for we were so weak that we could do little else, as nobody seemed to pay much attention to what we said, there being but two of us living on the disputed ground...."

The above was written by Judge Baldwin[53] and delivered at a meeting held in 1836 to celebrate Ohio's victory in the Toledo

Benjamin Franklin Stickney

War[54]. But it wasn't till 1867, almost 31 years later and after the Union's Civil War, that the full importance of Benjamin Franklin Stickney's involvement in the boundary dispute or Toledo War was fully realized. In a letter quoted from earlier for W. V. Way, February 9, 1867, Thomas W. Powell recalled some of the significant events of the Maumee Valley. The reminiscences first appeared in the Perrysburg Weekly *Journal* on March 13, 1868, and later in the Defiance *Democrat*, May 2, 1868.

"...... This settled the matter of jurisdiction, and the excitement produced by the [Toledo] war enabled Major Stickney to get the canal not only to Toledo, but even to Manhattan, five miles beyond where they wanted it, or had any use for it. Never, in either ancient or modern history, has there been an instance of secession and rebellion so successful, and no one is so entitled to be the hero of one of them, as Major Stickney of this."

Endnotes from Chapter Seventeen
a wedding, the stabbing, & a dead horse

---

[1]Major John Biddle was born in Philadelphia in 1792, graduated from Princeton College, and served with distinction in the War of 1812. His principal official positions were: Register of the Detroit Land Office from when the public lands were offered for sale to 1832, Territorial delegate to Congress from 1829-1831, member and president of the first Constitutional Convention 1835, a member and speaker of the House of Representatives in 1841. He was active in municipal and social affairs in Detroit; and being a fine scholar and elegant writer he contributed to the

instruction of the people of Detroit in the way of lectures, in connection with Gen. Cass, Henry Whiting, and Mr. Schoolcraft.

[2] Excerpts from *Maumee River 1835,* with the William C. Holgate Journal, edited by Louis Simonis, Defiance County Historical Society, 1979

[3] Commanded by Captain Chase.

[4] The Eagle Tavern was considered Toledo's third hotel when it opened in the Spring of 1834, and was owned by Ira C. Smith. It was purchased by J. H. Booth in 1837.

[5] Originally it was called the Port Lawrence House, with the merger of Port Lawrence and Vistula in 1833 it was renamed the Toledo House.

[6] The Mr. Daniels mentioned was William P. Daniels, one of Lucas County's first County Commissioners. Mr. Daniels sold the tavern in 1835 to E. Knapp. Mr. Knapp ran an ad in the December 12, 1835, issue of the Toledo Blade informing prospective customers that the Toledo House was under new ownership. In 1842, with the canal about to open, a third floor and broad porch was added and it was named the Indiana House.

[7] On Sunday, May 10, 1835, Stickney's youngest daughter Indiana married Platt Card.

[8] Platt Card in the ensuing years would be listed as property tax delinquent for the lands he owned in Toledo.

[9] In the author's opinion David White of Sylvania and or Whiteford had the most to gain in such an enterprise. A Michigan supporter this would give his mill access to the Michigan markets using the newly created Erie & Kalamazoo Railroad and its proposed connections to Monroe and Detroit.

[10] Lawyer later to become Associate Justice of the United States Supreme Court.

[11] Strong Democrat and supporter of VanBuren, favored Lewis Cass, from Cincinnati and former speaker of the Ohio Senate. Director of the Ohio Life Insurance and Trust Company.

[12] Ohio Democrat and strong supporter of VanBuren, United States Senator from Ohio 1837-1849.

[13] The occasion was the unveiling of the statue of St. Patrick at Father Edward Hannin's Institute adjoining St. Patrick's church in Toledo by Governor William Allen on March 18, 1874.

Benjamin Franklin Stickney

[14] David White accepted an appointment as a general in the Michigan Territory militia, while he kept his post office, established June 2, 1835, with postmaster James White, operating in Whiteford for as long as he could. Even as Toledo was returning to the use of Ohio postmarks, the Whiteford office continued to us the manuscript (ink cancels) bearing Michigan markings. David White eventually reconciled the fact that he was an Ohioan, lobbied for, and was appointed a Lucas County judge. The village of Whiteford also accepted the fact, and became the post office for Sylvania on February 12, 1859.

[15] Mary Matilda Way was the widow of Washington's Andrew Way.

[16] J. Baron Davis a young attorney, along with Dr. Clark, J. Irving Browne Jr., and J. W. Fellows erected what came to be called the "Bachelor's Hall" in May of 1834. Several other historians have argued that this location was nucleus of the Ohio agitation. "Bachelor's Hall" was located 150 feet north of Summit street and halfway between locust and Walnut.
J. B. Davis opened the Mansion House in 1835, located on the north side of Summit street and a little east of Locust street. The Mansion House was the location of the stabbing.
In 1837 he was Treasurer for the City of Toledo, and in 1838 Davis was appointed a School Examiner.

[17] Some sources have said that the knife that Two had was a dirk, which was described as a small pen knife with a blade of about two inches.

[18] Ira Smith opened the Eagle Tavern in 1834 on the south side of Summit street near Elm street. In 1836 Ira Smith built and managed the three-story brick hotel in Vienna, Michigan. The hotel was on the main stage route between Toledo and Detroit. Much later in 1847 he became the postmaster for Erie, Michigan.

[19] Started the Toledo HERALD, Toledo's first newspaper, with Mr. Browne. Further information comes from the recollections of Richard Mott, contained in H. S. Knapp's HISTORY OF THE MAUMEE VALLEY. "On the southeast corner of Summit and Lagrange streets, was a two story frame store, belonging to and occupied by Dr. Jacob Clark, the sign over the door being Clark & Bennett. This corner was then regarded as about the centre of business, ..."

[20] Dr. Clark based his diagnosis on Wood's barely perceptible and weak pulse.

Benjamin Franklin Stickney

[21] Moved to Monroe County, Michigan, from Elmira, New York, in 1835, and settled on a farm in Erie Township. Dr. Southworth had an extensive practice in the southern part of the county. He died from complications resulting from a fall in a barn on September 17, 1843.

[22] According to later testimony it was about 3 in the afternoon when the altercation took place, and there were about six to eight other patrons in the tavern. By the next morning a crowd of between forty or fifty residents of the disputed territory had gathered at Smith's Eagle tavern for a glimpse of the *"mortally wounded sheriff's deputy."*

[23]. On one occasion a Michigan *posse* attempted to arrest an individual in the dead of the night. After a flight down the river for about a quarter mile the pursued man jumped on a log near the shore and paddled across the Maumee River and freedom. It was generally believed that this man was Andrew Palmer, editor of the Toledo GAZETTE. Palmer was extremely active for Ohio, and kept Governor Lucas informed as to what was going on in the Toledo "strip." He was generally regarded as Lucas's right hand man in Toledo, and was knick-named by the Michigan group as "Governor Palmer."

[24] During the winter of 1835 and 1836 the GAZETTE & HERALD made their appearance, absorbing the original Toledo GAZETTE. This paper had a circulation of about 100 copies. At this time the Ohio Michigan Boundary Dispute was claiming the attention of all the inhabitants of the Maumee Valley, and any person who did not favor the cause of Ohio was termed a traitor by Andrew Palmer's GAZETTE. A paper was published at Perrysburg called the "Miami of the Lake." This paper's editor championed the cause of Michigan. The location of the first newspaper office was on the southwest side of Lagrange between the Maumee River and Summit, about 100 feet from the corner of Lagrange and Summit. Mr. Elias Fassett was Toledo's first news boy, he carried a route of 25 GAZETTE's within the territory bounded by Cherry and Elm streets, then called Vistula.

[25] Mr. Asa W. Maddocks, a Toledo pioneer in the Nursery business, was an apprentice typesetter, or "devil," in the office of the Toledo *GAZETTE* when the "Michiganders" wrecked the office in retribution for the paper's stand on the Ohio Michigan boundary dispute.

[26] Graduated from the United States Military Academy in 1818, plied his trade as an engineer in the United States Army constructing fortifications. He was responsible for the construction of the canal through the Dismal Swamp in Virginia, and served as astronomer in

determining the boundary line between Ohio and Michigan, 1832-1836. Talcott was always interested in practical astronomy, and while working on the Ohio Michigan boundary line devised a method of determining terrestrial latitudes through the observation of stars near the zenith, adapting the zenith telescope to the purpose. "Talcott's Method" was first described in the *Journal of the Franklin Institute, October, 1838.*

[27] Washington Hood was appointed to the United States Military Academy and graduated in 1827 as a topographical engineer. Worked at his trade from 1831 to 1836 resigning from the military in 1836. Reenters the military as Captain of the Topographical Engineers. With Robert E. Lee, in 1835, they determined the boundary line between Ohio and Michigan.

28 Born in Virginia, educated at West Point, graduating in 1829, Lee spent the next seventeen years as a second lieutenant of engineers. In the summer of 1835 he aided in running the boundary for Ohio and Michigan. His biographer Douglas Freeman, was in possession of a letter written by Lee in which he describes killing the keeper of the Pelee Island Lighthouse. A close examination of this letter will reveal that the keeper was nothing more than a snake common to the islands that they found when they entered the lighthouse.

[29] Please note that it was ten thousand more than Ohio appropriated for military action.

[30] Captain David Wilkison recollects that as a 15 year old deck hand for his Uncle, Captain Jacob Wilkison, the Mulhollen Family were passengers on their first voyage up the Maumee River to Maumee City in 1815. This is the same family whose hotel or inn located in Vienna was used by the Michigan troops during the Ohio Michigan Boundary dispute.

[31] This is the same Charles Schaler who as a young attorney from Cleveland, Ohio, delivered the message from Secretary of State to General Hull that war with Great Britain had been declared. The message was sent by mail to Cleveland where Schaler took on the duties of special messenger on June 28th finally catching up with Hull on July 2nd.

[32] Born in Virginia in 1802, graduated from Washington College and practiced law in Virginia till 1835. September 9, 1835, President Jackson appointed him Secretary and acting Governor of the Territory of Michigan.. In November of 1835 the people of Michigan elected a

legislature and state officers and hence refused to recognize the authority of Governor Horner.

[33] Actually in the middle of Horner's tenure as governor, the citizens of Michigan elected Mason as their first elected Governor under the state's constitution.

[34] Dr. George G. Baker was the first physician of Erie County, Ohio. Originally from Connecticut in 1822 he settled in Florence Township, later moving to Norwalk. He was quite successful in treating ague [Malaria].

[35] From a collection of five letters offered for sale by NB Books and Americana, Boston, Ma. Written on Tuesday, September 1, 1835 from Dr. George G. Baker of Florence Township, Erie County, Ohio, to George R. Lewis of New London, Connecticut.

[36] Was born in Monroe County, Michigan, in 1811. By occupation a farmer, lived first in Vienna, and afterwards in Erie. He was a Representative in 1849, 1857-8-9, and Senator in 1861-2.

[37] Came to Vienna, Monroe County, in 1830 from Lancaster, Pennsylvania. His son was later to become Senator from Monroe County.

[38] Charles Blivens had indicated in his address to the Maumee Valley Pioneer Society the 100 volunteers were in actuality arriving by the hundreds. Saturday 100, Sunday 1,000 volunteers with pieces of field artillery had arrived.

[39] VanFleet asked for twenty volunteers and received thirty.

[40] According to Andrew Palmer in a letter to Governor Lucas on September 8, 1835. "...*the forces of Michigan had to outwitted, since the Ohioans were out numbered, and reinforcements could not be brought up because of heavy rain which had rendered the Black Swamp impassible.*" This story may have some credence because of the heavy rain that also fell at Mulhollen's farm on the Michigan troops.

[41] Early Maumee Valley lawyer who later endowed the Way Public Library in Perrysburg. Wrote good early history of the "Toledo War." No relation to Andrew or George Way.

[42] "*The Blue Heron Council Ground turned into the Swan Creek Trading Post, once the Salt Beings [whites] pushed this far north. It is now a designated historic landmark in present day downtown Toledo, not because the old Council Grounds stood there, but because the site is occupied by the*

a wedding, the stabbing, & a dead horse
chapter seventeen

1853 Oliver House, a hotel, which has been deemed historic by the [white] settler government." From *Land of the Three Miamis,* Barbara Alice Mann, University of Toledo Urban Affairs Center Press 2006.

[43] Every year a lone person would introduce a bill to the Michigan Legislature asking for remuneration for the killing of his horse. In 1846, the Michigan Legislature finally settled his claim for $50.00 for the dead horse, and ten years interest on the $50.00 award.

[44] Lyman was attending Granville Literary and Theological Institute, later known as Dennison University, and would visit his parents as time would permit.

[45] The following is an excerpt from *Early Times* a monograph by Sara Rowsey Foley.

"..... Another original was our neighbor who lived just across the street -- Judge Draper. He had been a druggist at the corner of Lagrange and Summit streets for years; was made associate judge. When we came he had retired from all business except to make pills occasionally, and when he did, he always sent word to my mother that he had "some nice fresh pills," and she always laid in a stock and we had to take them. The judge had selected parts of such chapters from the Bible as appealed to him and declared that was the rule of his life. He did not believe in going to church, never entered one, and yet when he died he was taken there, and a funeral oration preached over him, which he certainly deserved, as he was, indeed, in every sense, a good, honest man, but I am sure he would have protested if he could. His wife, Grandma Draper, was the dearest old lady, whose tea parties were never slighted. ..."

[46] The author was always interested in how Lyman Draper had access to the historical figures of the northwest, and how he was able to interview them. Actually it was quite simple, his parents were friends with those people and they had probably shopped in their store, which was located on Lagrange between Huron and Erie. Lymans father, Luke Draper, was quite involved in the politics of the region. The first recorded instance was April 27, 1836, as a member of Lucas County's first Grand Jury. In 1839 he was the county's Tax Assessor, and in June of 1843 Lyman Draper was an Associate Judge of Lucas County. As late as 1872, Harriet Draper was still living in Toledo at 191 Superior Street with Lyman's brother Marvin.

[47] *Pioneer's Mission - The Story of Lyman C. Draper,* William B. Hesseltine, 1954, page20

[48] "The Oakland Whig," October 28, 1835

Benjamin Franklin Stickney

[49] From a letter dated October 13, 1835 from the Hon. Gustavus Swan to Ohio Governor Robert Lucas.

[50] In 1817 John Quincy Adams was Secretary of State for President Monroe, and as such was well acquainted with the principals in the Boundary Dispute. Elected to Congress in 1831, he was returned for eight successive terms.

[51] First elected to the Senate in 1820, and was responsible for the bullet in President Jackson from an earlier melee in a tavern in which Thomas supported his brother Jesse. Later Harts and Jackson's view came together when Hart supported Jackson's attempts to keep the union together.

[52] Working behind the scenes in Washington, Cass proposed that as a compromise Michigan be admitted as a state, that she surrender the Ohio strip, and accept as recompense that area north of the Straits of Mackinac, now known as Michigan's Upper Peninsula. It was the land that he and Schoolcraft explored; he knew its timber and mineral riches. Schoolcraft was privy to this plan and came to Washington to advocate it. He told a Senate Committee that the region would be *"found of far greater value and importance to the state than the seven mile strip surrendered."*

[53] Saturday, June 25, 1836.

[54] Two fictional accounts of the *"Toledo War"* can be found in literature. The first *The Wolverine: A Romance of Early Michigan* was written by Lansing native Albert Lawrence and published in 1904. *Curse of the White Panther* was the second book of a Michigan trilogy by Merritt Greene which had the "Toledo Strip" as its background.

Benjamin Franklin Stickney

Of all the questions concerning the Ohio/Michigan War that were circulating through the hotels, taverns, and back rooms of Washington, the one question that eluded even the insiders of the *Toledo Strip* was the armament of Michigan's militia.

Ohio Governor Lucas had always charged that the Michigan Militia under General Brown had received arms and ammunition from the Federal Arsenal in Detroit.[1] Col. Henry Whiting a career army officer and head of Detroit's federal arsenal was a close personal friend of Sec. Cass from his early days as territorial governor. Politically, once he discovered that the arms and ammunition had been issued, Sec. Cass went to great lengths to distance himself from the arms deal, and physically demand that the arms and ammunition were promptly returned. Sec. Cass always denied giving advice to anyone in the controversy, except in private letters, written as a private citizen, in a private way, and therein lays the response. Cass, contrary to the views of President Andrew Jackson's Administration, held that Michigan was entitled to the area in dispute, until possession had changed by due course of law.[2]

"In conversation with Messrs. Rush and Howard, in April last, they informed me that the President had ordered the public arms that had been issued by Col. H. Whiting to the authorities of Michigan Territory, to be forthwith returned to the Detroit arsenal. ... These arms were probably returned under said order at that time; but we find public arms again in possession of the people and authorities of Michigan, particularly at the time the attack was made on our boundary commissioners, on the 26 th of April.... In the course of conversation with him, I alluded to a report that Governor Mason had broken into the arsenal at Detroit, and taken possession of the U.S. arms and ammunition. General Haskil, in reply, observed that such were not the facts; he said that they did not take the arms by force; that Governor Mason applied to the keeper[3] of the arsenal for arms; that the keeper declined issuing them as being without authority from the Ordinance Department, but at the same time told Governor Mason that if he would take them on his own responsibility he might do so, and informed him where he might find the key of

Benjamin Franklin Stickney

the arsenal. General Haskil said that the key was procured by Mason, and that the authorities of Michigan took from the arsenal such arms and ammunition as they wanted." [4]

The ammunition and arms scandal running through the Nation's Capital only enhanced the image of the three conspirators in Michigan. Major Whiting was elected a director for the Bank of Michigan and the St. Joseph Railroad.[5] Later in his career he was brevetted a brigadier general. Whiting continued to publish articles in the *North American Review* which appraised Henry Schoolcraft's book on the Iroquois, and later a detailed article on General Zachary Taylor. He spent the greater part of the early 1840's writing two books: *The Revolutionary Orders of General Washington* and the *Life of Zebulon Montgomery Pike.*

Before traveling to the federal Capital at Washington, Benjamin Franklin Stickney[6] and several other leading businessmen[7], dismayed at the political leanings of Andrew Palmer and Governor Lucas, gathered at the Mansion House to discuss the need for another newspaper. Financial support was promised, and Dr. Wilson Everett hired George B. Way[8], Stickney's son-in-law by marriage, to be the editor of Toledo's second newspaper, the Toledo *BLADE* [9] in December of 1835. Contained in the BLADE's first issue Way and Everett would define the course of Toledo's newspaper of note.

"Our readers will immediately perceive that the name we have assumed was suggested by the notoriety of a certain city in Old Spain obtained for a peculiar kind of manufacturing, and when they are reminded that in the pending contest with Michigan, it has been and will continue to be the duty of the Toledo press to fight with that valor and ability which the justice of their causes deserves, they will not deem the selection inapt. ..... We may be accused of intending to be exceedingly piercing and polished -- we mean no such thing. We may be accused of challenging the rest of the world. We do not write for our motto "nemo me impune lacessit." We should prefer to keep our blade always in its scabbard, and hope not to be compelled to use it often in the offensive. We should not like, however, to have it rust in its

Benjamin Franklin Stickney

sheath so that it will not easily leap forth when necessity or honor demand that we should use it. Our blade has no elasticity -- it will break before it will bend. Neither is it a mirror, wherein every passerby may see his own peculiar and perhaps narrow whims and prejudices reflected. Neither is our blade a heavy broadsword, nor a malignant little rapier; but we intend it shall be as sturdy as a Scottish claymore -- an instrument better fitted for long and enduring service than for use in brilliant exploits." [10]

To the residents of the once *disputed strip,* 1835 ended with another cause for celebration. Since there was so much confusion over the actual Ohio/Michigan boundary, the residents of the *Toledo Strip* paid no property taxes that year. Putting a period to the *Toledo War,* a committee of the Michigan Legislature presented the bill for *"carrying into effect the laws relating to the southern boundary of their state,"* included in the estimate was the pay of 1,200 men in service at $8 per month, $9,600, for a total of $19,341.05. While Ohio's cost to enforce their rights over the Territory of Michigan was $8,837.[11]

Almost ten days had passed before Toledo knew that Congress had officially established Ohio's northern boundary. The report was first published in the *BLADE* on Saturday, the 25th of June 1836, and reproduced in the *GAZETTE "… by request, as that paper was in sympathy with the other side of the boundary question."*

According to the *BLADE's* issue of the 25th of June 1836: *"The day was ushered in at sunrise by the firing of cannon and ringing of bells, as we read. Appropriate banners waved from hotels and public buildings. At 8 P.M. the citizens such as had a mind to the occasion, with many distinguished visitors, assembled at the Mansion House, Daniel Segur proprietor, and marched to the school house in which the memorable court was held the year previous, where a short address was delivered by Emery D. Potter, Esq., when the procession returned to the hotel for a dinner prepared in Mr. Segur's best style. The cloth being removed, toasts were read by different gentlemen present."* [12]

Benjamin Franklin Stickney

Recollections of their glorious defeat came from many members of the Michigan Militia.

"Cone was captain of an independent military company from Oakland County, and while posting sentries at night, Captain Ingram, of the Farmington Greys, attempted to play a joke on Cone. Captain Ingram crept up on him in the dark, through the tall vegetation encumbering the banks of the sluggish Maumee at that time, and caught Captain Cone by the leg. In an instant Captain Cone drew his sword, striking Ingram on the head, giving him a scalp wound, which was the only blood spilled in the service of that uneventful war." [13]

"... yes, I was a soldier in the Toledo War. It is so long ago, however, that the whole affair seems to me just like a dream. It was a time of great excitement in Michigan, and when we won our glorious victory the Territory went wild with enthusiasm. The whole Toledo war may seem very funny to look back at, but most of us went down expecting to risk our lives. Everyone expected bloodshed. .... Some of us were armed with guns, but the great majority carried long broom handles....... We were as well as I can remember, something over two hundred strong. The advance on Toledo,.... occupied four days. ..... We had a vast amount of fun on the march down. The farming people en route generally welcomed us enthusiastically because we were fighting for Michigan. .... The first night passed away without hostilities, however, and next morning the city surrendered. I don't know as you would call it a surrender, but they called out to us that there had better be no disturbance, and that if we would come in peaceably there would be no opposition to our entrance. Under this arrangement we entered the town, and were very finely entertained there. We all got acquainted with each other and established many lasting friendships. ..... The only person hurt, to my knowledge, was a Frenchman from up the Maumee Valley. The only firing was done by some rowdies not belonging to either army, and he was wounded by one of these. It is claimed that he was shot because of an old grudge." [14]

Benjamin Franklin Stickney

> "If there had never been any Toledo War the development of railroading would have commenced earlier than it did. When hostilities were at the warmest point, I was a partner with my brother in the only store of Manhattan. In 1835 we obtained a charter for a railroad from New Buffalo, a small town on Lake Michigan, to Manhattan, under the name of the Maumee Land & Railroad Company....... I have always thought Michigan was right, and I believe Toledo would be a much larger city if she had been in Michigan. ...... We did our banking business in Monroe and Detroit, and all our commercial business of a larger scale was transacted in those two places. More than one half of the population between here and Fort Wayne were French, and they had intermarried with Monroe, so that all their sympathies were with Michigan. But the people who came from Cleveland and the East were strongly Ohio men in feeling....... The chief trouble was of a civil character in collecting taxes. Officers came upon us from both sections and levied there taxes. I refused to pay either until the matter was settled, and I gained considerable notoriety by throwing the sheriff of Monroe County out of my store one day. Others also refused, not that we were unwilling to pay, but we wanted to know from Washington whom to pay to."[15]

With the question of disputed territory legally settled, the land speculation continued to expand. Judge Salmon Keeney, and Daniel Miller, a grocer, paid Isidore Morin $1,050 for more than 150 acres one mile north of the state line proposed by Ohio, and adjacent to the Maumee Bay and Halfway Creek, and about two miles from the natural shipping channel and Lake Erie. Daniel Miller further hedging his land speculation purchased Indian Island at the mouth of the Ottawa River in 1834. It was also interesting to note that Sylvania's General David White who was a staunch Michigan supporter purchased 260 acres of land adjacent to Manhattan and the proposed town of Harve.

Though they were potential competitors for the same business dollar, Harve and Manhattan were closely linked by water and proposed rail transportation systems. Businessmen, shippers, and captains realized the importance of having a major port located within several miles of Lake Erie, as opposed to six to

Benjamin Franklin Stickney

ten miles required to get to Manhattan or Toledo. Daniel Bacon, a Manhattan planner, along with lawyers Platt Card and Daniel Chase, who had an office in Manhattan, and Levi Humphrey, commissioner for the planned Harve Branch Railroad, purchased land in Harve. The Harve planners even renamed Halfway Creek to honor Joseph Vance, Governor of Ohio.

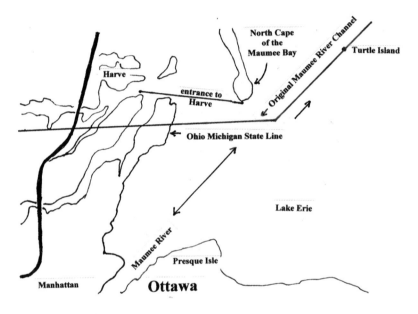

Proposed town of Harve, notice how it would link from Manhattan north to Monroe and Detroit. From the author's collection.

A close look at the Maumee River channel would note that the river's deep water course to Manhattan, Toledo, Maumee, and Perrysburg entered between Turtle Island and Wood Tick peninsula or the north cape of the Maumee Bay. Settlers from the Little Cedar Point area recalled that during times of low water they could drive their wagons on the sand bar all the way to Turtle Island. Even the Canadian Governor Simcoe recognized the importance of Turtle Island as the entrance to the Maumee Valley's interior. Simcoe placed several cannons and

Benjamin Franklin Stickney

fortifications to deny supplies to Fort Meigs from Lake Erie via the Maumee River.

Manhattan $3 bank note. From the author's collection.

Manhattan received another plus in its attempt to become a viable city on the Maumee River, when on Monday, the 8th of February a post office was established. Postmaster Daniel Chase, owed his appointment to the efforts of the Michigan authorities and postmarked his mail Manhattan, Michigan. The Manhattan post office switched to Ohio markings by November of 1836.

Daniel Chase also tried to help the development of Manhattan by visiting Detroit for the purpose of obtaining from the Michigan Legislature a *"State Charter"* for a bank. With the assistance of Governor Stevens T. Mason the charter was approved and issued. With the bank charter in his hand the first bank within the present limits of Toledo was brought into existence, and the Bank of Manhattan[16] was open for business. However, three years would pass before Ohio acknowledged the legality of the Manhattan Bank when it issued a State of Ohio charter to the bank in March of 1839.

The property on the west and northwest coastline of Harve began to sell rapidly, and on the 18th of May a notice appeared in the *Detroit Free Press*:

Benjamin Franklin Stickney

"We the undersigned do certify that said steamboat, MONROE, sailed up to the new city of Harve Thursday afternoon the 5th, where she landed the U.S. Engineers to survey the harbor. We found not less than eleven feet of water in the clear. It is a spacious, beautiful Bay, capable of containing a thousand sail of vessels, perfectly secure from all storms."

According to an early resident of the area Levi Morin, *"The colony was brought out on the steamer SUPERIOR. The people were prepared to start a good sized town, and they went to work at once to clear the wilderness. They came here in 1836."* Harve's graded streets soon boomed a warehouse, law offices, shops, two inns, and a hat maker along its 36 blocks. Michigan ordered two highways to be surveyed. One highway to Dundee and the other road to Indiana, both of which would be run through General David White's property in Sylvania.

The paper *Manhattan Advertiser*, which began in 1832, said that a natural spring was located in the waters east of Harve that contained all the healing qualities that are known to man. *"At present persons who wish to avail themselves to these waters, will find ample accommodations at Mr. VanDuzen's hotel at Harve...... Harve is only five miles from Manhattan and boats may be obtained here at any time."* [The spring can still be observed today west of present day Wood Tick Peninsula.]

Not only were the towns of Manhattan and Harve booming, but Toledo was receiving notice in the New York mail from Pierre M. Irving,[17] author Washington Irving's nephew.

"At the western extremity of Lake Erie, on the north side of the Maumee River, in the territory in dispute between Michigan & Ohio, stands a town which some with a modest & inventive taste in names have called Toledo. It has an excellent harbor; is rapidly rising into importance, & in the opinion of many is the germ of a second Buffalo. Here in all probability will terminate the Erie & Wabash Canal, & here also will terminate a rail-road already commenced running from the navigable waters of the

Benjamin Franklin Stickney

Kalamazoo River which empties into Lake Michigan. .... I go in company of John Berdan[18], the eldest brother of James, who removed to Toledo last autumn from his former residence in Ohio, & whose favorable representations have brought about this sudden determination." [19]

The winter of 1837-8 destroyed the fledgling town of Harve, with its unusual high water and ice. Not only was the Harve's Post Office flooded with two feet of water, but the entire town suffered the same fate. With the warming winds of Spring came an attempt at rebuilding the damage, but the winter of 1838-9 came with three feet of ice-clogged water throughout Harve. When the November storms subsided and the lake froze, the buildings of Harve were sold at auction, and hauled over the ice by teams of oxen to Manhattan. [20]

Not only was the speculation in the Maumee Valley coming from the wealthy authors of the time, but noted author, lawyer, and spokesman Daniel Webster, was receiving information on the available lands along the proposed rail line called the Erie & Kalamazoo to Adrian.

"..... I have located for you about 400 acres of land in the County of Hillsdale. ..... it is finely timbered good land and being in exact western course from this point may have a Rail Road pass through it which is chartered to extend from Sandusky to Toledo, thence to the western line of Ohio. You will perceive it is in the Disputed Territory.[21] .....'[22] signed [Toledo resident and attorney.] *Joseph R. Williams* [23"]

Another letter reached Daniel Webster with possible land offers. *"... Your remarks respecting lands upon great lines of communication at Government prices are certainly entirely correct, but it is difficult to get such, at least here. Good lands along the route of our Michigan & Illinois Canal are worth 5 to 10 dollars per acre. ...... When the canal is made, Chicago will be the outlet of the whole country on the Illinois river & its branches, one of the richest in the West. ..... I think no place West of Buffalo will rival Chicago, unless it be the Mouth of the Maumee*

Benjamin Franklin Stickney

in Ohio. Michigan Territory is promising, but lands are high there, & speculation, intense. ...[24] signed [Law student of Webster's and a Detroit resident.] *Fisher A. Harding* "[25]

"A small strip of country through that region must inevitably become as great a thoroughfare as any in the United States. I have reason to know that the Rail Road project will be pushed, ... Indeed before I left Toledo those principally interested in the charter for the Ohio portion of the Road offered to make me a Director. The land to be obtained however is near a continuation of the same line in Indiana. The soil through that country is "Openings" of fine quality & the country inviting to settlers. ..... From the information I had when I left the country I think 20,000 acres of land could be obtained which would promise greater returns than any country I know of at the west, especially as there are few speculators in it. Indeed I think the profits would be very great. ... signed Joseph R. Williams " [26]

And finally a letter from Pierre Irving on the 23rd of June really brings home the tremendous amount of speculation in the land available that had occurred since the boundary dispute was settled.

"....... P.S. Intelligence has just been received of the settlement of the boundary question in favor of Ohio. This decision is conclusive as to the termination of the Erie & Wabash canal at Toledo, over which point Ohio will now have undisputed jurisdiction. This place must now infallibly become the depot of the longest canal communication in the U.S. or indeed in the world, for the Wabash & Erie Canal with its various branches will exceed 1000 miles. ...."

With all the land speculation that was sweeping through the *disputed territory*, the population of the Toledo area was surprised when a Michigan sheriff by the name of Elijah Hayden, tried to take the horse of Thomas Carr [27] on the 15th of June to satisfy a judgment against him. Of all places in Toledo, the attempted legal seizure of property occurred at the white frame

Benjamin Franklin Stickney

building with green shutters of Ira Smith's Eagle Tavern, at Summit and Elm Streets.

Knowing that the patrons of the Eagle Tavern were Michigan sympathizers, Constable Hayden apprehended Carr's horse and took him to the Eagle Tavern. Thomas Carr known throughout Toledo as one of the rough and tumble *Ohio Boys* had been alerted that his prize horse was at the Eagle Tavern. Carr arrived just as Hayden was about to leave for Monroe. While Carr removed the horse's restraints, Hayden who had been watching from inside the tavern, rushed outside to the Eagle's hitching post. The hickory club [28] that Carr wore to protect him from the Indians, caught Hayden on the side of the head dropping him to the ground. Tavern keeper, Ira Smith and friends, took Hayden inside to keep Carr from really punishing him for stealing his horse.

Hearing that a horse thief masquerading as a Michigan sheriff had been caught, a large crowd began to gather in front of the American House. Driven by large quaffs of whiskey, the crowd was talking of breaking into the Eagle House and lynching the horse thief, when Carr with his hickory club bouncing off his leg marched off with his horse.[29]

With the last of the *incidents* firmly behind the fledgling Toledo, the Ohio Canal commission in late August of 1836 decided to continue the canal through Toledo to Manhattan for its terminus. Both Maumee and Toledo were to have connecting canals or side-cuts to the Maumee River. While the actual decision was made in August, the contracts for construction were not let for another nine months.

The canals were still in the construction phase in 1836 when the first passengers and freight were carried on the Erie & Kalamazoo Railroad. Until steel rails became available, the railroad used oak rails with strap steel spiked on the top. The first passenger cars looked like stagecoaches with steel wheels, and the entire "train" was pulled by horses.

Benjamin Franklin Stickney

harve, manhattan, & lectures
chapter eighteen

The first lady passenger on the E&K was Mrs. Clarissa Harroun of Sylvania on the 3rd of October 1836. Mrs. Harroun had been visiting relatives in the east when she arrived by passenger steamer in Toledo. Expecting a carriage ride for the rest of journey to her home[30], she opted to take the *"excursion train,"* from the foot of Monroe Street. The management of the line treated her with special care and dignity and placed a parlor chair on a flat car and with the rest of the gentlemen passengers sitting on the rough boards of the car, started on their way to Adrian via Mrs. Harroun's home in Sylvania. [31]

Ad for the Erie and Kalamazoo Railroad. Courtesy of the History of Toledo and Lucas County, Waggoner, 1888.

With Toledo now functioning as a fully incorporated city since Saturday, January 7th, 1837 Toledo's first election for Mayor took place on the 6th of March the same year. Whig candidate John Berdan beating the Democrat Andrew Palmer by one vote.

For the first year of the railroad's operation, the Erie & Kalamazoo Railroad terminated at the foot of Monroe Street, close to the beginning of Water Street. A meeting was held with

Benjamin Franklin Stickney

the Vistula land owners in 1837 for the purpose of extending the railroad east to Lagrange Street adjacent to the river. The residents decided to offer the Erie & Kalamazoo Railroad a strip of land which was then under water[32], on the south side of Water street, 50 feet wide, extending on a line between Lynn and Cherry streets, thereby making Vistula (Toledo) the first town west of the Allegheny Mountains to have a railroad. A steam locomotive, Number 80 of the Baldwin Locomotive Works, was brought from Philadelphia to Toledo by water and placed in service. It attained a top speed of 20 mph, and was used to carry the mail for the 33 mile run to Adrian.

During 1837, the track was extended along what is now Water Street, to the foot of Lagrange Street. The tracks were laid atop piles bridging the water, parallel to the shore line of the Maumee. At times the railroad was from 50 to 200 feet from the shore line. Water Street was not filled in till 1843. This railroad on piles would give Stickney an idea to boom Manhattan several years later.

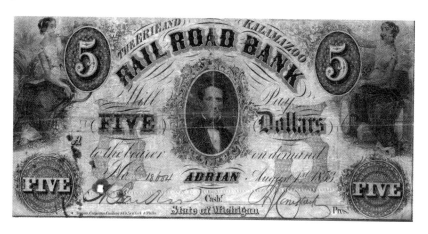

Erie & Kalamazoo Railroad's Bank. $5 note. From the author's collection.

Benjamin Franklin Stickney

Dresden Howard & Chief Winameg carved by Jim Stadtlander from the remnants of the 300 year old *Council Oak* from the Howard Farm near Winameg, Ohio. The carving is located in the Sauder Museum, Archbold, Ohio, Photo from the author's collection.

An interesting sidebar to the Erie & Kalamazoo Railroad was written by Dresden Howard and appeared in the March 20, 1895 issue of the Toledo BLADE. The article chronicles the appearance of the steam locomotive on the iron strapped tracks of the Toledo to Adrian railroad. The 20 year-old Dresden Howard and his friend Otis V. Crosby were riding their ponies with their Indian companions northwest of the city when they encountered the *Chim-mi-chim-min-i-too*, "Devil of the Woods," making its way towards Adrian. The horses were so startled by the *Pa-si-go-gi-she Pe-waw-bick*, "Iron Horse," that they refused to cross the tracks. *Reading between the lines, Howard indicates that by the mid 1830's, that both Indians and whites were on the most friendly of terms and enjoyed each other's company.*[33]

harve, manhattan, & lectures
chapter eighteen

In early May of 1837, Daniel Webster and his family set out on a tour through the Midwest to inspect the properties that had been purchased in their name. Their schedule was rather adventuresome, but accepted dinner invitations from Frederick Bissell, after turning down an invitation from Benjamin Franklin Stickney because of time constraints.

"I have the pleasure to inform you that the Hon. Daniel Webster has consented to partake of a dinner with his friends in Toledo on Thursday next - Mr. Daniels & myself will remain here to accompany down at that time - You will give this information to our friends, and take the necessary arrangements for his reception." [34]

Returning from his visit to Adrian, Michigan, famous orator and statesman Daniel Webster arrived in Toledo on board the steamer *Commodore Perry* at 1 pm on Thursday, July 13th, 1837. Webster received a rousing welcome, and was escorted to Perrysburg to tour the grounds of Fort Meigs. The entourage returned to Toledo for a 5 pm dinner at the American Hotel attended by Mr. Segur and Toledo's finest gentlemen and their ladies. They were rewarded with a one and one half hour speech.

Four weeks after squiring Daniel Webster, one of the Maumee Valley's newest land holders through the rich farm land and luxurious forests that once belonged to the Ottawa Indians, some of the earliest inhabitants of the Maumee Valley consented to finally leave for lands west of the Mississippi River.

Wasaonoquette, grandson[35] of Pontiac, in August of 1837 would lead one faction of the Maumee Ottawas consisting of 174 men, women, and children to the Kansas Territory. They boarded the steamboat COMMODORE PERRY for Cleveland, Ohio. From there they traveled by canal boat to Portsmouth on the Ohio River. They were under the care of Col. John McElvain, and John Mack, D. H. Forsyth, and C. Roby of Maumee City were attached to the expedition as commissary and interpreters.

Several members of the Ottawas under Ottokee, about 150 in number, decided to remain in the Maumee Valley for almost another two years before they finally left for the Territory of Kansas.

NOTICE,

IS hereby given, that arrangements are now nearly completed for the removal of the Ottawa Indians of the Maumee Valley, to their intended residence, west of the Mississippi. It is now confidently anticipated that they will depart on their journey in the course of a few days. These Indians are unfortunately considerably indebted to individuals in this section of the country, and it is their anxious wish, as it is that of all who are in any way connected with the business of their removal, that all who may have any just outstanding claims or demands *against any of the Nation now about to emigrate,* will take the earliest measures for their adjustment. They will please present their accounts, properly proven, to the undersigned, who will, at the request of the Indians, enter into an arrangement for the payment of the same by instalments of one, two and three years, if paid out of their annuity, and if paid out of certain funds due the Indians by treaty, the payments may perhaps be paid in bulk, and at a much earlier date.

It is most fondly hoped that all those who may feel interested in the future welfare and happiness of this miserable race of beings; all who regard their own well being, and have an eye to the success and prosperity of the poor unfortunate Indian, reduced to extreme degradation and want, as are the fallen Ottawas of the Maumee, will lend their counsel, aid and influence, in favor of their speedy removal to a better home, and a more promising land.

It is with deep mortification and regret, that the undersigned has to state from recent information received, that some of the emigrating Indians have been threatened with detention by some of their creditors. Can it be true that such intimations have been made! What Philanthropic, feeling heart, can indulge such feelings towards so poor, degenerate a race of Savage wanderers, as the suffering Ottawas. They have now no country or home here; may the removing agent ask, in the name of humanity, in the name of justice, in the sacred name of mercy, that if any are secretly working to discourage the emigration of these unfortunate creatures, they would pause and consider the impropriety of their course.

The undersigned seriously feels the high responsibility resting upon him as an agent of the government. He wishes to cast no imputations, to make no inferences of unlawful interference, and will continue as he has done, to practice moderation and forbearance in the fulfilment of his official duties. With this view, he hopes all the good citizens of the Maumee will accord, in giving complete success to his present arduous undertaking.

In conclusion, it is requested that those who have been in the habit of selling liquor to the Indians, do so no more, as it will be impossible to remove the dissipated if it is continued, and they must to their own ruin, and to the annoyance of the good citizens, remain.

JOHN McELVAIN,

MAUMEE EXPRESS July 25, 1839
"The last poor remnant of the once powerful Ottawas, that has lingered here around their ancient hunting grounds, and the graves of their kindred, departed on Thursday last, for the country west of the Mississippi, on board the steamer Com. Perry, by the way of Cleveland & the Ohio Canal and river. Judge Forsyth, the Indian Agent has had infinite trouble in collecting the disjointed fragments of the decayed nation, and

inducing them to undertake a journey, which is the last hook upon which to hang a hope for their preservation."

MAUMEE EXPRESS September 21, 1839
"The Ottawa tribe of Indians arrived at St. Louis, in the Monsoon, on the 13th. Among this band there are two chiefs, Au-to-kee, the head chief, and Petonoquette, a much younger man. Au-to-kee is a son of the celebrated chief, Tushquaquier, who was looked upon by the Ottawa as the father of the tribe. Petonoquette is half French, son of Loniscan, a distinguished chief, who was killed, when Petonoquette was a mere child, by that most barbarous and ferocious of all warriors, Kish-hau-go, who afterwards committed suicide in Detroit jail, in which he was confined for murder. Au-to-kee and Petonoquette are represented as very good men, well informed, and not much inclined to barbarity. –reprinted from the Louisville Advertiser"

The founding of Toledo was just in time to stumble from the depression resulting from the financial panic of 1837 caused by President Jackson's money requirements of gold and silver for government payments.[36] Even the founding of a Temperance Society by the Rev. Isaac Flagler[37], and commerce building regular steamboat service by the steamboat SUN[38] from Manhattan to Perrysburg, couldn't prevent the Maumee Valley from sliding into severe financial difficulty in 1838. Then once the businessmen began to see improvement, the *"Drought of 1838"* encompassed the Maumee Valley, which was followed by an epidemic of malaria fever.

Northwest Ohio and the Maumee Valley experienced one of the worst droughts in recorded history. From the 3rd of July till October of 1838 there was no rain fall of any consequence. The Black Swamp dried and developed great cracks in the muddy bottom lands of the surrounding territory. The St. Mary's River was so low that no supplies could be brought down from the Ohio River, and the smaller streams and creeks throughout northwest Ohio were reduced to a fine dust.

Benjamin Franklin Stickney

harve, manhattan, & lectures
chapter eighteen

Dr. Daniel Drake one the Maumee Valley's most respected physicians in 1842 wrote about the Drought of 1838 in excruciating detail.

"The Summer and Autumn of 1838 were signalized by a drought of longer duration and geographical extent than had been experienced from the first settlement of the country. It extended from the River Raisin, or some point further north, round to the end of the Huron River, on the south side of Lake Erie, if not still further east. The country, quite up to all the sources of all the Rivers lying between the Raisin and the Huron, suffered in nearly equal degree under its withering influence. On the Bay and Estuary of the Maumee, according to Professor Ackley, no rain fell from the 3 rd day of July until the 15 th of October. Drs. Calvin Smith and George R. Perkins of Toledo reckoned its duration at four months In the Upper Valley of the Sandusky River, as Judge John Carey informed me, the last rain was the 17 th of May, after which none occurred till October. At Tiffin, lower on the same River, the wells went dry before the middle of July. All the smaller streams throughout the whole region were exhausted, and their beds became dusty. Wild animals of every kind found in that region, collected on the banks of the larger Rivers, and even approached the Towns. Deer and raccoons were numerous between Toledo and Maumee City; quails passed over the town plat; the frogs of the shallow and sedge waters of the old bed of Swan Creek, now dried up, migrated in countless numbers through the streets of Toledo the Maumee River. The wet prairies of the interior were dried, and the grass of the dried ones withered, the marshes and pools of the post tertiary uplands; even those of the Black Swamp from the Maumee to Sandusky River, were evaporated, their bottoms cracked open from shrinking, the leaves of many of the trees growing in them perished, and, in some instances, the trees themselves were killed. Under this great drying process it was, that the ordinary Autumnal fever was raised into such an epidemic as never was known before. But its sway was not equal in all parts of the region in which the drought prevailed. The excavation of the Canal was at that time going on from its mouth at Manhattan to its head at Maumee. The laborers, 400 or

Benjamin Franklin Stickney

500 in number, were chiefly Irish, who generally lodged in temporary shanties, while some occupied bowers formed with green limbs of trees. It does not appear that a greater portion of these operators suffered than of the resident population; but a far greater proportion died. Professor Ackley mentions a circumstance which deserves to be recorded. One Canal contractor kept a liquor store and sold whiskey to all whom he employed, which was freely drank by themselves and their families. The mortality among these was very great. Another contractor lodged his operators on straw beds, in the upper rooms of a large frame house; made them retire early; kept them from the use of whiskey; and nearly all escaped disease. The occurrence of rain about the middle of October, with subsequent frost, put an end to the epidemic." [39]

Rival cities like Sandusky, Monroe, Detroit, and Adrian which were actively recruiting eastern and foreign immigrants, openly nicknamed Toledo and the Maumee Valley, *Death Valley*.

With the majority of the Indians headed to lands west of the Mississippi, Toledo's City Council passed an ordinance at the urging of the Rev. Isaac Flagler and the Temperance Society to control the sale of intoxicating beverages. Included in the Ordinance signed by Mayor John Berdan was the following provision. *".....prohibiting sale or gift to minors, servants, apprentices or Indians."*

One of the last mentions of the Rev. Flagler[40], pastor of the Maumee Valley's Presbyterian Church, was a marriage ceremony that he performed on the 22nd of May in 1838 which united a mulatto named Richardson to a white girl from Norwalk, Ohio.

"The groom was an industrious, respectable man, and the bride supposed to be the chief promoter of the union seemed to act upon clear convictions as to the propriety of such connection, she being of a respectable family, and having a brother a student at Oberlin College, then the most pronounced Anti-Slavery School in the country. Mr. Flagler no doubt acted

Benjamin Franklin Stickney

conscientiously in the matter, but evidently against the prevailing sentiment of the community and a large portion of his own church."[41]

With Toledo gaining in prominence in the region with the construction of a jail, Benjamin Franklin Stickney thought it only proper that Toledo should have its own cemetery. Eight acres of land were given by Stickney and named Forest Cemetery by Toledo in 1839.

One of the most fantastic projects that caught the excitement of Toledoans, especially those that lived in Manhattan, was the Ohio Railroad Project of 1836-42. Supported by the people of Manhattan, the railroad promised to link the Maumee Valley to the markets of eastern Ohio and New York. The Manhattan part of the plan was to build a railroad on piles across the great *Black Swamp,* linking Manhattan with Sandusky. The proposed railroad was to use proven construction techniques similar to those employed to extend the Erie & Kalamazoo Railroad along Water Street.

If the Ohio Railroad would have started at the Pennsylvania line, alone it would have been years before the tracks arrived in Manhattan. Nehemiah Allen[42], president of the Ohio Railroad with $52,000 worth of stock, proposed that the railroad's construction start from both ends. Also the Ohio Railroad was overloaded with investors who had financial interests in Manhattan who were hoping for a quick turn around on their investment.[43] Two gigantic pile-driving machines on railroad flat cars were the main instruments in the building of the railroad. In the spring of 1839, under the supervision of Two Stickney, one of these machines started eastward from the wharf on the Maumee across the river from Manhattan, while the other machine started westward from Sandusky. The two were expected to meet near the middle of the Black Swamp.

Encouraged by the State, the Ohio Company literally plunged into the building of the railroad. Benjamin Franklin Smead, editor

Benjamin Franklin Stickney

of the Manhattan *Advertiser*, wrote editorials entitled, "Locomotion Forever," on the 22nd of January 1840.

"Take this work for all in all, we shall seldom look upon its like again. It is in fact the greatest modern work of the world, and one of which Ohio will hereafter be able to boast without egotism. In the first place it is the widest track (seven feet) - in the next, the best constructed - next the cheapest - next with the greatest facility - and last with the most faithful supervision in all respects of any work that came under our observation....... There's no humbug about this. Nine months will enable us to travel the far-famed Black Swamp (thirty miles) in less than two hours, which now takes two days."

With an enterprise composed of great ideas and little engineering expertise to go with it, mistakes were bound to happen. The engineers expected five miles of track per day to be laid on the steam driven piles, but within the first month they had laid less than a 1,000 feet of track. As they gained experience, their trackage increased, and their confidence enlarged to the point that they began to doubt the engineer's strength requirements. Shortcuts were taken on the required depth of the pilings as they started across the swamp. And as a result the tracks which held the steam-driven pile driver, several flatcars, and steam engine gradually slanted and fell into the *Black Swamp*. Workers remarked that the pile-driver, work cars, and steam engine fell like stacked dominoes. [44]

By 1842 the Ohio Railroad Company was bankrupt, and in 1845 the Ohio Board of Public Works sought to recover its $249,000 investment. The Board found the pile drivers worth only the value of recovered scrap metal; the elevated railroad structure in a state of advanced decay, and its steel rails had been removed by adjacent farmers and sold for scrap. Finally, the railroad right of way was worth only $30,000. [45]

Also in 1842 English novelist Charles Dickens stopped at Upper Sandusky on Thursday, April 21st during his travels from Cincinnati to Buffalo, and wrote.

Benjamin Franklin Stickney

"It is a settlement of the Wyandot Aborigines who inhabit this place. Among the company at breakfast was a mild old gentleman (Colonel John Johnston) who had been for many years employed by the United States Government in conducting negotiations with the Aborigines, and who had just concluded a treaty with these people by which they bound themselves, in consideration of a certain annual sum, to remove next year to some land provided for them west of the Mississippi. He gave me a moving account of their strong attachment to the familiar scenes of their infancy, and in particular to the burial places of their kindred; and of great reluctance to leave them. He had witnessed many such removals, and always with pain, though he knew they departed for their own good. …. We met some of these poor Indians afterwards, riding on shaggy ponies. They were so like the meaner sort of gypsies, that if I could have seen any of them in England, I should concluded, as a after of course, that they belonged to that wandering and restless people."

Just a year after Charles Dickens' visit to Upper Sandusky, the first canal boat from Lafayette, Indiana, the ALBERT S. WHITE arrived in Toledo, on the Wabash & Erie Canal. The boat's captain, Cyrus Belden and crew were entertained at a banquet in their honor at the Ohio House. An address was delivered by Benjamin Franklin Stickney in honor of the event. Later, in the evening the event was moved to the Indiana House to round out the celebration. A packet or passenger boat followed the WHITE and was captained by William Dale of Fort Wayne.

Twenty six year old Oliver Hazard Perry[46], a namesake and no relation to Commodore Perry, boarded a steamboat in Cleveland on Sunday, the 29th of October 1843, for the 100 mile journey to Toledo, Ohio. Eager to hunt deer in the great Cottonwood Swamp area west and north of Toledo, Perry recorded in his journal detailed observations of his arrival in Toledo[47]. From his profession as grain merchant, he recalled the 60,000 bushels of wheat the Erie & Kalamazoo railroad carried for export through Toledo to the eastern markets. Perry traveled the 33 miles to Adrian on the Erie & Kalamazoo, where he noticed with

Benjamin Franklin Stickney

satisfaction the 30 farm wagons waiting to load grain on the railroad. From his Journal:

"..... The Maumee River Valley provided shelter for a multitude of wildlife. The year the railroad began found the valley still teeming with white-tailed deer, black bear, wolves, cougars, lynx, wildcats, foxes, and turkeys, as well as a variety of small game. Quail were so abundant that they sold for twelve cents a dozen live and eighteen cents a dozen dressed. White-tailed deer abounded. An oak ridge, where Toledo's first high school would eventually be built, provided a favorite resort for them when they were not sheltering in Stickney's Woods[48]. V. H. Ketcham, a pioneer resident, built his house in Toledo on a favored deer runway. ...... After finding that deer where scarce at Adrian, he took the train to Blissfield, Michigan, halfway to Toledo, where he hunted two days in the Cottonwood Swamp[49]. Near Blissfield, Oliver saw for the first time a flock of prairie chickens. The open country between Blissfield and Toledo boasted thousands of these prairie fowl. In Toledo itself, on Summit Street near Oak[50], over five hundred prairie chickens were seen flocked together at one time." [51]

Placed in high regard by his fellow residents and citizens Benjamin Franklin Stickney would often give lectures at the Young Men's Christian Association on his life's activities and on his recollections as an Indian Agent."

During one of Stickney's lectures everyone in attendance that night, in the standing room only crowd, thought that the program was so exceptional that no one took a transcription. Even the reporters put down their pads and were enthralled by Stickney's dialogue. Several small snippets of the evening survived and have been included.

"The remains of extensive works of defense are now to be seen near Lower Sandusky. The Wyandot have given me this account of them: "At a period of two centuries and a half since, or more, all of the Indians west of this point were at war with all the Indians east. Two walled towns were built near each other, and

Benjamin Franklin Stickney

each was inhabited by those of Wyandot origin. They assumed a neutral position, and all Indians at War recognized that character. They might be called two neutral cities. All of the west might enter the western city and all the east the eastern. The inhabitants of one city might inform those of the other, that the war parties were there, or had been there; but who they were, or whence thy came, or anything more must not be mentioned. The war parties might remain there in security, taking their own time for departure. At the western town they suffered the warriors to burn their prisoners near it; but the eastern would not. An old Wyandot informed me that he recollected seeing, when a boy, the remains of cedar post, or stake, at which they formerly burned prisoners. The French historians tell us that these neutral cities were inhabited and their neutral character respected, when they first came here. At length a quarrel arose between the two cities, and one destroyed the inhabitants of the other. This put an end to the neutrality." [52]

Another source has been found that recalls the same lecture and the second recorded version was slightly different.

"The tradition has been handed down that there were two fortified neutral towns here (Fremont, Ohio). One on the west and the other on the east bank of the Sandusky, evidences of which in the shape of earth works were visible to and described by the early settlers of Fremont. Major B. F. Stickney, Indian Agent in Northwestern Ohio, in a historical address delivered in Toledo in 1845, said that the Wyandots had given him an account of these two towns; that some time, perhaps early in the seventeenth century, all the Indians west of the Sandusky were at war with the Indians of this point. There were two walled towns here, constructed near each other, inhabited by Indians of Wyandot origin. All of the western people might enter the western town and all the eastern people the village on the east. The people of one town were permitted to inform those of the other town that war parties were there, but anything more as to who they were or where they were from must not be divulged. It was claimed for these neutral villages that during the entire period of contests previous to and after the advent of the whites,

Benjamin Franklin Stickney

during which the Iroquois contended for victory and their enemies for life, this band of Wyandot preserved their integrity as neutrals and peacemakers. "All who met at their threshold met as friends" and this nation of peacemakers was yet here when the French missionaries penetrated to the upper lakes more than two centuries ago. These villages were in the end destroyed by internal strife."

In a letter published in the *Toledo Blade* of July 17, 1846, Maj. B. F. Stickney, by request of Elisha Whittlesey, made the following explanation of the origin of the name "Maumee."

"At an unknown, but very remote period, the Wyandot Indians were acknowledged to have the most power and wisdom of any of the any of the Eastern part of the Continent - occupying all the country north of the Niagara River and Lakes Ontario and Erie - having an absolute Monarchical Government, with its seat where Montreal now is. The title of the monarch, in their language, was Sans-taw-rit-sa. He exercised a general superintending control East of the Mississippi, and probably further west. The Wyandots acknowledged no superior, on the continent, except the Mexicans; and communication was kept up between Sans-taw-rit-sa and Montezuma. The tribe we now call Miamis, came subsequent to the Wyandots. The King of the Wyandots, for some cause, sent a deputation from Montreal as far west as where Fort Wayne now is. There, for the first time, they saw some persons of this tribe, and they were very old or ancient people, Mi-a-mi. The name they use for themselves is Tweet-twee. The French took their name from the Wyandots and gave it their authority. In English the sound would be Mee-a-mee - the French sounding i as we do ee; and a as we do in father. We took the orthography from the French, and they called this River Mi-a-mi because they found people here whom they called Miamis. They found some of the name on the two rivers discharging into the Ohio, and called by the same name. To distinguish between them, they said "The Miami of Lake Erie," and the "big" and the "Little Miami of the Ohio." During the extensive military operations on this river in the War of 1812, much use was made of the name by persons who did not

Benjamin Franklin Stickney

understand French, and took the French sound of Mi-a-mi to be Maumee; and when the City of Maumee was named, this corruption was confirmed."

"The Miamis showed me a treaty on parchment, which they negotiated with William Penn at Philadelphia. They said this was their first treaty with the white people. It had a blue ribbon attached to the seal. In addition, there was a pressed dried heart attached to the ribbon. The end of the ribbon appeared to have been inserted into the heart in its undried state, and then dried and pressed. They told me this was the heart of the Indian who was the signer, and who held it in his possession until his death."

It only seems fitting that Benjamin Franklin Stickney's biography would end with his own words. Written for the BLADE in the twilight of his years, the monograph was published on the 20th of August 1850 less than two years before his death. In it, Stickney recalled his treks into territory that only the indigenous people had tread, wondered at its beauty, and at the same time yearned for their land. This duplicity coupled with the frequent use of liquor epitomized the unspoken conduct of the government's cavalier attitude.

"I was sent from Washington the 8th day of March, 1812, as an Indian Agent to Fort Wayne. I left Hon. Jeremiah Morrow[53] as the only representative in Congress; we had boarded together. At Pittsburgh I took a detachment of troops for the relief of Fort Wayne. We descended the river to Cincinnati in arks; arrived there 1st of April; found it a tolerable sized village. The Postmaster told me that the gross receipts for that year was $600 at that post office. It was 120 miles to Fort Wayne, which we, of course, marched by land, passing the places where are now large towns of Dayton, Troy, and Piqua -- a few white inhabitants at each. At Dayton they had a tavern kept in a log cabin. At this time the line dividing the State of Ohio and the Territory of Indiana had not been run, and Fort Wayne was supposed to be in Ohio, and Ohio did not extend North of the Black Swamp. Very little was known of the topography of the

Benjamin Franklin Stickney

country; Lake Michigan was supposed not to extend so far South by 40 miles as it is now known to be. The city of Toledo was assumed to be in Michigan, and she exercised government here up to 1836 when Congress settled the question, and Ohio was put in possession of the territory she had been deprived of. We arrived at Fort Wayne on the 11th of April, 1812, 80 miles North of the boundary of white population. This being but a short time after Gen. Harrison had his battle of Tippecanoe, the Indians of all this country were in a great state of excitement. The quarrel of Gen Harrison with the Indians had given the British Government a vast preponderance of influence over them; even before this occurrence, the balance of influence was against the United States -- the Indians always holding themselves up at auction to the highest bidder between the two great parties, and the United States being always over bidden. And more than this, the British could not buy their lands in the United States and the latter were constantly urging them to the relinquishment of their title, (that we called buying), while the Indians never gave any title to land willingly. As the white population advanced, they coveted more land, and desired to drive the Indians off. They now urged the government to go through the forms of buying the lands they desired; and the government ordered their agents to buy their lands honestly and peaceably if they could, but to use all the means in their power to extinguish their title. Added to this, the whole frontier were goading on the agents to use such means as were necessary to accomplish the end. If from compunction of conscience in the agents, or from any other cause, there is a failure, the coverers of the lands are present to observe the result and report to headquarters that proper means were not used. Now, the poor agents have to suffer under the lash. The Indians have the physical power to do as they please with the agents; but, as the agents know more than the Indians, they govern them, and they are ignorant of the means by which they are governed. Such have been the causes of Indian Wars, and such was the cause of the War of 1812, so far as the Indians were concerned, and in the northwest it was essentially an Indian War. By such means has empire advanced westerly, and by the same means will the advancement be made to the Pacific Ocean. The government of *the United States have not managed their Indian Department well, especially in as much as they have sent armies against them to destroy or drive them off. If the government should determine certain tribes should be destroyed, rather than send armies to kill them with powder and lead, wherein it would cost at least the life or one white man to kill one Indian, besides the cash amount, she should select any Indian agent who had been well educated in Indian affairs, with proper instructions, and furnished with plenty of good meat and bread, and a little tobacco, and if there was a little whiskey it would be all the better[54]. He could call the Indians together, within 500 miles square, at any point he should choose, and keep them during his pleasure. I have had a high number of opportunities of making experiments upon the high feeding of Indians, and of observing the effects. In about six weeks disease will commence, in eight or ten mortality will ensue, and during the summer months they would die at the rate of 20 per cent, at least, and through the year they would probably range from 15 to 20 percent per annum; and those who might remain would be so enervated that they would not be dangerous. Objections may be raised against the morality of this mode; but, would it be moral to shoot them down? Or would the morality be imposed by the Indians shooting the white men? In this mode all the lives of the troops would be saved, and at least three-fourths of the cash, and the Indians well satisfied with the mode of doing business. I communicated similar ideas to the government more than 50 years ago."* [55]

Benjamin Franklin Stickney's footprints will always be in the Maumee Valley .... the Gateway to the West.

Endnotes from Chapter Eighteen
harve, manhattan, & lectures

---

[1]Colonel Henry Whiting, in charge of the government arsenal at Dearborn, released one thousand stands of arms and five thousand rounds of ball ammunition to the Michigan patriots. Governor Lucas screamed foul and blamed Cass, accusing him of ordering the issue and

Benjamin Franklin Stickney

siding with Michigan. This the secretary (of war Cass) denied, but he admitted privately that "the state of affairs in Michigan has given me great uneasiness, both as a public officer and a private citizen." He cautioned Mason that "the crisis is one for calm deliberation & not for rash action," adding that a just regard for the President called for moderation.

[2] Letter from Secretary of War Lewis Cass to Secretary of State John Forsyth, November 19, 1835.

[3] Col. Henry Whiting.

[4] Letter from Governor Lucas to the Secretary of State John Forysth, November 10, 1835.

[5] Later to become after reorganization the Michigan Central Railroad.

[6] Benjamin Franklin Stickney and his wife Mary Matilda Way left for Washington D.C. for the winter season of parties and political opportunities.

[7] Edward Bissell, Joseph R. Williams, W. J. Daniels, Coleman I. Keeler, Dr. Wilson Evertt, and Emery Potter.

[8] George B. Way, son of Benjamin Franklin Stickney's second wife Mary Matilda, moved to Toledo and opened a law firm with his partner Richard Cooke. At the urgings of Stickney, Bissell, and others he bacame the Editor of the Toledo Blade, December 19, 1835.

[9] There are numerous stories concerning the derivation of the BLADE name. Grove Patterson, editor and long time friend of the BLADE, says that the name was suggested by the brother of author Washington Irving.

[10] Grove Patterson, I LIKE PEOPLE: The Autobiography of Grove Patterson, Random House, 1948.

[11] Jonathon Fletcher, the lad that was imprisoned in Tecumseh, received $100 for his troubles, and General John Bell received $228 for commanding the Ohio forces. While Swayne, Allen, and Disney received three hundred dollars to talk to President Jackson in Washington.

[12] The BLADE, June 25, 1836.

[13] Excerpted from the Michigan History & Pioneer Collection, Vol 5, p204.

[14] Excerpted from the Michigan History & Pioneer Collection, Vol 7, p69-73.

[15] Dr. H. A. Chase, Excerpted from the Michigan History & Pioneer Collection, Vol 7, p69-73.

Benjamin Franklin Stickney

[16] The legality of that bank was brought into question when the bank tried to collect on note that was in default by Judge James Myers. The case worked its way to the Ohio Supreme Court. The Court decided in 1852 that the bank never had a legal existence, thus was never authorized to do business. The Court reasoned that the bank's charter was issued in 1836 by the Legislature of the State of Michigan. There was no State of Michigan till January of 1837.

[17] Pierre was a research assistant for his uncle, Washington Irving the noted author. Pierre made good on his promise to return to the west. Later Pierre would become an Editor of the weekly Toledo *BLADE*. A story that was later attributed to Pierre was that a friend of his in Illinois shipped a carton of books to him in 1837. the most economic way was by way of Illinois, Mississippi, and Ohio Rivers, to the Erie Canal, and finally across Lake Erie from Cleveland to Toledo.

[18] John Berdan who was later to become the first Mayor of the city of Toledo, was the eldest brother of Pierre Irving's wife Margaret. His brother James, whose addiction to alcohol is not well known, had been Pierre Irving's law partner in New York City.

[19] A letter from Pierre M. Irving in Albany, New York, to his friend Daniel L. Roberts on the 20th of February 1836.

[20] It should be noted that the U.S.Government thought that the town of Harve would succeed because it purchased land for a set of range lights of the mouth of Mudjaw Creek and the Ottawa River. The earliest mention that I could find of property description is January 15, 1845. *"excepting 941/1000 of an acre from the 10 acres lying in the sw corner of the se quarter of the ne quarter of section number 9 town 9 south of range 8 east."*

[21] This is the area surrounding Toledo, which was settled by Congress on June 15, 1836.

[22] Letter from Joseph R. Williams to Daniel Webster, 24th of May 1836

[23] Williams graduated Harvard in 1831, studied law with John Davis and after passing the bar moved to Toledo and later Michigan in 1839. Ran twice for the Senate against Lewis Cass. Finally winning a Senate seat in 1860.

[24] Letter from Fisher A. Harding to Daniel Webster, 2nd of June, 1836.

[25] Harding was a graduate of Harvard and a law student of Webster's. Moved to Detroit in 1838 and formed a law partnership with Fletcher Webster.

Benjamin Franklin Stickney

[26] Letter from Joseph R. Williams to Daniel Webster, September 28, 1836.
[27] Thomas Carr appears later in the Lucas County history as a contractor for a section of the canal construction.

[28] Conflicts between the Ohio and Michigan factions occurred so often that Ohio boys often carried hickory staffs with a rope loop through a hole at one end so that they could be carried hanging from their arm. The Ohio boys said that the clubs were to protect them from the Indians, or the Michigan tax collectors.

[29] Taken from the *History of Lucas County, Historical Hand Atlas Illustrated*, H.H.Hardesty & Co., Chicago, 1882, page 203.

[30] The Harroun farm was located in Sylvania, south and east of Erie Road and Harroun Road. The present day Flower Hospital would be a good representation of their farm.
[31] History of the City of Toledo and Lucas County, Ohio, Clark Waggoner, p406
[32] The Water Street extension was built on pilings driven into the bottom land of the Maumee. The land would literally be filled in under the rails when the Hog's Back, the high land between Summit Street and Superior Street, was removed.
[33] THE OTTAWA INDIANS AND THE ERIE and KALAMAZOO RAILROAD, Dresden W. H. Howard, edited by Randolph C. Downes, NWOQ, V24:N3:p136

[34] Excerpted from a letter from Frederick Bissell in Detroit to Benjamin Franklin Stickney in Toledo Tuesday July 11, 1837.
[35] "Pontiac at this time had three known sons. They were Ne-gig, She-gen-e-ba, and O-tusa. ...... Comparative ages reveal the O-tusa was about thirteen years of age when his father, Pontiac was killed. O-tusa's mother was Kan-tuck-e-gun, probably much younger than Pontiac. Ottawa tribal history is that Kan-tuck-e-gun lived until after 1831. O-tusa had four sons who came west with the Ottawas from Ohio in 1831, 1837, and 1839. These sons were Waseon, Ottokee, Wassonquette, and Notino. *The Chronicles of Oklahoma, The Ottawa Indians of Oklahoma and Chief Pontiac, by Norman G. Holmes. Pg 192.*
[36] Called President Andrew Jackson's *Specie Circular*. The presidential order required that all land purchases had to be in gold or silver. This

37 situation was aggravated by the amount of gold and silver that was being transferred to Europe to settle American accounts.

37 Pastor of the First Congregational Church, and Toledo's Mayor, John Berdan as treasurer.

38 Captained by C. K. Bennett

39 The article was written by Dr. Daniel Drake[39] in 1842 in which he described in great detail the drought of 1838. Dr. Drake was formerly from Toledo, moved to Cincinnati and was one of the most respected physicians of the region.

40 Rev. Isaac Flagler was the father of Henry Flagler. Henry Flagler with others formed the firm of Rockefeller, Andrews, and Flagler, which is now known as the Standard Oil Company. Builder of the Ponce de Leon and Alcazar Hotels in Florida. He also built the railroad to Key West.

41 From the diary of James R. Osborn. The notes were written while he was practicing law in partnership with Myron H. Tilden. In 1839 he was Clerk of the Ohio Senate. He later returned to Toledo as Treasurer of the Wabash Railroad.

42 Allen was a State Representative from Geauga County who lived and owned property in Manhattan.

43 The known holdings of the Manhattan interests in the Ohio Railroad came to $435,333, out of a total of $1,875,951.

44 Everything was eventually salvaged and their were places along Route Two in Ottawa County where the rotted piles could still be seen as late as 1960. The Ohio Railroad was soon seen as a laughing stock and was unable to raise additional funds to continue.

45 According to Charles Frohman in Sandusky's Yesterdays as late as 1960 the wooden piles could be seen in Pipe Creek near the Cleveland Railroad Bridge. The New York Central Railroad west of Huron, Ohio is located on the Ohio Railroad's right of way. Page 77.

46 Claiming early Cleveland resident, Judge Nathan Perry, as his grandfather, and Black River fur dealer Nathan Jr. as his father, Oliver Hazard Perry was born April 12, 1817. Named after the hero of the Battle of Lake Erie, Perry kept detailed accounts of his hunting expeditions through the old "Northwest Territory," from 1836 through 1855

47 "Hunting Expeditions of Oliver Hazard Perry," was first published in 1899. This edition, published in 1994, was edited by John E. Howard, and published by St. Hubert's Press, DeForest, Wisconsin.

Benjamin Franklin Stickney

[48] Sara Rowsey Foley in her monograph *Early Times* states: ".....*Judge Potter stated that he killed deer in every ward of the city. There were many in Stickney's Woods, now that part north of Elm and Magnolia streets.*"

[49] The Cottonwood Swamp, while lesser known than the Great Black Swamp, was just as treacherous to travelers. Located to the north and west of the sand ridge that stretched between Sylvania, Ohio, and Adrian, Michigan. The sand ridge can be easily located by following the deserted train tracks of the Erie & Kalamazoo railroad. Riga, Michigan would be about the center of the swamp.

[50] Oak Street has been renamed to Jackson. Summit and Jackson was the approximate location of Stickney Hall.

[51] From "Hunting Expeditions of Oliver Hazard Perry," 1994 edition, page 12.

[52] HISTORY OF THE MAUMEE VALLEY, H. S. Knapp, Toledo 1877, page 506-7

[53] United States Representative (1803-1813, 1840-1843) and Senator (1813-1819) from Ohio. Jeremiah Morrow was born in Pennsylvania October 6, 1771. Trained as a surveyor, he moved to the Northwest Territory (Ohio) in 1795. He was a State Canal Commissioner for Ohio in 1822, and Governor of Ohio from 1822-1826. Chairman of the Committee on Public Lands for the 26 th and 27 th Congress. Elected as a Whig. Morrow County, Ohio is named for him. Died March 22, 1852, and is buried in Warren County, Ohio.

[54] Gladwin to Amherst, November 1763
> *They have lost between 80 and 90 of their best warriors; but if your Excellency still intends to punish them further for their barbarities, it may be easily done without any expense to the Crown by permitting a free sale of rum, which will destroy them more effectually than fire and sword.*

[55] Kitehi, a Delaware chief involved in the siege of Fort Pitt during Pontiac's reign, tried to get Captain Ecuyer, a British employed Swiss mercenary, to surrender Fort Pitt. Captain Ecuyer refused, but he suggested that Kitehi could persuade the other chiefs to make peace. To this end Ecuyer as a peace offering gave Kitehi some warm wool blankets to distribute among the Indians. Within days reports came back to Fort

Pitt of a terrible illness sweeping through the Indian Camps. The blankets had been infected with smallpox. Amherst applauded Ecuyer's efforts. (June 24, 1763)

In New York City, General Amherst, whom we left in a frenzy at the end of June, continued to receive a stream of bad news from the West. His rage and inhumanity increased as each Indian victory or depredation emphasized his seeming helplessness. He wrote sharp, impatient letters to the governors of New York, Pennsylvania, and Virginia, urging them to permit their militia to augment the regular army in its pursuit and chastisement of the enemy. He wrote to Gladwin that if any of the enemy Indians fell into his hands they should immediately be put to death, their extirpation being the only security for our future safety, and their late treacherous proceedings deserving no better treatment from our hands. (Amherst Papers, PRO, WO34, LIV, 171)

He (General Amherst) wrote to Bouquet that he wanted to hear of no prisoners being taken on his march westward to relieve Fort Pitt. As if in reply he heard from Bouquet on July 7 of the bloody loss of Verango, LeBoeuf, and Presqu'Isle. Detroit was now an isolated outpost in the savage wilderness beyond Niagara and Fort Pitt. In a postscript to his reply to Bouquet, Amherst made a startling proposal: "Could it not be contrived to send the small pox among the disaffected tribes of Indians? We must on this occasion use every stratagem in our power to reduce them." Bouquet answered that he would try to spread an epidemic with infected blankets and mentioned a wish to hunt "the vermin" with dogs. Amherst replied on July 16: "You will do well to try to inoculate the Indians by means of blankets, as well as to try every other method that can serve to extirpate this execrable race. I should be very glad your scheme for hunting them down by dogs could take effect, but England is at too great a distance to think of that at present."
(Transcripts of the Bouquet papers in the Canadian Archives, Series A, IV, 232; original in the Bouquet papers in the British Museum, Series 21634, f. 243. Oddly enough, neither postscript is mentioned in the calendar of the Bouquet transcripts in the Report of the Canadian Archives for 1889; nor is either one printed in the Bouquet Papers just published by the Pennsylvania Historical Commission from photostats in the Library of Congress. Francis Parkman's London agent, Henry Stevens, had no difficulty finding them among the Bouquet papers in the British Museum, and Parkman quotes them in his Conspiracy of Pontiac (6th ed.), II, 39-40.)

Benjamin Franklin Stickney

epilogue ...bush street...
chapter nineteen

With the winter storm gaining ferocity and strength as it traveled from Buffalo to the narrows of the Maumee Valley, it was bitterly cold that January morning in 1852 when Benjamin Franklin Stickney started for Mr. Fifield's[1] grocery store. It was only a half mile walk along the Maumee River, and with the storm at his back the wet snow quickly covered Toledo's Summit Street.

Many thoughts swirled through Stickney's mind as he thought about the forty years that he called the Maumee Valley his home. As Stickney approached Mr. Fifield's porch, portions of his frozen Wabash & Erie Canal were visible, waiting for the warmth of spring to resume. As he carefully mounted each step, Stickney was momentarily distracted by the shrill steam whistle of his Erie & Kalamazoo railroad's number two engine as it drove into the blinding snow. Stickney was proud of his achievements that benefited the Maumee Valley and Toledo, but he thought his greatest coup was the political decision that solved the *Toledo War* in Ohio's favor. As he gained the warmth of the pot bellied stove Stickney was aware of a crushing pain that drove the breath from his chest as he wavered, reached out and fell to the floor.

Benjamin Franklin Stickney died on a cold January morning in 1852 while talking politics as was his habit at Mr. Fifield's grocery store on Summit Street. The news of Stickney's death traveled throughout the Maumee Valley from business to business, home to home, and person to person as each of his acquaintances recounted numerous instances of friendship. But, what really brought the memories to the forefront were the instances of Stickney's eccentric behavior. His friends laughed while his detractors derided his mental acuity over his choices of names for his children. Who ever heard of naming sons One and Two and daughters after the States? While partially true and joined by their respective families; One, Two, Mary, and Indiana hastily traveled to their father's home on the Maumee.

Traveling one by one or in small groups, Stickney's friends and family trampled the freshly driven snow from Stickney's beloved Toledo to his home on the Maumee River bringing with them food and condolences.

Benjamin Franklin Stickney

> DEATH OF MAJOR B. F. STICKNEY.—
> Major B. F. Stickney an old and respected
> resident died very suddenly this moring. He
> was engaged in conversation with Mr. Fifield
> at his grocery store, when he was observed
> to totter, and falling, died instantly, probably
> from some affection of the heart.

Benjamin Franklin Stickney's Death Notice as it appeared in the Toledo BLADE. Courtesy of the Toledo BLADE.

Built along the Indian trail from Monroe, Michigan to Fort Industry, Stickney's two story brick mansion resided on the high north ridge of the Maumee River less than a mile from the shore line of Lake Erie. There were accounts that dated Stickney's brick home to 1818, but the first reliable narrative was from Giles Bryan Slocum in November of 1831.

Late in the month 1831
"...... and I put up for the night with Maj. Benjamin F. Stickney, a direct descendent of the celebrated Dr. Benjamin Franklin whose name he bears; and I would here remark, that Stickney bore a strong resemblance to the common portraits of Franklin which are to be found all over the country. Stickney prided himself in being of lineage to the great philosopher, and in the eccentricities of his manners sought to imitate in some degree that great man. Stickney I found ever kind and generous to me, and would receive no pay for stopping with him for several days. Stickney having lost his wife, a Mr. Parker and family ran the house (a good two-story brick mansion) for him very agreeably...." [2] Slocum's narrative provided the only description of Stickney as there were no paintings or sketches.

As Stickney's family and friends gathered in the main room under the guidance of Mary Matilda Way, Benjamin's second

Benjamin Franklin Stickney

wife, their was an under current of tension that caused each of Mary Matilda's comments to her adoptive family to be scrutinized for their true meaning. As the evening progressed and the stories lengthened the hospitality of Stickney's renowned *wine cellar* caused One, Two, and Mary to second guess their thoughts towards their step-mother.

Not only was Stickney's death unexpected, but in the evening when Stickney's will was read he had demonstrated one last bit of unconventional behavior. With one measured stroke of his pen, Stickney had abandoned most of his family. His will disinherited all of his sons and daughters, except for Indiana, and left the bulk of his estate to his second wife Mary Matilda [Way] Stickney.

"... My son One, my daughter Mary, and my son Two, having for a length of time acted toward me in an unfilial [3] and scandalous manner, and having bestowed upon them, in their education and otherwise, as much as I think proper to do, no farther provision is intended to be made for them. ..."[4]

Original clause from the Last Will and Testament of Benjamin Franklin Stickney. Courtesy of the Lucas County Probate Court.

Realizing the hold that their step-mother, Mary Matilda, had on their father, and that any possible inheritance whether in land or money was rapidly slipping from their grasp, One, Two, and their sister Mary retained Morrison R. Waite[5] on Wednesday, January 28, 1852 to break the will.

Benjamin Franklin Stickney

One of Ohio's most formidable attorneys by 1850, Waite was a recognized authority in real estate law and property titles and was thought by many to have the best chance at disputing the Baltimore, Maryland drawn will. Morrison R. Waite lost and a brokered peace was restored among the Stickney siblings through their sister Indiana. Mary Matilda [Way] Stickney retained title to Stickney's vast land holdings, while One, Two, and Mary received Stickney's brick home at Summit and Bush Streets and its contents.

Stickney's correspondence, political papers, and personal belongings had no interest to Mary Matilda [Way] Stickney and were abandoned to Stickney's eldest son, One. One Stickney still stinging from the rebuke of his father made his feelings known to his cousin Matthew A. Stickney in a letter almost 14 years later.

"…. As for the biography of my Father [Benjamin Franklin Stickney] I have neither the time nor talent. I take a very lively interest in the history of my Grand Father Stark and shall be very happy to have his biography. …"[6]

Morrison R. Waite. Courtesy of Knapp's History of the Maumee Valley.

Benjamin Franklin Stickney

epilogue ...bush street...
chapter nineteen

Two Stickney became the repository of his father's belongings by default when his brother One died, and consequently saved volumes of Stickney's historical letters and documents that would have otherwise been reduced to pieces of char in Stickney's burn pile.

Stickney's beautiful home overlooking his beloved Maumee River was soon reduced to rubble when Summit Street was realigned less than a year later. Judge Thomas Dunlap [7] salvaged the scarce bricks and used them to construct Stickney Hall.[8] Stickney Hall, while not a part of the Stickney Family, was Toledo's finest entertainment venue for the next six years.

Two Stickney, like his father, had married late in life to Lovina Cone from Vienna, Monroe County, Michigan. Two and Lovina's first child, Dorcas Franklin Stickney, was born in August of 1857 and died a month later. A son, Anthony Summers Stickney was born in 1859 three years before Two Stickney died in 1862. Having few prospects for support and no money of her own, Lovina Stickney widow of Two, married her neighbor James Entwhistle.

James and Lovina Entwhistle's home on Bush Street as it appeared in 2008. From the author's collection.

Benjamin Franklin Stickney

James Entwhistle [9] had the good fortune or common sense to build his home literally within feet of northwest Ohio's largest land owner.[10] With her three year old son Anthony, her luggage and family belongings, Lovina moved into Entwhistle's residence on Bush Street.

Bush Street, the home of the Entwhistle's, today stands defiant among its litter strewn neighbors. One of the last of Stickney's touchstones, the house remains alone, neglected, and guarded only by a rusted chain link fence with a long abandoned broken gate. Its empty windows gazed towards the Maumee River punctuating the years of neglect, while a hastily applied coat of white paint vainly tried to maintain what could have been. The last home of James and Lovina [Stickney] Entwhistle, one of the Maumee Valley's least memorable couples, stands alone, a shade of its forgotten past, and just a stone's throw from where Stickney's home cast its final shadow.

Tucked away in several large trunks were the majority of Stickney's correspondence, a silver tankard, and perhaps the most historically important find that would ever grace Toledo and northwestern Ohio. Mentioned by Toledo's Sunday TIMES BEE in 1903, the paper carried the first public mention of Stickney's traveled legacy, the silver tankard.

".... And there is still in the possession of the family, an engraved likeness, done in Paris, of Dr. Franklin, with his autograph, "For Dorcas Stickney[11] , in Newbury," on the back side; also his[Dr. Franklin's] Electrical Bells, and a letter from him [Dr.Franklin] to Anthony S. Stickney[12] , claiming that his first son should be named for him. He [Dr. Franklin] bequeathed to Anthony S. Stickney, a silver tankard, weighing about the equivalent of sixty Spanish milled dollars, bearing this inscription, "Legacy by the will of Benjamin Franklin to Anthony S. Stickney." ..."[13]

"... One of the most interesting relics owned in this city is a silver cup, photograph of which appears herewith, and which is owned by Mrs. J. Entwhistle ... The cup has descended from father to son and is now the property of Mrs. Entwhistle who has the

Benjamin Franklin Stickney

precious relic in a safety deposit vault in one of our local banks....",14

Benjamin Franklin Stickney's silver tankard as photographed in 1903. Courtesy of the TIMES BEE and the Toledo BLADE.

There was an earlier mention of the tankard during the probate of Anthony Summers Stickney's estate in 1883 where his entire holdings consisted of a gold watch, chain, and charm that was evaluated at $ 75 and a silver tankard at $25. Being of legal age when he died, Anthony Summers Stickney would have inherited the loose ends of his father Two, and his grandfather Benjamin Franklin Stickney.

Inventory and Appraisal for Anthony S. Stickney for gold watch and tankard. Courtesy of the Lucas County Probate Court.

Benjamin Franklin Stickney

The TIMES BEE might have been somewhat in error when it represented the tankard as belonging to Mrs. Entwhistle because in 1884 James Entwhistle purchased the gold watch, chain, and tankard from the estate of his step-son.

Having no sons or daughters with Lovina, James Entwhistle in his 84th year, in the company of his attorney, presented to the Toledo Museum of Art the silver tankard given to Benjamin Franklin Stickney by legacy from Dr. Benjamin Franklin.

Benjamin Franklin Stickney's silver tankard as it appeared in the Toledo Museum of Art in 1997. From the author's collection.

Inscribed with *"Legacy by the will of Benjamin Franklin to Anthony S. Stickney Presented to the Toledo Museum of Art by Mr. James Entwhistle,"* the silver tankard was proudly displayed by the Museum from 1915 till January of 1962 in *Director George F. Steven's Museum Collection*. Close inspection of the combined monograms and hallmarks of the tankard's silversmiths George Smith and Thomas Hayter of the Goldsmith

Company determined that the tankard was handcrafted in 1792. Mr. Riefstahl suggested to the Museum that since Dr. Benjamin Franklin died in 1790 the piece should be removed from display "... *since it no longer has any relationship to Franklin.*"[15]

Although Benjamin Franklin Stickney was buried in Forest Cemetery the exact location of the grave has been lost. The monument marks the Family Plot. Courtesy of Fred Folger.

The once proud possession of the Stickney Family now resides on a shelf in one of the Museum's basement storage facilities, locked away to be viewed by appointment only. Except for his name on a weathered and much repaired Toledo Street, one of the last touchstones of Benjamin Franklin Stickney's journey through the Maumee Valley had slipped into historical oblivion.

The biography of Benjamin Franklin Stickney and the growth and maturity of the Maumee Valley are so intertwined as to be almost inseparable. Therefore the narrative of Stickney's travels through his beloved Maumee Valley cannot be told without the stories of those native people that lived along the broad expanse of the Maumee River. They were the first to recognize the possibilities of the Maumee Valley, and they were the people that originally shaped the Maumee Valley.

Endnotes from Chapter Nineteen
epilog ...bush street...

[1] Mr. Fifield's neighborhood grocery store was located on the north side of Summit Street between Elm and Lagrange Streets.

[2] Taken from *"The 1831 Narrative of Giles Bryan Slocum."* The reminiscence was written in 1875. Courtesy of the Toledo Lucas County Public Library.

[3] *Unfilial*: not having acted in a respectful manner towards their father...

[4] *Last Will and Testament of Benjamin Franklin Stickney*, Lucas County, Ohio, Probate Court, April 26, 1852.

[5] Chief Justice of the Supreme Court of the United States graduated from Yale and began the study of the law in the offices of Samuel M. Young in Maumee, Ohio. His father was Chief Justice of the State of Connecticut, and his grandfather was a justice of the peace. In 1839 he was admitted to the bar, and in 1850 he moved his practice to Toledo, where he was joined by his brother, Richard. Waite became a recognized authority in real estate law and legal titles. Waite was extremely active in the campaign of Harrison for President and at 29 he was an unsuccessful candidate for congress. In 1863 he was offered an appointment by the Governor to the Ohio Supreme Court but refused. In 1871 Waite was appointed by President Grant to serve with Cushing and Evarts as American counsel in the Geneva Arbitration. On January 20, 1874, he was appointed by President Grant as Chief Justice of the Supreme Court. The nomination was well received by the bar across the country. In 1875 he refused to let his name be considered for the Presidency, he believed that the court should not be used as a stepping stone for political office.

[6] Letter from One Stickney to Matthew A. Stickney May 2, 1866.

[7] Judge Thomas Dunlap married Jeanette Allen on May 9, 1842. He was considered a Whig in politics and was an attorney with an office in Maumee in 1844. Dunlap was a Lucas County prosecuting attorney from 1845 to 1947.

[8] Designed for theatrical amusements the Hall's official dedication was October 9, 1855 with music provided by Louis Mathias and his Toledo Musical Society. It's interesting to note that the following week 12 year old violinist prodigy Adelina Patti [8] brought out the best in Toledo's sophisticated society.

[9] James Entwhistle was first listed as a drayman [large wagon pulled by a powerful team of horses] in 1872 and by 1894 his occupation is listed as Real Estate.

[10] Benjamin Franklin Stickney's home was located along the Indian Trail [Summit Street] at the foot of Bush Street overlooking the Maumee River. Entwhistle's home was located on Bush Street just south of Erie Street. About 400 feet.

[11] Anthony Stickney: Born 05.12.1724, married Dorcas Davenport 11.16.1747. They had a son Anthony Somerby Stickney, born 03.02.1748, who married Ruth [Brown] Coffin on 03.06.1770. Anthony Somerby Stickney and Ruth [Brown] Coffin were the parents of Benjamin Franklin Stickney born 04.01.1773. Dorcas Davenport would be Benjamin Franklin Stickney's grandmother.

[12] Anthony Somerby Stickney was Benjamin Franklin Stickney's father, and Anthony Somerby Stickney was Dorcas Davenport's husband.

[13] New England Historic-Genealogical Society, prepared by Wm. B. Trask, Historiographer of the Society, Volume 21, April 1867, pp 187-8.

[14] Excerpt from the Sunday, December 27, 1903 issue of the Sunday TIMES BEE.

[15] Memo to Mr. Wittman From Mr. Riefstahl, January 25, 1962. Toledo Museum of Art.

Benjamin Franklin Stickney

1800 & Froze to Death: 127, 135n8, 135n9
1831 Narrative of Giles Bryan Slocum: 236, 240
Abbey, Private: 303
Abbott, Mr: 59
Adams, James Q.: 307, 316n50
Adams, President John Quincy: 63, 65, 213
Adams, Secretary of State John Quincy: 170
ALBERT S. WHITE: 338
Algonquin Indian[s]: 45
Allen, Col.: 92
Allen, Nehemiah: 336, 345n11, 348n42
Allen, Capt. Samuel: 237, 243, 253n11, 261
Allen, Mrs. Samuel: 239
Allen, Seneca: 240, 253n12
Allen, William: 277, 286n36, 289p, 290, 310n13
Algonquin Indian[s]: 14
American Fur Company: 201
American House: 327
American Philosophical Society: 63, 66n10, 196
American Revolution: 45
Amherst, Lord Jeffery: 20, 22, 23, 349n54, 350n55
Ancient Forts of Northern Ohio: 13n4
Ancient Monuments of the Mississippi River: 13n4
An-ouk-sa: 89
Ancient Forts of Northern Ohio: 13n4
Ancient Monuments of the Mississippi Valley: 13n4
Andrews, General S. C: 301
Anti-Masonic Party: 252n2
Appasesab: 124
Applegate Farm: 15
Armstrong, Secretary of War John: 103, 113n18, 93, 103n18
Atawang: 38
Atwater, Mr.: 209n10
Auglaize River: 215, 225
Au-to-kee: 333
Bachelor's Hall: 252, 260-261, 288, 311n16
Bacon, Elizabeth: 256n40
Bacon, Judge Daniel S: 250-251, 256n40, 289, 306, 322
Bacon, Rev. Daniel S: 110
Badger, Rev Joseph.: 205
Bailey, Lewis E.: 303
Baker, Dr. George C.: 299, 314n34, 314n35
Baldwin, John: 197, 248, 302, 308
Ball, George: 183, 191n18
BALTIMORE & OHIO RAILROAD: 248
Bank of Michigan: 318

Barker & Holt: 288
Barker Jacob A.: 288-289
Barry, William T.: 224, 231n24
Battle of Fallen Timbers: 53, 56, 58n27, 59, 60
Battle of Lake Erie: 154
Battle of Mud Creek: 304
Battle of Phillip's Corners: 274, 276, 285n31, 304
Battle of Presque Isle [present day Waterville, Ohio]: 53, 58n28
Battle of Thames: 107
Baxter, Benjamin: 274-275, 285n33
Belden, Cyrus: 338
Bell, General John: 267, 301
Bellestre: 10, 11
Benton, Thomas: 308, 316n5
Berdan, John: 325, 328, 335, 346n18, 347n34, 348n37
Between the Logs: 108, 117n6
Biddle, John: 287, 309n1
Biddle, Owen: 63-64
Biddle, Major: 213, 229n3
BILL OF PAINS AND PENALTIES ACT: 250-252, 256n39,n263, 267, 269, 271, 274, 277, 280n7
Birds of Lucas County: 157n16
Bissell, Edward: 214, 219n6
Bissell, Fredrick: 331, 345n8
Black Hawk: 244p
Black Hawk Indian War: 244
Black Robes: 45, 110
BLACKSNAKE: 119-120, 145
Black Swamp: 168, 170, 333-334, 336-337, 342
Black Wolf : 53
BLADE, the Toledo: 2, 7, 23n2, 123-127, 318, 330, 341, 342, 345n8, 345n9, 345n12, 346n17, 352
Blanchard, Judge: 305
Blivens, Charles: 264, 281n10, 299, 314n38
Blodget, Samuel: 67, 80n1
Blue Jacket: 51, 54, 59-62, 65n1
Bomford, Chief of Ordinance Col.: 266, 268, 282n14
Bondie, Antoine:86-89, 91, 101n6
Bowman, Judge Baxter: 302
Braddock, General Edward: 12, 17-20, 28n14
Brady, Col: 74
Brant, Joseph:55
Brighthorn: 89
Brock, General Isaac:85, 95, 104n23
Brown, General Joseph W.: 263-264, 268, 272, 274, 276, 280n9, 298,

300-301, 304
Brown(e), James Irving: 311n16
Brown, Noah: 164
Brown, Senator Ethan: 196, 206, 212n40
Brownstown: 22, 62
Burying Ground: 246
Butler, Attorney General Benjamin: 265-266, 270, 281n12
Butler, General: 49
Calhoun, Secretary of War J. C.: 161-162, 165-166, 171n1, 199
Camp Seneca: 96, 104n24
Campbell, Captain: 22-23,
Campbell, Louis W.: 157n16
Canneff, Joseph: 15, 27n5
Captain Johnny: 60, 89
Carass, Mr.: 183
Card, George: 288
Card, Platt: 288-289, 303, 310n7, 310n8
Carr, Thomas: 326-327, 347n27
Carter, John:120
Cass, Lewis: 298
Cass, Secretary of War Lewis: 224, 233, 245, 251, 254n29, 262, 266-267, 277, 283n21, 300, 310n11, 316n52, 317
Cass, Territorial Governor of Michigan Lewis: 91, 100, 103n13, 105n30, 114, 128, 131-133, 136n9, 139, 142, 152-153, 157n10, 158n23, 161, 163, 165-166, 168, 173n18, 175-176, 179, 181-188, 191n13, 191n14, 193-194, 199, 201, 208n3, 213, 215-216, 219-220, 224-226, 229n7, 230n10, 230n14, 230n15, 232n29
Chaine, Isadore: 75-76
Chandler, Howard: 54
Chase, Alexander Ralston: 165, 173n15
Chase, Daniel: 322, 323
Chief Orontony: 8, 13n13
Chief Tussan [see O-Tussa]: 195, 212n42
Chippewa Indian[s]: 16, 17, 24, 28n15, 53
Cincinnati's Western Immigration Society: 140, 156n5
Clark, Dr. Jacob: 261, 294, 311n16, 311n19
Clark, Henry: 292
Clay, General Green: 96
Clayton Act or Bill: 308
Clayton Street & Oliver Streets: 3, 4
Clinton, Governor of New York DeWitt: 141-142, 14, 157n9, 165, 198
Coe, Avin: 205, 211n34
Coffin, Ruth [Brown]: 13n1
Collins, Sanford L.: 238, 253n10, 265,

281n11
COMMODORE PERRY: 119, 331, 332
Common Sense: 68
Conant, Horatio: 196, 202, 206, 209n18, 216n39, 264-265, 301p, 302
Cone, Lovina: 355
Concise Account of North America: 21
Conquest, the: 5, 13, 14n17, 236
Cornplanter: 48, 57n15
Corsellius, George: 233, 234
Corydon: 142
Cottonwood Swamp: 274, 285n30, 338-339, 349n49
Council Oak: 330
Coueurs de Bois: 1, 6
Cowdrey, Mr. Roselie: 5, 15
Cram, Rev.: 112
Crane Charles: 1, 2
Crary, Isaac: 307
Crawford, Secretary of the Treasury: 165
Crawford, Secretary of War William: 121, 129, 134n2
Creek Indian[s]: 79
Crescent Street: 2
Croghan, George: 9, 10, 14n20, 20, 21, 26, 28n14, 29, 32, 96-99, 104n25
Crosby, Eleanor: 201
Crosby, Otis V.: 330
Cuerie, Mushett: 39, 43n18
Cuillerier, Alexis: 39-40, 43n18
Cuillerier, Antoine: 40
Curtis, Lt. Daniel: 88-89, 101n7, 128-129, 131-132, 135n13
Custer, General George Armstrong: 256n40
Cuyahoga River: 9
D'Iberville, Pierre le Moyne Sieur: 7
Dale, William:338
Dallas, acting Sec. of War Alexander J.: 117, 118n18
Dancing Ground: 110, 117n9
Daniels, Mrs. Harriet: 262
Daniels, Munson: 262, 302
Daniels, William P.: 288, 310n6
Davenport, Dorcas: 13n1
Davids, Tice: 224
Davis, J. Baron: 252, 256n43, 260, 261, 288, 292, 293, 311n16
de Cadillac, Antoine de la Mothe Sieur:, 45
de Callieres, Count: 7
de Celoron, Pierre Joseph Sieur: 9, 13n9
de Champlain, Samuel: 13n10
de Troit: 7
Death Valley: 335
Defiance, Ohio: 181, 215, 222,

Defiance DEMOCRAT: 309
Delaware Indian[s]: 14n27, 17, 24-25, 29, 45, 47, 59, 142
Depot Station: 182, 191n17, 207
Detroit: 16-17, 20, 22-23, 26, 78, 82n21, 151
Detroit FREE PRESS :259, 299, 323
Detroit GAZETTE: 154, 179, 186, 196, 259,
Detroit River: 16, 22, 25, 79, 181
Detwiler Golf Course: 157n16
Dickens, Charles: 337-338
Disney, David T.: 278, 290-291
Dodge, Engineer: 273
Doty, James Duane: 165, 172n13
Douglas, Capt. David Bates: 166, 173n16, 181, 191n12, 191n14
Downes, Dr. Randolph: 5, 6, 14n7, 236,
Dragoo, William: 110,
Drake, Dr. Daniel: 334
Draper, Dr. Lyman: 15, 27n7, 42n5, 153, 159n27, 159n28, 159n29, 215, 230n9, 304, 315n45, 315n46, 315n47
Draper, Luke and Harriett: 304, 315n46
DROUGHT OF 1838: 333-334, 348n39
Dunlap, Judge Thomas: 355, 360n7
DuPonceau, Pierre: 196, 209n14
Duquesne, Governor: 17
EAGLE: 120
Eagle Tavern: 287-288, 294, 310n4, 311n18, 312n22, 327
Ecuyer, Captain: 349n54
Edwards, Abraham: 196, 209n17
Eel River Indian[s]: 59-60
Elliot, Matthew: 75-77, 82n21, 83n27
England, Col. R. G.: 51
Entwhistle, James: 355-356, 358, 360n9
Entwhistle [Stickney Cone], Lovina: 356, 358
Erie & Kalamazoo Railroad: 248, 255n34, 289, 310n9, 325, 327330, 336, 338-339, 349n49
Erie Canal: 141, 198, 249
Erie Indians: 6, 186, see Cat Indian[s] also
Eustis, Secretary of War William: 71, 73, 75-76, 82n14, 82n16, 85, 93
Everett, Dr. Wilson:318, 345n7
Expedition of Exploration: 165
Ewing, Nathaniel:
EXPEDITION OF DISCOVERY:,165
Fassett, Elias: 1, 312n24
Falls of the Niagara: 141
Fellows, J. W.:311n16
Fifield, Mr.: 351, 360n1
First Methodist Church – Perrysburg: 127

First Presbyterian Church of Christ Maumee: 179
Fish, Jacob: 172n8
Fisher, Betty: 37-39, 40
Fisher, Dexter: 228, 235n35
Fisher, Marie: 37
Fisher, Millie: 37
Fisher, Sergeant James: 35, 37
Five Medals: 209n9
Five Nations: 6
Flagg, Sheriff Junius: 301-302
Flagler, Henry: 348n40
Flagler, Rev. Isaac: 333, 335, 348n40
Fletcher, Jonathan E.:274, 276, 304-305
Foley, Sara Rowsey : 315n45, 349n48
Folger, Fred: 359
Follet, Oran:262
Foot of the Rapids:
Forest Cemetery: 336, 359
Forrer, Ohio Canal Commissioner Samuel: 273
Forsyth: 246
Forsyth, Ann:78,
Forsyth, D. H.: 331, 332, 345n4
Forsyth, Major Robert: 165, 172n12, 213, 228n1
Forsyth, Sec of State John: 266-267, 282n15, 282n16, 283n19, 283n21, 298
Fort Chatres: 37
Fort Dearborn:85, 166
Fort Defiance: 52-53, 59, 91-92
Fort Deposit: 31, 35-39, 41, 53
Fort Detroit:, 7, 21
Fort Duquesne: 17-18, 20, 27n13, 28n14
Fort Gratiot: 166
Fort Greenville: 54
Fort Hamilton: 49
Fort Harmar: 46
Fort Harrison: 70, 81n9
Fort Industry: 352
Fort Industry Chapter of the D. A. R.:3
Fort Jefferson: 49
Fort Mackinac:8
Fort Malden: 77, 79, 83n27, 85, 92-93, 96, 100
Fort McArthur: 92, 103n16
Fort Meigs: 94-96, 113-114, 120, 141, 144-145, 179, 182, 199, 206, 323, 331
Fort Meigs A Condensed History:
Fort Miami[s] [British]: 8, 53, 58n24, 60, 65n5, 94, 143, 179, 190n8 267, 283n20, 302

Fort Michilimackinac: 8, 14n22, 21, 85
Fort Pitt: 35
Fort Sandouski: 8
Fort Stephenson: 96-98, 107
Fort Street: 2, 13n2
Fort Washington: 46, 48, 50, 57n8,
Fort Wayne: 49, 57n10, 60, 73-79, 82n16, 83n29, 85, 87, 90, 113, 116, 120, 131, 135n10, 139-143, 148, 156, 161, 167, 179, 181, 182, 190n7, 213
Fort Wayne, Indiana: 8
Fort Winchester:, 91, 115, 181, 191n15,
Forts of Anthony Wayne:
Fox Indians: 7, 13n12, 53
Fox River: 7
Franklin, Dr. Benjamin: 1, 13n1, 356, 358-359, 360n15
Freemasonry: 173n20
French and Indian War: 14n26, 31
Frenchtown: 92-93,
FROST BITTEN CONVENTION: 308
Fulton, John A.: 257
Fulton Line: 168
Galloway, Todd B.: 269
Gano, General John: 99, 104n27
Gardner, Indian Agent James B.: 228, 232n31, 232n32, 232n34
GENERAL BRADY: 303
George Croghan Journal of 1760:
Gibbs, Lt. Almon: 113-114, 120, 182, 199-201
Gilbert, G. K.: 4
Gilbert, Stephen: 199
Gladwin, Lt. Henry: 349n 54, 350n55
Gladwin, Major: 35, 43n8
Goddard, Lewis: 236, 240-241, 253n7, 254n17
Goldsmith Company: 358
Goodsell, Naaman: 271-272, 284n24, 284n25, 284n26
Goslin, Francis: 36-37
GOVERNOR MARCY: 287
Grahm, Clerk the War Department George: 137n27
Gratiot, General Charles: 249, 256n38
Grave Island: 44
Green [Stickney], Mary: 123-127
Greenville, Ohio: 49, 52
Grouse Land: 69, 81n8
Grower, Robert: 302
Gunckel, John E: 207
Halfway Creek: 321-322
Hall, Henry: 15-16, 27n8

Hardin, Col. John: 46-47
Harmar, General Josiah: 46-49, 57n11, 59,
Harris & Fulton Line: 214p
Harris Line: 168, 257, 258p, 262-263, 266-271, 273, 277, 296
Harris, Mr.: 175-176
Harris, William: 257
Harrison, General William Henry: 68-71, 80, 85, 87, 89-90, 92-97, 99, 102n11, 113-114
Harroun, Mrs. Clarissa: 328, 347n30
Harve: 321-325, 346n20
Harve Branch Railroad: 322
Harvey, Journal of B. J.: 241, 254n20,
Hathaway, Dr. Harrison: 13n2
Hathaway Street: 13n2
Hawkins, Lt. Thomas L.: 95, 103n20, 104n22, 199
Hayden, Sheriff Elijah: 326-327
Hayter, Thomas: 358
Hecox, Ambrose: 199
Hecox, Chloe Spafford Gilbert: 199, 201
HENRY CLAY: 213, 229n2
Hertzler, Christian: 300
Heth, Captain John:
Hewitt, Justice Charles: 274
Higgins, Judge D.: 222, 230n18, 297
HISTORICAL SOCIETY OF NORTHWESTERN OHIO: 5, 13, 14n17
History of Michigan: 31
History of the Maumee River Basin:
History of the Maumee Valley: 64, 354p
Hog Island: 36-37, 42n7
Holgate, William C: 287-288, 310n2
Holloway, Cyrus: 272-273, 284n28, 302
Hood, Lt. Washington: 297-298, 313n27
Hopkins, Gerald T.: 107, 117n1
Horner, John S.: 299, 304, 306, 313n32, 314n33
Hosack, Dr. David: 165, 172n10
Hosmer, Hezekiah Lord.: 30, 116, 118n17
Howard, Benjamin: 266-273, 277, 282n16, 283n22, 283n23, 285n29
Howard, Dresden: 4, 118n10, 178p, 190n5, 205, 217, 224, 228, 230n11, 245, 330
Howland, Elisha: 199
Hudson Bay Company: 201
Hudson, J. T. : 288
Hull, Governor William: 76, 78, 83n24
Hull, Levi: 127, 135n7
Humphrey, Levi: 322
Hunt, General: 85, 100, 101n1, 101n2
Hunt, John: 107, 117n3, 117n4

Hunt, Major: 59
Hurd, Lyman: 293-294
Huron Indians: 6, 17
Hutchins, Thomas: 29
Indian Island: 44
Indian Removal Act: 219, 222, 236n20
Indiana, State of: 213
Indianola Island: 43n17, 44
INDIANS OF THE MAUMEE VALLEY:
Ingersoll, Charles J.: 196, 209n15
INQUIRIES: 187, 196, 209n16
Iroquois Indians: 6, 7, 13n10, 17-18, 20, 45, 55, 59, 186, 192n29
Irving, Pierre M.: 324, 326, 345n9, 346n17, 346n18, 346n19
Irving, Washington: 324, 345n9, 346n17
Isle au Cochon: 35
Jackson, General Andrew:
Jackson, Indian Agent James: 246, 248, 254n30, 255n36
Jackson, Miss Anna Marie:
Jackson, President Andrew: 177, 189n3, 217, 219, 222-224, 230n12, 230n20, 231n23, 231n24, 231n25, 233, 254n30, 258-259, 263, 265-270, 277-278, 281n12, 282n15, 290-291, 296, 298-300, 303, 306308, 317, 333, 345n11
Jay's Treaty: 55, 58n31, 59, 65n3
Jefferson, Vice-president Thomas: 63,
Jennings, Governor of Indiana Jonathon: 142, 157n10
Jerome, Judge Jonathan H.: 302
Johnson, Sir William: 20, 22, 26
Johnston, Indian Agent John: 73, 78. 85, 93, 113, 115, 130, 133, 153, 159n27, 161-162, 171n3
Johnston, Stephen: 87-88, 102n9, 114
Jones, N. F.: 119
Joliet: 16
Kanakee: 48
Kaweahatta: 61
Keeney, Salmon: 321
Kekionga: 47
Ken-tuck-ee-gun: 32, 42n4, 195
King George III, 15
King George's War: 8
Knapp, H. S.: 64, 301, 312n27, 354p
Kosciosko, Thaddeus:64, 66n12
LaDemoiselle: 9, 10, 11, 14n15, 14n16
Lake Erie: 15, 17, 25p, 27n1, 76, 141, 143, 175, 177, 181, 213-214, 223, 258, 262-263
Lake of the Cat: 6, 15

Lake Michigan: 175-176
Lake St. Clair: 25p
Langford, Joseph: 120, 131
Langlade, Charles: 11, 12, 14n22, 14n25, 17-19
Larned, Charles: 137n26
LaSalle, Antoine: 7
Lansing, Jacob B.:
LAST WILL & TESTAMENT OF BENJAMIN FRANKLIN STICKNEY: 353
Law, Rev.: 183, 191n21, 201, 203
Lawrence, Lt. William : 74
Lee, Lt. Robert E.: 292p, 298
Lewis, Col: 92
Lewis & Clark: 107
Little Cedar Point: 32
Little Turtle: 47-52, 55, 58n19, 58n20, 59-65, 66n7, 66n8, 75, 77, 79, 83n29, 208n6
Little Turtle: 63
Little Turtle the Great Chief of the Miami Indian Nation:
Lloyd, Lemuel L.: 219, 220, 221
Logan, Captain John: 85
LORD's PRAYER: 184, 191n25
Loramie Creek: 10
Louis XIV: 55, 45
Lower Sandusky:
Lucas County Historical Series: 5, 13n11, 14n17
Lucas, Governor Robert: 189n4, 258-259, 259p, 262-264, 267-273, 276-279, 279n2, 279n3, 283n19, 286n37, 290-292, 295-297, 300, 304-305, 314n40, 317-318, 344n1, 345n4
Lykins, Samuel: 219, 230n13
Lyman, Darius: 259
Lyon, Lucius: 251, 256n41
Mack, John:331
Macomb, General: 186, 192n28
Maddocks, Mr. Asa W.: 312n25
Madison, President James: 68, 71, 73, 77, 82n16
Maiet, Jean: 39-40, 44n19
Manhattan ADVERTISER: 324, 337
Manhattan & Harve Railroad: 289
Manhattan Ohio: 208, 288-289, 321-325, 327, 333-336, 348n43
Manor [Menard, Minor], Pierre [Peter]:
Mansion House: 288, 293, 311n16
Marietta, Ohio: 46, 57n4, 57n5
Marquette, Father James: 16, 109
Mashkeman: 152-153

Mason, John: 189n3, 224, 231n25, 231n26
Mason, Michigan Territorial Governor Stevens T.: 291-296, 298-300, 303-304, 307, 314n33
Mason, Secretary of the Michigan Territory Stevens T.: 233, 251, 252n2, 256n42, 259-260, 260p, 262-271, 277, 279n1, 280n8
Mason, Stevens Thomson: 189n3,224, 231n25, 231n26
Maumee Rapids: 143
Maumee River: 2, 10, 12, 15-17, 23, 27n2, 27n3, 38-39, 47, 54, 76, 161-162, 175, 177, 179, 181, 183, 214, 214p, 216, 221, 222, 226, 228, 213, 214, 223, 226, 235, 240, 247-249, 261, 351, 352, 355
Maumee River Basin: 2, 4, 257, 262-263
Maumee Valley: 1, 7, 9, 15-16, 20, 27, 59, 73, 107, 108, 110, 140, 143, 144, 153, 154, 177, 179, 180, 182, 185, 190n5, 216, 217, 219, 222-224, 228, 235, 244-246, 248, 262, 351, 359
Maumee Valley Historical Society: 299
McAfree, Captain Robert B.:
McArthur, Duncan: 114, 118n14, 226
McCoy, Rev. James: 182,
McDougall, Lt. George: 39
McElvain, Col. John: 331-332
McHenry, Sec of War James:
McKay, George: 271-272, 284n24, 293-294
McKee, Alexander: 47, 51, 57n12
McKenney, Thomas L.: 148, 158n23, 158n25, 213, 229n3
McKinstry, John: 75-76, 83n23
McNair, William: 274, 285n34
Me-au-me: 178
Meck-ke-sic-ko-qua:
Meigs, Commissioner of the General Land Office Josiah: 139, 156n1, 156n3, 156n4,165
Meigs, Governor Return Jonathon: 86, 99, 104n28
Meigs, United States Comptroller Josiah:
Menard, Peter: 246
Merrill, David E.: 145, 158n22
Meta: 85-86
Miami Canal: 223, 249
Miami & Erie Canal: 197, 261-262
Miami & Fassett Streets: 2, 3,
Miami Indians: 7, 9, 10, 12, 14n20, 14n23, 14n27, 17, 45, 47, 51, 59, 61, 65, 77, 79, 80, 142, 148, 162, 178

Miami of the Lake: 50
Miami River: 9, 12
Michigan Branch Railroad: 289
Michigan Historical Society:302
Michigan SENTINEL: 196
Miller. Daniel: 321
Miller, Sheriff James H:292, 293
Minavavana: 24, 28n15
Mingo Indians: 14n27, 24, 30, 45,
Missionary Herald at Home and Abroad, 205, 216, 226, 232n31, 232n33, 246
Missionary Island: 43n17, 44
Missionary [Mission] School: 205, 216-217, 232n30
Mitchell, Dr. Samuel Latham: 146, 165,
Mitchell, John: 176, 189n2
Mohawk Valley: 6
Monhollens: 119
Monocue: 117n6
Monongahela River: 18-19, 28n14
Monroe, Michigan: 352
Monroe, President James: 100, 163, 170, 190n11, 199
Monroe, Secretary of War James: 68, 82n14, 115-116
Morin, Isadore: 321
Morin, Levi: 321
Mounds at Winameg: 4
Mud Creek: 15, 27n4, 244, 262
MudJaw Creek: 346n20
Muir, Major: 91
Mulhollen, Samuel: 300, 314n36
Mulhollen's Farm: 299-301, 304, 314n40
Nason, Captain William: 2
Nation of Bobcats: 6
NATIONAL HISTORIAN, St. Clairsville: 223, 231n22
NATIONAL INTELLIGENCER:,
Navarre, Mr. Peter: 16, 153, 154p
Ne-gig: 110-111, 117n8
Nelson, Dr. Larry: ii, iii
Neolin: 7, 24-26, 28n17, 29
Newcomer: 24, 29
Newell, Miss.: 226-227, 232n31
NEW ENGLAND PATROIT: 68
NEW HAMPSHIRE REGISTER: 68
New Madrid Earthquake: 79
Neyon, Mons: 37
Nichols: 13n13
Nichols, Judge Francis L.: 207
Niagara Falls: 23
Niagara River: :
Nichols, Judge Francis L.:
NORTH AMERICAN REVIEW: 186

Norvell, Senator John: 266, 283n18
Obwondiyag: 16
Odel, Jeremiah: 292
Ohio Archaeological & Historical Quarterly; 10, 11
Ohio Canal Project: 223, 230n21, 249, 261,
Ohio Company: 46, 57n6
Ohio Historical Society: 54
Ohio House: 338
Ohio Indian Trails: 18p
Ohio Legislature: 176
OHIO-MICHIGAN BOUNDARY DISPUTE: 175, 177, 223
OHIO-MICHIGAN REGISTER AND EMIGRANTS GUIDE: 242, 254n21, 254n22
Ohio Railroad Company: 336-337, 348n43, 348n44
Ojibwa Indian[s]: 59, 185
Old Betsy: 98, 104n26
Old Britain: 9, 10, 11, 12, 14n15
Old New England Farmer's Almanac & Register:
Old Northwest Territory: 20-21, 24, 29, 35, 68, 181, 186-187, 213, 214p, 218, 222, 234
Oliver, Mrs. William: 262
Oliver, Pete: 87
Oliver, William: 89, 102n10, 102n11, 247, 255n32
On Canada: 71, 82n16
ONTWA the Son of the Forest: 160p, 186, 192n29
Oquanoxa [Oquinoxey]: 215, 229n8
Oral Tradition of the Ottaway Indians: 32
Ordinance of 1787: 176, 226
Orleans of the North: 165
Osborn, James R.:
Ostrander, Lt.: 90
OTTAWA INDIANS: 11, 14n27, 15-21, 32, 37-38, 45, 53, 59, 179, 183, 186, 193, 215, 218-222, 228, 230n15, 244-246, 248
Ottawa River [Ohio]:50, 177
Ot-ta-wa-sepe: 177
Ottokee [Ot-to-kee]:207
Otussa: 16, 32, 42n4, 42n5, 215, 229n8
Outaoues: 16-17
Paine, Thomas: 68, 81n6
Palmer, Andrew: 260, 264, 284n27, 294-295, 312n23, 314n40
Panic of 1837: 223, 231n23
Park [Pake or Parker], Judge Benjamin: 142, 157n10

Parkman, Francis: 30, 42n8
Patchin, Sheriff James: 274
Patrick: 200, 210n25
Patterson, Commissioner: 273
Patterson, Dr. Michael: 274-275, 285n32
Peckham, Howard: 31, 38, 43n11, 43n12
PEGASUS: 199
Peltier, Charles: 86
Perry, Commodore Oliver H.: 99-100, 107, 164, 235
Perry, Oliver Hazard [Hunter]: 338-339, 348n46, 348n47, 349n51
Perrysburg: 27n3, 156n2, 179, 267-269, 273
Perrysburg WEEKLY JOURNAL:309
Philadelphia UNION: 167
Pianguisha: 14n15
Piankeshaw Indian[s]: 59
Pickawillany: 9, 10, 11, 12, 14n20, 14n21, 18
PIONEER: 240-241, 254n18
Pitcher, Dr. Zina: 307
Pondiac: 16, 111
Pontiac: 7, 11, 12, 14n25, 15-23, 26, 27n9, 28n18, 29, 32, 35, 37-41, 41n2, 41n3, 43n16, 68, 81n12, 153, 159n29, 195, 213, 215, 331
Pontiac and the Indian Uprising: 38, 43n11, 43n12
Pontiac's Rebellion: 31, 41
Pontiague: 16, 20
Porter, Michigan Territorial Governor George: 221, 230n16, 233, 245-246 252n1, 254n29, 255n31, 255n36
Port Lawrence: 143, 157n17, 165, 169, 176, 179, 182-183, 197, 213, 219, 230n14, 234p, 235, 238, 247, 261, 267-268, 288, 310n5
Port Lawrence HERALD: 260, 280n5
Potawatomi Indian[s]: 17, 53, 59, 71, 81n12, 85, 88, 127, 139, 142, 148, 182
Presque Isle [Maumee-Waterville]: 16, 127
Presque Isle [Pennsylvania]: 135n4
Presque Isle [Toledo east]: 32, 43n16, 127, 135n6, 195, 214-215
Proctor, Col. Henry: 48
Proctor, General Henry: 93-94, 96, 98-99
Prophet: 71
Prophetstown: 68, 70, 71, 81n10
Provost, Sir George: 77, 82n15
Quinousaki, Chief: 17
Race, John: 120
Raisin River: 92-93, 262
Randall, E. O.: 78
Rathburn, Benjamin: 145, 158n21

RECOLLECTIONS: 243
Recollections of old Winameg: 245
Red Jacket Seneca Chief: 112, 118n11
Red Pole: 59, 62, 65n1
REGISTER: 163
Remember the Raisin: 100
Removal of the Indians from Ohio 1820-1843:
Reynards: 13n12
Rhea, Captain James: 75, 78-79, 85-86, 88-90,101n4, 101n5, 101n6
Richardson, Isaac: 200, 221
Richardville, Jean de Baptiste: 130, 132-134, 136n20, 137n23, 142, 171n2
Riefstahl, Mr.: 359, 360n15
Riley, James: 67
Roby, C.: 331
Roche de Bout: 17, 38, 44, 221
Rodgers, Robert: 32
Rogers, Robert: 21-22
RUSH-HOWARD PROPOSAL: 298
Rush, Dr. Benjamin: 63, 66n10
Rush, Richard: 266, 269-270, 272, 277, 282n17, 283n23
St. Clair, General Arthur: 48-50, 57n15, 59,
St. Joseph River: 7, 17, 23, 37
St. Joseph Railroad: 318
Sandusky Bay:17
Sandusky Bay Navigation Company: 262
Sandusky REGISTER:
Sandusky River: 8, 9, 23
Sannillac, A Poem: 185
Saux Indian[s]: 53
Schaler, Judge Charles: 289, 313n31
Schoolcraft, Henry R.: 74, 165, 179, 182, 184-187, 196, 199, 201
Schoolcraft's Narrative Journal:
Scioto River: 9
SCOOUWA: 57n1
Scott, General Charles: 48
Scott, Jesup: 242-244, 254n23, 254n24
Scott, J. Austin: 244
Sears, Richard:288
Seely, Commissioner: 273
Segur, Daniel: 319
SENECA INDIANS: 23, 48, 57n15, 182
Shaw, Cornelius: 240, 253n15
She-wu-naw: 246
Shabonee: 71, 81n12
Shane, Anthony: 210n27
Shaw, Indian Agent John: 93, 130,
SHAWNEE INDIANS: 14n27, 17, 25, 30, 45, 59-60, 90, 177
Shelby, Secretary of War [?] Isaac: 131,

Sherman, R. B.: 10
Shetrone, H. C.: 10, 11
Shetoon: 75-76
Shinga: 12
Silliman, Benjamin: 165, 172n11
SILVER TANKARD: 6, 356, 357p, 358p
Simcoe Governor John Graves: 51, 58n21, 322
Simmons, David: 221-222
Sketches of a Tour to the Lakes: 213, 229n3
Slocum, Dr. Charles E.: 2, 3, 4
Slocum, Giles Bryan: 236, 240, 253n8, 253n9, 352, 360n2
Smallpox: 29, 37, 43n9, 63
Smead, Benjamin Franklin: 336
Smith, George: 358
Smith, Ira: 294, 310n4, 311n18, 327
Soldier: 60
Southworth, Dr.: 294, 312n21
Spafford, Amos: 120, 127, 139-140, 156n2, 156n4, 199
Squire and Davis: 13n4
Stadtlander, Jim: 330
Stark, Caleb: 75-76, 83n22
Stark, General John: 67-68, 71, 73-75, 80n4, 81n7, 82n16, 83n23, 354, 360n6
Stark, Mary: 67, 81n5
Stevens, George F. Museum Collection: 358
Stickney, Anthony Somerby: 13n1
Stickney, Anthony Summers: 13n1, 355-358, 360n12, 360n13
Stickney, Benjamin Franklin: 1, 13n1, 16, 32, 42n3, 67-68, 71-79, 81n5, 81n7, 82n16, 82n19, 82n20, 83n22, 83n25, 83n30, 85-91, 93, 98, 100 101n3, 103n14, 107-108, 113-16, 118n15, 120-121, 129-134, 136n19 139-148, 156n8, 157n9, 157n12,157n13, 157n14, 158n24, 158n25, 161-163, 167, 169, 171, 175, 179-187, 189n1, 190n6, 190n9, 190n10, 190n11, 191n17, 191n22, 191n23,192n26, 192n27, 192n30, 193-194, 197, 207, 208, 215-216, 220, 228, 229n7, 230n10, 230n13, 235-236, 242-243, 247-250, 252n4, 253n11, 255n34, 256n40, 259, 261, 263, 271-272, 278-279, 284n27, 286n37, 288, 292-295, 303-304, 308-309, 318, 329, 331, 336, 338-342, 345n6, 345n8, 347n34, 351-

Benjamin Franklin Stickney

359, 360n2, 360n4, 360n10, 360n11, 360n14
Stickney, Dorcas Davenport: 355-356, 360n11
Stickney, Indiana: 132, 351, 353, 354
Stickney, Louisa: 67
Stickney, Mary [daughter]: 351, 353-354
Stickney, Mary [wife]: 68, 83n22, 161, 215-216
Stickney, Mary Matilda [Way]: 352, 353, 354
Stickney, Matthew A.: 354, 360n6
Stickney, One: 67, 81n5, 351, 353-354, 360n6
Stickney, Two: 68, 241p, 293-296, 304-306, 336, 351, 353-354, 357
Stickney Avenue: introduction
Stickney Elementary School: introduction
Stickney Hall: 355, 360n8
Stickney's Woods: introduction
Stuart, Gilbert: 63
Sugden, John: 78
SUN: 333
SUPERIOR:324
SWAN: 60
Swan Creek: 3, 60, 120, 143-146, 157n16, 161, 167, 179, 235, 247, 288
Swayne, Noah: 277, 290p, 291
Swift, Rev. E. Pope: 183, 201-203
Tahquamenon River: 179
Talcott, Capt. Andrew: 297, 312n26
Tambora Volcano: 127
Tarhe the Crane: 208n7
Taylor, Commissioner: 273
Taylor, Captain Zachary: 86, 101n5
Taylor, General Zachary: 318
Tecumseh: 7, 53, 68-71, 77-79, 81n12
Tecumseh: 78, 94, 96, 99, 100
Tecumseh, the Shawnee Chief: 78
Tenskwautawa: 71, 81n11, 81n13
Territory of Michigan: 331, 332
Thirteen Fires: 45, 50, 57n3
Thomkins, Governor Daniel: 72
Thomkins, Vice President Daniel: 165
Thornton [Brodeau], Mrs. Anna Marie: 67, 80n2
Tiffin, Governor Edward: 173n21
Tiffin, Surveyor General Edward: 168, 173n21, 257p, 257
TIMES BEE, the Toledo: 356, 358
Tippecanoe and Tyler too: 71, 97
Tippecanoe River: 68, 70
Toledo: 15-16, 176-177, 261-262, 268-274, 277
Toledo COMMERCIAL: 290
Toledo GAZETTE: 265, 272, 280n5, 284n27, 295, 312n23, 312n24, 312n25
Toledo HERALD: 311n19
Toledo House:288, 310n5, 310n6
Toledo Museum of Art: 358
Toledo Strip: 249-250, 257-258, 261, 263, 265, 268, 287, 290, 292, 295, 306, 307, 317, 319
TOLEDO WAR: 177, 258-259, 261, 287, 299, 304, 308, 319, 320-321, 351
Too Long On A Lonely Isle Neglected: 154
Topinbee: 55
Tradition of the Ottaway Indians: 30,
Treaty of 1817: 140
Treaty of 1831: 28
Treaty of 1833: 246
Treaty of Fontainebleau: 41n1
Treaty of Fort Meigs: 247
Treaty of Greenville: 54-55, 59, 62, 68, 70p, 78-79, 140, 143, 156n3
Treaty of Paris: 20, 29
Treaty of St.Marys': 161-162
Treaty of the Foot of the Rapids: 151, 153
Trowbridge, Charles C.: 165, 173n14
Tupper, General: 92, 103n15
Turner, Dr. William: 129, 131, 134, 135n14, 136n16, 171n5
Turtle Island: 214, 297-298, 322
Tussan, Chief [see Otussa]: 195
Tutle, Charles Richard: 31
Twightees: 14n20
Underground Railway: 224, 231n27, 231n28
University of Michigan: 247
Upper Peninsula: 179
Upper Sandusky: 193
VanBuren, Governor of New York Martin: 217, 230n12
Vance, Governor of Ohio Joseph: 322
VanFleet, Col.: 301-302, 314n39
VanTassel, Rev. Isaac: 204-205, 211n36, 216, 226-227, 232n33, 245-246
Van Tassel, Lucia B.: 204
Vincennes: 68-69
Vistula: 1, 197, 210n19, 234, 235p, 236, 242, 247-248, 252, 252n6, 254n22, 260-261, 265, 287-288, 304, 310n5
Vollmar's Amusement Park: 43n17, 44
Volney, Constantine: 111
Waashaa Monetoo: 59
Wabash/Maumee Corridor: 7, 8
Wabash & Erie Canal: 142, 143, 197-198, 223, 288, 308, 324, 326, 338, 351
Wabash River: 7, 23, 48, 68, 70, 76, 77,

140-142, 182, 213
Waite Morrison R. : 353, 354p, 360n5
WALK-In-The-WATER: 164-165, 172n6
Walk-in-the-water [Chief]: 208n8
Walpole Island: 245
Wapakoneta: 62
War of 1812: 178, 268
Washington, Lt. Col. George: 18, 28n14,
Washington, President George: 49, 57n15, 62
Wassonquette: 248, 255n35, 288, 331
Water Street: 328-329, 336, 347n32
Way, George B.: 318, 345n8
Way, Mary Matilda: 293, 311n15
Way, Willard V.: 210n20, 302, 309, 314n41
Wayne, General Anthony: 50-54, 57n26, 59-62, 65n5, 69
Wea Indians: 59, 142
Webster, Daniel: 325-326, 331, 346n22, 336n24, 326n25, 347n26
Wells, Ann: 162, 11n4
Wells, William: 61-63, 66n7, 66n8, 75, 79, 83n29
Wenzislaus: 236
Western Hemisphere: 260
WESTERN IMMIGRANT: 233
Western Immigration Society: 140, 156n5
Western Missionary Society: 203-204
Western Spy: 140-141, 156n6, 156n8,
Whisky: 51, 55, 59, 62, 66n8, 77, 113, 133-134, 171n2, 201, 221, 224, 294
Whistler, Major John: 74, 100, 101n3, 105n29, 114-115, 117, 120-121, 128-131
White, Dr. Oscar: 245, 254n26, 254n27
White, General David: 292, 310n9, 311n14, 321, 324
White Pigeon: 115, 118n16
White Population: 228
White Raccoon: 87
White River: 8, 13,
Whiteford: 292, 310n9
Whiting, Captain Henry: 154, 160n30, 186, 187, 196
Whiting, Col. Henry & Mrs.: 213, 228n2
Whiting, Quarter Master Detroit Federal Arsenal Henry: 266, 268, 281n13, 283n21, 317, 318, 344n1, 345n3
Whittlesey, Col. Charles: 2, 6, 13n4
Whittlesey, Elisha: 269-271, 341
Whittlesey Focus People: 6, 13n4, 13n5
Wilcox, Frank: 18
Wilkinson, Col. James: 48
Wilkinson, General James: 60, 63-64
Wilkison, Amelia: 179

Wilkison, Captain David: 119, 134n1, 179
Wilkison, Captain Jacob: 119, 145
Will, George: 52
Williams, Micah T.:143, 157n15
Wilson, Judge William: 302
Winameg, Chief: 5, 330
Winimac: 55, 88-91, 102n8
Winchester, Major: 91-93, 120,
Wing, Austin E.: 207, 212n41, 249-250, 255n37, 262, 280n9, 287
Wood, Captain Eleazer D.: 94
Wolcott, Dr. Alexander: 165, 173n17
Wolf's Rapids: 203, 204
Wood, Deputy Sheriff Joseph: 293-295, 304, 306
Woodbridge, Michigan Territorial Governor William:168-170, 173n22
Worthington, General: 86
Wyandot Indians: 8, 13n13, 14n15, 14n27, 17, 21, 45, 59, 75-76, 82n21, 99, 107-108, 115, 127, 139, 161, 193
Yeslin Farm: 15
Young, Calvin: 63